Coherent Chiastic Oeuvre in the Unity of Luke–Acts

Coherent Chiastic Oeuvre in the **Unity** of **Luke–Acts**

Two Volumes Conjoined as a Single Book

BY
John M. Powell

FOREWORD BY
Ron C. Fay

WIPF & STOCK · Eugene, Oregon

COHERENT CHIASTIC OEUVRE IN THE UNITY OF LUKE–ACTS
Two Volumes Conjoined as a Single Book

Copyright © 2025 John M. Powell. All rights reserved. Except for brief quotations in critical publications or reviews, no part of this book may be reproduced in any manner without prior written permission from the publisher. Write: Permissions, Wipf and Stock Publishers, 199 W. 8th Ave., Suite 3, Eugene, OR 97401.

Wipf & Stock
An Imprint of Wipf and Stock Publishers
199 W. 8th Ave., Suite 3
Eugene, OR 97401

www.wipfandstock.com

PAPERBACK ISBN: 979-8-3852-4554-3
HARDCOVER ISBN: 979-8-3852-4555-0
EBOOK ISBN: 979-8-3852-4556-7

VERSION NUMBER 06/18/25

Scriptures marked CEB are from the COMMON ENGLISH BIBLE. © Copyright 2011 COMMON ENGLISH BIBLE. All rights reserved. Used by permission. (www.CommonEnglishBible.com).

Scriptures marked (CEV) are from the Contemporary English Version Copyright © 1991, 1992, 1995 by American Bible Society. Used by Permission.

Scriptures marked CSB are from The Christian Standard Bible. Copyright © 2017 by Holman Bible Publishers. Used by permission. Christian Standard Bible®, and CSB® are federally registered trademarks of Holman Bible Publishers, all rights reserved.

Scriptures marked (GNT) are from the Good News Translation in Today's English Version- Second Edition Copyright © 1992 by American Bible Society. Used by Permission.

Scriptures marked ESV are from The Holy Bible, English Standard Version®, copyright © 2001 by Crossway Bibles, a publishing ministry of Good News Publishers. Used by permission. All rights reserved.

Scriptures marked KJV are from the King James Version, public domain.

Scriptures marked NASB are taken from the NEW AMERICAN STANDARD BIBLE®, Copyright © 1960, 1962, 1963, 1971, 1972, 1973, 1975, 1977, 1995 by The Lockman Foundation. Used by permission

Scriptures marked NIV are taken from The Holy Bible, New International Version® NIV® Copyright © 1973, 1978, 1984, 2011 by Biblica, Inc.™ Used by permission. All rights reserved worldwide. The "NIV" and "New International Version" are trademarks registered in the United States Patent and Trademark Office by Biblica, Inc.™

Scriptures marked NKJV are from The Holy Bible, New King James Version Copyright © 1982 by Thomas Nelson, Inc. Used with permission.

Scriptures marked (NLT) are taken from the Holy Bible, New Living Translation, copyright © 1996, 2004, 2015 by Tyndale House Foundation. Used by permission of Tyndale House Publishers, Carol Stream, Illinois 60188, USA. All rights reserved.

Scriptures marked MSG taken from THE MESSAGE. Copyright © 1993, 1994, 1995, 1996, 2000, 2001, 2002. Used by permission of NavPress Publishing Group.

Scriptures marked NRSV are from the New Revised Standard Version Bible, Copyright © 1989, Division of Christian Education of the National Council of the Churches of Christ in the U.S.A., and are used by permission. All rights reserved.

Contents

List of Tables | ix
Foreword by Ron C. Fay | xi
Preface | xv
Acknowledgments | xix
Abbreviations | xxii

Chapter 1: Introduction | 1

Chapter 2: Elucidating and Explicating Luke-Acts in Canonical and Greco-Roman Literary Structure | 42

Chapter 3: The Unity of Luke-Acts and Theory Behind Luke's Intention and Purpose | 67

Chapter 4: Narrative Criticism in the Construction of Luke-Acts | 97

Chapter 5: Backgrounds—The Literary and Cultural Context of Luke-Acts | 127

Chapter 6: Exploration of the Themes of the Lukan Travel Narratives from Galilee to Rome | 167

Chapter 7: Juxtaposition of Ascension Narratives in Luke 24 and Acts 1 and Introduction to Chiasmus | 201

Chapter 8: Stitching Luke and Acts Together at the Seams | 232

Chapter 9: Climactic Denouement of Christ's Ascension in the Coherent Narrative of Luke-Acts | 274

Conclusion | 297

Bibliography | 303
Index | 317

List of Tables

Table 1. Length of Luke and Acts | 142

Table 2. Four Great Uncials Containing Luke and Acts | 147

Table 3. Regional Travel Circuits in Luke's Volume 1 (9:51—19:48) | 184

Table 4. Regional Travel Circuits in Luke's Volume 2 (1:1—12:25) | 184

Table 5. Regional Travel Circuits in Luke's Volume 2 (13–28) | 185

Table 6. Westcott-Hort's Alignment with P^{75} | 220

Table 7. Westcott-Hort's Alignment with the Byzantine Text-Type | 221

Foreword

I WAS LUCKY ENOUGH to have John Powell as one of my first doctoral students to mentor. His ideas on displaying the unity between Luke and Acts, moving back toward Luke-Acts, are compelling. Of course, the problem with books like this, those converted from a dissertation, comes from the style of writing. Dissertations tend toward boring, drawn-out arguments. The wonderful thing about this work, however, is that Powell's writing displays fluidity and comprehensibility instead of the expected opacity and jargon. Powell has combined a few different methods to reach a literary conclusion. This is more than a response to Parsons and Pervo.[1]

Rather than making a theological or lexical argument, Powell has focused primarily on structural issues. He begins by looking at how Greco-Roman literary works function. In doing so, he considers theological writings and earlier biblical writings (specific episodes in the LXX). With the help of authors like Burridge, Powell turns to look at genre issues in Luke as well.[2] In terms of the genre of Acts, Powell interacts with the main arguments and typical foils, such as Pervo.[3] Powell makes certain to focus on authorial intent with respect to his hermeneutical principles, which clarifies the trajectory of the book. Powell does not read against the grain of Luke and Acts; instead he looks for the intended meaning, which then should lead toward the intended structure. In looking at the purpose of each

---

1. Parsons and Pervo, *Rethinking the Unity of Luke and Acts*.
2. Burridge, *What Are the Gospels?*
3. Pervo, *Profit with Delight*.

book individually, Powell can compare the theological and historical traits and tendencies of each book in order to gauge the likelihood of unity. In other words, John Powell does not impose an outside will or agenda on the text, rather he seeks to elucidate Luke's own purpose and make it discernible to the reader. This allows any reader of this book to access, however indirectly, insight into not just what Luke did with his writing but why he did it.

The idea of Luke and Acts moving to Luke-Acts, along with all the various back and forth arguments, comes to a climax in how each reader of the Bible approaches the writings. Does Luke intend for them to be understood together? Scholarly consensus has moved from no to yes to we are not sure. John Powell has put together an argument that can move the opinion back toward the side of seeing them as a unified work. Does that really matter, though? In terms of how one would read and understand the Bible, yes. Seeing Luke and Acts as Luke-Acts brings the story of the church into closer connection with the story of the church's founder, Jesus Messiah. Just as Luke begins with the birth of Messiah, so does Acts begin with the birth of the church, founded strangely enough by that same Messiah being taken up into the clouds. Once one understands the unity of these stories, one can see how Luke's themes from his Gospel connect, continue, and are even enhanced by Acts.[4]

I have not yet touched on what I think constitutes the most significant aspect of this work, Powell's use of narrative/literary criticism. He looks at the possible areas of connection, not limited to theological or thematic but structural, and shows how Luke and Acts weave to form a completed tapestry only when together. He does not demonstrate Luke or Acts as unfinished on their own, rather he shows the necessary and intentional connectivity between the two based on specific passages, echoes, and seams left behind in the texts. Powell argues that in placing those different passages together, a completed picture then emerges. His most compelling work surrounds the ascension, a notoriously difficult set of passages to put together.

Though biased, I believe that any reader who values the historical and theological significance of Luke and Acts will value John Powell's

4. E.g., Fay, "Narrative Function of the Temple," 255–70.

helpful contribution to the discussion. More importantly, I think Powell correctly utilizes the tools of a literary critic to make his case. He looks to past scholarship without overreliance. He breaks new ground without being radical. This book primarily focuses on literary and narrative ideas, yet he makes theologically significant points as well. The reader of Powell's work will come away with more knowledge, see connections that have not been made this way before, and likely find themselves with more of an inclination to see Luke-Acts as a two-volume work, which Powell argues is what Luke intended.

Ron C. Fay, PhD

Preface

THE UNDERTAKING OF THIS project produced a glaring obviousness how only a few have long been drawn to the life and literary contributions of Saint Luke, whose remarkable erudition produced two divinely inspired works within the New Testament. Much fascination with his writings has been a driving force behind this research, compelling a desire to explore their depth and significance. Additionally, the yearning interest has also been motivated by the unique position he occupies as the only known gentile author in the New Testament, offering a perspective that bridges Jewish and Greco-Roman audiences. His meticulous historiography and theological insights continue to shape Christian thought, making his works indispensable to biblical scholarship.

While Luke holds as the only gentile writer in the New Testament, such a distinction underscores the inclusive nature of God's redemptive plan. His writings serve as a powerful testament to the equal standing of gentiles and Jews within the unfolding narrative of salvation, offering profound encouragement to believers across all generations. Moreover, his perspective provides a unique lens through which the expansion of the gospel beyond Israel can be understood, highlighting the universal scope of Christ's mission and the church's role in carrying it forward.

Unlike the other three inspired Gospel writers—Matthew, Mark, and John—Luke did not assume that gentiles were inherently familiar with God's historical narrative as understood by the Jews of the Old Testament. Recognizing this, he took a unique approach by tracing Jesus's genealogy all the way back to Adam. In doing so, Luke emphasized the universal scope of God's redemptive plan, illustrating that all of humanity shares a fundamental connection to God through Adam.

When examining Luke's background, he often appears to be less recognized than Paul or other first-century biblical writers who physically walked with Jesus during his earthly ministry. It is also highly probable that Luke never saw Jesus in person. This realization serves as a driving force behind this study, which seeks to offer a fresh perspective on this remarkable author, historian, and theologian. In particular, it focuses on his two literary masterpieces—the Gospel of Luke and the Acts of the Apostles—shedding new light on their significance and contribution to the New Testament.

The Gospel of Luke and the Acts of the Apostles exist today as two separate books within the New Testament canon, maintaining their distinct placement and authority since its formation. This division has persisted throughout history and remains the standard in modern Bibles. However, the final chapter of Luke and the opening chapter of Acts serve as a literary bridge, seamlessly stitching the two volumes together into a unified narrative. Furthermore, Luke's writing contains structural and thematic connections that reinforce their continuity, demonstrating his original intent for them to be read as a single work. This is evident in Acts 1:1, where the author explicitly refers to his *former book*, unmistakably identifying the Gospel attributed to Luke.

Modern Bible translations present the Third Gospel and Acts as distinct, independent books, separating them with the Gospel of John. However, this study provides substantial research and evidence affirming their common authorship by Luke, whom Paul refers to as "the beloved physician" in Col 4:14. Widely acknowledged as both a physician and a close companion of the apostle Paul, Luke demonstrates remarkable historical precision and literary skill. Under the inspiration of the Holy Spirit, he meticulously composed these works, crafting a unified and theologically rich narrative that bridges the life of Christ with the birth and expansion of the early church.

Although later canonical divisions have led to their separation, a close examination of their structure, themes, and rhetorical design reveals a cohesive narrative framework that underscores their unity. The prologues of Luke (Luke 1:1–4) and of Acts (Acts 1:1–5) also suggest a common authorship and purpose, with Acts serving as a natural continuation of the Gospel's story. This continuity is further emphasized by the parallel use of language and thematic elements, reinforcing the idea that both volumes were intended to be read as a unified work. The deliberate connection between the two volumes highlights the continuity of the narrative from the life of Jesus to the early church's mission.

In contrast to those who continue to criticize Luke's historical accuracy, Luke and Acts are indeed historically accurate but not solely because of their biblical inspiration, but also due to their acceptance into the canon, which subsequently affirmed them as authoritative Christian doctrine for the church. Additionally, there is clear evidence suggesting that these writings were not the product of anonymous authors claiming to be Luke. This book will explore this issue further, as it is crucial to understanding the concept of biblical inspiration and the authenticity of these texts.[1]

No amount of credible or sustainable historical evidence exists to suggest that the Third Gospel and Acts were written anonymously or that they were originally intended to be separate, independent works. On the contrary, they are connected in several significant ways. Their unified literary design reveals a cohesive structure, with events unfolding in a way that reflects the author's intentional narrative progression. Luke likely wrote his works in a chronological order, which highlights his intention for both volumes—the Gospel as volume 1 and Acts as volume 2—to be read as one continuous story.

The ascension of Jesus Christ is strategically positioned at the conclusion of the Gospel and the beginning of Acts, forming a chiastic

---

1. Those books in the Bible that were accepted as Scripture are those writings that were recognized to be authoritative Christian doctrine. These books were yielded as possessing apostolic authority because they were written by people who were personally chosen by Christ for this work, while those authors wrote under the Holy Spirit's inspiration. Other works in this period with unknown authorship were deemed pseudepigraphic.

structure. This chiastic design serves to unite the two volumes, creating a seamless hinge that links the gospel of Christ with the early history of the church. Central to both works, Christ's ascension is pivotal not only to the narrative's progression but also to the theological and historical framework Luke establishes. This book explores how Luke wrote in a culture that was hostile to Christianity, while building up to the ascension of Christ. In the final three chapters, it will exclusively focus on the ascension by exploring its crucial role in shaping the continuity and flow of Luke's two-volume work.

A critical analysis of Luke-Acts reveals a chiastic design that unites both volumes, with the ascension as the central axis around which the narrative pivots. The Third Gospel progresses from Galilee to Jerusalem, culminating in the passion, resurrection, and ascension of Christ, while Acts extends the movement outwardly from Jerusalem to Rome, tracing the expansion of the gospel message through the church. This symmetrical structure strengthens the argument that Luke-Acts was conceived as a single historiographical project, reflecting the unfolding of divine salvation history from Israel to the nations.

Beyond their literary structure, Luke's theological vision remains consistent across both volumes. Key themes such as the universality of salvation, the role of the Holy Spirit, the fulfillment of Old Testament prophecy, and the legitimacy of the Christian movement before both Jewish and Roman authorities pervade the entire work. The emphasis on continuity—from Jesus's mission to the apostle's ministry—reinforces the notion that Luke-Acts is not merely a sequential pairing but an interconnected theological treatise designed to affirm the reliability and expansion of the Christian message.

This monograph aims to explore the unity of Luke-Acts by examining its structural, historical, rhetorical, and theological dimensions. By reevaluating the ascension as the central hinge of the narrative and considering Luke's literary craftsmanship, it seeks to demonstrate that Luke-Acts is best understood as a single, continuous work, providing an indispensable foundation for interpreting the early Christian movement. Ultimately, this work invites readers to reconsider Luke-Acts not as two separate entities, but as a harmonious and intentional narrative that shapes our understanding of the origins and mission of the Lord Jesus Christ and his church.

Acknowledgments

THIS BOOK IS DEDICATED to all who genuinely love and cherish the Lord Jesus Christ and his written word. His unwavering care and guidance have graciously equipped me to present a level of understanding that is intended to bless and edify his church. It is my sincere hope that those who read this book will be moved to a deeper understanding and appreciation of the profound theological truths embedded in the Gospel of Luke and the Acts of the Apostles, and that the insights presented here will motivate a greater commitment to the call of Christ in their own lives.

First and foremost, I owe an immeasurable debt of gratitude to Dr. Ron C. Fay, whose mentorship has been indispensable throughout this entire process. His countless hours of guidance, wisdom, example of scholarly excellence, and deep faith have left an indelible influence on my academic journey. His unwavering belief in my potential and invaluable advice have continually encouraged me to push past obstacles, fostering an environment in which I could flourish both as a scholar and as a person.

I would also like to express my heartfelt appreciation to my family. To my wife, TaMara, your love, patience, and unyielding support have been a constant source of strength throughout this entire endeavor. Your sacrifices and encouragement have been the foundation of my ability to pursue this calling. To my children, Evan and Chloe, you have brought joy and inspiration to my life every day. Your laughter and presence have always reminded me of the greater purposes beyond academia and have strengthened my resolve to continue seeking God's purpose for my life. You are a continual blessing and source of motivation.

A special thank you to my brother Norman for always being there, supporting me through every season of life. Your friendship and encouragement have meant the world to me, and I could not have asked for a better companion on this journey. I would also like to acknowledge the friendship and support of Rich Thin, Kevin Patton, and Al Cambric. Your sincere friendship has enriched my life in countless ways, and your unwavering support has been invaluable in helping me navigate both academic challenges and personal trials. Thank you for being such steadfast and encouraging friends.

The professors I had the privilege of learning from during my graduate studies have also played an integral role in shaping my academic development. Their teaching, guidance, and scholarly example provided the foundation on which I built my PhD program. Their dedication to their craft and their investment in my growth moved me to continually strive for excellence. Beyond imparting knowledge, they nurtured my intellectual curiosity and challenged me to think critically and deeply. Their mentorship went beyond the classroom, offering invaluable advice and encouragement, which helped me navigate the complexities of academic research. Through their support, I developed not only as a scholar but as a person, better prepared to contribute meaningfully to my field and to the church.

Additionally, my deepest gratitude goes to the exceptional faculty, scholars, and theologians at Liberty University, whose mentorship and guidance were instrumental in the successful completion of the program. I am especially grateful to Dr. Richard Fuhr for his insightful guidance throughout my studies, and to Drs. Adam McClendon and James Gifford for challenging my critical thinking and pushing me to refine my academic approach. I also owe much to Drs. Jordan Jones, Daniel Gurtner, and Jeffrey Dickson for their unwavering encouragement and support during the time I spent with them, helping me navigate challenges and providing invaluable perspectives that have shaped my academic journey.

Finally, I express the sincere gratitude to all those not mentioned by name. Your encouragement, advice, and intellectual contributions have profoundly influenced both my academic and personal journey. It has been an honor to collaborate with such brilliant minds, and the lessons I've learned from each of you will remain with me throughout my life. As Matt 23:34 reminds us, Jesus sent prophets, teachers, and scholars as gifts to his church, and I am deeply thankful to have encountered such gifted individuals along my path.

·

Abbreviations

CEV	Common English Version
CSB	Christian Standard Bible
AYBD	*Anchor Yale Bible Dictionary*
BDAG	Arndt et al., *A Greek-English Lexicon of the New Testament and Other Early Christian Literature*, 3rd ed.
ESV	English Standard Version
GNT	Good News Translation
KJV	King James Version
JAAR	*Journal of the American Academy of Religion*
JBL	*Journal of Biblical Literature*
JBTS	*Journal of Biblical and Theological Studies*
JETS	*Journal of the Evangelical Theological Society*
JPS	Jewish Publication Society
JSNT	*Journal for the Study of the New Testament*
LBD	*Lexham Bible Dictionary*
LCL	Loeb Classical Library
LXX	Septuagint
MSG	The Message translation
MS(S)	manuscript(s)
NA^{28}	*Novum Testamentum Graece, 28th Edition*

NASB	New American Standard Bible
NET	New English Translation
NIV	New International Version
NKJV	New King James Version
NLT	New Living Translation
NRSV	New Revised Standard Version
NT	New Testament
OT	Old Testament
UBS⁴	*The Greek New Testament*, United Bible Societies, 4th ed.
WH	Westcott-Hort

Chapter 1: **Introduction**

DOCTRINAL DISCUSSIONS SURROUNDING THE ascension narratives in the Bible do not appear to be as popular of a subject in comparison to other doctrines like the crucifixion and resurrection.

One reason is because most people are unfamiliar with it. A central reason results from it not being discussed much by the biblical writers. The human interest for knowledge and understanding often attempts to associate itself with things, ideas, and realities familiar to them, or with things that can be relatable.

In modern discussions of ascensions, they are not things that have occurred to anyone that have either been witnessed or that can be pointed to in their lifetime for enlightenment or relativeness. Such events are only read about in the past, in the Bible, or through extrabiblical literature, and in ancient myths of the sort. Such lack of discussions in no way diminishes their reality or can take away from the factuality of such events.

Human cognition naturally desires to associate supernatural experiences with realities that can be logically explained or understood. However, God seldom operates in the realm of reason or logic, but in the realm of things unreasonable and illogical because he is a supernatural being. In this aspect, he challenges people to believe in what cannot be understood or explained away by natural means, to things that are irrational to the end that it takes faith on the part of an individual to please him (e.g., Heb 11:6).

The biblical narratives regarding the ascension of Jesus Christ from earth to heaven are often treated by Bible readers and believers as irrelevant or discarded as unimportant as if the ascension has no relevance or practical application that can be experienced by them in this life. In other words, those who believe that Christ ascended from earth to heaven might often feel like it happened, and now it is time to move on to another discussion, without realizing the significance of this event. The ascension is essential to this book because it seeks to prove that the two ascension narratives in the Gospel of Luke and the Acts of the Apostles connect both volumes together as one book.

The significance of the event itself benefits people in several ways. In Luke-Acts, the author intended to relate the fulfillment of the OT Passover with the crucifixion and the NT outpouring of the Holy Spirit on the day of Pentecost. Both events are divided by the ascension of Christ, whereas the ascension joins the crucifixion in the Gospel and Pentecost in Acts together, as dependencies upon it. Pentecost, or the Feast of Harvest (Exod 23:16), Weeks (Exod 34:22), and first fruits (Num 28:26), fell on the fiftieth day after the Passover. The forty days given by Luke in Acts 1:3 included a ten-day lapse until the Holy Spirit descended and filled all who were prepared in Jerusalem (see Acts 2:1–4).[1]

When examining the end of the Gospel and the beginning of Acts, this book conjectures that both Luke and Acts are sewn together by the finished work of Jesus Christ using the ascension narratives in both volumes. As "he was taken up" (Luke 24:51), or as "he was going up" (Acts 1:9), the event became the ultimate sign of his passing the propagation of all he accomplished on earth to his apostles. It became an event that vindicated his message and ministry.

It is at this juncture where the crucifixion comes more into focus. While the crucifixion made it possible for God to atone for all sins permanently, all the way back to Adam, it was needed for the resurrection and ascension. Where these is no crucifixion there is no resurrection, and where there is no crucifixion and resurrection, there is no ascension. The resurrection proved his power over death and the grave, and the ascension proved his eternal reign as King and Lord of all creation. The ascension proves a future return to earth as the risen Lord and conqueror (see Rev 17:4).

1. Metzger, *New Testament*, 181.

The ascension becomes one of the several connection features that stitch Luke and Acts together, and will be scrutinized, and is one of Luke's major themes that span both volumes which will be examined. A valid question to Luke would be, What did he intend between the Gospel and Acts? It becomes more of an answer to the question rather than simply a question as his intention is unfolded as God's salvation history to humankind.

In Luke's theology, God's salvation history of Israel (OT) is the culmination of the Gospel and Acts, which also becomes the inclusion of the gentiles (NT), both encapsulated into God's eternal plan (cf. Rom 11:25). It is what the apostle Paul would later call "the mystery of the church that was hidden in all ages and was revealed to the apostles and prophets by the Holy Spirit" (Eph 3:3–6; Col 1:26–27).

In this context, Jesus had to ascend for the Holy Spirit to descend. In Luke's producing of Luke and Acts, by a latter designation Luke-Acts, the importance of a comprehensive study of the two volumes demonstrates a chiastic arrangement that discloses what the author intended. As such, Acts cannot be separated from the Third Gospel any more than the Gospel can be separated from Acts. The unity existing between both volumes attests to a single story among the two-volume work.

Thesis

Luke's coherent chiastic oeuvre in the unity of Luke-Acts as two volumes conjoined as a single book is examined in this book. It builds upon the thought and concept of other scholars who believe that Luke and Acts (fashioned Luke-Acts) were intended as a single book to Luke's first audience.[2] It will consider points that have not been examined by any others. For instance, a chiasm in the ascension

---

2. David Moessner believes the designation Luke-Acts owes its origin to the work of Cadbury, *Making of Luke-Acts*, originally published in 1927. The designation, according to Moessner, did not have much popular usage until the rise of redaction criticism and after World War II. The emphasis on the designation Luke-Acts, with Luke as the author, further emphasizes how he worked independently and creatively on gathering and compiling his sources. Also see Moessner, *Jesus and the Heritage of Israel*.

narratives of Luke 24 and Acts 1 is a literary link that ties both volumes together as one, forming a bridge between Luke to Acts is what this book will seek to substantiate.

The author of Luke-Acts uses themes throughout Jesus's travel-route (also called travel narratives) from Galilee to Jerusalem (additionally from Jerusalem to Rome) as this was a divinely intended circuit. These themes are essentially markers that speak to the author's intention. The author's intention for Luke-Acts is/was to take Jesus from Galilee to Rome. Such are major themes in the ministry of Christ whether he was physically present or working in or through the church in the background.

Luke's Gospel and Acts have traditionally been upheld by many as two separate books. Yet, some still view them as separate and independent works today, ever since they were separated during the formation of the canon. They were made separate and independent in the way they are canonized among the additional remaining twenty-five NT books. This book does not attempt to convert Luke-Acts into one book from their modern detachment. It argues that their author intended for them to be read as one single work.

In addition to the previous point, rather than cleping Luke-Acts as First and Second Luke, both the Gospel and Acts are designated correctly and are unique with specific genres. Aune agrees with the single-work hypothesis as it was not the author's intention for Luke and Acts to disassociate into separate, independent works. "The Acts of the Apostles" was not named as such at its onset.[3] Whereas together, Luke-Acts could also have been appropriately titled *Ad Theophilum*.[4]

The placement and appearance of Luke-Acts as two separate books in the NT canon does not present a problem with their trustworthiness or any gaffe between the two. It, however, was advantageous for later readers of Luke and his modern readers to understand the connection, for which this book is intended to aid in filling this gap. The ascension narratives will be seen as pivotal to this book's

---

3. Cadbury, *Making of Luke-Acts*, 2nd ed., 10.
4. Aune, "Text-Tradition of Luke-Acts," 70.

thesis in forming the primary chiasm that connects both volumes as a single book.⁵

The Gospel comes into the chiasm from Galilee to Jerusalem, and Acts goes out of the chiasm from Jerusalem toward Rome, thereby making Luke-Acts a continuous story with no break in the narrative. The primary chiasm, the ascension narratives, forms the central point of Luke's literary structure and design. In addition to chiasmus, this book proves the single author, intention, and objective adjacent to Luke's coherent literary structure and design.

The chiastic structure of Luke-Acts strengthens its thematic unity and narrative cohesion, with the ascension serving as the central hinge between both volumes. It marks the conclusion of Jesus's earthly ministry (Luke 24) and the beginning of the apostolic mission (Acts 1, followed by the church of all ages until the return of Christ), thereby highlighting the transition from Jesus's messianic work to the disciples' commission (Luke 24:50, Acts 1:8), reinforcing Luke's overarching chiastic design.

First-century biblical writers were deeply influenced by Greco-Roman rhetoric and Jewish traditions, shaping both their oral and written communication. They employed techniques such as *parallelism* (synonymous, antithetical, and synthetic) to structure ideas, *inclusio* to construct unity by framing passages with similar themes, and *amplification* to emphasize key points through repetition or elaboration. Classical rhetorical (the art of persuasion) appeals were three persuasive strategies identified by Aristotle such as *ethos* (credibility), *pathos* (emotional appeal), and *logos* (logical argumentation).⁶ Luke employed these techniques to make his works both persuasive and compelling to Jewish and Greco-Roman audiences within their historical and cultural context and beyond.

In addition to Luke, the biblical writers utilized *midrashic interpretation* by expanding upon and reapplying Old Testament and Jewish traditions to new theological insights.⁷ The *diatribe* was also used

---

5. Luke and Acts are two volumes of a single work. See Rayan, *Holy Spirit*, 1.

6. Corbett, *Classical Rhetoric*, 35, 459.

7. In Matt 2:15, he quoted Hos 11:1 ("Out of Egypt I called my son") and applied it to Jesus's return from Egypt, portraying him as the fulfillment of Israel's history.

to engage in rhetorical dialogue, and *chiasmus* (ABBA structure) to enhance memorability and coherence.[8] New Testament writers inherited the style from Hebrew literary traditions and Greco-Roman rhetorical structures to enhance memorability, reinforce themes, and create literary symmetry.

The rhetorical function of the ascension shapes Luke's narrative flow, theological argument, and engagement with both Jewish (e.g., Enoch, Elijah) and Greco-Roman (i.e., apotheosis) traditions. It contains theological implications for Christology and eschatology within first-century thought structurally, theologically, and historically. Structurally, it serves as the central pivot in the Luke-Acts chiastic design. Theologically, it affirms Jesus's exaltation, divine authority, enthronement, and the transition to his Spirit-led church. Historically, it interrelates with Jewish and Greco-Roman traditions regarding the transition of individuals from one state of being to another, particularly in similar concepts of divine exaltation, apotheosis, and heavenly enthronement.

Recognizing the ascension as the chiastic stitching point reveals Luke-Acts as a unified, intentional work, where Jesus's earthly ministry seamlessly gives way to the disciples' Spirit-led mission. Rather than serving as an ending, the ascension functions as a turning point, reinforcing Luke's broader narrative structure and theological vision. This key contribution is in demonstrating that it acts as the chiastic hinge that binds both volumes together, affirming their unity as a single, continuous narrative. This perspective moves beyond treating Luke and Acts as separate works but rather highlights the deliberate continuous narrative and theological continuity he intended to construct.

Understanding Luke's personal background and the context of his writings is crucial for accurately interpreting the text and fully grasping its central message as he is the author. It involves

---

In 1 Cor 10:1–4, Paul interpreted Israel's wilderness journey as typological of the Christian experience, with Christ as the spiritual rock that sustained them. The Dead Sea Scrolls and New Testament writers used a pesher (interpretive) approach to apply past prophecies to their own time. Example: In Acts 2:16–21, Peter interprets Joel 2:28–32 as being fulfilled at Pentecost, reframing it to their time.

8. Paul often used diatribe in his epistle of Romans (e.g., Rom 2:1; 6:1; 9:19–21).

examining the author's purpose, intended message for the original audience, and future implications of the text, but through the lens of the historical context in which the work was written. Additionally, considering external environmental and sociological factors helps date the audience and situate the message within its broader hermeneutical historical framework.

By examining both Luke's structural design and theological intent, the ascension emerges as both a literary hinge and a theological climax. Luke's background as a physician, historian, and theologian informs his writing, making his use of medical language and sources important to an investigative historian where eyewitnesses to the event and Old Testament references (e.g., Enoch, Elijah) became integral to the ascension narratives. His reliance on sources (people that knew Jesus personally and were eyewitnesses to his works) (Luke 1:1–2; Acts 1:1–3) or scriptural allusions (e.g., Dan 7:13–14 and Ps 110:1) strengthens both his theological message and literary framework.

Understanding Luke-Acts within the Greco-Roman context is crucial for fully appreciating its literary style, historical setting, and rhetorical techniques. He skillfully engages with the literary and cultural conventions of his time while preserving a distinct authoritative theological message. This makes his writing both accessible to his audiences (present and future) and subtly, subversively challenging, prevailing against cultural norms, redefining power (Caesar versus Christ), authority, and divine rule through the theological lens of Jesus Christ.

Finally, the limitations of first-century scroll length influenced the reason continuous texts were written on separate scrolls (as two separate volumes) rather than a single continuous work. While scroll length contributed to their division, Luke intentionally structured his works as complementary counterparts. His adaptation to Greco-Roman literary conventions ensured readability while preserving a unified message, reinforcing the case for Luke-Acts as a single, continuous narrative. He was not merely constrained by physical limitations—he deliberately designed the ascension as a literary hinge that conjoined both volumes.

Analysis of the Problem

Despite the overwhelming and strong evidence supporting the connection between Luke and Acts, some scholars continue to dispute their unity. Since the second century, Luke and Acts have been separated and seen as two separate, independent books, particularly with their appearance in the canon. The separateness and singleness of Lukan unity is explored in a great amount of detail. The separation of both volumes resulted in a challenge to Lukan authorship, specifically of Acts.[9] This resulted in Luke's Gospel having been given more precedence than Acts, and Acts is often treated as an anonymous work.

The book of Acts, as it is recognized in the canon today, has often been isolated from the Gospel because of its association with this disconnection.[10] The disparaging effect has resulted in proof-texting Acts, thereby taking scriptures and/or entire passages in Acts out of their intended context, and causing Acts to lose the contextual narrative presented in the Gospel. This book explores this as a method the author never intended, resulting from Acts being separated from the Gospel.[11] The author's intentional bridge forms both volumes to continue reading from the Gospel into Acts on an unbroken hinge.

Another problem exists in the way that the work of Christ and the work of the Holy Spirit are separated to the point that Christ appears in a limited role or nearly vanishes altogether in Acts. Considering that Jesus is the first-person actor, presently working in the church through the indwelling Holy Spirit among Christians, it is unfruitful to disconnect Jesus and the Holy Spirit into independent and separate entities, thus making the Holy Spirit begin a new work apart from the work Christ completed in the Gospels and while Christ becomes nearly absent as the first-person actor in Acts.

Consequentially, Acts should be seen as a continuation of the salvific work that Christ started in Galilee in the Gospel of Luke.

---

9. Padilla, *Acts of the Apostles*, 21.

10. Padilla, *Acts of the Apostles*, 31.

11. Parsons and Pervo agree with the notion that "several scholars have recently affirmed that the author of Luke and Acts intended them to be one continuous unified narrative from the perspective of the newer narrative criticism." See Parsons and Pervo, *Rethinking the Unity*, 45.

Even though Matthew, Mark, and John contain a narrative that also continues the story of Christ into Acts, Luke's Gospel provides the smoothest transition that allows readers to continue reading into Acts with an unbroken narrative. It is naturally what is intended when writing a single story.

This gets to the heart of Luke's narrative agenda, for his intentions and purpose behind writing Luke-Acts. He had a desire to take Jesus from Galilee to Rome, thereby sharing him with a world where polytheism and idolatry were normative.[12] At this point, God's salvation history with the Jews had extended to the gentiles. The Jesus presented in Luke-Acts is the only divine Lord and Savior, and God is calling the whole of humanity to turn away from current lifestyles and turn to Christ.

Jesus told his disciples it was to their benefit for him to leave them physically (see John 16:7). The limitations placed upon God in the incarnation made Jesus subject to limitations in the flesh. The theological association with this doctrine is called the *kenosis* as seen in the so-called Philippian hymn (2:5–8). To express that God personally underwent a process of self-emptying of his divine attributes in the incarnation is likely not the best way to explain it.[13]

The NT explains how the kenosis or κενός was necessary for God to become a genuine human being to die for all the sins of humankind (past, present, and future). While Jesus was God manifested in human

---

12. Parsons and Pervo highlight Joseph Tyson's argument that Luke and Acts were intended to tell a single story that began with Zechariah in Jerusalem and ended with Paul in Rome. See Parsons and Pervo, *Rethinking the Unity*, 45.

13. The entire context of Phil 2:1–11 is about Jesus Christ. In contrast to other English Bible translations, the NASB uses the word "emptied" in Phil 2:7. ἐκένωσεν ἑαυτὸν or "emptied himself" implies that God renounced or divested himself of divinity in the process of taking on humanity. Even though self-emptying is derived from *kenosis*, a literal self-emptying of God may not provide the best example of the incarnation. Paul Enns says kenosis means emptied. It was not "self-emptying" like in an example of a full glass of water, where the water is completely poured out of the glass. In Ps 139, David hints at describing God as an omnipresent Spirit. Such limitations set upon Jesus in the incarnation placed limitations upon the divine attributes of God. Consider the omnipresence of God manifest in human existence; as such, Jesus could only be in one place at one time as a human being. He did not surrender the absolute or immanent attributes because he was always holy, just, merciful, truthful, and faithful. See Enns, *Moody Handbook of Theology*, 228, 639.

existence (see 1 Tim 3:16), he did not cheat in human existence as a man but relied on faith and on the Holy Spirit to perform a successful three-year earthly ministry (see Acts 10:38; 2 Cor 5:19).[14]

This process of self-emptying means to empty, to make empty, to abase, neutralize, make of no effect, of no reputation, or to make something void.[15] The term "humiliation" is a more accurate way to describe it.[16] God's humiliation involved his taking on the form and nature of a human being thereby placing all the human limitations upon himself to fulfill the service of God, without ceasing to be God. The desire to save human beings required him to surrender the independent exercise of relative or transitive attributes voluntarily, specifically omniscience (Matt 24:36), omnipotence (John 5:30), and omnipresence (Ps 139:7–10; Prov 15:3; Jer 23:23–24; Heb 4:13–5:10).[17]

Another problem exists in the way that Luke and Acts are juxtaposed in terms of genre. Since Acts has been viewed by many as history, it would be equitable to do the same for the Gospel rather than designating it as something else apart from its companion volume. One primary reason is a result of the historical appellation of their prologues (Luke 1:1–4; Acts 1:1).[18] In this perspective, it should make sense to view both volumes collectively as history.

Was the Gospel written for the sake of doctrine, and was Acts intended to be treated as a history of the church? Such designations are likely okay and are reckoned to be distinct genres, but Acts is not always treated as equally authoritative as the Gospel. They are often treated as two different and separate works. Acts, in some circles, is given less authority than the Gospel. Luke begins with the Gospel and continues through the work of Jesus Christ in and through the church, and since the author has this intent, one's hermeneutics should treat both as equally authoritative Scripture.

---

14. In the *Theological Bible Commentary*, O'Day and Petersen refer to the Holy Spirit as being the Spirit of Jesus. See O'Day and Petersen, *Theological Bible Commentary*, 328.

15. BDAG 539.

16. Enns, *Moody Handbook of Theology*, 228, 639.

17. Enns, *Moody Handbook of Theology*, 639.

18. Pitts, *History, Biography, and the Genre*, 1.

An example in modern Christianity involves water baptism as it is seen in the Gospel of Matthew in comparison to the way it is performed in Acts. In Matt 28:19 Jesus told the apostles to "πορευθέντες οὖν μαθητεύσατε πάντα τὰ ἔθνη βαπτίζοντες αὐτοὺς εἰς τὸ ὄνομα τοῦ Πατρὸς καὶ τοῦ Υἱοῦ καὶ τοῦ Ἁγίου Πνεύματος" (NA[28]).[19] The Acts version spoken by Peter is different from the Matthean version quoted by Jesus.

Beginning in Acts 2:38 and repeated throughout additional parts of Acts, these verses do not use the phrase "Father, Son, and Holy Spirit." Instead, they use "the name of Jesus," "the name of Jesus Christ," and "the name of the Lord Jesus" (e.g., Acts 8:12, 16; 10:48; 19:5). In Acts 2:38, Luke recorded Peter as saying Πέτρος δὲ πρὸς αὐτούς Μετανοήσατε [φησίν] Καὶ βαπτισθήτω ἕκαστος ὑμῶν ἐπὶ τῷ ὀνόματι Ἰησοῦ Χριστοῦ εἰς ἄφεσιν τῶν ἁμαρτιῶν ὑμῶν καὶ λήμψεσθε τὴν δωρεὰν τοῦ Ἁγίου Πνεύματος (NA[28]).[20]

If Acts and select Pauline Epistles (e.g., Acts 2:38–39; 4:12; 8:12, 16; 10:48; 19:5; 22:16; Rom 6:3–4; 1 Cor 1:13; Gal 3:27; Col 2:11) are placed on par with the words of Jesus recorded by Matthew, it may be that the Acts version of water baptism exercised by the apostles is either taken for granted, not practiced by the church at all, or is rejected altogether as not being on par with the recorded words of Jesus in Matthew.

Another way to look at this is the way Luke's Gospel does not use a baptismal message as did Matthew in the Great Commission (see Matt 28:19), but he intended to record it in Acts as the apostles quoted it. Since the Third Gospel and Acts are read as a single book, he wanted to teach that the Gospel is discipleship in training and Acts is discipleship in action. As Jesus taught and commanded them in the Gospels, the apostles carried out what he commanded in Acts.

When Jesus commanded water baptism in the Gospel recorded by Matthew, Luke bridged from the ministry of Christ in his Gospel to the ministry of the apostles in Acts. The version in Matthew's Gospel

---

19. Matt 28:19, "Go therefore and make disciples of all the nations, baptizing them in the name of the Father and of the Son and of the Holy Spirit" (NKJV).

20. Acts 2:38, "Then Peter said to them, 'Repent, and let every one of you be baptized in the name of Jesus Christ for the remission of sins; and you shall receive the gift of the Holy Spirit'" (NKJV).

has led some scholars to ignore the baptismal name in Acts as the apostles used it, and have stated that Jesus's words in Matt 28:19 carry more weight by using the terms "Father, Son, and Holy Spirit." It, however, should not be a surprise that Jesus did not write Matt 28:19, but tradition holds that the apostle Matthew wrote it.[21]

For as much as it is the case, it would have been so that Matthew and the rest of the apostles in Acts understood Jesus's words in their Great Commission by Christ (also see Matt 28:16) the same way that Peter understood them in Acts. The term τὸ ὄνομα in Matt 28:19 carries a singular noun usage in Acts. The apostles, after the composition of the Gospels, appear more concerned with connecting water baptism with *ordo salutis* throughout the NT.

To respond to the problems or answer the questions presented requires a further examination of what Luke intended with the Gospel and Acts. An answer is essentially a rhetorical one as this book continues to unfold the literary structure in the way both volumes are written through the examination of narrative and rhetorical analysis, socio-environmental elements, connection features, and chiasms. Rather than using an ancient Homeric style, he writes in a Hellenistic Greco-Roman style prevalent in writing styles of his day.[22]

Specifically, regarding connection features, they are presented as primary themes and reveal important highlights in the literary narrative of Luke-Acts, as they are also rhetorical devices. In addition, the connection features are also identified in travel narratives Luke uses as a divine circuit to take Jesus from Galilee to Rome. The chiastic arrangement through Luke-Acts is essential in revealing what he intended. The coherent structure in the literary narrative of Luke and Acts brings out all the chiastic and connection features intended to join both volumes into a single book.

This book argues that the two volumes form one book and not two separate, independent works. The Gospel is volume 1, and Acts is volume 2. Luke's narration is not broken when reading from the

---

21. The title ΕΥΑΓΓΕΛΙΟΝ ΚΑΤΑ ΜΑΘΘΑΙΟΝ denoted by Papias ca. AD 125 is one of the first post-biblical voices to ascribe the Gospel of Matthew to Matthew the apostle of Jesus named in Matt 9:9; 10:3; Mark 3:18; Luke 6:15; and Acts 1:13. See Davies and Allison, *Critical and Exegetical Commentary*, 7–8.

22. Parsons and Pervo, *Rethinking the Unity*, 14.

Gospel into Acts. Luke's Gospel is the first story, and Acts continues that story, which is why his literary writing style appearing as narrative is key to understanding the narrative flow between both volumes.

Another issue revolves around the view of Acts today in terms of how it is read and interpreted. Today, Acts is often proof-texted with specific scriptures yanked out of their context and used to support a specific view, agenda, or doctrine. It is read with a common intent on supporting a specific supposition without consideration of the Gospel. If Luke were here today, anyone could ask him directly. But if Acts is going to be understood and interpreted today as it was among a first-century audience, it must be read in the inclusion of the Gospel.

This book is also accomplished by juxtaposing the prologues of Luke and Acts to demonstrate how the author intentionally focused on the birth of Christ in the Gospel and the birth of the church in Acts. Such parallel structure on the part of the author is prevalent throughout both volumes. The parallelism used in Luke's writings is common in ancient writing.

The first-century literary and cultural context is explored to examine how it contributed to Luke's writing style as a historian and theologian. Some scholars would like to compare it to the ancient Greek poet Homer. But further examination brings him closer in similarity to the Hellenistic Greco-Roman literature of the first century. Narrative criticism is important in reading Luke-Acts.

Additional key elements to his writing style are revealed in themes he uses to take Jesus's message from Galilee to Rome. It is essentially the beginning of his ministry, where he traveled from Galilee to the Jordan River to be baptized by John the Baptist.[23] Luke's overt concern is with the spread of the message, the gospel of Christ. He highlights an extensive travel narrative from the beginning of Jesus's ministry in Galilee to the end of Paul's ministry in Rome. "The world" in Luke 2:1 was likely expressed as the boundary within the confines of the Roman Empire. In Acts, the Roman world was vast and was thought to have extended "to the ends of the earth" (see Acts 1:8), but

---

23. Luke, in his Gospel, does not name this location, but Matthew specifically notes that Jesus traveled from Galilee to the Jordan River where John was baptizing (see Matt 3:13).

not exclusively, by implying that the gospel message would eventually extend beyond the empire's capital.

He ingeniously connects the end of the Gospel to the beginning of Acts using an ascension narrative in both books (Luke 24:45–51; Acts 1:6–11) with the term ἀναβαίνω. Using Sailhamer's expression of two garments being sewn together at the seams, Luke-Acts is similarly stitched together at a seam running down the middle, in a similar fashion to two pieces of a quilt sewn together at their two seams, making the quilt one garment.[24]

The chiastic structure of Luke and Acts also bridges Jesus's death and resurrection with the outpouring of the Holy Spirit on the first disciples. Jesus's travel narrative throughout Luke's Gospel arrives at Jerusalem. A chiasm is a place where Luke's Gospel narrows out to this epicenter, Jerusalem, where it focuses on the culmination of Jesus's mission, and branches outwardly from that epicenter, that is, from Jerusalem to Samaria, to Judea, and the outermost reaches of the earth.

Although the gospel message continued branching outwardly in the post-apostolic age of the church, Luke, however, stopped writing after Paul reached Rome. The Gospel of Luke is coming into the chiasm and Acts is going out of the chiasm in this coherent structure and design. Several chiasms exist in both the Gospel of Luke and Acts. The ascension narrative formed at the end of the Gospel and the beginning of Acts is the main or primary chiasm. It is a literary device or parallel structure used to aid readers in understanding both volumes as one book.

In Acts 1:8, the disciples seemingly asked a bad question, "Will you now restore the kingdom of Israel" (as it was in the glory days of David and Solomon)? As a result, Jesus set forth their missional statement that the Holy Spirit is coming to the witness on their behalf. Luke uses Jesus's tripartite missional statement death, burial, and resurrection in Luke 24 to connect it to his ascension in Acts 1:8. The disciples' mission has its foundation on this fact. Acts, therefore, does not begin with the church; it begins with Jesus. Acts becomes a continuation of Jesus's work that Luke recorded in his Gospel.

---

24. Sailhamer, *Pentateuch as Narrative*, 35.

In addition to the crucifixion and resurrection of his gospel message, the ascension narrative is the primary chiasm that connects both books, as Acts continues the work of Christ through salvation and the outpouring of the Holy Spirit. When Jesus healed people on his journey from Galilee to the epicenter of Jerusalem, the church continued his mission and healed people going outwardly from Jerusalem to Rome.

Henceforth, Jesus's extensive travel narratives in Luke's Gospel bring him inwardly into the middle of the chiasm. Luke does so by also emphatically demonstrating this chiastic structure as the continuation of Jesus's ministry. And where deliverance was needed, the church did not simply pray for it; the Holy Spirit endowed them with the courage and power they needed to boldly speak as witnesses of Christ's message (i.e., the gospel).

In addition, and throughout the travel narratives in the Gospel, Luke demonstrates that Jesus preached and taught the people out of his mission. The church in Acts, therefore, lives out Christ's mission through the Holy Spirit (and the mission of Christ that had been committed to them in Matt 28:19). The reality of that mission lived out through the Holy Spirit becomes a practical expression and a lived-out experience in the life of God's children.

Finally, Luke develops a syllogism in his compositions of his chiastic structure and design. More broadly speaking, the Gospel of Luke is the front end of the chiasm, and the Acts of the Apostles is the back end of it. His chiastic structure in the literary narrative is his style of writing that bridges this continuity of Luke and Acts. They can both be read as one book in a chiastic arrangement. Additional links joining Luke and Acts as a continuation of his story are examined as literary and theological links between the two volumes intending to demonstrate how both should be read together as one book as the author intended.

Methodology

The research is meticulously conducted with great attention to detail, very carefully, and with preciseness. Any commitment to the in-depth study of Luke-Acts can be seen as like other things in life. Becoming a professional at a craft requires one to invest time in deep hermeneutical study and exegesis to understand and appreciate their beauty. Once this has been done, only then can one begin to see and unfold the beauty of such great works God has given to the church through this servant.

An in-depth understanding causes the mind to wonder if God himself grabbed the pen of the author and unrolled back some richness and glory of his eternal words and wisdom. Those who have done the same through hermeneutical exegesis can understand and come to enjoy what is truly being expressed in so few words. It does not discount the gap between first-century readers of Luke-Acts and modern readers. Textual critics have done an admirable service in bringing today's version with that which was read and appreciated by Luke's original audience.

All too often, as Luke and Acts have been separated and read as two separate and independent works, they have been read out of their intended context. It has often been a harmless common practice to proof-text both Luke and Acts like a shotgun. Just as a shotgun when it is fired at close range sprays bullets all over a target aimlessly, Luke and specifically Acts have been treated in a similar way where scriptures are often pulled out or detached from their intended context and aimlessly misapplied. The problem and answer to the problem or question are explored through careful exegesis with interpretative methods of narrative, literary, and rhetorical criticism.

Background analysis-synthesis includes the socio-environmental elements (historical-cultural criticism and social-scientific analysis). Such include authorship, date of writing, writing style, and cultural backgrounds in at least the first three centuries of the NT that all contributed to the shaping of Luke-Acts in the environment producing his two-volume work. Finally, it involves examining an additional literary element such as genre.

Things of interest include the flow of Lukan theology throughout both volumes, Luke-Acts. Luke's information also harmonizes with data supplied by Matthew and Mark that also proclaim Jesus as the Davidic Messiah and Savior of the world. Not every biblical critical method is used in this examination. A few methods that are used for research and data gathering are narrative, literary, rhetorical, and socio-environmental critical analysis in the overall process of examining Luke-Acts.

The reason for narrative criticism is that it focuses on the narrative, whereas Luke is telling a story about something to someone. The hermeneutical engagement of the method seeks to reveal various attempts to be a means of access to the world behind the text and within it and as a medium and means of communication between the author and reader. A textual flow within the narrative of the text is experienced by the reader as the narrative unfolds and flows in an allusion to a chronological sequence of events.[25]

The method is used in this book in accordance with other rhetorical and social-scientific critical methods as the flow of Luke's story unfolds the plots, themes, motifs, characterization, style, figures of speech, symbols, text repetitions, and language within and behind the text. The story is unfolded to disclose what the author means and what he has told the reader, whereas narrative criticism has been regarded as an extended type of rhetorical criticism.[26]

Using a rhetorical critical method draws attention to the text, to what is happening in the text, as well as the real world within which the intent of the text is doing its work. It is a language aimed at persuasion on the part of the speaker and/or writer, the context, and the subject being presented by the speaker and/or author.[27] The method is not original to Luke or to writing in the first century. It was an ancient practice used by rhetoricians to capture the attention of an audience and dominate it. It is an ancient practice that spanned to the Greeks and Romans in first-century Hellenism, as a tool to capture an audience and/or reader's undivided attention.[28]

The literary critical method is used to identify and uncover hidden assumptions (not meanings) and contradictions that shaped the

---

25. McKenzie and Kaltner, *New Meanings*, 107.
26. Porter, *Dictionary of Biblical Criticism*, 375.
27. McKenzie and Kaltner, *New Meanings*, 80, 87.
28. Porter, *Dictionary of Biblical Criticism*, 381.

text of Luke-Acts.[29] Narrative criticism is akin to literary criticism because it analyzes the literary structure and style of the text. Any kind of intellectual study of literature is a form of literary criticism.[30] While narrative criticism focuses on the narrative, the focus for readers is on the story being told by the author.

As such, the literary critical method is used in this book to examine the literary structures of the written texts of Luke-Acts. As specific passages are studied contextually, a literary analysis of the author's "original and current text" is needed for examination to see the whole story of it.[31] In addition, acute literary structures that make up the text such as words, phrases, sentences, and paragraphs are examined in this book to aid in the determination of the meaning of what the author wrote and is communicating to his audience and readers.

Finally, socio-environmental critical analysis has two methods of aiding in the examination of the history in the text, the history around the text, and the history outside the text. It uses a historical-cultural analysis and social-scientific criticism.[32] The reason for conducting a historical-cultural analysis of the text of Luke-Acts is to gather background information that includes dates, authors, recipients, contributing historical events, and extrabiblical historical information that contributed to the author putting the words on the scroll.[33]

In addition, a social-scientific analysis is conducted to deal with the historical elements and the history at the same time the author wrote Luke-Acts. These methods are exclusively in chapter 5 regarding backgrounds. These include cultural values, social relationships, religious and political systems, and other social events and patterns of

---

29. Porter, *Dictionary of Biblical Criticism*, 74.

30. Barton, *Nature of Biblical Criticism*, 1–2.

31. The meaning behind the expression "original and current text" has to do with the original autographs written by Luke versus the current text that exists today in the Bible. It does not imply that the author wrote a different text than it is today. It does mean that the original text was written in a geography, culture, and language different from today's languages. As such, it opens this subject for analysis and examination.

32. Blomberg, *Handbook*, 63.

33. Blomberg, *Handbook*, 66.

behavior at the time the biblical account happened in history to help clarify the way the author presents the text.[34]

The primary question for Luke-Acts centers around the ascension narratives at the end of the Gospel and at the beginning of Acts, used by this book to connect Luke-Acts as a single book. To avoid this agreement, some scholars attempt to attribute the ascension narratives to anonymous interpolations over the original and the same author as the rest of the text. All such problems and questions will be solved and answered as all chapters leading up to the final three chapters will seek to accomplish this humongous task.

The last three chapters are written around an examination of "ascension," whereas chapter 8 is the analytical discussion on the ascension narratives in Luke-Acts and the chiasmus associated with those ascension narratives. Again, as the previous chapters build up to a full exegetical study of the ascension narratives in the final three chapters, chapter 8 of this book is intended to make the literary connection between both volumes.

Literature Review

Some sources are difficult to read, whereas some others are excellent. Some authors appear to write or comment on the New Testament with a negative agenda, aimed against a specific biblical author's historical data, such as accusing him of being uneducated, illiterate, or inaccurate in his research. In the case of Luke, author of the dual work Luke-Acts, he used sources for his research and did not become an actual eyewitness of the events he reported on until the middle point of Acts 16. Because Luke conducted his investigation and research on matters he reported, his data is sometimes attacked as being inaccurate.

Modern sources such as those of modern authors are not helpful at all and some of their writings appear at times or sometimes give the appearance of being agnostic or atheistic. It also appears that a select number of modern authors do not approach the Bible from a Christian position of faith, but from a point of view that sees the Old and New Testaments as just another piece of ancient literature. Those

---

34. Blomberg, *Handbook*, 66.

holding such positions veer from the internal message of the biblical author as he has presented to them and his readers.

The author of Luke-Acts wrote autographs that express an internal witness of Scripture and that claim inspiration (God-breathed) from the Holy Spirit (e.g., 2 Tim 3:16–17; 2 Pet 1:21). From the aspect of biblical inspiration, there are two modes or methods of getting to what the NT is today. One is the original author, and the other is the copyist. The original author was inspired, not the copyist. The extant manuscripts contain copies of the author's original autograph and contain some errors during the copy process, such as grammar, spelling, or word choices. Overall, scribes have done a great service in producing and maintaining those manuscripts.

Critics of the Lukan texts argue that Luke was not concerned with facts and history, as he was with theology.[35] But an inaccurate theology is derived from an inaccurate history, which then argues that a historian must be accurate in his record of the history he is writing. The non-faith approach of a non-biblical author is fine if that is their position, but the attack on a biblical author's research and data as being inaccurate does not serve any practical purposes on the part of other readers. It is likely arrogant for a modern scholar to assume they know more than the Bible author about the event he reported close to two thousand years ago. Granted, the Bible to people who have faith in it is the word of God.

Edward D. Andrews, *The New Testament Documents* (2020)

Andrews should be highly respected for his research on the NT, and his book is an excellent, invaluable source. In *The New Testament Documents*, he supports and apologetically writes to defend the historicity

---

35. Ramsay appears critical of Luke, accusing him of being a poor historian and of misrepresenting facts. See Ramsay, *Luke the Physician*, 46. Forbes and Harrower accuse Luke of being more concerned with having good theology at the expense of historic accuracy. Forbes and Harrower, *Raised from Obscurity*, 40. Walaskay, in contrast, sees Luke as concerned about historical context, whereas Luke not only sought to present the facts of history but also an interpretation of those facts so the reader could understand his historicity as presented in the same manner as other historians in antiquity. See Walaskay, *Acts*, 11.

of the NT while presenting historical and physical (archeological) evidence to support his research. He starts with the formation of the Gospels and explores their process and the people. In his research, he presents evidence of the manuscript tradition for support of the abundant evidence that confirms the trustworthiness of the NT. For those who are merely critical of the accuracy and historicity of the NT, he attempts to write a contrasting accurate account of the transmission of it and processes regarding the formation of the canon to dispel many of the suppositions and errors in their criticism.

Andrews attempts to conduct a complete survey of the NT manuscripts. Even though he poses a negative view of the Textus Receptus, he believes that MSS earlier than the Received Text are more accurate because of the way the latter was translated (sources used and translation made). The author analyzes the transmission of the NT and the formation of the canon while defending how the books of the NT have been preserved over centuries. Andrews attributes the names of NT books to the original author of those books bearing their name. Andrews appears to keep an open mind to not be swayed by popular opinions. An apologist of the NT, he proves the reason the NT is completely trustworthy and dispels unsupported opinions aimed against it.

Henry J. Cadbury, *The Making of Luke-Acts* (1927, 1999)

In *The Making of Luke-Acts*, Cadbury was helpful and became an additional layer of support to the defense that the same author wrote the Third Gospel and Acts. He also concludes that Luke used sources for his work, and it is these sources and the way that Luke used them where Cadbury appears to place more of an interest. To Cadbury, Luke-Acts is a unity, not separate and different works. A majority if not all scholars credit Cadbury with the famous hyphen between Luke-Acts, and the designation is used this way throughout this entire book. Cadbury's research expresses that Luke-Acts centers around four distinct areas: the sources the author had at his disposal, the language and genre used for his writings, his own individual personality, and his specific conscious purpose in its composition.[36]

Bart D. Ehrman, *The New Testament: A Historical Introduction to the Early Christian Writings* (2012)

Ehrman claims that nearly 90 percent of the people in the first century were illiterate and could not read, write, or a combination of the two. Ehrman, along with other skeptical modern writers, also charged Jesus as being illiterate and that the apostles did not write their books because they too were illiterate.[37] Moreover, Ehrman believes the books making up the NT canon were not written by the first-century biblical authors bearing their names or based on their internal inscriptions, but were written by later anonymous persons. Ehrman's research was not helpful to assist with any accurate investigation of the NT.

In contrast to Ehrman's view on education in the early Roman Empire, there is so much overwhelming evidence that proves an opposite view to that held by Ehrman. In the first century, education was flooded with institutions of higher learning. Let alone, many Greek and Roman structures such as libraries were well known. Such availability to places of education and learning alone proves that a significant number of people went to school and were educated, contrary to Ehrman's views. Based on the many documents, newspapers, commercial documents, letters of poetry, military documents, pseudepigraphic books, and miscellaneous letters of the common people in society (of which hundreds of thousands have been discovered by archeologists), these writings are additional evidence to prove the high literacy rate.

---

36. Cadbury, *Making of Luke-Acts*.

37. Most people in the first century spoke at least two, three, or more languages, more than many people speak today. For someone to criticize the literacy of Jesus and his apostles is disconcerting. According to Col 1:16–17 and Heb 1:3, all things (that also includes knowledge) were created by Jesus Christ. To say that Jesus was illiterate moves so far away from the truth of anyone holding such a view.

David E. Garland, *Luke,* Zondervan Exegetical Commentary of the New Testament (2011)

Garland's commentary was helpful. It provides a complete verse-by-verse commentary on the Third Gospel. Before the commentary portion of the book, the introduction provides a historical background of Luke regarding authorship, his sources, the genre, dating, provenance, and readers. Although the commentary is on the Gospel, Garland assumes that Luke-Acts are a unity, which view became an important source to this book. The historical section concludes with the author's purpose behind Luke-Acts while seeing both as a unified work, and the structure of the Gospel. The book was a valuable source of historical data and information on Luke's background.

Joel B. Green, *Luke as Narrative Theologian: Texts and Topics* (2020)

Green sees Luke as the author of the two-volume work Luke-Acts, a theological and narrative unity. Green uses a collection of scholarly writings and essays as one of the few approaches to decipher Luke's message, regarding how he writes it and his intentions behind the style of his writing. While Luke is a theologian who writes his accounts in the form of a narrative, Green examines several highlighted themes in the Gospel for what he calls theological discourses. *Luke as Narrative Theologian* is a valuable source for deciphering Luke's narrative-theological unity of his Gospel.

Larry W. Hurtado, *Destroyer of the gods* (2016)

Hurtado's book was a good source in reflecting upon early Christianity. The author addresses a variety of topics in the early history of Christianity, and their distinctiveness among non-Christians, in the first three centuries of its existence. It reveals how Christianity survived and that the church grew exponentially despite the persecution it endured in the early stages of its existence. The historical setting of Christians, Jews, and gentiles were vastly different, whereas the

Christians residing within the early Roman Empire were labeled as atheists because they did not believe in the gods of the world.

While a large proportion of Judaizing Jews rejected Christ as Messiah and Lord, the Christian plight to hold Christ as the only divine being competed with reverence to Caesar and the Roman and Greek gods, which gentiles believed was strange. The Jews of OT Judaism were indoctrinated as a monotheistic race of people. Christians of the NT period were also monotheistic but envisioned Jesus as the God of the OT made known in human existence. The irony in the title is what Christianity became in the eyes of a polytheistic society, where it prevailed in an empire where others did not survive.

Craig S. Keener, *Acts: An Exegetical Commentary, Volume 1* (2012)

Kenner's commentary was a valuable reference and source. It presents a mountain of evidence for the historicity of the Acts of the Apostles. The commentary is a two-volume set. Volume 1 covers the first two chapters of the Acts of the Apostles as the source that deals with the ascension in this book. Keener supports the historicity of Acts and does not agree with the position of those who claim it is a novel. The first commentary reviews, examines, and explains historical sources that contributed to Acts.

Keener also supports the traditional Lukan view of authorship. One criticism aimed against the commentary is that it is not exegetical as the title purports. Keener agrees and states it is what the publisher wanted. He introduces historical questions related to Acts and provides a so-called detailed exegesis of Acts in the opening chapters. Another benefit of this commentary is that it does not fill up the pages with Bible verses with the author's opinion of their meaning.

Gail R. O'Day and David L. Petersen, *Theological Bible Commentary* (2009)

Theological Bible Commentary is not an exhaustive commentary on any specific subject, but it is an excellent resource for deducing scholarly discussions on the books of the Bible and select theological subjects. It also focuses on biblical studies and theology and attempts to merge relevant scholarly theological conversations around the biblical texts. The focus on biblical books wants to answer questions about God: Who is God, and what does each book say about God? The commentary provides exegesis and theological reflection attempting to engage readers hermeneutically on varied theological subjects today and how the books of the Bible engage those scholarly conversations theologically.

Mikeal C. Parsons and Richard I. Pervo, *Rethinking the Unity of Luke and Acts* (1993)

The listed source was helpful in the collation of a contrasting scholarly view. Parsons and Pervo accepts Luke's single authorship but assert that this alone does not imply that there is canonical, generic, narrative, and theological unity among both volumes. Lukan authorship has been seldom questioned; however, one issue with Luke-Acts involves their being written in different literary genres and the employment of different theological constructs between the two. The assertions presented in this book do not agree with such ideas employed by Parsons and Pervo but take a different approach from them.

Arthur G. Patzia, *The Making of the New Testament: Origin, Collection, Text and Canon* (1995)

The Making of the New Testament was another good source for history. It discusses the origin, collection, copying, and canonization of the NT books. It also examines how those books were produced in the first century and what motivated the early Christians to commit their teachings and writings to papyrus. Additional analysis examines how the early stories about Jesus were circulated and shaped into what became the four Gospels, in addition, what techniques were used to classify the NT books including when, where, and why they were written; the reason for there being four Gospels; the letters of Paul; and the methods used for inclusion of books in the canon.

Eckhard J. Schnabel, *Acts,* Zondervan Exegetical Commentary on the New Testament (2012)

Schnabel's commentary is essentially a commentary on the Acts of the Apostles. It looks like a companion to Garland's volume on the Gospel of Luke and is written in this similar format. It is indeed a complete verse-by-verse commentary on Acts. It is written as a commentary for those who are not familiar with or do not know Greek. After examining the historical background associated with Acts, like Garland's commentary on Luke, he then provides a commentary on each verse in Acts the same as Garland does with the Third Gospel. His explanation of each verse is accomplished by introducing the question that Paul and others were addressing that led to their answering it or resolving the problem at hand.

Patrick E. Spencer, "The Unity of Luke-Acts: A Four-Bolted Hermeneutical Hinge" (2007)

Spencer supports and defends the unity between Luke and Acts. He argues that out of all attempts to dissolve their unity it cannot be dissolved. The unity that exists between them should not and cannot be dissolved because such unity is upheld by a four-bolted hermeneutical hinge known as genre, narrative, theology, and reception history. The hyphen inserted by Cadbury connects them together as a unity, and each bolt will have to be removed, which cannot be done because each bolt fastening its hinges continues to remain fastened securely.

Robert C. Tannehill, *The Narrative Unity of Luke-Acts: A Literary Interpretation* (1986)

Tannehill was helpful as a source and he is often quoted. *The Narrative Unity of Luke-Acts* is a two-volume set of Luke and Acts. The second volume is a sequel to the first one, as they both feel like commentaries to the reader. Tannehill also views Luke-Acts as two volumes of one single work, but written and recognized in a literary and narrative bodywork. He thinks they are works of history that highlight the values, beliefs, and role models of a specific era. And the characters were influenced out of divine purpose for which activities much bigger than the characters arose and gave shape to the narrative unity of Luke-Acts.

For Tannehill, much of the words and meanings were developed by themes. The screenplay, however, of the Gospel and Acts differs in a sense. Jesus is the main character in the Gospel of Luke, which is highly episodic. Acts, on the other hand, has a focus on plots, and the plots of the narrative (story being progressed) contribute to Luke's overall literary structure. His point of view that Acts does not have a main character, however, is not entirely accurate. The main characters that surface in the first half of Acts are Peter, John, Stephen, and James (the Lord's brother), while the entire second half of Acts has Paul as the primary character.

Ben Witherington III, *The Acts of the Apostles: A Socio-Rhetorical Commentary* (1998)

Witherington's *Acts of the Apostles* was helpful and useful as well. It is essentially a commentary on the Acts of the Apostles. The author's purpose in the commentary is to provide a social and rhetorical analysis of the Acts of the Apostles. In addition, it focuses on the major historical and theological issues in and around Acts regarding early Christianity, the relation of Acts to Paul's Epistles, the Jews of Judaism, and secular people, and issues in the Roman Empire regarding its emphasis and effect on the history in Acts. It was helpful as a good source for history.

Research Summary, Structure and Design Considerations, and Substructural Framework

The layout of this book consists of nine chapters and a conclusion. Chapter 1 deals with introductory material and lays the groundwork for all the remaining chapters that follow. Chapter 2 continues the discussion from the introduction. Chapters 3 and 4 examine the literary connections between Luke and Acts. In addition, chapter 4 examines Luke's narrative design using narrative criticism.

Chapter 5 deals with cultural background–related studies in the first three centuries of the Roman Empire. Chapter 6 explores Luke's major themes or motifs along with Jesus's three-year travel itinerary, which is a divine circuit he traveled during his messianic ministry. The final three chapters, 7, 8, and 9, specifically examine Jesus's ascension. Chapter 7 examines the ascension, chapter 8 builds chiasms with the ascension, and chapter 9 climaxes the study of the ascension structure within Luke and Acts.[38]

As it was briefly summarized, chapter 1, "Introduction," and chapter 2, "Elucidating and Explicating Luke-Acts in Canonical and Greco-Roman Literary Structure," introduce this book and set the structure and framework for it. These beginning chapters are important to present some common problems with the view of Luke-Acts and explain the methods involved in solving all those problems and how the questions that are presented will be answered. Chapter 3 will move into a narrative unity and interconnectedness of Luke-Acts. It will analyze specific features unique to both volumes that connect the two as a running narrative.

Chapter 3, "The Unity of Luke-Acts and Theory Behind Luke's Intention and Purpose," suggests that Luke and Acts are a unity. The unity within Luke-Acts discloses his intentions and purpose for writing. There are primary themes identified as connection features throughout both volumes. The connection features in the unity of Luke-Acts are grouped literary narratives in the coherent structure of Luke-Acts that reveal what he intended.

The prologues of Luke (1:1–4) and Acts (1:1–5) prove intentional on the part of the author to begin with this information rather than his simply filling of ink on the page. Another motivation is to consider the audience, that is the designation to whom both volumes were first directed.[39] Specifically Luke and Acts were directed to an important

---

38. The terms "Luke's Gospel," "the Gospel of Luke," and "the Third Gospel" are all used interchangeably throughout this book.

39. The same author makes the point that Luke-Acts was directed to a predominantly gentile audience by way of Theophilus, even though they are generally intended for all believers, both Jew and gentile, rather than a narrow Christian

person such as Theophilus who was instrumental in financing the works, as they were intended for a broader Christian audience.

Funding was important for large projects like Luke-Acts. The development (and copying) of scrolls was expensive. It was common in the Greco-Roman world for writers to rely on professional scribes. According to Joseph Fitzmyer, when Luke uses the expression κράτιστε Θεόφιλε, it takes the vocative in Greek which is "most excellent Theophilus."[40] While Fitzmyer does not want to assume Theophilus was a patron of Luke, he does affirm however that dedication of a work or works to someone meant patronage in the Greco-Roman world of Luke's time. The biblical author's dedication to Theophilus implies that he was a wealthy Christian that financed the publication and distribution of Luke-Acts.[41]

The Bible or specific books of the NT are plentiful in the modern world but were not easy to possess in the first century. Richard Randolph states that most local churches in the Greco-Roman world may not have possessed a complete copy of any Gospel. It is because autographs had to be copied by hand. As a result, Christian congregations possessed only parts or portions of the autograph or manuscript to make it useful for their specific functions.[42]

Luke brilliantly sets the introductions with his use of the prologues. Loveday Alexander does not think Luke's prologue includes the first four verses of chapter 1 (see Luke 1:1–4). He calls this a preface, and calls the first four chapters, beginning at verse 5, a narrative prologue.[43] The verity apart from Alexander's view is their theological significance. To this point, the prologues of Luke and Acts were likely intended to set the stage for the birth of Christ and the birth of the church in the author's purview.

In contrast to the prologue to John's Gospel, Luke appears more apologetic.[44] He sought to establish a defense of Christ and Christianity

---

community of believers.

40. Fitzmyer, *Gospel According to Luke*, 300.
41. Fitzmyer, *Gospel According to Luke*, 300.
42. Richards, "Reading, Writing, and Manuscripts," 364.
43. Alexander, *Acts*, 211.
44. Maddox, *Purpose of Luke-Acts*, 4.

in an empire that was hostile to it. Both prologues provide internal evidence, traditionally accepted, that Luke was the author. Maddox would like to compare this to our modern-day printing press.[45] In the first century, a patron like Theophilus played a key role in getting Luke's message into the hands of many.

In modern times, writers intend for the first part of a book to capture the reader's interest to keep them reading. It was the same for Luke.[46] The contrast between Luke and the other writers, Matthew, Mark, and John, is different. He was not a direct witness of the life and works of Christ but rather relied on accurate sources for his data. It is not an epoch-making conclusion. He simply wanted his readers to know that his account had been carefully and thoroughly researched and investigated by gathering his data from those who knew Jesus personally and from those who were with him from the beginning of his ministry.

To this point, Luke was not physically present to witness the events about which he wrote. It is the same with the first part of Acts. Most of it consists of speech relayed to him from others. These include, for instance, Peter's Pentecost sermon (Acts 2), the apostles' defense before the Jews (Acts 4–6), the calling of the first deacon-like leaders (Acts 6), Stephen's speech before the Sanhedrin (Acts 6:8—7:53), Phillip's witness in Samaria (Acts 8), the calling of Paul and his conversion (Acts 9), Peter's experience at Joppa and his witness to the household of Cornelius (Acts 10), the martyrdom of James (Acts 12), the first missionary journey of Paul and Barnabas (Acts 13–14), and the first Jerusalem council (Acts 15).

Following the Jerusalem council, Paul and Barnabas departed to Antioch. Paul suggested that they return on the previous circuit to visit the Christian believers in the towns they had evangelized (Acts 15:36). Luke likely joined them when they left Antioch en route to Phrygia and Galatia. Regarding a disagreement over John-Mark, Paul and Barnabas separated. Barnabas took John-Mark with him and sailed to Cyprus, and Paul took Silas with him and traveled through Syria and Cilicia (Acts 15:39). Timothy joined them when they reached Lystra, and

---

45. Maddox, *Purpose of Luke-Acts*, 3.
46. Harris, "1 Gospel," 3–20.

they traveled through the regions of Phrygia and Galatia (Acts 16:1, 6). While being divinely directed from Asia to Macedonia, they went to Troas where Luke was with them (Acts 16:11).[47] It is here that Luke begins writing in the first-person using the plural pronoun "we."

An examination of the background information behind Luke's writing is a necessary part of Luke-Acts. It will also juxtapose the prologues of Luke-Acts in contrast to other NT Gospel writers to find commonalities as well as differences. There is a theological significance to the prologues that will need to be discovered and examined. In essence, Luke's way of using prologues lends credence to their unity and to the way both volumes are connected through this literary hinge.

Chapter 4, "Narrative Criticism in the Construction of Luke-Acts," examines the narrative within Luke-Acts and allows for discovery and examination of the way those narratives flow like the reading of a story. The Third Gospel story flows into the Acts story with an unbroken hinge. Following the prologues of Luke-Acts, he introduces the birth narrative of Christ in the Gospel and the birth narrative of the church in Acts. He proves himself a capable theologian, as his primary intention and objective is to tell these stories as he intended them to be read. The chapter provides the opportunity to examine the narrative of Luke-Acts in comparison to other narrative-style writing in the first century. The style he uses is common in Hellenistic writing.

The scholarly work entitled *Luke as Narrative Theologian* by Joel B. Green examines the views of several scholars in attempts to uncover Luke's narrative theology. He uses narrative criticism as his methodology for examining the theological and narrative unity of Luke-Acts by examining selective topics within the Lukan texts.[48] Kavin Rowe denounces that Luke and Acts were intended to be read as a single work.[49] The conclusions reached in this book stand in contrast

---

47. Acts 16:10 is where the author first uses "we" to indicate that he was accompanying Paul, Silas, and Timothy at that time.

48. Green, *Luke as Narrative Theologian*, highlights these topics as "salvation, wealth and poverty, baptism, resurrection, conversion, the birth narrative, Jesus's crucifixion, Jesus' ascension, the Pentecost episode, and the stories of Cornelius and Lydia."

49. Rowe, "History, Hermeneutics and the Unity"; Rowe, "Literary Unity." See Green, *Luke as Narrative Theologian*, 7–8.

to those presented by Rowe and others who share simular views. The structure of the narrative in the literary style that bridges Luke-Acts as a narrative unity is examined.

Narrative is one of the primary ways of reading Luke-Acts as an unfolding sequence of events happening one after the other. The discussion on narrative criticism in this chapter also ties back into chapter 3 regarding the question of what Luke intended. The chapter in no way attempts to make Luke-Acts a narrative genre. It is simply one of the methods used to examine his writing style when reading Luke-Acts while also examining the connections made between them.

Chapter 5, "Backgrounds—The Literary and Cultural Context of Luke-Acts," examines the literary and cultural context for Luke's writings as an author, historian, and theologian. Establishing the historical background of Luke-Acts in chapter 5 is important to determine when both volumes were written. In this chapter, Luke's literary and cultural context was formed by his being reared in the first-century Greco-Roman Empire, at a time when Christianity was outlawed by the state.[50] The Third Gospel and Acts were written by him in those days when there was no printing press as it exists in modern society. Writing in Luke's day was an expensive as well as time-consuming endeavor. This is because most authors hired a professional amanuensis to hand copy an autograph or manuscript.

Many socio-environmental and economic challenges and elements manifested themselves that ultimately influenced the writers of the NT, particularly in Luke's writing at a time the Christian church was being persecuted. While many Christians were being martyred, Luke was divinely guided to complete this two-volume work, Luke-Acts. The Gospel and Acts contain sociolinguistics not only because of the environment that they originated in but also based on Luke's

50. Hurtado examines Christianity in the first century and the writings of Roman authors to determine the cause of hate of a religion they despised so much. Pliny and Trajan wrote about how Christians were badly treated in an empire and society so hostile to it. In the first century, it was illegal to be a Christian, a crime that was punishable by the state. The crime of being a Christian or participating in the religion was placed in a different category from all other crimes committed in the empire. As much as it was illegal to a Christian, the charges could be erased by a person's change of heart by publicly renouncing their position. See Hurtado, *Destroyer of the gods*, 25–26.

profession as a physician. To show this or to bear this out, some of the Greek word choices will be examined. H. E. MacDermot stated, "It is not difficult to show that the medical terms used by Luke were those of the Greek medical literature of his time."[51]

Two areas of background analysis considered are what Craig Blomberg refers to as historical-cultural analysis and social-scientific criticism.[52] Ben Witherington uses a socio-rhetorical approach to examine Luke and Acts, which will also be examined, in detail, in chapter 5 of this book. These two studies presented by Blomberg, when used in examining the background of Luke-Acts, help to aid our examination and understanding of the historical context of the NT writer. An examination of the historical-cultural analysis of Luke-Acts gathers the writer's background information. It examines the history behind the text, such as author, date, recipients, and the historical events that contributed to the writing of his autograph(s).[53]

A study of extrabiblical historical information is important for understanding the history in the text, behind the text, and outside the text around the time of the biblical author. A social-scientific analysis also examines the history at the same time as the text. But it will include specific elements associated with the text such as the cultural values, social relationships, religious and political systems, and other social events and patterns of behavior at the time the biblical account occurred in real time.[54]

The rhetorical world around the Bible and Luke's use of it in Luke-Acts is examined in the way it was used in writing in the ancient world. The use of rhetoric in writing is an old practice. It was essentially a literary device and structure used throughout the ancient world. Aristotle defined it as the ability in the means to the art of persuasion.[55] While rhetoric was commonly used in ancient writing, Greco-Roman and Hellenistic writers were well acquainted with rhetoric and used it.

51. MacDermot, "Medical Language of St. Luke."
52. Blomberg, *Handbook*, 63.
53. Blomberg, *Handbook*, 66.
54. Blomberg, *Handbook*, 66.
55. Copeland, "Pathos and Pastoralism."

A writer's use of rhetorical criticism in the Bible was commonly used by them with the intention of persuading readers to their message. The first-century literary and cultural context contributing to Luke's writing style used rhetorical criticism. A message that Luke reported was often accompanied by a supernatural miracle that confirmed the message that was being spoken by the primary character in the message that was reported.

In classical or attic Greek rhetoric as seen in Homer, speeches reportedly take up more than half of the *Iliad* and the *Odyssey*.[56] This is not to assume that Luke imitated Homer; it simply means he made use of the *attic* style of rhetoric. He uses discourses to report the oratorical speeches of others. As stated earlier, Luke predominantly writes in the third person and switches to several "we" passages in Acts. Acts was intended to persuade his audience. Ancient and Hellenistic oratory was a powerful skill common among the learned in society. Luke does not use poetry as seen in Greek philosophy, but Luke-Acts has commonalities in the narratives of his telling his story in the form of speeches impelled by rhetoric. While Green will use a narrative-theological approach to Luke-Acts, Witherington will use a socio-rhetorical approach to examine Acts, which chapter 5 will examine in detail.[57]

The chiastic structure Luke uses is also a rhetorical device. It is rather unfolded to see his erudition. Early first-century readers were familiar with the way rhetoric worked within Hellenistic literature. There are similarities and differences, but letter writing, in general, rendered a common format. The Bible code for each biblical writer emphasized its message to those who had an ear to hear. As stated earlier, the art of persuasion in Greek and Hellenistic rhetoric was meant to persuade the readers to hear what the author had to say and what he told them. The idea is often developed in Jesus's speeches and reverberated throughout the NT.

The Bible, which people of faith call the word of God, is presented in a way that intends to capture the audience's attention to what God has to say to people. Such includes biographical,

---

56. Kremmydas and Tempest, "Introduction," 2.
57. Green, *Luke as Narrative Theologian*; Witherington, *Acts of the Apostles*.

historical, theological, sermonic, and apocalyptic, including various sub-genres. But it is also left up to each person to respond to it based on their faith in its message (cf. Matt 11:15; Rev 2:29). These similarities are predominantly found in Luke's writings resounding how the same author wrote the two volumes.

Chapter 6, "Exploration of the Themes of the Lukan Travel Narratives from Galilee to Rome," examines the primary themes used by Luke to take Jesus from Galilee to Rome. The epicenter, Jerusalem, culminated the end of Jesus's earthly ministry and the beginning of the church. From Jerusalem, the Gospel begins to spring from the Jews to the gentiles, as it is taken from Jerusalem to Rome.

The immediate readers of Luke were a small Christian community, but he wrote to a predominantly gentile audience where he wanted them to know that Jesus was fully human in every way of the term except that he had no sin. He also convinces them Christ died for all the nations and that they were also included in God's plan of salvation like the Jews were included in it. He presents Jesus as the Son of Man and traces his genealogy back to humanity's beginning with Adam.

In the Third Gospel, Luke wants to bring Jesus's messianic ministry from Galilee to Jerusalem (the epicenter).[58] Throughout the travel narratives in the Third Gospel, he documents Jesus's travels from Galilee to the epicenter, and in the process highlights important themes in Jesus's ministry. These themes are important for understanding the route Jesus was divinely directed on a specific circuit for three years of earthly ministry, ultimately leading to his crucifixion in Jerusalem. The circuit from Galilee to the epicenter was a ministry to the Jews, and the circuit from the epicenter to Rome was to the gentiles.

Luke culminates Jesus's three-year earthly ministry in the Gospel with his long-awaited arrival to Jerusalem, beginning with passion week. During this final week Luke continues highlighting important

---

58. Some scholars argue that this epicenter is the temple. The point is that Jesus came into the world to be a human sacrifice for the sins of the world. As such, his mission was to get to Jerusalem. It is also true that the prophet Malachi's visitation of YHWH was the manifestation of Jesus Christ in the Jerusalem temple (Mal 3:1). So, whether it was Jerusalem or the temple, both are true within the mission of Christ in the world.

themes such as the Last Supper with Jesus's disciples in the upper room (also cf. Acts 1:13), his arrest in the garden of Gethsemane, his trials and persecutions by the Jews and gentiles, his crucifixion, death, burial, resurrection, and ascension.

These events are crucially important to the Lukan literary narrative in as much as Jesus's ascension to heaven forms the primary chiasm that connects Luke 24:45–51 and Acts 1:6–11. After celebrating his pending departure in an upper room with his disciples, Christ's physical presence was replaced by the immanence of the Holy Spirit descending upon his disciples in an upper room in Jerusalem (Acts 2:1–4). A chiasm connects Luke-Acts to be read from the Gospel into Acts as a continuous story elucidating the concept of a single book.

To reiterate as it will be presented in chapters 4 and 5, background studies are an important component to understanding Luke's narrative of Luke-Acts and a historical-critical-grammatical exegesis of Acts 1:8. They are important to see Luke's further intentions of taking Christ from the Jerusalem epicenter and then to Rome. When reading Acts, Rome might be what Luke considered as the outermost reaches of the earth. If this is the case it likely becomes the reason he stopped writing when the church (specifically Paul) reached it. Jesus Christ and his gospel have been taken from Galilee to Rome as Luke intended.[59]

Chapter 7, "Juxtaposition of Ascension Narratives in Luke 24 and Acts 1 and Introduction to Chiasmus," builds a discussion on the ascension of Christ as it introduces the ascension as the main or primary chiasm connecting Luke-Acts. The ascension narratives Luke uses in Luke 24:45–51 and Acts 1:6–11 connect both volumes (Luke-Acts) as one book. The term meaning ascension is used in the LXX, in Greco-Roman literature, and other parts of the NT. The implication of the term involves someone who is moving toward an objective and/or going in an upward motion. In Revelation, the apostle John uses the term to describe how the two witnesses went up in a cloud while their

---

59. Luke's writing account of Acts ended in chapter 28 when Paul reached Rome. Luke accomplished his mission here by tracing the gospel of Christ from Galilee to Rome. The Gospel and Acts are connected in an unbroken hinge, bridging the two volumes together.

enemies looked upon them going upwardly.[60] According to the *LBD*, in Eph 4:8–9, the apostle Paul directly connects Jesus's descent with his ascension (ἀναβαίνω): "far above all the heavens."[61]

Throughout the OT, the idea of ascension was used in a lesser sense, described as someone walking up to a throne on an elevated platform (and within Isaiah and Ezekiel's ascension narratives it was used regarding Lucifer's rebellion). It coincides with Jesus's point in John 3:13 that "no one has ever ascended into heaven except the one [Son of Man] who came from heaven."[62] And Caesar, who usurped claims to divinity, made claims of ascending. Though Caesar was not a god but a man, he was heralded as a god, whereas Jesus was the true Son of God who ascended to heaven, not Caesar. In an ironic twist to Greco-Roman thought, Jesus was the true God who ascended for the benefit of Caesar.[63] Jesus is the only one who proved he was divine because he ascended in the sight of many witnesses (see Acts 1:9; cf. 1 Cor 15:6).

In contrast to Caesar, Jesus Christ is the one who ascended upward into heaven, which is used mostly by the NT writers in the context of his going upward into the sky. The use of ἀναβαίνω in Greco-Roman culture and its use in Luke always carried a sense of someone or something moving toward an objective. Both Luke and Paul use ἀναβαίνω to emphasize how Christ went up to heaven (cf. Luke 24:51; Acts 1:9–10; Eph 4:8–9). It essentially becomes divine "ascension" terminology based on the premise of a divine being ascending to heaven.[64]

---

60. "Then they heard a loud voice from heaven saying to them, 'Come up here.' And they went up to heaven in a cloud, while their enemies looked on" (Rev 11:12 NIV).

61. Brasfield, "Jesus, Ascension of."

62. An understanding of this statement made by Jesus will need to be harmonized with John's entire message on the divinity of Christ. It is clear from Jesus's statement that he was God manifested in human existence if he pre-existed the incarnation of God in Christ (cf. John 1:1, 14; 1 Tim 3:16).

63. "He will manifest in His own time, He who is the blessed and only Potentate, the King of kings and Lord of lords" (1 Tim 6:15 NKJV).

64. An apotheosis was used in ancient myths to describe a legendary hero who became a divine being at the time of an upward ascension after physical death. See Green and McKnight, *Dictionary of Jesus*, 780.

Chapter 8, "Stitching Luke and Acts Together at the Seams," examines how the ascension narratives in Luke and Acts are not the only connection points for both volumes. It examines and explores the chiasms around the ascension narrative in Luke and Acts. As discussed earlier, the themes within the travel narratives are Luke's coherent structure and design for taking Jesus from Galilee to Rome. Both Luke and Acts or Luke-Acts are stitched together around Jesus's ascension. The thread is the ascension narratives (Luke 24:51 and Acts 1:11), which bridges both volumes together as one book. In both the Gospel and Acts, Jesus is standing on the Mount of Olives giving his last in-person speech to the disciples who remained with him up to the time of the ascension (see 1 Cor 15:6).

When considering how two quilts (or two garments) are stitched or sewn together to make one garment, the concept is the same with Luke-Acts sewn together. The main chiasm will stitch together the two volumes so it can be read as one book as the author intended. The example of stitching and sewing garments together is metaphoric and practical. For instance, the left side of the quilt is the Gospel of Luke. And the right side is the Acts of the Apostles.

Consider the OT Pentateuch scholar John H. Sailhamer, who uses compositional literary analysis in narratives also called compositional seams for connecting chapters and books.[65] The same concept is also good for constructing Luke-Acts. It helps determine the key point of a passage in the middle of the chiasm. One part is Luke's arrival with Christ at the epicenter (Jerusalem or the temple in Jerusalem). The Gospel comes into the chiasm by coming from Galilee to Jerusalem. It then goes out from the epicenter to Rome. Christ's ascension, which takes place in Jerusalem, is the thread that sews both volumes together, and the needle is the Holy Spirit.

The chiasm also helps to see the parallel structure to what the author is aiming is a main chiasm that joins together Gospel and Acts as one book. It exists in the ascension narratives of Luke and Acts. It is also a rhetorical literary device that helps readers understand how both volumes are connected as one. Literary connection points also exist in the resurrection narrative and the travel narratives that

---

65. Sailhamer, *Introduction to Old Testament Theology*, 165–66, 192.

began in Christ's ministry in Galilee and continue through Acts, from Jerusalem to Rome.

Jerusalem is the centerpiece between Galilee and Rome. From the centerpiece, readers go back into the past to Galilee when Jesus first began his ministry in Nazareth or progress forward into the future when Paul is under house arrest in Rome. Luke continuously demonstrates how Jesus was progressing forward from Galilee to Jerusalem during his earthly ministry, and the gospel is taken to Rome by the church. It is what Luke intended to accomplish in Luke-Acts.

The epicenter is what Luke reveals as the melting pot for the gospel of Christ and essentially becomes its center of activity. Several events transpire when Jesus arrives at this epicenter. Jesus is arrested in the garden of Gethsemane where he then goes on trial before the Jews and Romans. He is then crucified, resurrected, and ascends to heaven. The first members of the church receive the Holy Spirit on the day of Pentecost, and they begin the Christian witness to the nations (see Acts 2:5).[66]

Chapter 9, "Climactic Denouement of Christ's Ascension in the Coherent Narrative of Luke-Acts," is the final chapter. The chapter distinctly underscores my central contribution and foundational thesis regarding the ascension narrative, particularly its role as the theological and literary hinge that unites Luke and Acts. The discussion reaffirms the ascension's profound significance across both volumes, not only as the culmination of Christ's earthly ministry but also as the inaugurating event of the apostolic mission, with implications for the created order. Additionally, the chapter engages with opposing viewpoints, addressing potential objections that challenge this thesis. By critically evaluating these perspectives, I reinforce my argument, demonstrating how the ascension serves as the structural and theological linchpin of Luke-Acts.

---

66. While beginning in Galilee, Jesus's messianic ministry begins branching outwardly toward Rome (and the outermost reaches of the earth, see Acts 1:8), while first taking it all the way to Jerusalem. Another rhetorical device used by Luke in Acts involves the Christian witness by Philip the Evangelist in Samaria where his witness of Christ is backed up with a miraculous event. Then Judea, where Saul of Tarsus enters the scene as the greatest persecutor of the church. The gospel message continues branching outwardly to Judea and continues toward Rome.

Furthermore, I continue exploring first-century rhetorical techniques, particularly how Luke employs narrative summary to bridge his two volumes. The argument advances to an examination of the literary relationship between the conclusion of Luke and the opening of Acts, illustrating how the ascension forms a chiastic transition. Acts 1:1–11 not only concludes the chiastic structure initiated in Luke 24 but simultaneously inaugurates the broader chiasm spanning Acts—from Jerusalem (Acts 1) to Rome (Acts 28). This structural unity further solidifies the ascension's role as the narrative and theological fulcrum of Luke-Acts.

The conclusion will reiterate and review the thesis statement that examined the *Coherent Chiastic Oeuvre in the Unity of Luke-Acts: Two Volumes Conjoined as a Single Book*. The majority traditional view has always recognized these two volumes as two independent works because of their current placement in the NT canon. There is no intention or attempt to attach new genres to them nor make them of the same genre. The Gospel of Luke still belongs to the Gospel genre (and each has specific sub-genres), and Acts is still more of a historical work.

Luke chapter 24 and Acts chapter 1 contain a literary seam where the ascension of Christ is the thread that stitches together both volumes as one book. The connection features identified in travel narratives as well as the major themes have become part of Luke's literary structure and design. Volume 2, the Acts of the Apostles, continues the work Christ started in Galilee. Luke's narrative agenda is exposed in both volumes, where he brings Jesus from Galilee to Rome.

Luke's intended purpose is disclosed in this book as it reveals the reason he stopped writing shortly after Paul reached Rome. For Luke, his mission was accomplished. He had successfully taken Jesus from Galilee to Rome, which is from the beginning of Christ's ministry in Nazareth to the end of Acts in Rome. Luke could have included more detail on Paul's state and condition but it is clearly not what he intended in writing Acts, noticeable with its abrupt ending.

The narrative culminating with Jesus's ascension does not end in the last chapter of the Gospel but continues into Acts as a completely unbroken story. The role of the Holy Spirit is central, unique throughout both volumes. The genre and authority of both volumes will also be examined. Regarding Luke's narrative theology, it examines how and why Luke wrote for theological purposes as he is telling a story in the order of a chronological sequence of events. It would appear to modern readers as a never-ending story, a story that is continuing today.

In a metaphoric example, the Holy Spirit is the needle, and the ascension narratives are the thread. He sews Luke and Acts together like a hem in a garment. Luke and Acts is a magnum opus because of its purpose and intent.[67] The way Luke and Acts appear in the NT today differs from how it was before the second century. Modern views of it have adopted this later view while not realizing how much different it is than the way Luke's first-century audience viewed it.

The Third Gospel and Acts were also written in a different genre. The author appears to have switched his discussion from a theological-biographical discussion of Christ to a set of historical-theological motifs of the apostles. The Gospel has been seen by some as being more authoritative than Acts. If both have canonical acceptance then both should be equally authoritative; one should not be seen as more authoritative than the other.

The discussion on "genre" in the next chapter, in the section "Analysis of Literary Genre of Luke-Acts," explores the literary genre of both volumes and how they differ. It should also be noted that works of differing genres does not prove an intended separation of the two works. While the Gospel of Luke is popular for a biography of Christ, ancient biographies were also associated with history. While modern distinctions may exist between them, a link or association between the two was synonymously recognized as far back as Plutarch and Nepos, and any difference between these two in antiquity is nearly nonexistent.[68]

---

67. Comfort, *Encountering the Manuscripts*, 15.
68. Cadbury, *Making of Luke-Acts*, 132.

Chapter 2: Elucidating and Explicating Luke-Acts in Canonical and Greco-Roman Literary Structure

ACTS CONTINUES WHERE THE Gospel of Luke leaves off, beginning with the ascension and a discussion on the impending Holy Spirit, the ministry of the apostles, the genesis and expansion of the nascent church, and the missionary journeys of Paul, finally ending with Paul living and preaching in Rome. Acts is a sequel to the Gospel, but it is more than that; it is volume 2 of a unified work, extending the story of Jesus's ministry through the work of his followers as the Holy Spirit empowers them. In interpreting the two volumes, the narrative and thematic unity between them is noted.

The unity is evident in the prologues (Luke 1:1–4; Acts 1:1–5), where Luke explicitly connects the two works, indicating that Acts continues the story that began in his "former account" (see Acts 1:1). Such unity is woven into the fabric of Luke's narrative theology. Common themes and motifs such as the role of Jesus as the messianic prophet, the Holy Spirit, the response toward persecution, ministry, healing, prayer, rejection and acceptance, wealth, Christ's crucifixion, resurrection, and ascension run through both volumes reinforcing their interconnectedness.[1]

---

1. Johnson, *Acts of the Apostles*, 28; Tannehill emphasizes what the critical nature of Peter's Pentecost Sermon meant to the witness of Jesus's identity as Messiah (Acts 2:31) and Lord (2:34), and how 2:36 combines those titles to emphasize what the resurrection, ascension, and outpouring of the Holy Spirit are taken together culminating in the fulfillment of the Scripture. See Tannehill, *Narrative*

The parallel unity of the ascension narratives forms a narrative bridge that connects the two volumes. The narrative serves as a structural and thematic link, a kind of literary stitch that binds both volumes together, underscoring their standing as a single unified work. The ascension narratives elucidate a significant theatrical role in stitching Luke-Acts together as a unified, cohesive story.[2] As such, the Gospel is intrinsically designed to be read in tandem with Acts, positing that they both exist with a natural narrative progression from one into the other as in an unbroken narrative hinge. Luke's deliberate iteration of the ascension narrative goes beyond mere repetition and serves as a literary bridge.[3]

While tying together the conclusion of the Gospel to the beginning of Acts, this literary hinge emphasizes the seamless continuum between both volumes where the ascension becomes the pivotal event between Jesus's tangible earthly presence and his ethereal manifestation through the Holy Spirit, profoundly reverberating this narrative arch.[4] Luke's intertwining of the two volumes advocates for their cohesive reading as an integrated opus and augmentation for comprehension of the intricate theological constructs inherent in this work.[5]

Early Views of Luke-Acts and Controversy Surrounding Its Text Today

When parsing out modern views and perceptions associated with Luke and Acts, one of the few questions is regarding authority. The Gospel is commonly seen as having more authority than Acts because

---

Unity of Luke-Acts, 37.

2. Tannehill, *Narrative Unity of Luke-Acts*, xiii.

3. Cohesiveness, in the context of Luke-Acts, should be understood as all its parts fitting together well to form a unified whole. When reading Luke-Acts as a narrative and as a single narrative, its unified cohesiveness emerges when each episode is read considering the whole. Throughout, the abundance of evidence demonstrates how their unity is maintained through the narrative developments that take place, as they continue to unfold and progress forward. See Tannehill, *Narrative Unity of Luke-Acts*, 8.

4. Tannehill, *Narrative Unity of Luke-Acts*, 263.

5. Tannehill, *Narrative Unity of Luke-Acts*, 23, 263.

it contains the words from Jesus's earthly ministry. The question of authorship, therefore, becomes an important consideration. For one reason or the other, if Luke wrote the same Gospel bearing his name and including the Acts of the apostles, then why would one seemingly have more authority than the other? Furthermore, why would one book in the Bible have more authority than another one that is part of the same canon?

When the Gospel of Luke was separated from Acts, Luke was added to the *Tetrevangelium*.[6] It brought about the perception that some would rather trust the words spoken by Jesus in the Gospels over those spoken by the apostles in Acts while forgetting that Jesus did not write any of the words the Gospel writers said that he had spoken. When challenging the authority of Acts versus that of the Gospels, it is like saying that a person trusts what Matthew, Mark, Luke, or John have written in their Gospels over those written by Luke in Acts.

In addition, if one assumes the words of the *Tetrevangelium* are more authoritative than those written by Paul, Peter, James, or the letters of John, it would make it difficult to determine if the person believes the entirety of the NT is indeed written under God's inspiration. If the same author wrote both Luke and Acts, both seemingly should bear the same authority and not one over the other, just because of their terms of genre or placement in the canon.

Another determination regarding the way Luke and Acts are viewed today is the consideration of what they are today versus the way they were viewed by Christian believers in the first century AD.[7] For example, were these two separate, independent works, and separate books, written by different authors, or were they the same? It is not an easy answer on the surface but one that is examined in this book. Considering the authority of Luke and Acts in the first century, it would not be a surprise for the rejection of their authority in comparison to the books in the OT.[8]

---

6. Aune, *New Testament*, 77.

7. The book that modern readers know as Acts was known as *Apostle* among the first Christians. See Cadbury, *Making of Luke-Acts*, 2.

8. It is possible that the apostle Paul did not realize he was writing Scripture that would be on par with the OT Scriptures he often quoted. The apostle Peter recognized all Paul's writings as Scripture which "ignorant and unstable people distort,

In this aspect, Luke and the NT writers may not have realized they were writing Scripture that contained the same authority as the Torah. When it was recognized that Jesus was the prophet like unto Moses (Acts 3:22–23; cf. Deut 18:15, 18–19), and even greater than him, they affirmed the words of the Torah were fulfilled in Jesus. Judaizing Jews specifically would not have considered Paul's writings as equal to those of Moses and others.

But to those who believed on Christ, the message of the apostles was just as authoritative as the prophets of old because the Lord commissioned them as he commissioned the prophets. Regarding the writings of Paul, for instance, Peter considered his writings Scripture and on par with the OT (2 Pet 3:16). In another instance, the apostles even envisioned the NT perhaps superseding the OT, by their reading new meanings and fulfillments, at times, back into it.

In the second century, the view of Luke and Acts significantly changed. They were no longer seen as a continuous single story, because both were separated from each other, and the Gospel of Luke was enveloped into the genre books making up the fourfold Gospel collection. Acts was left alone as a history of the church and became seen in a different way, other than the way the Gospel of Luke was seen.

Considering the four written canonical Gospels, Mark wrote to a first-century audience in Rome, and John's audience was to congregations in and around Ephesus in Asia Minor.[9] Unlike Luke's Gospel, Matthew is specifically a Jewish Gospel, as he wrote to Jewish believers around Jerusalem in Judea. In early Christianity, some started considering Matthew the lead Gospel because Jesus's first message was to the Jews before it came to the gentiles (Matt 10:5–6).

Upon Jesus's ascension to heaven, the apostles and disciples camped around Jerusalem. The gospel message of salvation did not leave Jerusalem until Philip was led to proclaim it in Samaria (Acts

---

as they do the other Scriptures, to their own destruction" (see 2 Pet 3:16 NIV).

9. Blomberg assumes the apostle John, the author of the Gospel named after him, wrote in the first century to the churches in and around Ephesus during the latter part of his life. The pure gospel message as it was taught by those who knew Jesus personally was being assaulted by the twin attacks of incipient Gnosticism and Jewish excommunicators, and perhaps an emerging form of Ebionite Christianity. See Blomberg, "Gospels for Specific Communities," 113.

8:5, 14). It extended from Judea and Samaria to Antioch during the ministry of Paul and Barnabas (see Acts 13:2; Gal 2:9). Mark eventually took the central role in the *Tetrevangelium* as it was claimed as the first Gospel to be written.[10] Some assumed that Luke and Matthew used a hypothetical Q source and Mark to write their Gospel.[11]

For form critics who envisioned specific shaping at their early development, it is assumed that each Gospel was initially written in and for their own *Sitz im Leben*, which Edward Klink thinks must be defined if they are to be read correctly.[12] Based on modern social-scientific methods of reconstructing the backgrounds of early Christian communities behind each of them, each of the Gospels was concerned with their unique, specific community and situation of their environment.[13]

When the biblical authors wrote their autographs for what eventually became scriptures on par with the OT, their writings did not contain chapter and verse numbers, nor in some cases book titles (names). Later, stylometry analysis was able to associate any anonymous or unknown writing to the author based on internal content and associations. In some cases, words and sentences were written with no spaces between the words in sentences.

The internal witness of the text was more important to the early readers of the text than the name or title of it. The addition of verses, chapters, and book names did not require nor cause a change in the original text, or to it, from the translated autograph or manuscript. Such additions were added for clarity and readability, which aided in making the text easier to read, whereas chapter and verse numbers added to the adroitness of finding specific information in the text.[14]

The primary reason attributing the way Luke-Acts looks today compared to the first-century version is language, writing style, and all the nuances contained within a source language that are difficult

---

10. The assertion that Mark was the first Gospel to be written is referred to as Markan priority, whereas apostolic priority would affirm that Matthew and John are the lead Gospels because apostles wrote them.

11. Bock, *Luke and Acts*, 28.

12. Klink, *Audience of the Gospels*, 4.

13. Klink, *Audience of the Gospels*, 4.

14. Smith, *After Chapters and Verses*, 19.

to translate in writing from that language to another. The original autograph was not rewritten, but translated many times over again, into a target language or languages to enable more people to read it in their language.[15]

Many who are not familiar with the way the Bible was handed down through generations are unaware of the process of translation, whereas skeptics and denigrators of the NT for instance often bewilder the work of translation with a rewriting of the text or with corruption of it. Latter translations of Luke-Acts mostly involve discussions around the source text used in translating Luke and Acts into the target language (detailed discussion on this in chapter 5).

One point of debate for scholars also comprises the early text of Acts. Debate surrounding the distinction of textual type and their families contributed to the popularity in the scholarly study of the text of Acts, which today has been studied more than that of any other book in the NT.[16] For instance, the Western text is a little longer than the Alexandrian textual type, which Metzger believes was the Greek text of Acts that circulated among the first Christians called *the way*.[17]

No manuscript or manuscript family is rightly absolute in determination of the original text. But on the same token, no family should be outright rejected for determination of the original text since the many others also contain all or portions of Luke and Acts.[18] Admittedly so, the *Tetrevangelium* became the earliest witness to the life and ministry of Christ, for without them, it would be difficult in the case of later and modern generations to know or have known much about Jesus outside the witness of those texts.

Luke wrote his two-volume work to give him certainty of the truth that he had learned from the many "declarations" being purported in the first century (Luke 1:1). The confidence Luke gave to Theophilus was that the persecution of the church in the then

---

15. The case of a biblical writer such as Paul, who references one or more of his letters that cannot be found, would require a rewrite on his part of the seemingly lost letters (cf. 1 Cor 5:9 and 2 Cor 2:3–4).

16. Roth, "Text of Luke and Acts," 51.

17. Metzger, *Textual Commentary* (1994), 222.

18. Aune, "Text-Tradition of Luke-Acts," 69, 80.

Roman Empire was not a sign of judgment or rejection.[19] It was a counter-cultural message lived by those who proclaimed it, to and in a hostile world. It was a living message that condemned the ungodly lifestyles and practices of many and challenged all to forsake all and turn only to Christ for salvation.

Jesus predicted the persecution of Christians, and it was a means by which the gospel message could go out to even the outermost reaches of the world (cf. John 15:18–27; Acts 1:8). The work details how Jesus is at the center of God's plan, a plan that anticipated not only his death but also his resurrection and ascension on the right hand of God (Acts 7:56; Heb 10:12), the one having all authority in heaven and earth (Matt 28:18–20), where he offers the benefits of salvation as Lord to all who come to him by faith (John 6:37–40).[20]

Luke-Acts is the story of God in Christ and the new era of promise spoken by the prophets (Joel 2:28–29; Ezek 36:26–27). The helper and enabler will guide and provide God's elect (those faithful to God's divine call) as God's chosen people in the hostile world. For Theophilus, and those chosen in Christ, are expected to continue in faith as his faithful community in a world that persecutes it and that rejects the message of Christ in the world with the realization that all will give an account to him.[21]

Luke's use of titles such as "Kurios" and "Son of Man" introduces the idea that he wanted to show a real and human Jesus to Theophilus, a Jesus to whom others who have only heard or read about him could relate. The NT uses κύριος approximately 717 times, whereas Luke uses the term more than any other NT writer.[22] The term did not reference someone who was necessarily divine, but it was used many times as a respectable gesture such as mister or sir.

Luke does something unique in his texts. The understanding of Jesus as *Kurios* exceeded that of a respectable gesture. It is that YHWH is the Lord God of Israel that became human (Mal 3:1; John

---

19. Bock, *Luke and Acts*, 29.
20. Bock, *Luke and Acts*, 29.
21. Bock, *Luke and Acts*, 30.
22. The term κύριος is used by Luke 211 times in Luke-Acts. It is used 104 times in his Gospel. Matthew uses it 80 times, Mark uses it 18 times, and John uses it 52 times. See Blackaby, *Experiencing the Word*, 186.

1:1, 14).²³ Luke then replaces the *Kurios* in Hellenistic emperor language and understanding and applies it to Jesus.²⁴ Luke then begins presenting Jesus as the human identification of YHWH to Theophilus, as the term takes on a whole new meaning by revealing Jesus to Theophilus and his audience.

The Gospel quotes of Jesus's use of "ὁ υἱὸς τοῦ ἀνθρώπου" were an applicable case of referencing himself as the human Messiah, a human descendant of David, born of a virgin, and anointed as the Messiah for a mission to die for sins (cf. Acts 10:38; Luke 4:18; Isa 61:1). Apart from direct quotes of Jesus using it for himself, the phrase never became a confessional title among early Christians other than Stephen's attribution of it to Jesus when he was being stoned. He said, "I see heaven open and the Son of Man standing at the right hand of God" (Acts 7:56).

The apostle John applied it to Jesus in the book of Revelation when he saw "one like a son of man" (Rev 1:13; 14:14). For John, the one enthroned in Daniel's vision he called "the Ancient of Days" is who John applied to Jesus (Rev 1:13–15; cf. Dan 7:9–10).²⁵ For Luke, such terms and phraseology were likely used as a reference to the "Son of Adam" (see Luke 3:38) who was also "ὁ κύριος" from the tetragrammaton of the LXX.²⁶ In addition, Jesus was not simply a person being born into the world like any ordinary person; he was the only human being who was able to take away sin, an exclusively divine function (Luke 2:11; cf. Isa 43:11).

Luke's highlight of Jesus's human descent from Adam was intended to underscore the universal scope of his mission, to the Jews and gentiles.²⁷ A predominant fulfillment of OT prophecies by Jesus shows that Luke is thorough and methodical in showing his fulfillment of a unified witness of Scripture in the Law, Prophets, and the Psalms (Writings) (Luke 24:44).²⁸ However, Luke, like Matthew, is

23. Staples, "Lord, Lord," 2.
24. Mundhenk, "Jesus Is Lord," 55.
25. Hardin and Brown, "Son of Man"; Reynolds, *Son of Man Problem*, 431.
26. Mundhenk, "Jesus Is Lord," 55.
27. Köstenberger and Goswell, *Biblical Theology*, 452, 458.
28. The term "Old Testament," abbreviated OT, is a non-existent term in the

steeped in the OT, and grounds Jesus's messianic mission proclaimed in the Hebrew Scriptures.[29]

For Luke, Jesus came to establish his kingdom with Adam's seed by his coming into the world (Luke 24:44). Köstenberger and Goswell state that Luke's writings constitute the glue that holds together the entire NT because the Gospel is uniquely joined from the OT by the birth of John the Baptist. And Acts transitions into the Epistles as a foundational background.[30] Luke's writings proclaim Jesus's identity and mission as a unique work binding together God's work among the Jews in the OT and the Holy Spirit's work in the days of the early church's mission.[31]

The ascension of Christ as it was viewed and told in the first century was based on previous ascension stories in the OT and ancient myths. Such stories would have made Jesus's ascension more believable with the examples preceding him. Uniquely in the case of Jesus, however, many witnesses saw him alive after his resurrection. In addition, it became a celebrated event by Christians in the first century, whereas the crucifixion, resurrection, and ascension are separate events yet all connected.

The author uniquely flanked the ascension in Luke and Acts with the Holy Spirit. The ascension became the visible, tangible, and concrete expression of Jesus's exalted status and reality as the divine Lord and Christ.[32] Jesus did not just leave earth for someone else to take his place. The Holy Spirit is none other than the presence of Jesus (Acts 16:7) albeit in another dwelling.[33] Paul's farewell message to the elders in Ephesus noted that the church is God's flock and that God purchased it with his blood (see Acts 20:28).

Hebrew Bible. It became *old* based on the existence of the New Testament or NT. These terms (OT, TaNaK, LXX, Septuagint, Hebrew Bible, and Hebrew Scriptures) are used synonymously throughout this book.

29. Köstenberger and Goswell, *Biblical Theology*, 450.
30. Köstenberger and Goswell, *Biblical Theology*, 442–43.
31. Köstenberger and Goswell, *Biblical Theology*, 442–43.
32. Green and McKnight, *Dictionary of Jesus*, 50.
33. Green and McKnight, *Dictionary of Jesus*, 50; O'Day and Petersen, *Theological Bible Commentary*, 328.

The Holy Spirit is not mentioned as such in the final chapter of the Gospel, but Luke specifies in Acts 1:2 that it was through the Holy Spirit that Jesus had given instructions to his apostles. The scene Luke prepares in Christ's ascension begins with bringing the Holy Spirit to the forefront of his theology as it is significant for the day of Pentecost. In the speech-act recorded by Luke, Peter considers this as significant an event in human history as the crucifixion, resurrection, and ascension (Acts 1:15–24; 2:14–40).

The long-awaited fulfillment of the OT Pentecost was manifested by the descent of the Holy Spirit on Jesus's first disciples (Acts 2:3–4, 16–21; cf. Joel 2:28–32). The pneumatological theology used by Luke in Acts corresponds to the period known as the ecclesiastical age, but it can also be identified as "the age of the Spirit."[34] According to Luke, Peter notes the outpouring of the Holy Spirit on the day of Pentecost (Acts 2:1–4) as "the last days" that await the fulfillment of Acts 1:10–11.

The Holy Spirit is the consequence of Acts, and not the other way around, as he takes more of a highlighted role in the lives and ministry of believers in the Roman Empire.[35] The promise of the Spirit coming to them did not become a substitute or fulfillment of Acts 1:10–11 (cf. John 16:7), whereas a return of Christ to earth constitutes a return in the same manner that he ascended in a physical human body. The intermediary period of a Spirit-Paraclete *logia* serves as an immediate and definitive solution to the problem of delayed *parousia*.[36]

---

34. Green and McKnight, *Dictionary of Jesus*, 50.

35. The Holy Spirit is the central point of God's redemptive activity, the heart of the gospel, and Christian hope, which only became available to everyone in Acts. See Rayan, *Holy Spirit*, 2. Justo González believes Luke's work, which has been traditionally called the "Acts of the Apostles," is the "Acts of the Holy Spirit" and is also an insight that has stood the test of time and proves to be the vital key to it. See González, *Acts*, book jacket. Köstenberger and Patterson also agree that the Acts of the Apostles would be better titled the Acts of the Holy Spirit. See Köstenberger and Patterson, *For the Love of God's Word*, 76.

36. Breck, *Shape of Biblical Language*, 229.

Consequence of Acts, the Holy Spirit, and Its Significance Given by Luke's Gospel

Acts serve a critical role in the modern understanding of the early church. It is not merely a historical record; it provides valuable theological insights into the growth and development of early Christianity and the central role of the Holy Spirit in the divine plan of salvation history. Acts elicits a unique perspective on the early church. Unlike Paul's letters, Acts offers a broader narrative of the church's expansion. It traces the journey of the gospel from Jerusalem to Rome and provides a narrative context for the NT Epistles, and that from a largely Jewish milieu to a gentile context, reinforcing the universality of the Christian message.

Regarding the epistolary narrative context, it discloses situations and events that gave rise to the issues addressed in the letters.[37] It helps readers understand the dynamics of the early Christian communities, their struggles, conflicts, and achievements. Beyond its historical role, Acts also has significant theological value. The narrative demonstrates the power of the Holy Spirit in the life and ministry of believers as the driving force behind the church's expansion, empowering the apostles to witness the risen Christ, as a guide for the church in its early decisions, and as an enabler of believers to live out their faith in challenging circumstances.

The writing of Acts is important because of its historical and theological contributions.[38] By providing a narrative of the nascent church and highlighting the Holy Spirit's role in it, Luke offers a model for the church's mission and life. He portrays the church not as a static institution but as a dynamic, Spirit-led community engaged in proclaiming and living out the gospel message in a world extremely hostile to it. The time frames provided by the author enhance an understanding of his narrative.

He grounds the events in a historical context and connects them to significant biblical themes and events, enhancing their theological

---

37. Acts provides the canonical, historical, essential background, and a logical foundation for reading the Epistles. See Köstenberger and Patterson, *For the Love of God's Word*, 77.

38. Köstenberger and Patterson, *For the Love of God's Word*, 39.

resonance. He uses time frames not merely as chronological markers but as narrative tools that deepen the meaning and impact of his account. The writing of Acts and the time frames provided are crucial for understanding the early church's historical context and theological vision. They shed light on the church's mission, its reliance on the Holy Spirit, and the significance of its foundational events in the light of biblical history and symbolism.[39]

By presenting a comprehensive and theologically rich account of the gospel and the nascent church, the author stitches together a tapestry of faith that continues to instruct and inspire Christians throughout every generation in time. In both the Gospel of Luke and the Acts of the Apostles, the author intends to emphasize various critical events that reflect the Holy Spirit's role. From the annunciation, conception, and birth of Jesus, through the birth of the *ecclesia* on the day of Pentecost, each of the events showcases the Spirit's transformative work.

Luke's Gospel account of Jesus's human life begins with the Holy Spirit's intervention. In the annunciation, the angel Gabriel tells Mary that she will conceive a son by the Holy Spirit's power, and he will be called the Son of God (Luke 1:35; cf. Matt 1:18). The divine conception serves as the foundation for the high Christology of Luke's Gospel, establishing Jesus as fully divine from his conception.

The baptism of Jesus, as narrated by Luke, marks the beginning of Jesus's public ministry. Here again, the Holy Spirit plays a crucial role. As Jesus prays after being baptized, the heavens open, the Holy Spirit descends on him in bodily form like a dove, and a voice from heaven declares, "You are my Son, the Beloved; with you, I am well pleased" (Luke 3:22 NRSV). Following his baptism, Jesus was led into the wilderness by the Holy Spirit for forty days of testing (Luke 4:1–2).

The episode not only underscores Jesus's reliance on the Holy Spirit but also sets the stage for his victorious mission. Upon his return from the wilderness, Jesus, "filled with the power of the Spirit," enters a synagogue in Nazareth and reads from the scroll of Isaiah, declaring, "The Spirit of the Lord is upon me because he has anointed me to bring good news to the poor" (Luke 4:14, 18 NRSV).

---

39. O'Day and Petersen, *Theological Bible Commentary*, 360.

It solidified the public initiation of Jesus's mission, clearly guided and empowered by the Holy Spirit.[40]

Moving into the Acts of the Apostles, the descent of the Holy Spirit on the day of Pentecost marked one of the most significant events in history apart from the crucifixion (Acts 2:1–4). The event, which takes place fifty days after Jesus's resurrection, marked the birth of the NT church. The Holy Spirit gifted the disciples to speak in various languages (cf. 1 Cor 12:10, on Paul's explanation of the gift of various kinds of tongues or languages), enabling Christians to live out the gospel more effectively as chosen by God.[41] The event echoes Jesus's empowerment in Luke's Gospel and establishes a pattern for the mission of the church.

In Acts 6:1–7, the Holy Spirit moves the apostles to select deacons to ensure the equitable distribution of food and support among the Greek and Hebrew-speaking widows in the community. Those chosen are described as being "full of the Spirit and wisdom," reiterating the Spirit's guiding role in the church's administration and decision-making.[42] The account of the Ethiopian eunuch's conversion and baptism in Acts 8:26–39 demonstrates the Spirit's action in bringing non-Jews to faith. Prompted by the Spirit, Philip interprets Scripture for the eunuch, leading to his baptism. The event emphasizes the Spirit's role in understanding Scripture as well as pointing to the inclusiveness of the gospel.

Saul's dramatic conversion on the Damascus Road (Acts 9:1–19) is another transformative event prompted by the Holy Spirit, where Paul sees Christ and is converted to the Christian faith. After three days, Jesus sends Ananias to heal Paul, to water baptize him, and to guide him in receiving the Holy Spirit (see Acts 10:10–19). Following the encounter, Saul (later Paul) becomes one of the most fervent proclaimers of the Christian faith, demonstrating the Spirit's power to change hearts and lives.

---

40. O'Day and Petersen, *Theological Bible Commentary*, 329.
41. O'Day and Petersen, *Theological Bible Commentary*, 366.
42. O'Day and Petersen, *Theological Bible Commentary*, 366.

These events reveal Luke's emphasis on the Holy Spirit's crucial role in the life and mission of Jesus and the early church.[43] Whether it is the initiation of Jesus's ministry, the birth of the church at Pentecost, or the conversion of individuals like the Ethiopian eunuch and Saul of Tarsus, the Holy Spirit is consistently portrayed as the empowering and guiding force throughout Luke-Acts. Through the Holy Spirit, the threads of faith, mission, and community are stitched together, constructing a narrative quilt that shapes the entire Christian identity and witness.

Considerations Significant to the Expansion of Luke's Theological Narratives

The LXX version of the TaNaK was important to the expansion of Luke's narrative theology.[44] The methodology in the salvation history of OT Israel contributed to the shaping of his theology as crucial to seeing its culmination in Christ. He sees David as having a key role in the Messiah that he introduced in the Gospel and Acts (Luke 1:32–33; Acts 2:25–36). OT prophecies often carried a two-fold meaning, present and future. In David's desire to build God a house (cf. 2 Sam 7:2–3), Nathan told him that the Lord would establish it. The present fulfillment was the temple built under the reign of Solomon (see 2 Sam 7:13). The future fulfillment was in the incarnation where Jesus, called the son of David according to the flesh (John 2:19–21; Rom 1:3), was God's temple.

The Gospel of Luke attempted to present Jesus to a gentile audience as a real, genuine human being, the Son of Man. The God that spoke to David, the OT patriarchs, and the prophets no longer dwelt among his people in a temple made with human hands (see Acts 7:48). At the time of Jesus, he referred to it as (his) "my house" and "a house of prayer" (see Matt 21:13; Isa 56:7), howbeit, now in human flesh as an act of divine mercy, grace, and love toward humanity.[45]

---

43. Köstenberger and Patterson, *For the Love of God's Word*, 73–76.
44. Muraoka, "Luke and the Septuagint," 13.
45. Köstenberger and Patterson, *For the Love of God's Word*, 31.

Regarding Christ's resurrection, Brandon Crowe sees this event as a key element in Luke's theology. Accordingly, it became one of the greatest of turning points in *historia salutis*, which helps parse out the relationship between Jesus's resurrection, his ascension, and exaltation.[46] The resurrection is tied to the crucifixion and ascension in equal ways to God's purpose of providing salvation to humanity.

Christ, the son of David according to the flesh (see Rom 1:3), is both Lord and Christ (see Acts 2:36 and Phil 2:11). Now, the grace of God that offers salvation to all people has appeared to all, indeed. It is effectuated upon all of those who accept Jesus Christ as their Savior (see John 3:16; 11:25–26; Titus 2:11). It was important to Luke for gentiles to understand this truth and accept the reality that they were and are also included in God's plan of salvation equally with the Jews.

Chapter 4 of Luke's Gospel is significant to the beginning of Jesus's ministry. After being kicked out of a synagogue in Nazareth, he relocated to Capernaum, near the home of Phillip, Andrew, and Peter in Bethsaida (see John 1:44). It is in this region called Galilee where the thrust of his public messianic ministry begins. He selects the disciples that were to be with him, and then he begins traveling about from one town and village to another, proclaiming the good news of the kingdom of God (cf. Luke 8:1). Luke is unique in his identification of three prominent women: Mary Magdalene, Joanna, and Susanna. They followed him closely, even up to his crucifixion and resurrection, and assisted him financially (see Luke 8:1–3).

Analysis of Literary Genre of Luke-Acts in the New Testament Canon

The Gospel of Luke and Acts give the appearance of being a narrative when they are read, but they are likely quasi-narratives. They are interjected joined-together discourses with the appearance of being read as narrative genres. The Gospels are about what Jesus did as the Holy Spirit empowered him to do so; whereas Acts is about what the church did as the Holy Spirit empowered them.

---

46. Crowe, *Hope of Israel*, 106.

Richard Burridge notes that the Gospels emerged out of Greco-Roman biography contexts and that the Gospels are like them.[47] He assumes if one is to accept a genre of or as βίοι (life, biography, life-story), it would be seen as it appeared in Greco-Roman writing styles, and not in a way that is similar with contemporary writing biographic styles,[48] and that genres reveal a lot about an author's writing. Burridge stands reserved on assigning a genre to any of the Gospels.

For Burridge, the Gospels are genre-less. In addition, they can be compared to first-century Greco-Roman βίοι (i.e., life, biography, life-story).[49] Although Burridge does not appear to set a clear fixed methodology of genre for the Gospels, to him, they are indeed genre-less Greco-Roman βίοι. At some times he would acknowledge a Greco-Roman biography (life story), whereas it is slightly possible to recognize one, a couple, or a few in a labor-intensive combing through their reading to discover something regarding it.

If one is to take Burridge's perspective it would mean that a literary genre is therefore not easily recognizable. He dismisses the notion of any early developments of literary forms and units of material recognized by form critics such as Hermann Gunkel. The notion of form criticism is from the consideration that the gospel of Jesus Christ was proclaimed before there was any written account. It is the formation and development of the teachings they were instructed by Christ to proclaim his words to the lost world around them.

An oral witness of any early gospel form that seemingly gave rise to later written accounts had to be a gospel story about Jesus based on eyewitness testimony of those that knew him personally (Luke 1:2). Before Luke's written account, it is obvious that many other writings about Jesus were already in circulation based on the GNT version of Luke 1:1: "Many people have done their best to write a report of the things that have taken place among us [them]." And for those who never saw him, accounts in some shape that eventually gave rise to the later written accounts were already prevalent.

---

47. Burridge, *What Are the Gospels?*, 105.
48. Burridge, *What Are the Gospels?*, 105.
49. See Burridge, *What Are the Gospels?*, 105.

To some scholars, this hypothesis became designated as the German word *Quelle* (shortened Q) meaning source.[50]

On the other hand, Rob James believes it is unlikely that any of the Gospels existed in whole in written form before any of them were written down in their canonical form.[51] In contrast, however, it seems likely that parts existed as the witness of Christ was proclaimed by the apostles and early church that testified to the works, words, and deeds of Christ. It presented an opportunity for Luke to highlight one of his sources when he states καθὼς παρέδοσαν ἡμῖν οἱ ἀπ' ἀρχῆς αὐτόπται καὶ ὑπηρέται γενόμενοι τοῦ λόγου, affirming that a Q source was likely available to him.[52] The conclusion makes it highly likely that an oral tradition regarding the words and deeds of Christ was available to Luke as an additional source to use for constructing his Gospel.

Although James denies the existence of this Quelle source, it is possible to observe it as a collection of sayings by the apostles of Christ.[53] If Q materials were essentially *the sayings* of the apostles (those things that the apostles said about Jesus before any canonical NT Gospel was written) whether they were oral or written, hypothetically, their sayings would more likely have been the teachings they directly received from Christ.[54]

What is true for the Gospel must also be true for Acts, given the credence of both volumes having the same singular author. The Third Gospel is a collection of the oral traditions handed down by Luke (Luke 1:2) to a small community of Christians,[55] in continuation of the traditions through Acts as jointed discourses mostly in the form of

---

50. Wansbrough, *Jesus*, 213.

51. Although James denies the existence of a Q source, he thinks Luke gathered his material from elsewhere or that he made a deliberate change in some of his narratives. See James, *Spiral Gospel*, 2.

52. Holmes, *Greek New Testament*, Luke 1:2. "Just as they were handed down to us by those who from the first were eyewitnesses and servants of the word" (NIV).

53. James, *Spiral Gospel*, 143.

54. Some hypothesize that Matthew had a sayings source before he wrote his Gospel. Mark wrote his Gospel, and then Matthew and Luke wrote their Gospels based on Mark's sayings sources. The commonalities and similarities among the three make them Synoptics.

55. James, *Spiral Gospel*, 14.

speech-acts. Such is common for Luke because he was not physically present to witness any such activities.

Luke becomes an obvious eyewitness of later recorded events when the text of Acts begins expressing the personal plural pronoun "we" on at least three occasions (Acts 16:10–17; 20:5—21:18; 27:1—28:16).[56] For Christians, including Luke, who had not met or seen Jesus in the flesh during his earthly life, nor were eyewitnesses of his deeds and teachings, the Gospel text was an invaluable document as it is also for Christians today.[57]

Regarding the way Burridge suggests how the Gospels looked in the first century, he believes they were similar (and did not appear strange) in comparison to all the other kinds of biographical compositions in the Hellenistic era.[58] An additional aid for Luke's Gospel is to consider its classification. For example, is it a letter or a sermon, is it a book of prophecy, or does most of the book contain poetic, metaphoric, or symbolic discourses? In addition to sorting this all out (even though the Gospel contains a majority or all of these aforementioned elements), one should ask for the most purposeful way in which it can be classified.[59]

When considering the Gospel genre, the best and clearest appearance of genre for the Gospel of Luke is a biographical-theological narrative. It is biographical because it presents the life of Jesus Christ (although he omits any of Jesus's biographical data between the ages of twelve to thirty), his ministry (works and deeds), his death (trials and crucifixion), and his resurrection and ascension to heaven. It is theological because it directly teaches and proclaims to people the words, commands, and divine will of God. And it is narrative because it reads like a story.

In comparison to Luke's Gospel, Acts is different. The closest that it comes to being biographical is by intruding into the life and works of Paul. But Paul's life is not on full display in Acts. Luke provides no record of his birth, childhood, or anything specifically

---

56. Porter, "We Passages," 162–63.
57. James, *Spiral Gospel*, 16.
58. Burridge, *What Are the Gospels?*, 211.
59. Burridge, *What Are the Gospels?*, 211.

about his life. Paul does not come on the scene until the martyrdom of Stephen in Acts 7:58–60. In contrast to Paul, Luke does however attempt to record the history of the entire early Christian church. In a similar fashion to the Gospel, it is also clear that he intended it to be read as a story.

Although many scholars have adopted a biographical thesis for the genre of Luke's Gospel, others have adopted similar arguments for the genre of Acts as biographical discourse.[60] But not all; some others hold to Acts as history.[61] From all appearances, Acts has the appearance of a historical-narrative work of Christ among the church. The biblical history according to Parsons and Pervo is not of a specific type. In league with Aune and Balch, they say it contains pliable, fluid, and disparate types of historical writing, which may be too difficult to obtain any specific model.[62] They attempted to compare Luke and Acts with Diodorus and Dionysius, as their goals rested on the hope of uniting dissimilar people-groups that were under Greco-Roman rule.[63]

Luke's intentions expanded beyond that of the Roman rule itself because his writings were certain to out-survive the Roman Empire, realizing someday that God was to bring it to an end. Instead, he sought to bring all humans under the rule of Jesus Christ. When placing Luke's works, the Gospel and Acts, among the three first-century historians like Diodorus, Dionysius, and Strabo, Luke is, with bias, criticized of being an amateur with only some rhetorical training.[64] If, however, the others are prominent authors based solely

---

60. In the work of Pitts, *History, Biography, and the Genre*, he identifies several scholars that identify Luke and Acts as biographies. Accordingly, C. W. Votaw, Charles Talbert, Philip Shuler, Albrecht Dihle, Richard Burridge, and Justin Smith are among those who adopted Luke's Gospel as biographical. Stanley Porter, Richard Burridge, and Sean Adams are among those who adopt Acts as biographical. See Pitts, *History, Biography, and the Genre*, 1–2.

61. Pitts, *History, Biography, and the Genre*, 1–2.

62. Parsons and Pervo, *Rethinking the Unity*, 30.

63. Schmitz and Wiater, *Struggle for Identity*, 17.

64. Pitts, *History, Biography, and the Genre*, 1–2. Schmitz and Wiater in *Struggle for Identity* highlight Diodorus and Dionysius along with Strabo as the most prominent authors of the first century based on substantial parts of their works that were produced and preserved. See Schmitz and Wiater, *Struggle for Identity*, 17.

on substantial parts of the works they produced, then why is Luke accused of being an amateur?[65]

His historical technique indeed attempted to explain the origin and growth of Christianity into a worldwide movement, which may have been questionable to those who were hostile to it. But to assume this subject was contemptible and directed toward an unworthy readership cannot be substantiated any more than the notability of those previously mentioned.[66] As with the Third Gospel, Luke desires for his readers to read it as if they are reading a story about something.

Regarding its history, the author is presenting a story (narrative) about the history of the church built by Christ as a continuation from the Gospel of Luke (see Matt 16:18). And not only does Acts compare to a genre of history, regarded in the traditional view, but it indeed reveals the history of the Christian church that began on the day of Pentecost (see Acts 2:1). The historical view of the church portrays, in narrative style, a focus not on a specific congregation but on the church entirely.

In contrast to the opinion of literary critics, an author's history must be accurate, otherwise it becomes their own fabricated account of a story of the past. Those essentially accusing Luke of being historically inaccurate take it upon themselves to know more about the history of Luke's time than the first-century author himself. The critics appear to produce little to no convincing evidence that supports arguments against the Lukan history which some reprove.

Osvaldo Padilla, among others as well, associates Acts as a historical monograph. The ideal became a bearing on modern readers to understand Luke as an eyewitness and as one who participated in the events he narrated.[67] Although the term "historical monograph" did not exist in antiquity, it is essentially a modern label. Padilla's suggestion for Acts is that it is a Hellenistic historical monograph in the Jewish tradition.[68] Luke first collected stories from trustworthy sources until he became a literal eyewitness to the events he later reported.

65. Parsons and Pervo, *Rethinking the Unity*, 31.
66. Parsons and Pervo, *Rethinking the Unity*, 31.
67. Padilla, *Acts of the Apostles*, 73.
68. Padilla, *Acts of the Apostles*, 61.

However, if historical accuracy is not important for Luke, as some modern scholars assume, it builds upon a problem that potentially challenges the inspiration of his writings.[69] The historical-critical aspects become even more of a problem. It tends to focus on the human aspects of history while ignoring or even removing the divine aspects. In contrast to a historical-critical method of Acts, Luke intended for people to hear God speak to them through the text.

The historical critical approach is important to aid a reader's understanding of the history in, around, and outside the text of Scripture. One of its inadequacies, however, is its resolve to overemphasize the humanness of the text itself, while downplaying the divine prerogatives that make it God's word.[70] If inspiration is brought into question, the Bible will become the mere word of humans in place of it being the word of God (see 1 Thess 2:13). If this were the case, its trustworthiness for salvation and all the promises God has made to humanity would have simply been a trick contrived by people to deceive others for less than divine reasons.

Smith and Kostopoulos propose that Luke-Acts belongs to a single literary genre.[71] The structure and design of its varied literary elements, most assuredly their single authorship, presents a wide collection of Greek prose narratives.[72] It is another way of envisioning how Luke-Acts is read as a single unified narrative.[73] A writing's literary genre is important wherewith it aids in understanding an author's writing. The literary genre in the narrative of Luke-Acts preserves a collective unity by intercalating both volumes into categories revealing the author's intention of reading them as a single book.[74]

---

69. Padilla stated that "the author of Acts does not guarantee accuracy but encourages the reader to view the events narrated as having occurred." See Padilla, *Acts of the Apostles*, 72.

70. Grenz, Guretzki, and Nordling, *Pocket Dictionary of Theological Terms*, 59.

71. Smith and Kostopoulos, "Biography, History and the Genre," 390–410.

72. Smith and Kostopoulos, "Biography, History and the Genre," 390–410.

73. Smith and Kostopoulos, "Biography, History and the Genre," 390–410.

74. Smith and Kostopoulos, "Biography, History and the Genre," 390–410.

Authority of Luke-Acts in the New Testament Canon

The historical reliability of both volumes elicits more credibility because of the reputation of the author who wrote them. In the Third Gospel, he says, "σοι γράψαι, κράτιστε Θεόφιλε."[75] He uses quite similar phraseology in Acts 1:1: "πρῶτον λόγον ἐποιησάμην περὶ πάντων, ὦ Θεόφιλε."[76] The author of both volumes provides the strongest evidence of a singular author. Acts is attributed to the same author as the author of the Gospel of Luke.[77] As Luke was a careful investigative historian (Luke 1:3), people can be assured of the historical accuracy of Acts just as certainly as they can be with the Gospel of Luke.

A historical-critical approach to the Gospel of Luke is often harmonized with that of Matthew and Mark. The three have been called synoptic because of their similarities to each other establishing Luke, the beloved physician and companion of Paul, as the author of the Third Gospel. It gives credibility to Acts in establishing it, and essentially gives both volumes credible historical and canonical authorial authenticity. They are not the pseudepigraphic works of an anonymous or unknown person.

As an emphasis regarding scholars who believe that historical accuracy is not important for Luke, it is important for inspiration, trustworthiness, and reliability of *Sanctus Scriptura*. It is one example of why Luke's historical record must be accurate. A first-century reader of Luke-Acts would more likely have a different view of inaccuracy in Luke's history than modern readers. It mainly is because Luke's contemporary audience was well attached to much of the history in Luke's day. With this in consideration, it would have been easier for them to verify Luke's sources. If they deemed his messages contained inaccuracies, this would have potentially damaged his character as a credible

---

75. Harris, *Lexham Greek-English Interlinear New Testament*, Luke 1:3: "to write [them] down to you most excellent Theophilus."

76. "The first account [Gospel of Luke] I composed concerning all things O Theophilus...."

77. According to the *Dictionary of Early Christian Biography*, "The first line of the Muratorian fragment concludes a notice of Mark's Gospel, as it speaks of Luke's as in the third place, and the Gospel of John in the fourth place." Wace and Piercy, *Dictionary of Early Christian Biography*, 744.

eyewitness, which, thereby, would also have caused great harm to the historicity of Christianity.

The overarching purpose of Luke's writings is an attempt to bring human beings to a place of faith in Jesus Christ, regardless of national origin, background, and culture. With this in consideration, the historicity of Luke is important for his readers, otherwise it would likely shatter the faith of many. The result would bring about a condition that would likely prevent many from even accepting the truth of Scripture. Similarly, many alleged inaccuracies in the proclamation of that message have already seemingly dismantled the faith of some.

If Luke falsified events that he reported to have happened, his testimony would be no more than any other uninspired fictitious writer to fulfill their agenda. If Luke-Acts were simply a collection of epic tales or an ancient novel to entertain people as claimed by Bonz and Pervo, his writings could not have been backed by the inspiration of the Holy Spirit. To this end, God does not operate in deceit and falsehood. And the information he claimed to be true would be mere lies (cf. Luke 1:1–5).[78]

Luke's historical accuracy is important. It is important not only for the testimony of the Scriptures but also for the building of a person's faith in Jesus Christ, as Luke proclaims in his written testimony (see Luke 1:4). Historical accuracy is essential for the proper interpretation of Christian doctrine. Luke must be accurate in his history not only for it to be a trustworthy account of things he says happened, but for it to be theological. In telling a story it is not history to the writer. When it is read in the future, it is history to the reader.

The demand placed upon the chronicler by those accepting the writer's account as an accurate record of those events he is reporting is great, as he is responsible for telling the truth about the accounts he is making about his context. If Luke was trying to deceive his readers regarding the history of/in the text, so could Matthew, Mark, John, and perhaps others potentially do the same.

In the annals of a historical past, Luke wrote two volumes of one narrated story for an early Christian community to appropriate and transform their lives to a message that once began out of an ancient

78. Padilla, *Acts of the Apostles*, 53–58.

corporeality of Jewish culture. It was a marvelous undertaking by appropriating and transforming the sacred traditions of Israel's past as written in the TaNaK and translated in the Septuagint to scattered monotheistic Jewish communities.

It is unfounded to assume that Luke was writing epic stories like that of Virgil and Homer as Bonz has concluded. To view Luke and Acts of the same genre as Greco-Roman epic is an unsubstantiated claim and cannot be substantiated only because a person wills it to be the case. For Virgil, who wrote the *Eclogues*, *Georgics*, and *Aeneid*, his epics were foundational for appropriating and transforming the lives of the Roman people by imitating Homer. For Bonz, Luke and Acts are epic because he essentially imitated Homer as did Virgil.[79] Bonz uses lots of parallels adduced between the *Aeneid* and Luke and Acts that are wholly superficial. As a result of the circular reasoning, she comes very close to parallelomania.[80]

In addition, Pervo, in his commentary on Acts, does not think that the literary style of Acts matches up to that of the ancient historians. Rather, he argues that it fits much better with the popular writings of ancient novels.[81] However, a little more than a decade later, Pervo, according to Padilla, appeared to have changed his mind about Acts and called it history.[82] Accordingly, the achievements of Luke as a historian do not reside in his ability to create but to accurately record it.[83] While Theophilus continues to be the central figure around the prologues of the Third Gospel and Acts, it becomes important to modern readers to have an idea of the identity of this character that Luke appeals to, to which he was somehow indebted.

According to James, the Norwegian theologian Halvor Moxnes suggested that "most excellent" was an appellation given to a real person named Theophilus whose designation was highly used in

---

79. In *The Past as Legacy*, Bonz argues that Luke and Acts are epic stories like those of Virgil and Homer. See Bonz, *Past as Legacy*, 26.

80. Padilla, *Acts of the Apostles*, 54; Bonz, *Past as Legacy*, 26.

81. Pervo, *Acts*, 7.

82. Padilla, *Acts of the Apostles*, 59.

83. Padilla, *Acts of the Apostles*, 59.

the Greco-Roman world.[84] Even though most scholars also believe Theophilus was a person, it would not be too much of a stretch to imply that anyone who is "a friend of God," as is the meaning of Theophilus, is who Luke was also intending to address.[85]

Chapter 5 of this book on "Backgrounds," where Luke's literary and cultural context are examined, will explore and identify the reason why Theophilus had a real purpose and the reason he was important to Luke's research. Is this Luke's intention in writing this two-volume work, or did he have other intentions in mind? This is what the next chapter will explore, the unity of Luke-Acts and the theory behind his intention to write this two-volume work.

---

84. James, *Spiral Gospel*, 2–3.
85. James, *Spiral Gospel*, 3.

Chapter 3: The Unity of Luke-Acts and Theory Behind Luke's Intention and Purpose

Luke's two-volume work consisting of Luke-Acts makes up a quarter of the entire NT.[1] The ancient title for the Gospel is rendered the *Gospel according to Luke*. The title appears at the end of Bodmer papyrus XIV and XV instead of in the beginning, as is common with other books.[2] It is designated P75 and is the oldest surviving Greek manuscript, dated between AD 175 to 225.[3] In contrast to the Gospel, Acts is preserved in fourteen papyrus Greek manuscripts dating between the third to the eighth centuries AD. It mainly consists of three primary text types, Alexandrian, Western, and Byzantine.[4]

The occasion for the writing of Luke-Acts appeared to be primarily for gentiles. According to Craig Evans, Luke aimed to answer four questions for his readers. (1) Why has Jesus not yet returned as he promised? (2) What was the task of believers while they waited for the Lord's return? (3) Why were the Jews continuing to reject Christ and his gospel? (4) How do the gentiles relate to Israel and God's promises?[5] The answer to these questions becomes the occasion be-

---

1. Evans, *Luke*, 14.
2. Comfort and Barrett, *Text of the Earliest New Testament Greek*, 2:75.
3. Evans, *Luke*, 15.
4. More discussion on this in chapter 5. Refer also to Schnabel, *Acts*, 41.
5. Evans, *Luke*, 18.

hind his theory and intention for writing a two-volume work that he intended to be read as a single book.[6]

Both apostles Paul and Peter give reasons why Jesus has not yet returned as he promised. It is highly likely that the early church expected Jesus to return in their lifetime.[7] And when there were no signs of this happening, some of the Christians showed signs of weariness (see 2 Thess 2:2). Because of the fact the Lord had not returned, some believers in Thessalonica thought that he had already returned unexpectedly (see 2 Thess 2:1). As time progressed, both Paul and Peter received more insight on this subject (see 2 Thess 2:3; 2 Pet 3:9).

According to Paul, he emphasized how it accomplished nothing for the apostles to write about the dates and times of his coming because when it happened it would be like a thief in the night (cf. 1 Thess 5:1–2). It would be like sudden destruction manifesting in times of peace. And when a pregnant woman does not know when her labor pains will occur, that is how the Lord's coming would be, unexpectedly (2 Thess 5:3). Peter defers it all to the Lord's will, in saying that the Lord has not yet returned because he does not want people to be lost. He is giving the unrepentant people more time to repent of their sins and turn to him. Many would perish if the Lord returned to the earth's present state of humanity. His delay comes out of his longsuffering toward humanity (see 2 Pet 3:9).

The believers were given a God-given task while they waited for the Lord's return. Paul warned those in Thessalonica to not live in darkness so that day would not unexpectedly come and overtake them. The point is that the children of God do not live in darkness (sin). They do not belong to the world, but to God. People sleep during the night and even get drunk. But God's people do not belong to the night but belong to the light. Even as others were sleeping, it is important for them to remain sober and alert.

The believers must stay sober and let their faith and love be like a suit of armor, and their firm hope that they will be saved is their helmet (see 1 Thess 5:5–8 CEV). And because it is Jesus who died for their sins, whether they are in heaven or on earth, they must encourage one

---

6. Evans, *Luke*, 18.
7. Moore, *Parousia in the New Testament*, 109.

another with such words of comfort (see 1 Thess 5:4–11). And to the Corinthians, he encouraged them to "be steadfast, immovable, always excelling in the Lord's work, because you [they] know that your [their] labor in the Lord is [was] not in vain" (1 Cor 15:58 CSB).

Finally, their personal responsibility was to walk upright before God and others and to excel in Christ. To go back into a life of sin (live in the dark) is what others do who are asleep (dead in trespasses and sins). Such lifestyles did not exemplify a witness for Christ where Paul, to the contrary, told the Corinthians they were living epistles known and read of others, and manifested epistles of their ministry (see 2 Cor 3:2–4), that went against God's purpose for them, who desires them to be ready when he returns (cf. 1 Thess 5:5–9).

In Romans, Paul reveals the reason that the Jews were continuing to reject Christ and his gospel.[8] Paul made this clear in the book of Romans that God allowed Israel to be blind and to remain blind until he brings in the fullness of the gentiles. But Israel's blindness was only temporary, only until God brings in all the gentiles predestined to be saved.[9] It is what he called a mystery, meaning that it was God's plan that was revealed to him (see Rom 11:25).

In John 3:19, Jesus gave the verdict on the Jews who continued to reject him. He said that he was the true light that had come into the world, but people loved darkness instead of light because their deeds were evil (see John 3:20). Jesus is the light that exposes all sin, and the Jews did not want their sins to be exposed by him. And they continue to not believe in Jesus because they were not his sheep (see John 10:26). The Gospel writers convey the anger vented toward Jesus. The more he condemned them, the more it appears to have caused resentment toward him, which is also part of what led to Stephen's death (see Acts 7:51–58).

The sentiment also resonating among the Jews appeared to be the loss of their tradition and culture. The chief priests and Pharisees of the Jewish Sanhedrin wanted their traditions to continue while ousting the Romans from their homeland. Those of the Sanhedrin felt that if they let Jesus go on working miracles and raising the dead

---

8. Schreiner, *Romans*, 461.
9. Schreiner, *Romans*, 560.

then everyone would believe in him, and the Romans would come and take away both their temple and nation (see John 11:48). The sentiment appears to be another fear they had of Jesus, and the fear they put into the mind of their followers who also continued to reject Jesus and the gospel.

The way gentiles related to Israel and God's promises is an assignment that Paul was sent to resolve among the Jews, by interpreting God's plan to them (cf. Eph 1:9–10; 3:1–6; Col 1:25–28). He used metaphors to describe their relationships.[10] He called Israel a holy branch broken off an olive tree. But the gentiles were simply like a wild olive tree grafted in among Israel. And with them, they are made partakers of the root and fatness of the olive tree (see Rom 11:16–21). The gentiles remain a part of the olive tree because of their faith in Jesus Christ. But if they abandon their faith, they, too, like the faithless Israelites would be also broken off. And when those Jews begin to come to Christ in faith, they will be grafted back into the fold of God.[11]

Thomas Schreiner uses an analogy to describe the root, lump, and branches. Accordingly, the first fruits are the OT patriarchs made holy by their faith in YHWH. The lump is the Jewish descendants of the patriarchs who are also holy. And the branches are also Jewish descendants of the twelve tribes that are also made holy, naturally.[12] Jesus was the Messiah from the line of David of the tribe of Judah that came from the Jews and to the Jews (Rom 9:5). The gospel was for the Jews first (see Rom 1:16; 2:9–10); the promises made to the Jewish people will be fulfilled (see Rom 9–11).[13]

According to Schreiner, the image of the OT patriarchs being the first fruits and the remaining part of Israel being the lump is also like the patriarchs being the root and Israel being the branches.[14] Paul is getting at that, by placing faith in Jesus Christ as their Savior, the gentiles are made partakers of salvation and eternal life in Christ.

10. Schreiner, *Romans*, 66.
11. Schreiner, *Romans*, 603.
12. Schreiner, *Romans*, 593.
13. Schreiner, *Romans*, 41.
14. Schreiner, *Romans*, 601.

They, like Israel, are made inheritors of all the promises to Abraham extended to the Jews.

What Was Luke Intending?

Based on those questions presented by Evans, Luke wrote his Gospel while revealing the Jews were rejecting Jesus, and Acts reveals the gentiles being grafted into God's plan that the Jews rejected. During Jesus's time on earth, he ministered to people from the regions of Galilee, Samaria, Judea, the Decapolis, Perea, and Phoenicia. According to Matthew's Gospel, Jesus sent his twelve apostles out with the following instructions: to "not go among the gentiles or enter any town of the Samaritans," but to "go rather to the lost sheep of Israel" (Matt 10:5–6 NIV).

Luke now sees an expanded mission Jesus commanded beyond the locality of the Jews (see Acts 1:8). Following the resurrection, he commanded the apostles to make disciples of all nations (Matt 28:19). Luke's original audience was composed of Jews, Samaritans, and gentiles. These consisted of all who had an ear to hear and a mind to obey God's words, the gospel.[15]

As the gospel spread (cf. Acts 6:7), the question fitting more into the mind of the apostles had to do with the place for the gentiles and how they fit into God's plan of redemption (see Acts 11:18). It became increasingly direr as more gentiles began accepting the gospel and joining the posthaste developing *ecclesia*.[16] The idea of an imminent return of Jesus to earth as was witnessed in Acts 1:11 appeared to become clearer to Luke that God was intending to work out his plan in their present and their future by saving the gentiles. For Luke, it was an additional challenge faced head-on by the nascent church. In addition to persecution from unbelieving Jews, their next challenge is the issue of the gentiles (see Acts 6:1).

The first answer to this challenge was to select deacons that could assist in such matters (see Acts 6:2–4). Another challenge had to do with their taking the gospel message to them, and explaining

---

15. Evans, *Luke*, 21.
16. Evans, *Luke*, 15.

to the Jews that the gentiles are placed on an equal basis with them through Christ and the gospel (see Acts 10:5–29; cf. Rom 9:24 and Gal 3:28). The positive evidence of gentile legitimacy, membership, and participation in the Jewish messianic promises was signified through their reception of the Holy Spirit.[17] An explicit reason for the missionaries' turning to the gentiles was Jewish unbelief and rejection of the gospel (see Acts 11:18).[18]

The genius of Luke with Acts is like that of the author of 1–2 Chronicles in the OT.[19] As Chronicles retells Israel's history from Adam to Cyrus's decree for the Jews in Babylon, Luke reiterates the message of the gospel, that it is offered to everyone. Luke's retelling of Christ's message was not just for the Jews. It is simply a message to all who have the faith to receive it. It is what he sets out to accomplish in Acts. Luke's intentions in Luke-Acts are not only to chronicle the events of early Christian history. It does so by most importantly retelling the history of its origins, being retold through the prism of the Third Gospel. It is a message of the kingdom being offered to everyone.[20] With Acts, he intended to chronicle the spread of the gospel as it was then apportioned beyond the commonwealth of the Jews.

Alongside other ancient historical literature, Luke's writings are placed within the framework of both sacred and secular histories.[21] As an able biographer of history, he should not be seen as measured for the sake of style, but regarding the great range of his subject matter that covers several decades. Regarding some first-century historians like Josephus, Pliny, Suetonius, and Tacitus, Tacitus is one who mostly resembled Luke as a historian.[22] And the closest writings in

---

17. Evans, *Luke*, 19.

18. Evans, *Luke*, 20.

19. According to the *Baker Illustrated Bible Handbook*, 1–2 Chronicles was written by Ezra or a priest like Ezra. With the former likely the case, he retells Israel's history from Adam to Cyrus for accomplishing two goals. The first is the Davidic covenant has a focus on Israel's messianic hope for the future. Second is the temple, its proper worship and its handling of those issues in the present while establishing them for the future. See Hays and Duvall, *Baker Illustrated Bible Handbook*, 212.

20. Cadbury, *Making of Luke-Acts*, 4.

21. Evans, *Luke*, 18.

22. Cadbury, *Making of Luke-Acts*, 2.

comparison to Luke's style and aim are the canonical Gospels of Matthew and Mark.²³ Henry Cadbury favors Luke's works as being extremely important to Christianity and that the Christian movement would greatly suffer without them. Even with the loss of the two other Synoptics, it would not reduce the amount of the information about Jesus as seriously as it would with the loss of Luke.²⁴

When considering how indispensable the Gospel of Luke is among the Synoptics, Cadbury agrees that Acts is an even more indispensable work because no other narratives have survived that could parallel it.²⁵ Acts or Πράξεις chronicles the background to understanding the history, theological importance, and story behind the Gospels.²⁶ It links, connects, and bridges the Gospel and the Apostle (the original name among early Christians).²⁷

Λουκάν and Πράξεις are understood as good news. Λουκάν is the good news of Jesus and Πράξεις is the good news about Jesus. Πράξεις takes Λουκάν from teaching to a practical application of the teachings of Christ by the apostles and by the members of the body of Christ. In the early stages of the church, the believers did not have a Bible of the NT so the members held to the teachings of the apostles about Christ. When the church started to see martyrs among their members, and when they realized that Jesus's return was not as imminent as they originally hoped, the necessity for a permanent record also likely became imminent. However, in the early beginnings of its novice establishment, an oral tradition was durable next to a written message.

The first written record of the twenty-seven NT books began with Paul's Epistle to the Galatians.²⁸ In addition to his writing, Paul eventually became one of the greatest leaders of the NT church. Luke

---

23. To this point, Cadbury believes that the Gospel of Luke contains the largest part of the unique material among the Synoptic Gospels. See Cadbury, *Making of Luke-Acts*, 2.

24. Cadbury, *Making of Luke-Acts*, 2.

25. Cadbury, *Making of Luke-Acts*, 2.

26. Cadbury, *Making of Luke-Acts*, 2.

27. The term "Apostle" is the name used in early Christianity to refer to Luke's second volume before it became Acts in the canon. See Cadbury, *Making of Luke-Acts*, 2.

28. Gundry, *Survey of the New Testament*, 318.

joined him in Troas during a ministry that has been called a second missionary journey (see Acts 20:5).[29] Luke chronicled the life of Jesus and the life of the church in what became known as Luke-Acts. Apart from the remaining twenty-five books that make up the NT canon, this two-volume work proved itself to be different from any other historical works in the world then. The idea that makes this special is known as inspiration. The inspired books are not the mere contrivance of human authors, but they are also the works of God.

Another reason the inspiration of Scripture is important is because it guarantees that the story being told to the readers is trustworthy. Without inspiration, the transmission of information handed down through decades and perhaps centuries of time can be challenged as unreliable. Unless one believes in inspiration, an inerrant oral tradition and a supernatural church as organs of transmission of that historical data, handed down by way of unchecked oral repetition and during a meal held in remembrance of their master, could be questionable or challenged if it was reliable.[30]

Another occasion for Luke was to bridge the OT and NT with his Gospel. He picks up from the OT where Malachi, the last of the writing prophets, ended his prophecy, that God was going to send the prophet Elijah (4:5-6) to avoid him smiting the earth with destruction. The messenger, which is the meaning of Malachi's name, pointed to someone besides him as God's messenger of the covenant (see Mal 3:1). He says that God will send his messenger before the face of Israel to prepare the way before the Lord. In the Gospel of John, he attributed this work to John the Baptist who "confessed and denied not" (KJV's rendition; see John 1:19-28).

Those priests and Levites sent to John were bright enough to understand that Malachi predicted the appearance of Elijah. God would send this prophet to "turn the hearts of the parents to their children, and the hearts of the children to their parents" (Mal 4:6a NIV). If his ministry was unsuccessful, the entire land would face

---

29. The author uses the personal pronoun "us" thus implying that Luke joined Paul during their arrival at Troas. It says, "These men went on ahead and waited for us at Troas" (NIV).

30. Cadbury, *Making of Luke-Acts*, 2.

destruction. This is precisely where Luke begins his testimony, with the appearance of the prophet Malachi's Elijah-like prophet, John the Baptist (see Mal 4:5–6; cf. Matt 11:14; Luke 1:13–17), and ends it with Paul under house arrest in Rome.

Apart from the Lukan history, further information that chronicled the early Christian history, outside of the church letters, was nearly extinguished for a generation.[31] No other person during the period of the first-century church history as presented in Acts has been clearer in their knowledge of Jesus and the church than Luke.[32] Other first-century writers like Josephus and Tacitus chronicled partial accounts of Jesus and the church but intermingled scattered accounts with Jewish (Josephus) and Roman (Tacitus) history.

A scholarly study of Luke's writings has been the subject of a lot of criticism in accordance to the points made earlier. The challenge was mainly to those who do not believe in biblical inspiration or hold to the inspiration of the text. Without inspiration, the transmission of the NT information handed down through time was perhaps viewed as unreliable if it was not checked like modern conventions of historiography.

Apart from his critics, Luke, with the help of others, set out what he intended to accomplish. He was able to produce a historical account that took Jesus from Galilee to Rome for all who wanted to know the truth. The great amount of detail that takes up one-quarter of the entire NT was provided to everyone so that they could know with certainty of the truth about Christ that was taught, accepted, and believed by the early Christian community (see Luke 1:4).

The Separation of Luke and Acts

According to Cadbury, one of the first causes for the separation of Luke from Acts and Acts from Luke happened in the post-apostolic church, which had to do with the style, scope, and type of writing of all the

---

31. It is not until perhaps the second century AD that extrabiblical writers outside the twenty-seven inspired NT books write on the history of the church.

32. Cadbury, *Making of Luke-Acts*, 4.

NT books that were later regarded as *Sanctus Scriptura*.[33] And with the emergence of three other Gospels (i.e., Mark, Matthew, and John), Luke was also regarded as εὐαγγέλιον because they were solely about the life and ministry of Christ. The four Gospels unanimously passed into the NT canon. Cadbury believes that the four, while the original name for them is unknown, were collectively known and identified as Gospel, whereas the ordering of them was transmitted as a single group and not based on the date they were written.[34]

In contrast, Parsons and Pervo identify two ways that led to their separation. But first, to assume that a lack of documentation proves the early church did not read them *as a single continuous narrative is making an argument from silence*.[35] To assume also that their canonical split in the current canonical form is evidence that the first readers read them separately is also unwarranted.[36] A further hypothesis is that "the first readers read them separately and either intentionally split them from a one-volume work into two to create them as two books, or passively introduced the individual books at different points in the canonical order" is a theory that goes against the argument of a single, continuous unity of Λουκᾶν and Πράξεις.[37]

A second point regarding their separation had to do with scroll length. And because the limit to the length was placed on scrolls in the first century, it contributed to their division. Regarding the twenty-seven books that make up the canon, Λουκᾶν-Πράξεις makes up one-fourth of the entire NT.[38] To this point, longer writings required divisions into detached volumes. Limitations placed upon scroll lengths required a new scroll for Πράξεις. It, according to Juel, placed Λουκᾶν-Πράξεις in a special class, that Λουκᾶν was the only known papyrus scroll in the early church to combine the story of Jesus (Λουκᾶν) with the story about Jesus (Πράξεις).[39]

33. Cadbury, *Making of Luke-Acts*, 10.
34. Cadbury, *Making of Luke-Acts*, 10.
35. Parsons and Pervo, *Rethinking the Unity*, 12.
36. Parsons and Pervo, *Rethinking the Unity*, 12.
37. Parsons and Pervo, *Rethinking the Unity*, 12.
38. Evans, *Luke*, 14.
39. Juel, *Luke-Acts*, 12; Parsons and Pervo, *Rethinking the Unity*, 12.

Finally, Parsons and Pervo also make mention of a quote from Josephus in *Against Apion*. It is suggested by Josephus that Luke may have simply run out of space at the end of the Gospel.[40] Another alternative, in contrast to Josephus, is that Luke simply reached the end of his scroll at the same time he completed the end of the gospel message he was seeking to convey.[41] And to repeat an earlier point, the scroll (or volume 1) had reached its mandatory length after the resurrection narrative.

The memorabilia of εὐαγγέλιον were completely about Jesus Christ. They emerged out of and were compared to the first-century Greco-Roman biographies or βίοι, which tell about the life, a biography, or life-story of someone. In the case of the Gospels, this person is Jesus Christ.[42] The authorship of Luke's Gospel has been attributed to Luke the physician and companion of the apostle Paul. While this has long been the traditional view, there were also many arguments aimed against it as well. Whereas the Third Gospel was grouped with Mark, Matthew, and John, Πράξεις (or Acts) was in a category of Christian writings and memorabilia about the apostles.

In contrast to the four Gospels, Πράξεις became the earliest writing of its class, and it alone was canonized apart from the Third Gospel. In the selection of authorized and authoritative books that belonged in the NT canon, Πράξεις was severed from the Gospel of Luke, and its subsequent textual history as well as its canonical position were determined by other factors, according to Cadbury.[43]

Volumes 1 and 2, so-called Luke-Acts, were written a few centuries before they were placed into what is now called the NT canon. Parsons and Pervo make a correct assertion that Luke and Acts were added and formed a canonical disunity.[44] In other words, these two works never stood side by side in the authorized canonical listing of NT books, and their canonical ordering had never formed

---

40. Parsons and Pervo, *Rethinking the Unity*, 11.
41. Parsons and Pervo, *Rethinking the Unity*, 11.
42. Burridge, *What Are the Gospels?*, 105.
43. Cadbury, *Making of Luke-Acts*, 10.
44. Parsons and Pervo, *Rethinking the Unity*, 8.

one continuous narrative.[45] The correlation is not quite accurate, however, because Luke-Acts contains readability in the likeness of a continuous narrative regardless of their placement in the canon divided by the fourth Gospel.[46]

A fourth-century listing of the NT books in the "Cheltenham Canon and the Stichometry of Codex Claromontanus" places Luke's Gospel last among the four canonicals, and Acts is placed at the end of the Pauline Epistles in the Cheltenham and at the end of the NT in the Claromontanus.[47] While Luke and Acts were also divided by the fourth Gospel, the arrangement caused even more confusion for those to be viewed as companion volumes. It made possible the idea for a juxtaposition of Luke and Acts out of mind. Cadbury believes it is not known for certain what the original name was of the autographs as Luke would have called them. He suggests that they all indeed carried a common name distinguishable as Book 1 and Book 2. But when they were first written they did not carry the same appellations as they do today such as Gospel, Luke, Acts, etc.[48]

The Use of Intentional Prologues That Tie Luke-Acts Together

The Bible used by NT writers was a Greek translation of the Hebrew TaNaK called the Septuagint. As with any language, writings capture the idioms, nuances, and expressions of the language that cannot be avoided in either oral or written communication. Prologues are not new to the NT but were used in the OT and throughout the ancient world. The writers of the NT made use of the common Greek language to communicate with a diverse multilingual world.

---

45. Parsons and Pervo, *Rethinking the Unity*, 8.

46. González also states that Luke and Acts are two volumes of a single work. The continuity throughout both volumes suggests they were originally a single book that was divided so that the first section would be parallel to the other three Gospels. See Rayan, *Holy Spirit*, 1–2.

47. Parsons and Pervo, *Rethinking the Unity*, 8.

48. Cadbury, *Making of Luke-Acts*, 10.

In classical Greek, for instance, prologues have been seen in works dealing with Demosthenes and Greek oratory.[49] The prologue was meant to balance the conclusion to a speech, which summarized the case and attempted to persuade the audience to be well-disposed to the speaker. In doing so, it captured the goodwill of the audience by captivating it with eloquence. However, to avoid roughing up or perhaps losing one's audience, it was important that the information being given was accurate. Equally important with prologues was their rhetorical value. It was a means to an end, to provide insight into the Grecian (Athenian) attitudes to their democracy as well as to the reactions and even expectations of the audience at an assembly.[50]

Prologues had rhetorical value and when used by the Gospel writers emulated language used in the ancient world with its rhetorical features. Aristotle used rhetoric to gain the audience's goodwill from the outset of communication with his audience.[51] Prologues in ancient languages are one of four parts of speech in classical rhetorical theory.[52] Douglas Ehninger defines rhetoric as "an organized, consistent and coherent way of talking about written or oral discourse that sought to inform, evaluate, persuade, or entertain" an audience.[53] Plato envisioned rhetoric as a clever technique for persuading an ignorant crowd that the false is true, that it was not borne out by the speeches, and the legal system does not appear to have produced many arbitrary or clearly unjust results.[54]

Green and McDonald identified parallels in the works of Luke and Josephus.[55] The Lukan prologues (Luke 1:1–4 and Acts 1:1–3) are like those of Josephus in *Against Apion* (1.1–5; 2.1–3), and both

---

49. Demosthenes, *Speeches 60 and 61*, 57.
50. Demosthenes, *Speeches 60 and 61*, 56.
51. Demosthenes, *Speeches 60 and 61*, 55.
52. According to Demosthenes, the use of prologues in classical Greek is one of the four sections of making up ancient rhetoric. These four sections are the prologue (προοίμιον), the narration (διήγησις), the proof (πίστις), and the conclusion (ἐπίλογος). In this arrangement (τάξις), each section has its distinct role. See Demosthenes, *Speeches 60 and 61*, 55.
53. Ehninger, "On Systems of Rhetoric," 15–28.
54. Demosthenes, *Speeches 60 and 61*, 25.
55. Green and McDonald, *World of the New Testament*, 401.

have patrons, Theophilus for Luke and Epaphroditus for Josephus.[56] Throughout their discourses, both writers refer to similar people, places, and events. In keeping with the accuracy of Luke's history that has been criticized by scholars, Josephus appears to either quote Luke or provide his own account of the events regarding the census under Quirinius, and political leaders like Pontius Pilate, Herod Antipas, and the revolutionary account of Judas the Galilean (see Acts 5:37), Theudas, and the Egyptian (see Acts 21:38).[57]

Luke and Josephus wrote apologies on history to defend a group against baseless accusations and to demonstrate the essential virtue of a particular group's way of life. While Luke focused on Christians in the Roman Empire, Josephus focused on Jews, not specifically Christians.[58] Luke intentionally uses prologues to Luke-Acts with an intention to tie both volumes together as one book. Intentional prologues are also used by other Gospel writers, respectively Mark and John. Matthew is the only Gospel without a prologue. Joseph Kelly believes that it is likely that Matthew included a prologue, but no extant version exists.[59] However, it is thought that Matthew's prologue is referenced in Luke's prologue.[60]

The prologues in ancient writing provided some information about the writer, but those of Mark, Luke, and John do not provide any information about an author.[61] Those of Mark (1:1–8 or 15) and John (1:1–16) are relatively longer than Luke's, if one considers Luke 1:1–4 as a prologue to his Gospel. Luke's preface and prologue are often used interchangeably. But sometimes his preface is seen as a short prefix added to his lengthier section of chapters 2 and 3. The prologue to Luke-Acts extends beyond the preface (Luke 1:1–4; Acts 1:1–5), whereas the preface is his introduction. When comparing the opening lines of Luke and Acts it becomes transpicuous to readers how both volumes appear

---

56. Green and McDonald, *World of the New Testament*, 401.
57. Green and McDonald, *World of the New Testament*, 401.
58. Green and McDonald, *World of the New Testament*, 401.
59. Kelly, *Concise Dictionary*, 13.
60. Stadel, "Gospel Prologues,"; Kelly, *Concise Dictionary*, 13.
61. Kelly, *Concise Dictionary*, 13.

to come from the same author. He opens his work with a preface (or introduction) relaying how and why he wrote it.

The prologue to Luke's Gospel is widely believed to contain an anti-Marcion bias. This is because the prologue is traditionally believed to have been written to oppose the views of one Marcion of Pontus.[62] If one takes this position, it would either designate a late date for the original Gospel autographs or the prologues in the original autographs would simply be redactions to the front of them. In the case of Luke, his authorship has not been questioned to any point of controversy. As such, it seems unlikely that the prologues were aimed against Marcion.

Marcion of Sinope in Pontus was regarded as a heretic based on his view of the gospel and of God. As the son of a rich shipmaster, he arrived in Rome in AD 140 to bring his version of the gospel. To Marcion, Paul was the one and only true apostle because the others elapsed back into Judaism. And the version of the gospel proclaimed by Paul, Luke's Gospel, was the only gospel. The version of Marcion's gospel is what he called *The Gospel of the Lord*.[63]

To Marcion, there were two gods. One was the creator of the earth and the other was the creator of the universe, while the first one was inferior to the second one. The god of the universe sent his son to rescue humanity from subjection to the creator, from his laws and penalties. In the OT, the patriarchs and prophets belonged to the inferior God, and their prophecies did not point in any way to Jesus as the Messiah whom the demiurge intended to send to earth.[64]

According to one tradition, Marcion mutilated Luke's Gospel by removing all the birth narratives of Jesus along with his teaching and discourses. He also persuaded his disciples to think of him as more trustworthy than all the apostles who passed down the gospel. He did not give his listeners a complete gospel, but only a fragment of Luke's

---

62. Kelly, *Concise Dictionary*, 13.
63. Hill, *Gospel of the Lord*, ii–iii.
64. Hill, *Gospel of the Lord*, iii.

Gospel that he revised.[65] Marcion was eventually excommunicated as a heretic and he died circa 170.[66]

The so-called anti-Marcionite prologues found as late as the eighth century were the Latin Codex Toletanus manuscripts. Donatien de Bruyne designated them "anti-Marcionite Prologues" in an essay entitled "Les plus anciens prologues latins des Evangiles" in the *Revue Bénédictine* (a peer-reviewed academic journal published since 1884).[67] He argued that they formed a single literary unit, that they were anti-Marcion in sentiment, and that they were written near the end of the second century (ca. AD 160–180). Some scholars argued that they were written by one and the same author in the fourth century. The view was abandoned, however, as Koester contended that Luke's prologue was written much earlier than a fourth-century date as originally argued by modern scholarship.[68]

Bruyne also argued that Irenaeus knew about them and that they depended on their Latin translations. However, Bruyne conjectured that they were originally written in Greek and that the only surviving Greek MS contains the Lukan prologue.[69] Nearly every book of the NT contained a prologue according to Bruyne. Their purpose was to give the reader personal information about the author, his addressees, and his occasion of writing because of how the Epistles are written. Bruyne said when Marcion published his NT it included Luke's Gospel and ten of Paul's letters. The *ecclesia* at Rome responded with a counter edition of its own and added an anti-Marcionite prologue to each of the Gospels; he was convinced that he had found those belonging to Mark, Luke, and John. In the case of the Pauline letters, Marcion's own prologues were inadvertently taken over and used.[70]

---

65. Bettenson and Maunder, *Documents of the Christian Church*, 41.

66. Hill, *Gospel of the Lord*, ii–iii.

67. Haenchen, *Commentary*, 17.

68. Koester, *Ancient Christian Gospels*, 243. In addition to Koester, Dr. Fay, at Liberty University, commented that manuscripts of Luke's prologue that are part of the Gospel have been found that date from around 300 or so, meaning that those prologues would have taken longer to have been originally written if they were separate.

69. McDonald, "Anti-Marcionite (Gospel) Prologues," 162–69.

70. Haenchen, *Commentary*, 17.

Theological Significance of the Prologues of Luke and Acts

As stated in the previous section, if a person is to take the position that someone wrote the Gospel prologues other than the author of the Gospel in question, this argument would either designate a late date for the original Gospel autographs or contend that the prologues in the original autographs were simply redactions to the front of them. In the case of Luke, his authorship has not been questioned to any point of serious controversy. If they were indeed written by the authors of the books bearing their name, it would seem unlikely that they would have been aimed against Marcion as emphasized by Bruyne, Koester, and others. But this does not exclude the proposition that they could not have been used to be aimed at him a century later.

Another way that the anti-Marcionite prologues have been used is by scholars to gather extrabiblical information on Luke's writings. It would not be absurd for those who believe in unadulterated Lukan authorship, specifically of Luke-Acts. The Gospel prologues and prologue to Acts are short introductions prefixed at the beginning of their tome. They were all written in Greek, but at least forty Vulgate manuscripts contain them.[71] The supposition by scholars is that they helped by shedding light on the origins of the Gospels themselves.[72] However, since Luke's works were already in circulation, several copies of the manuscript, widely circulated, protected it from corruption by Marcion and others.[73]

Koester agrees with Bruyne that the anti-Marcionite Gospel prologues were composed in Greek, having dozens translated and appearing in Latin Bible manuscripts. And only prologues for Mark, Luke, and John are extant, whereas the prologue for Luke is also preserved in Greek.[74] In early twentieth-century scholarship, some argued that the three were composed together as a response to

---

71. Wace and Piercy, *Dictionary of Early Christian Biography*, 698.
72. Cross and Livingstone, *Oxford Dictionary of the Christian Church*, 77.
73. Wace and Piercy, *Dictionary of Early Christian Biography*, 698.
74. Koester, *Ancient Christian Gospels*, 243.

Marcionism.[75] Comparative linguistic examination by William Sanday concluded that a portion of Luke that Marcion acknowledged, along with portions he omits, revealed or provided clear proof of a common author. The text of Luke that was used by Marcion contained readings acknowledged by Irenaeus.[76]

The Muratorian canon is one of the earliest references to the Gospels outside the NT. It highlights Luke's as the Third Gospel, and Luke as a companion of Paul. It states that after the ascension of Christ is when Paul took Luke to himself as one that was studious and upright. And while traveling is when he wrote in his own name what he had been told (in order) although he had not ever seen the Lord Jesus in the flesh. He recorded all the Acts of the Apostles in one book because he was present to witness them. Luke was with Paul when they landed in Rome (see Acts 28:16). He does not provide any history past Rome, only that Paul rented a house for two years and continued preaching Jesus Christ and the kingdom of God (see Acts 28:30–31).[77]

In Acts 13, Luke is not mentioned by name when Paul and Barnabas landed there to begin their mission activities to the gentile world. It follows the notion stated in Acts 13:48 that they were destined to begin spreading their knowledge of Jesus Christ to all gentiles who were appointed to eternal life.[78] A Christian community existed in Antioch prior to the arrival of Paul along with Barnabas in Acts 11:26. Barnabas recruited Paul in Tarsus for help with the mission in Antioch. It is this location in which the believers were first called Christians.[79]

Another suggestion for Luke is that he was among the converts of Paul and Barnabas in Antioch, a view questionable at best. The only evidence to support this view is an old variant in Codex Bezae at Acts

---

75. Hall, *Doctrine and Practice*, 37–39.

76. Wace and Piercy, *Dictionary of Early Christian Biography*, 698; Sanday, *Gospels in the Second Century*, 211.

77. Luke avoids writing history beyond Paul's two-year stay in Rome. This is one of the reasons Luke has been criticized as not being a historian. All other data outside Acts and the Epistles (limited, and not intended to be historical) will have to consult with extrabiblical literature.

78. Huffman, "Luke, Gospel of."

79. Cross and Livingstone, *Oxford Dictionary of the Christian Church*, 78.

11:28 that implies that he was one of the early members of the Christian community at Antioch. Plummer identifies this as a plausible hypothesis supported by Eusebius, Jerome, and others.[80] While Luke witnessed the manifestation of the Holy Spirit, he took great interest in their ministry notating the activity among the novice church. Paul then made note of Luke and essentially made use of his profession as a physician. Paul needed him due to the many physical hardships forthcoming in his travels to those lands where they were persecuted.

In Acts, however, Luke is not mentioned by name, nor does he give any evidence that he was with Paul prior to their arrival and stay in Troas (cf. Acts 16:8–12). From Troas, Luke (along with Timothy and Silas) accompanied Paul to Philippi (Acts 16:10–17), and on a third circuit, from Philippi to Jerusalem (Acts 20:5–21; 18), and then to Rome, where he was imprisoned before appearing before Nero (Acts 9:15; cf. Col 4:14; 2 Tim 4:11; Phlm 24).[81]

In Col 4:14, Paul calls Luke "the beloved physician." The word "physician," translated from the Greek word ἰατρός, implies the act of mending wounds by stitching, providing cures by means of medicines and physical care, and reversing symptoms to make a person physically whole.[82] It is likely that Luke used something like diaries to chronicle events along the way, whereby, in the final analysis, he proved to the world to be a capable and notable historian and writer. It would be unusual to assume that he became a historian at the time he became a Christian, but nevertheless, his writings prove he already had this talent. It, however, was not apparent at first, whereas there are not any ancient sources to support his idea of authoring other books apart from Luke and Acts.

Luke's identity is certain in extrabiblical sources, but not specifically definite in his writings due to the fact that he did not write about himself in the NT. According to one source, it is said that he was a Hellenistic gentile from Antioch, Syria.[83] He was an Antiochene Syrian, a

---

80. Plummer, *Critical and Exegetical Commentary*, 2.

81. Plummer, *Critical and Exegetical Commentary*, 2.

82. The other places where ἰατρός appears in the New Testament are in Matt 9:12; Mark 2:17; 5:26; Luke 4:23; 5:31; 8:43; Col 4:14.

83. Dicken, "Luke."

doctor by profession, and a disciple of the apostles. He followed Paul until his martyrdom in Rome and served Jesus blamelessly. According to later legends, he was one of the seventy disciples Jesus sent out in Luke 10:1 and the unnamed disciple of Emmaus in Luke 24:13–15.[84]

The former and latter points, however, are purely suppositional along with the lack of historical documentation and evidence to support them. The theory behind another traditional record of events alleges that he was martyred.[85] He was never married and had no wife or children, and died in Thebes, a then metropolis of Boeotia, being full of the Holy Spirit, at the age of eighty-four.[86] Further *acta* implies that Constantias II had his remains moved from Thebes in Boeotia to Constantinople to be monumented for all time. The church of the apostles was built soon afterward between AD 356–357 in honor of him.[87]

Two Volumes, One Book, One Message in Continuous Historical-Theological Narrative

Loveday Alexander agrees that Luke-Acts should be accepted as a single work.[88] It is a single two-volume work that has been acknowledged as a phenomenal achievement on part of Luke.[89] Instead of directing a Gospel to Jews (Matthew), gentile believers in Rome (Mark), or believers in Asia-Minor (John), Luke directed his Gospel to Theophilus with intentions of it being read by a much wider and broader audience consisting of both Jews and gentiles.

Luke-Acts was for a reading public.[90] His dedication in style and choice of words closely resemble the opening of ancient literary and secular writings with readers in mind that appreciate and enjoy

---

84. Cross and Livingstone, *Oxford Dictionary of the Christian Church*, 1005.
85. Cross and Livingstone, *Oxford Dictionary of the Christian Church*, 1005.
86. Huffman, "Luke, Gospel of."
87. Plummer, *Critical and Exegetical Commentary*, 2.
88. Alexander, *Preface to Luke's Gospel*, 205.
89. Alexander, *Preface to Luke's Gospel*, 205.
90. Alexander, *Preface to Luke's Gospel*, 6.

catchy rhetorical focus in opening communication.[91] In the way he makes his address to his readers in the preface to his prologue, there must have been many additional Gospel writings and types already before or around the year 60.[92]

There have been few questions regarding the meaning of the former treatise in Acts 1:1, but no serious dispute on the matter. But many have accepted without too much contention that it is a reference to the Gospel of Luke. No historical corroboration has been produced that has disputed this resolve to the contrary. Quite apart from the similarities of style with Luke-Acts, the identity of the dedicatee suggests that Luke's Gospel is the only canonical candidate that could ever fit the description in Acts 1:1. The propinquity of their relationship and its literary consequences have been variously assessed in recent scholarship. An estimate of the literary significance of the prefaces has tended to treat both together. Along with this ascertainment also comes a precaution. It falls under the assumption that any genre indications implied by the Gospel are mistakenly taken to be the same for Acts as well.[93]

Frank Dicken assumes that the Third Gospel was one of the last of the Gospels to be written.[94] The notion is likely agreed upon by interpreting Luke 1:1 to imply that others have already preceded him in such a project.[95] It, however, is not sufficient proof to Dicken's point, especially in the case that Luke may have been written before the Gospel of John. For John, he had all appearances of being a late writer, being that he was one of the early church members that was not martyred. Prior to Luke's εὐαγγέλιον, the Gospel of Mark was already written in Italy, and Matthew was written in Judea. While in Achaia, the Holy Spirit moved Luke to begin a two-volume work called Luke-Acts.[96]

---

91. Alexander, *Preface to Luke's Gospel*, 6.
92. Alexander, *Preface to Luke's Gospel*, 152.
93. Alexander, *Acts*, 23.
94. Dicken, "Luke."
95. "Many have undertaken to draw up an account of the things that have been fulfilled among us" (Luke 1:1 NIV).
96. Dicken, "Luke."

W. Ward Gasque dates Acts in AD 65 and that it was written from Rome.[97] If Gasque is correct, then Luke's Gospel would have been written prior to the year 65. According to another source, the Third Gospel was written in AD 60 while Paul was in prison in Caesarea.[98] The attestation is highly probable particularly when Luke documents Paul's events, and Paul would have been using Luke's Gospel prior to his death. It was not the original name given by Luke to this two-volume work, but the name of its later designation for them as they were attributed to him.[99] Luke's emphasis on the word "many" (πολλοί) appears to imply that there were other writers, apart from Matthew and Mark, who attempted this project.

Luke's reference to the "many" in Luke 1:1, who he implies have already drawn up an account of the things fulfilled by Christ among them, is translated from πολλοί. According to Luke 1:1, this implies that there were many other accounts that existed before he decided to undertake a writing project himself. He does not, however, specify whether those accounts were oral, written, or a combination of both.

It is possible that the πολλοί Luke is referring to are the oral reports plus a combination of the writings of Matthew, Mark, and John. It also argues for the existence of the hypothetical *Quelle* source covered in the introduction to this book. It is possible that *Quelle* was the oral traditions about Christ, his life, work, and deeds that were passed from the apostles that knew him personally, including his family (e.g., Mary and James). The oral testimony of witnesses was all that existed until those things were written down.

David Guzik comments on the subject that Luke wrote his Gospel knowing that many others had already written accounts of the life of Jesus. Guzik also thinks this may be a reference to the works of Mark and Matthew (most people think John was written after Luke), and/

---

97. Gasque, *History of the Interpretation*, 22.

98. Halley, *Halley's Bible Handbook*, 485–86.

99. In addition was the suggestion for Achaia as the place of origin for the Third Gospel. During the Roman Empire, Achaia was part of Greece, and it was the Roman name of the province that included most of Greece. It was one of the two provinces into which Rome divided Macedonia and Greece in 27 BC and established Achaia as its administrative province. Also see Unger, *New Unger's Bible Dictionary*, 20.

or other biographies that were written about Jesus in the first century that are not directly inspired by the Holy Spirit.[100] Alfred Plummer suggests that πολλοί should not be taken to include writers of apocryphal or pseudepigraphic works, being that those are all much later writings after Luke.[101] Advertently, those who have undertaken (the task to) ἀνατάξασθαι διήγησιν (draw up a narration) is what Plummer assumes are the three other canonical Gospels.[102]

To Horst Balz and Gerhard Schneider, the term πολλοί in Luke 1:1 stands out on the form-critical literary level regarding literary units of sayings that existed in oral transmission prior to being written down as Scripture. And that πολλοί (meaning many) is nothing more than a stylistic device (figure of speech), whereas the many also appear between the eyewitness reports (first generation), oral reports (first generation), and Luke-Acts by Luke himself. Balz and Schneider believe this essentially leads to a further hermeneutical-theological problem of the *polymorphous* nature of the NT witnesses like a canon within the canon.[103]

It is highly likely when Paul made reference to "my [his] Gospel," he was referring to the Gospel of Luke. This would imply that it was either written or in the progress of being developed during the time of Paul's references in Romans and 2 Timothy (Rom 2:16; 16:25; 2 Tim 2:8).[104] A second point also has to do with Paul's definition of the gospel he received directly from Jesus in 1 Cor 15:3–4, "For I delivered to you . . . that Christ died for our sins in accordance with the Scriptures, that he was buried, that he was raised on the third day in accordance with the Scriptures" (NIV). Paul's reference, "in accordance with the Scriptures" is likely a reference to the gospel message reported to him by Luke he deemed on par with the OT.

During his close companionship with the apostle Paul, Luke documented history based on interviews with others who witnessed the events personally and based on his own experiences as a personal

100. Guzik, *Luke*, 7.
101. Plummer, *Critical and Exegetical Commentary*, 2.
102. Plummer, *Critical and Exegetical Commentary*, 2.
103. Balz and Schneider, *Exegetical Dictionary*, 133.
104. Maier, *Eusebius*, 94.

eyewitness to those events. It is only natural to conclude that there were a lot of tête-à-têtes in between the texts of Scripture that would be impossible to reconstruct unless it is noted in Scripture or by extrabiblical sources, where someone other than the biblical writers was made privy to those conversations. Readers can, however, develop the gist of a lot of the narrative with a historical-critical approach to the text.

Purpose of Acts in the Overall Scheme of the Third Gospel

In this chapter, a lot of attention and focus has been directed to the unity behind Luke-Acts and the intention behind his theory and purpose for writing both volumes. It sought to discover his intentions for writing volumes 1 and 2 and his purpose behind writing them. Another concern that needed to be examined involved the cause and reason Luke-Acts were dissected as they entered the NT canon and the theory behind their separation. There was then a focus on the prologues, their importance, and their significance to not only proving Luke's authorship but also on the prologues to the unity of both volumes.

The book, up to this point, has been partly seeking to prove that Luke-Acts was intended to be read as a single book. On this premise, it was important to establish Lukan authorship by tying evidence in the prologues to the author of Luke-Acts. The prologues of any ancient writer were intended to tell the readers a lot about the author. Unfortunately, however, the Gospel prologues reveal nothing about their authors. The purpose of Acts fits in the overall scheme of the Third Gospel. In *Luke-Acts in Modern Interpretation*, Porter and Fay makes a case that the Gospel of Luke tells the story of Jesus's founding of the church, and Acts tells the story of the development of it.[105] Acts, in this prism, is connected to the Gospel as it continues the story of what Jesus started in the Gospel(s).

The tension of Luke-Acts presented by Parsons and Pervo is not really tension that some scholars conjure in two questions. Why was

---

105. Porter and Fay, *Luke-Acts in Modern Interpretation*, 338.

the Gospel written, and why was Acts written? It is under the assumption that either/or can survive without the other. It, however, is not the case when examining this from a thousand-foot level. It is because the Gospel is dependent upon Acts and Acts upon the Gospel for its complete story in a mere existence of two volumes. Both exist because of the Christ event and the church event, which revealed Luke's intentions and purpose for writing two volumes instead of just one.[106]

In further regard to Luke's purpose and intentions, some believe that he did not intend to write Acts as an account of history. Gasque argues that in Acts, Luke did not intend to narrate a historical account of the church.[107] It is because Luke did not go into enough detail on the Palestinian church and the activity of the other apostles. While this information is present in extrabiblical sources such as Josephus, Tacitus, Suetonius, and Pliny for instance, it requires the reader to go outside of Acts.

Further on Gasque's point, Luke skips over or does not bother to cover additional events in the history of the early church such as the spread of the gospel eastward into the region of the Euphrates and the Tigris, the foundation of the church in Rome, activities of the church in the Roman Empire, or events that Paul mentions in some of his letters that are not mentioned in Acts.[108] One of the problems with Acts as history is that it does not provide enough of a historical narrative to call it history. It does provide historical information, but only from the perspectives of a few people; and Paul surrounds the story from more than the latter half of the entire volume.

Pervo is correct in his assumption that if Luke really intended to describe a historical account of Christianity, rather than the deeds of the apostles, his narrative must show his meaning to do this.[109] In other words, the life, works, and deeds of the *ecclesia* should have been given full coverage, rather than half of the narrative focusing on those words and deeds of Paul. Luke used Jesus's quoted statements in Acts 1:8 as his launching platform to write Acts where the

---

106. Parsons and Pervo, *Rethinking the Unity*, 86.
107. Gasque, *History of the Interpretation*, 22.
108. Gasque, *History of the Interpretation*, 22.
109. Pervo, *Profit with Delight*, 131.

beginning of the narrative is set in Jerusalem. From here, it goes to Samaria, to Judea, and then out to Rome.

Pervo does make good points on the narrative of Acts, however; after the first two chapters, the narrative is mostly about Peter and John, where Peter still appears to get most of the focus. The first five chapters in Acts are given to the church's mission and concerns, rather than the missions of a few individuals.[110] Luke fills in smaller narratives of others such as Philip (8:26), Stephen (6:8—7:60), Barnabas (4:36; 14:14), James Bar Zebedee (12:12), James the Lord's brother (15:13–21; 21:17–25), Apollos, Priscilla, and Aquila (18:18–28).

Apart from Peter and Paul, Stephen is given one of the longest narratives. But to Pervo's point, what of Andrew, Phillip, Nathaniel, Thomas, or the others? It is as if at least the other nine apostles are entirely absent from the text. Apart from Peter, John, and his brother James, the remaining apostles, based on the narrative flow of Acts, appeared to simply fade away from the story, which is what essentially happens to those three as well.[111]

He is, however, a chronicler of the activities of specific people, but most of Paul begins in chapter 13 to the end of the book. Gasque says that Acts has been mostly viewed as a defense of Paul, a testimony of God's help in the spread of Christianity, a history of Christian missions, or an attempt to persuade Jews to become Christians. But various scholars all agreed that the information given by Luke is historically reliable.[112]

The first twelve chapters of Acts focus on Peter, the church, and the persecution of the apostles by the Jews. Following Jesus's ascension (see Acts 1:8), the next prominent voice heard is that of Simon Peter. Luke places the three prominent speakers in Acts as Peter, James (the Lord's brother), and Paul. Peter is staged at the beginning of Acts, James as leader of the church in Jerusalem in the middle, and Paul is placed from the middle all the way to the end of Acts.[113]

---

110. Pervo, *Profit with Delight*, 131.
111. Pervo, *Profit with Delight*, 131.
112. Gasque, *History of the Interpretation*, 23.
113. Buttrick, *Interpreter's Bible*, 161.

Koester says that Luke wrote Acts as if he was speaking directly to a pagan world as seen in his dedication to Theophilus, who was not a Jew.[114] He supports the apostles and their mission and writes Acts from an apologetic position. To Koester, Acts is an epic story because of its fulfillment of OT promises as it reaches back into Israel's past to the prophets, to which John the Baptist belongs.[115] The view is partially misleading because the story of John the Baptist ends in the Gospels (see Matt 14:1–12; Mark 6:14–29; Luke 9:7–9), and Acts simply continues the story of the Third Gospel.

Acts, in contrast to the OT and the story of John the Baptist, progresses forward from the day of Pentecost (cf. Acts 2:1) and does not go back into the past. In Koester's use of the term "epic," it does not appear that he is referring to Acts as epic-fictional, but to a story over a long period talking about great events. However, when referring to epic, a person more likely has a hero in mind. If Paul and Barnabas were an example of epic heroes as read about in classical Greek and as argued by Bonz, it still would not make Acts an epic tale.[116] An example of this point is from the NLT version of Acts 14:12: "They decided that Barnabas was the Greek god Zeus and that Paul was Hermes since he was the chief speaker."[117]

Acts is not full of epic tales, and it is a chronicle of limited or select historiography of specific acts in the first-century church. Since a lot of historical information is either omitted, passed over, or not covered, Luke did not appear to have a purpose in writing history, but he was a chronicler of specific events in the lives of specific people with a theological purpose in mind. The Acts of the NT are more like the First and Second books of Chronicles of the OT. The author only gives his readers enough information that he wants them to know that he deems important for their faith in the Lord and/or a belief in the specific story he is trying to narrate to them. He appears to want history to

---

114. Koester, *History and Literature*, 314.

115. Koester, *History and Literature*, 315.

116. It was discussed in chapter 2 that Bonz argued that Luke and Acts were simply epic stories, like that of Virgil and Homer. See Bonz, *Past as Legacy*, 26.

117. The NLT uses the Greek terms Zeus and Hermes, whereas the KJV and ESV use the Latin translation of Jupiter and Mercury.

be narrated within the events in his address to Theophilus. He narrated a first account and desired to narrate a second one.

Luke's first-century audience, however, would have had a different view of Acts than readers have today. To them, Luke was not writing history because those events likely occurred in their present time. But to twentieth-century readers, Acts is historical because they are reading about events that happened in the past. Although Luke does not give an exhaustive account of Acts from a historical point of view, he provides information from one dominant perspective, mostly with Paul in view.

If a person wishes to read about the exploits and martyrdoms of James (the brother of the Lord) or Peter, he or she would have to read one or more of the ancient historians discussed earlier. For Luke's future readers or readers of his present to get a complete account of church history, they will need to supplement other sources of historical dialogue along with Acts because Acts alone does not provide all the information about the church in the first century. Was Luke biased, was he writing based on God's plan, or both, or neither? These are valid questions a learned person would likely inquire of for answers.

The historical setting of Luke-Acts is in the first-century Roman Empire. The life of Jesus up to the arrival of Paul in Rome to appear before Caesar (Acts 9:15) covered the reign of five Roman emperors. In volumes 1 and 2, he names all except for Caligula and Nero (see Luke 2:1; 3:1; Acts 18:2). He likely based the second volume on his goals of the first one. The NLT version says, "I also have decided to write an accurate account for you, most honorable Theophilus, so you can be certain of the truth of everything you were taught" (Luke 1:3b–4). As with the first volume, Theophilus and others needed to rely on the second one as it was with the first one. But for Acts, were Luke's intentions of writing it based on a desire to write a historical account of church history?

Up to this point, this book has also been examining Luke's desire to give Theophilus a comprehensive account of what he has been taught about the Christian faith in Christ (cf. Acts 1:1–2). Acts was helpful to Theophilus as well as to others because the church did not have any NT Scripture to refer to or to read regarding their faith. They only had the oral testimonies of the apostles and the words of their witnesses. The teaching and preaching of the apostles were based on what they learned from Jesus. For those who were scattered throughout the world, many converts or newcomers to the faith had never seen nor heard Jesus or his apostles directly.

The things the apostles taught people were the words of Christ, and as they heard them they handed down those teachings to others. And those who heard the witnesses of the apostles passed their teachings down to others who continued to transmit the information. Without a written account, the accuracy of information had the potential of becoming inaccurate by the time it reached its destination. It made the urgency of written accounts (or Scripture) necessary for first-century believers and for Christian believers of all time. Based on an oral schematic, the original words of Christ and the apostles could easily get misconstrued.

Another intention of Luke, as will be examined later in the chapter covering travel narratives, was to share Jesus with the world. It was done in Luke's time by taking Jesus and the good news of Christ from Galilee to Rome. While Jesus was born in Bethlehem of Judea and grew up in Nazareth, his ministry began in Galilee as signified by the Holy Spirit descending on him in bodily form like a dove (see Luke 3:22–23). Luke takes Jesus from Nazareth of Galilee to Jerusalem, the epicenter of Christianity. And in Acts, he takes him from Jerusalem to Rome. And when Paul and Christ's gospel message reached Rome, he stopped writing, as if he completed the goal he set out to accomplish.

Christianity began in Jerusalem, as it was also signified by the Holy Spirit filling all of them (see Acts 2:2). The epicenter of NT believers in Christ was not only the epicenter of Christianity but also Judaism. Ron C. Fay states how Luke's narrative from the Gospel to Acts traverses continued activity toward the temple, which is essentially the epicenter of activity in Jerusalem.[118] It was where the temple was stationary for nine hundred years.

At the time of Solomon, a stationary temple replaced the mobile tents or tabernacles where worship and service to YHWH had been

---

118. Fay, "Narrative Function of the Temple," 255–70.

done since the time of Moses. When David and his men captured Jerusalem from the Jebusites in 869 BC, he named one of its hills Mount Zion (see 2 Sam 5:6–10).[119] It remained the centralized location where worship and service to the LORD would be accomplished until the coming and appearance of the Messiah (John 4:20–21). Luke becomes a trustworthy witness to the fact that Jesus Christ was/is the Messiah foretold in the Hebrew Scriptures (see Luke 24:44–48 NIV).[120] The next discussion leads into the narrative criticism of Luke-Acts.

---

119. David captured the fortress of the people of Jebus (Yevussi or Yevusi, מבצע יבוסי) within Jerusalem (Yerushalayim, יְרוּשָׁלַיִם) and called it the city of David. See Kantor, *Jewish Time Line Encyclopedia*, 47.

120. "He said to them, 'This is what I told you while I was still with you: Everything must be fulfilled that is written about me in the Law of Moses, the Prophets, and the Psalms.' Then he opened their minds so they could understand the Scriptures. He told them, 'This is what is written: The Messiah will suffer and rise from the dead on the third day and repentance for the forgiveness of sins will be preached in his name to all nations, beginning at Jerusalem.'"

Chapter 4: Narrative Criticism in the Construction of Luke-Acts

CADBURY SAYS THAT LUKE and Acts are not two independent writings but a continuous story from the pen of the same writer.[1] The fine point brings readers into the discussion of narrative criticism in the construction of Luke-Acts. Mark Powell defines a narrative as any work of literature telling a story.[2] In Luke-Acts the story is unquestionably being told to a person named Theophilus (Luke 1:3; Acts 1:1), and all readers are invited to listen in on the telling of it.[3] Narratives have two aspects, the story and the discourse. The story refers to the content of the narrative. It consists of the events, characters, settings, and plot. The discourse refers to the rhetoric of the narrative, specifically how the story is being told.[4] This explanation may qualify the four Gospels and Acts as narratives, though they are perhaps more accurately described as quasi-narratives.[5]

In *Introduction to Biblical Hermeneutics*, Kaiser and Silva express that between one-third to one-half of the Bible is written in the style of narrative, and it is the most common genre and framework of both testaments.[6] It is a framework that spans from the creation (Genesis) through the exile of Judah (2 Kings). The narrative picks

1. Cadbury, *Making of Luke-Acts*, 8–9.
2. Powell, *What Is Narrative Criticism?*, 23.
3. Powell, *What Is Narrative Criticism?*, 27.
4. Powell, *What Is Narrative Criticism?*, 23.
5. Powell, *What Is Narrative Criticism?*, 23.
6. Kaiser and Silva, *Introduction to Biblical Hermeneutics*, 123–24.

up following the post-exilic years to the NT, i.e., the Gospels running to Acts.[7] In this aspect of reading the Bible as narrative, it is easy to see how Acts is connected through the gospel stories and how the Gospels (Luke specifically) flow together as a continuous story. In a broader sense, the narrative framework is an account of specific spacetime events. It is a story of all participants involved in the stories being told, forming God's one grand plan and purpose with each having a beginning, a middle, and an ending.[8]

Köstenberger and Patterson believe a narrative is a literary framework that builds sentences and paragraphs around discourses, episodes, or scenes.[9] These literary types are present throughout both testaments. As such, narrative studies recognize that meaning is found in the text rather than in isolated scriptures. They describe three different modes of narrative texts appearing throughout the Bible: a story, an account, or a report.[10] It goes without saying that a lot of the historical information in the OT and in the Gospels through Acts is presented in narratives to be read like a story.

Apart from genres, such as poetry, wisdom literature, simile, metaphor, parable, allegory, or symbolism, for instance, the literal sense of a story being told is based on facts that the author is presenting a true account to his readers.[11] Natan Elgabsi cites Plato regarding the idea that a writer's integrity in writing is everything and it is most of all a moral quality. As such, honesty and dishonesty in a historian say a lot about the moral quality of the person when they are purporting to give information to others.[12] In ancient writing, it was not uncommon for authors to develop a story with speeches and dialogues around them as turning points for events in the surrounding narrative. For reasons such as these, it is important for readers to recognize the words

---

7. Kaiser and Silva, *Introduction to Biblical Hermeneutics*, 123–24.

8. Kaiser and Silva, *Introduction to Biblical Hermeneutics*, 123–24.

9. Köstenberger and Patterson, *Invitation to Biblical Interpretation*, 186–88.

10. Köstenberger and Patterson state that recognizing the various ways a narrative can be presented in any biblical book is one of the necessary but important steps to understanding the author's message contextually. See Köstenberger and Patterson, *Invitation to Biblical Interpretation*, 186.

11. Köstenberger and Patterson, *Invitation to Biblical Interpretation*, 186–88.

12. Elgabsi, "Is There a Problem," 225.

of the actors who are speaking for awareness of the larger narrative. It increases the reader's understanding of the author's plot, makes the reader feel like they are part of the story being told, and allows the reader to follow the entirety of the context.[13]

A reading of Luke-Acts reveals a narrative unity between the two volumes. In *Luke as Narrative Theologian: Texts and Topics*, Joel B. Green presents a collection of essays to discover if Luke was a theologian and to examine the use of theology through his style of narrative. In essence, Green takes it for granted that the relationship between history and theological interpretation is crucial to understanding Luke as a writer.[14] Some scholars say that narrative theology dismisses objective truth.[15] In other words, a reflection of theological claims is embedded in stories.[16] To interpret the writing style of Luke, Green uses miracles told by Luke to interpret them as theology.

It was already pointed out that between one-third to one-half of the Bible is written in narrative.[17] Green has not shifted into a post-liberalist position while making his arguments. As a result of the new narrative criticism, some scholars are now calling narrative theology "post-liberalism." Green is not using this sort of theory to interpret Luke but believes Luke is simply a theologian who writes in a narrative style. For a narrative theologian like Luke, which Green identifies him as, he writes theology that he intends his readers to take in as if they are reading a story and to apply its truths to their lives.[18] The style was not original with Luke but an ancient practice that predated him. Green's examination of the deeds of Christ are theologically driven by Luke's narrative.

In the introduction to this book, a discussion on the literary genre for Luke-Acts was covered in a fair amount of detail. Both genre and context (immediate, historical, literary) are important to

13. Köstenberger and Patterson, *Invitation to Biblical Interpretation*, 186–88.

14. Green, *Luke as Narrative Theologian*, 24.

15. A modern trend has developed by associating narrative theology with post-liberalism and charging it with using narrative over systematic theology and objecting to the truth of Scripture.

16. Comstock, "Two Types," 687–717.

17. See Kaiser and Silva, *Introduction to Biblical Hermeneutics*, 123–24.

18. Green, *Luke as Narrative Theologian*, 97.

understand the biblical author's message. Apart from this, the prooftexting of select passages within the purpose and design of the overall book is left up to the reader in the making of poor hermeneutics and thereby leads to a grave misinterpretation of the text.

Meaning should not come from the reader but from the text.[19] However, pursuit of this line of thought and the attending controversy is outside the bounds of this book. In addition to developing a proper hermeneutic of Luke, "a study of the literary context, literary forms (genre), and backgrounds (historical, cultural, geographical, authorship) are important keys that aids the reader to understanding the message of the author."[20]

Fay comments on narrative analysis whereas the kind of analysis seen in Luke-Acts typically focuses on specific characters, such as Jesus in Luke, and the early church and Paul in Acts.[21] Therefore, it stands to reason that Luke's idea for the Gospel was the same idea he held in mind for Acts. Whereas the Gospel was on scroll 1, Acts is a continuation of the Gospel's narrative of scroll 1 onto scroll 2. His goal was to write a διήγησις concerning the events that took place among them.

The furtherance of this was to persuade readers of the full certainty of the truth of the traditions about Jesus and their significance for salvation.[22] Luke's use of the term αφήγημα literally translates in English as "narrative." The term describes the type of writing that those before him have already attempted (1:2). For instance, "inasmuch as many have taken in hand to set in order a narrative," (1:1a), his desire was to also set in order a narrative in his statement, "it seemed good to

---

19. In a reader-response method of interpretation, the meaning of the text does not originate from the text but from the reader of the text. See Kaiser and Silva, *Introduction to Biblical Hermeneutics*, 34. The danger of this theory is that it allows the reader to determine what the text means. A danger to this approach is that the text cannot convey meaning and interpretation but is left up to the reader. It is a flawed approach to biblical hermeneutics that appears to place any reader in the position to make the text mean what it means to them as they read it. See Poirier, "Some Detracting Considerations," 250–63.

20. Womble, *Bringing the Depths into Focus*, 12–13.

21. Fay, "Narrative Function of the Temple," 255–70.

22. Garland, *Luke*, 49.

me also" (1:3a), after he had gotten "a perfect understanding of those things" (1:3a) "fulfilled among us [them]" (1:1b).

The birth narrative of Christ and the birth narrative of the *ecclesia* are important beginnings for Luke's narrative and aim for telling his story. They are placed at the beginning to show how the stories develop from these established premises. The birth story of Christ in the Third Gospel and the beginning of the church in Acts are both presented in the form of a narrative. These two narratives at the beginning of both volumes are important in Luke building the narratives to both volumes as a single story. Without the birth of Christ, there would be no gospel and church. And without the church, there would be no purpose for Acts.

These birth narratives in Luke and in Acts can serve as introductions, and broader narratives are developed within the framework of the stories as they progress and develop, using them as hinge pins into the larger narratives of the author's purpose. These two accounts are the glue that holds together the Third Gospel and the history of the church; Luke's birthed, crucified, and resurrected *Kurios* entered the physical world as a real, genuine, and authentic Lord and Savior on the specific mission of reconciling all things back to himself (Col 1:20a).

The resolve of the divine purpose was for Christ to be born, to die for all sins, and to reconcile humanity with God. Whereas the first Adam led the creation away from God in exerted infringement of sin into the world, the last Adam brought it back to God (1 Cor 15:21–22). Wherefore instead of originating Christ's genealogy with Abraham as Matthew does with a Jewish Gospel, Luke extends it back to Adam where the problem of sin and rebellion against God first began.

Birth Narratives in Luke's Gospel and Their Aim to His Larger Gospel Narrative

The virgin birth is essential not only to Luke's entire narrative of Luke-Acts but also to the entirety of the NT. Without it, there would be nothing for Luke or any other Gospel or NT writer to discuss any further. The virgin birth disclosed in the birth narratives of Jesus hinges on the premise that Jesus was a sinless human being. As such, he was born by a natural physical human birth to save all humans by dying for all the sins of mankind.

The story that Jesus was and is the Savior of the world is the central message of the Gospel writers. If Jesus had a biological human father, he would have also inherited the sinful nature that was passed down from Adam through his descendants to all humans. He escaped the sin nature in conception and birth (cf. Ps 51:5) by a supernatural conception by the Holy Spirit (cf. Matt 1:18, 20; Luke 1:35). What is necessary to the foundation of the NT is the virgin birth, on the premise that Jesus was born of a virgin, that he was sinless, and that he was and is qualified to be humanity's Savior.

The Gospel of Luke provides more detail about the birth of Jesus Christ than any other book in the Bible. Luke understood its importance as necessary and essential to the knowledge of humanity that a savior needed to come into the world (see Luke 2:10–11). To the virgin birth of Christ, there was no other alternative nor any other perspective to compare to it. And with it, the prophecy of the prophet Isaiah was fulfilled (see Isa 7:14; cf. Matt 1:23). Its authenticity is and was directly expressed in the OT, as it was also confirmed by Christ's mother, Mary (see Luke 1:34–35) and witnessed through Elisabeth (see Luke 1:41–44) and Zechariah (see Luke 1:67–80).

Prior to Christ's birth, Malachi's messenger was on Luke's cognizance. His purpose of starting with John the Baptist was an attempt to connect Malachi, the last of the writing prophets, to the front of his Gospel (see Matt 11:14; cf. Mal 4:5–6). His Gospel would therefore bridge Mal 4:5–6 while Acts would bridge his Gospel. The uniqueness of this bridge using John the Baptist, from Malachi's Elijah-like prophet (as Luke's intertextual fulfillment), was his ability to connect both testaments better than any other writer on the subject.[23] Luke's Gospel presentation provided the longest birth narrative on the birth of Christ in the whole Bible.

---

23. Whereas John 1:1 connects Jesus to Gen 1:1, his Gospel and Genesis do not flow as a unique transition of the OT into the NT, as Luke's does uniquely with Malachi. Genesis 1:1: "בְּרֵאשִׁית בָּרָא אֱלֹהִים" ("In the beginning God created ..."), whereas John 1:1: "Ἐν ἀρχῇ ἦν ὁ λόγος" ("In the beginning was the Word ...").

Even though Mark and John begin their narratives with the ministry of John the Baptist, both John and Jesus are complete adults at the beginning of them. Neither Mark nor John provides a birth narrative, unlike Matthew and Luke. Each of the four Gospels and other NT books uses intertextuality to read NT meaning (interpretation and fulfillment) into OT Scripture from a christological position of Jesus Christ.[24] The OT prophets hinted at the revelation but it was not yet realized until its prophetic fulfillment as recorded in the NT (see 1 Pet 1:11). Luke's purpose was to provide a realized eschatological revelation to the birth of Christ and the fulfillment of the prophets in the first century.

Luke gives his readers nearly three chapters on this subject of birth narratives. In chapter 1 verses 26-38, Christ's birth is announced, and in verses 39-56, he discusses how Mary and Elizabeth handled their situation as the burden of God placed upon them as a miracle granted to them only by the Lord. Chapter 2 of Luke's Gospel presents the *Sitz im Leben* of early Bethlehem at the turn of the century. It precedes the early life of shepherds tending their flocks in the fields of Bethlehem, the miraculous appearance of angels, the infant Jesus at the temple, and the socio-cultural conflict surrounding all the events that followed. Even though Luke discards the connection between Herod and his commanding the murder of Jewish infants, it is, however, given by Matthew (see Matt 2:1-18).[25]

---

24. Beale underscores how the NT writer's use of OT texts was not out of line with the meaning of original OT passages, but their reading of NT meaning back into the OT was determined by a wider, overriding perspective that viewed redemptive history considering Jesus Christ and that it was unified by God's divine wisdom. See Beale, *Handbook on the New Testament*, 87-89. In addition to Beale, some scholars argue that the apostle Paul, for instance, was at liberty to interpret the OT considering the NT, as they saw Jesus Christ as the fulfillment of OT messianic texts. It was a process of taking the original OT meaning of texts and applying them to later events and people. See Moyise, *Paul and Scripture*, 124. This is a theological practice of intertextuality, which involves reading NT meaning and interpretation back into the OT as the NT writers interpreted OT text as applied to Jesus Christ. Another example of intertextuality comes from Luke 24:44, "This is what I told you while I was still with you: Everything must be fulfilled that is written about me in the Law of Moses, the Prophets, and the Psalms" (NIV).

25. Refer to the work of Chen for a more detailed discussion and historical analysis of this subject. See Chen, *Luke*, 34-45.

In Luke chapter 3 following the introduction to the ministry of John the Baptist, verse 23 adds the genealogy table of Jesus all the way through the end of the chapter. Luke's account of John's and Jesus's births are so detailed to the point that it seems like he sat down with Elisabeth and Mary and got firsthand information for himself.[26] Many of the myths surrounding Roman and Greek deities and how they gave birth to humans were well known in Greco-Roman culture and society.[27]

Most gentiles had gods for nearly everything in public and private life. When the Greek gods gave birth to humans, the individual was not like normal humans, but he or she was a supernatural part god and

---

26. Brown points out that Luke's infancy narrative has no parallel with that of Matthew, which implies that both used independent sources. In Streeter's four-document hypothesis theory (Mark, Q=*Quelle*, M=Matthew, and L=Luke), Funk argues unique material in the so-called L and M sources more likely came from oral tradition. See Funk, Hoover, and Jesus Seminar, *Five Gospels*, 15. In as much as there is only one birth narrative, the question emerges as to how both Luke's and Matthew's became fragmented. Brown suggested since Mary dominates Luke's account of the events, and Joseph dominates Matthew's, Luke simply gives Mary's remembrance of the events, as Matthew gave Joseph's remembrance of them. Another point to Luke's narrative, even if he had not spoken directly with Mary, his account of the infancy narrative is what scholars recognize as a family tradition believed in a community and passed on to others. And since Mary treasured all these things in her heart (Luke 2:19), she was the only person who revealed the details in Luke's account until she felt the need to reveal them to others. Mary was also among the other disciples up to the day of Pentecost in Acts (cf. 1:14). See Brown, *Birth of the Messiah*, 35. It would imply that she was available for testimony at the time of the establishment of the church, and had relocated to Ephesus with the apostle John particularly after Jesus willed them to be mother and son (see John 19:26). See Alaharasan, *Home of the Assumption*, 19. If this was the case, it is not a farfetched idea that Luke would have had ample opportunity to meet and talk to her, particularly while possessing historical tendencies for research.

27. In Greek mythology, Zeus, for instance, was thought to be the greatest of the deities and was considered by Homer as the father of gods and men, the ruler and protector of all. See Hartog, "Zeus," 1419. According to Greek mythology, Zeus impregnated some human women, one of whom also bore the demigod Hercules (from whom some Roman emperors thought they also descended). A demigod is/was seen as a mythological figure who was half god and half man, or a human that became divine. See Barry et al., *Faithlife Study Bible*. Around the era of the Maccabees (Hellenistic period), the city of Rome was personified as the main deity of the Romans. It was around this time when they began assimilating Greek deities into their culture while assuming Latin names for them. Westfall, "Roman Religions and the Imperial Cult."

part human. The lengthy narrative on John, specifically on Jesus, was not a myth as Luke wanted Theophilus to understand.[28] He wanted to provide details of these narratives in an orderly fashion. It is seemingly the reason that he goes about providing so much detail.

Jesus was a real human being in every way it is meant to be human (Heb 2:16) except he did not possess a sin nature passed down in human descendancy.[29] The sin nature resident in every other human being was passed down from copulation and conception. In Ps 51:5, David understood this reality about human nature by saying, "Surely I was sinful at birth, sinful from the time my mother conceived me" (NIV). It however was not the case with Jesus seeing that he did not have a biological human father. His conception was not caused by Joseph but by the Holy Spirit (see Matt 1:18; Luke 1:31–36); therefore, God was his Father (see John 3:16, where he is called "the only begotten son"). The ESV of 1 John 3:5 says that

28. Theophilus was a name that was common in the first three centuries AD. Two others named Theophilus were Theophilus of Antioch and Theophilus of Alexandria (who was said to be a Jew). But the Theophilus in Luke's reference does not fit these two because they lived much later than the Theophilus Luke addresses. Several people with the name Theophilus existed at the time of Luke's writing, therefore the person being referenced by him is addressed as "most excellent" to distinguish him from all others. It stands to show that Luke's reference is to a gentile who loved God and wanted to know more about God's truth that was being taught by the apostles of Christ. It is also possible that "most excellent" alludes to an official position he held within the Roman government (cf. Acts 23:26; 24:2; 26:25). See Nelson, "Theophilus," 1298. In addition, Luke 1:4 suggests that Theophilus might have sought details that would enhance his limited knowledge of Jesus's life and the early church. The NT does not provide any clues as to how Luke met or even had known him. A possible indication was a result of his esteemed character and highly favorable reputation as a physician, which opened a door for him even within the Roman government. Such a direct inquiry by Theophilus to Luke was possible for prompting Luke to write his Gospel and Acts, being that there were more people in Theophilus's position who wanted to know more about Christ and the Christian faith. The assertion that Theophilus was a gentile is highly likely due to the aim of Luke's Gospel, whereas he was not writing to Jews. Roman Garrison also speculated that Theophilus was a gentile since the tradition says that Luke wrote when he was in Greece, and Jerome speculated that the recipient might be a famous official in Athens by the same name. See Garrison, *Significance of Theophilus*, ii, 4, 8. However, the tradition that Luke's "Most Excellent" Theophilus was bishop of Antioch or Caesarea cannot be substantiated. See Miller, "Theophilus."

29. All human beings are biological descendants of Adam, whereas Eve, the mother of all living (Gen 3:20), also came from Adam (Gen 2:22).

there was no sin in him.³⁰ It is what qualified him to be God's Lamb sacrifice for sins (see John 1:29).

Even though Jesus was divine, he was also human. The Romans appeared to have tolerated the monotheistic Jewish religion at the time of Jesus. But after his departure, the disciples worshiped him as divine (see Matt 28:17). When the Christians (a later designation from the time of Paul and Barnabas, see Acts 11:26) started preaching the gospel of Christ, after Jesus's departure, they were labeled throughout the Roman Empire as atheists.³¹ In regard to the gods giving birth to humans, Luke had the desire to present a genuine human Jesus to Theophilus. He often used the phrase "Son of Man" in quoting words spoken by Jesus more than any other Gospel or NT writer except for Matthew.³²

But Luke reveals Jesus as being unlike the humans that were born of the Roman and Greek gods, as it is often told in Greek mythology. And rather than the myths, he was called "the Son of the Highest" (see Luke 1:32 NKJV). The supernatural activity that came with the anecdotes of old were probably not at all too convincing, especially to one Theophilus who desired to know the truth and its certainty surrounding Christ (see Luke 1:4).³³ It is likely the reason Luke took great interest in Paul's ministry, because the operation of miracles in the ministry of believers was real.

To Luke's point, Jesus's birth was not a myth like the gods of old. While being the only gentile writer, he was likely not reared in a monotheistic theocracy as were his Jewish counterpart writers. The gentile culture and upbringing were predominantly or possibly all polytheistic for gentiles. The gentile upbringing of Theophilus

---

30. Additional NT passages bear out the fact that Jesus was a sinless human being, such as Rom 8:3; 2 Cor 5:21; Heb 4:15; and 1 John 3:5.

31. Young, "Persecution of the Early Church," 234.

32. Jesus often used the phrase "ὁ υἱὸς τοῦ ἀνθρώπου" to describe himself and his ministry. See Hardin and Brown, "Son of Man." The phrase occurs eighty-one times across the four Gospels. Luke uses it more than the others: twenty-five times. It is used in Matthew thirty times, in Mark fourteen times, and twelve times in John. Every time the expression is used in the Gospels, each writer is quoting Jesus as the one using the expression. See Hurtado, *Lord Jesus Christ*, 291.

33. Luke wanted Theophilus to know the truth about Christ, and "so that [he] [would] know the certainty of the things [he] [has] been taught" (Luke 1:4 NIV).

lends to the apparent reason to render such great amount of detail in the birth narratives, as to prevent their stories from sounding like another Greek myth to Theophilus.[34] In other words, the God-man presented to Theophilus was born to die. It was a divine purpose and not simply another Greek tragedy.

Many have offered various points of view about intertextuality, mostly because of the semantic range involved with terms and passages to denote meaning. Although there are still lots of discussion over the term, a suggestion is being offered here to briefly explain how it is sometimes used theologically to understand a NT author's intent in specific passages used to emphasize meaning from an older passage of Scripture. According to Moyise, intertextuality as used in theology became a textual emendation introduced into biblical studies in 1989. It was intended to contrast the relationship that exists between different texts, in different authors, and different textual sources.[35]

NT writers such as Luke, on occasion, connected and read new meaning back into OT passages to emphasize the original author's theorized empirical meaning; but in terms later to the interpreting NT author (Luke), it was the OT author's intended meaning. The original author (the OT passage or passages) and the NT author (Luke) understood motifs, genres, literary expressions common to their culture, which modern readers are not privy to experiencing, resulting from time of writing and differences in culture and language.

Luke uses intertextuality to represent the framework of his narrative that allows his readers to make sense of what he or she might perceive as inexact, unclear, or unsettled by both the divine and human author.[36] An example that expresses this point is seen in Luke 4:19 where he interpreted Jesus's triumphant return to Nazareth, to proclaim the "favorable year of the Lord." The Jubilee year was well known among Jews of the OT period seeing that it was an acceptable time for God and for people.

---

34. While narrating Jesus's life story from beginning to ending, Luke does not make him another Greek tragedy like gentiles read in the myths. He was born to die, to save humanity from sin and eternal damnation.

35. Moyise, "Intertextuality and Biblical Studies."

36. Plottel, *Intertextuality*, xix.

According to Mosaic law, practice, and ancient Hebrew custom, the Jubilee year was the "year of release" from all bondage and was proclaimed throughout all the land to its inhabitants. During the celebration, everything including people and property that was in possession of another had to be returned to the original owner (see Lev 25). Luke intertextually reads a spiritual fulfillment of the OT Jubilee as God's release year of Israel (and for all people) from the spiritual bondage of Satan and sin (see Luke 4:18–19).[37]

The final theological meaning between texts in Old and NT passages was not just limited to inter (between)-textual (the testaments) passages, but NT writers also improved upon each other's ideas to bring harmony among each other's writing. This is an idea that appears common among the Synoptic Gospels. Intertextuality involved not only the conflation of an old passage with new meaning but also a connecting of those NT passages with OT passages. Luke's καθὼς παρέδοσαν ἡμῖν οἱ ἀπ' ἀρχῆς did not only include interviews with people that knew Jesus personally. It also included OT writings that spoke of Jesus as the Christ (i.e., Messiah, Anointed One).

Luke's treatment of the birth narrative of Christ is the root and foundation of his first (Luke) and second (Acts) treatises.[38] As John's Logos was made flesh (John 1:14), Luke's *Kurios* is the Son of Man.[39] The term, as it was used in the first century, was a common

---

37. When Jesus returned from the wilderness of temptation in the power of the Spirit, one of the six anointings that rested upon him was the ability "to proclaim the favorable year of the Lord" (NASB). The year of the Lord's favor is the Jubilee year. And because Jesus quotes from Isaiah and not from Leviticus, the imagery used for Jubilee refers to the day of salvation. Garland believes it was intended to invoke signs of eschatological redemption that were manifesting by the advent of Jesus Christ instead of the political and social reforms of Jubilee under the OT era. Jesus therefore read and applied Isa 61:1–3 as the dawn of salvation, release from the bondage of sin, and deliverance from Satan. See Garland, *Luke*, 200.

38. A consensus of Luke-Acts scholars believes that both volumes should be interpreted as two volumes that are read together as a single unit. It is built on the insight that the unity of both books is interpreted by telling a single story that includes both Luke and Acts. See Keener, *Acts*.

39. The Gospel writers use Jesus's expression "Son of Man," in view of the interpretation of Dan 7:13 (also Ezek 3:4) as it applies to Jesus. The KJV translates Daniel as saying, "I saw in the night visions, and, behold, one like the Son of man came with the clouds of heaven, and came to the Ancient of days, and they brought him near before him" (cf. Matt 26:64 and Luke 21:27).

masculine expression in Greek, equivalent to the English words "mister" or "sir." It became one of the christological titles used in Luke for Jesus, meaning Lord. Some extant Greek manuscripts contain papyrus fragments (second or third centuries) of the NT ranging from only a few verses to entire fourth-century codices. Some date from the late first to second centuries AD and have the term χυριος (Gk. *kurios*, Lord) as direct quotations of OT passages when translating the Tetragrammaton הוהי (YHWH). It is believed that these copies are manuscripts that originated from various regions in the Mediterranean that reflect different manuscript families (or textual traditions) tracing back to the first century.[40]

Scholars purported to use a method to help understand the Bible considering its historical and cultural backgrounds arising out of a real, authentic human context. A variety of possibilities are involved to determine what happened in the history behind the text. A problem that can be argued against a historical-critical method in understanding Luke is based on its perceived ideal to downplay the scriptures as a divinely inspired revelation while attempting to overemphasize only the humanness of them. It is helpful to a certain extent, but there is danger involved with any attempt to remove the divine prerogatives from the text. If this happens, it could better be defined as the word of man rather than the word of God.

A historical-critical method for understanding Luke aids the reader's understanding of the logorrheic history behind and around the text of the author. But in the process of reading, one should come to the realization that the Holy Spirit guided Luke in his writing of the Third Gospel (see 2 Tim 3:16 and 2 Pet 1:21). Using a historical-critical method alone to interpret Luke apart from considering biblical inspiration of the text would certainly not be a fair treatment of it, unless one is seeking to draw out the author's primitive original meaning in its original historical context.[41] But even then, the reader must seek to find and understand Jesus in the text because he remains the focal point of Luke's entire writing strategy.

40. Bowman, *Putting Jesus in His Place*, 159.
41. Soulen and Soulen, *Handbook of Biblical Criticism*, 78–79.

The purpose then is to interpret Luke by repeating what he said, by contextually interpreting what he meant, and by interpreting him within the larger context of the book. His goal was to present a very real human Jesus to his readers and the world. He devotes nearly three chapters to the birth narrative of Christ alone to suit his purpose of making Jesus a real human being, and to dispel myths associated of God's fathering of a human based on the way it is conveyed in Greek thought. For Luke, the gentile recipients and readers needed to understand the humanness of the Lord that Luke was presenting in the Gospel. He presents his information in a way that he does not purport to overwhelm either Jesus's divine nature or human nature.

The κύριος of Luke is ὁ υἱὸς τοῦ ἀνθρώπου when he (and the three additional canonical Gospel writers) referred to Jesus, and is a term adopted from the LXX.[42] To reaffirm Bousset's point here, the designation "ὁ κύριος" alone is used more frequently in the Gospel of Luke.[43] Luke, in his brilliance, presented a text for readers to understand Jesus as being fully human and fully divine. In keeping with the theology of the OT, God is the only Savior. The NT writers continued their discussion of salvation by applying it to Jesus as the only one who is indeed Savior.[44]

In times prior to Luke's writings (particularly to the OT era), there was an awareness of κύριος as it related to the exalted one of Israel. Independent of Judaizing Jews, the apostles of Christ correlated it with Jesus as his identity became lucid, to which they heralded him ὁ κύριος without hesitation. And with that, it became a designation given to ὁ Ἰησοῦς. For Bousset, the transition to the divine name

---

42. See the earlier section under "Literature Review" in the introduction, where I demonstrated that some of the extant Greek manuscripts contained portions of the New Testament that refer to *kurios* as YHWH. The inspired text of Mal 3:1 also proclaimed that YHWH would visit the temple. It was manifested in the Lord Jesus Christ when YHWH physically and visually came to the temple, fulfilling Malachi's prediction.

43. Bousset, *Kyrios Christos*, 123.

44. Second Peter makes it clear that Jesus had a divine nature. Being that he was human, it should be also understood that he had a human nature (see 2 Pet 1:4). The overwhelming NT evidence makes it clear that he was both God and human where it was essential that the two natures did not conflict nor become overwhelmed by either of the other.

ὁ κύριος had its influence from the LXX, which even more proved that it, in a religious and theological sense, was used for Jesus only in Hellenistic Christian communities. The Judaizing Jews would not use this designation for anyone other than YHWH (they quoted as Adonai) on assumptions of blasphemy.[45]

It has been shown how Luke provided an in-depth account of the birth narratives of John and particularly Jesus. The data was παρέδοσαν (passed down or handed over) to him from those who knew Jesus personally from the beginning of his ministry. Luke's use of the Septuagint was at an advantage. While considering his language choice, he was highly capable of mediating the Greek version in the language common to everyone in his day.

The authenticity of the Lukan birth narrative of Christ is not only given in Luke's Gospel. It was proclaimed well in advance by the Hebrew prophets (Isa 7:14 and Mic 5:2). The LXX version of Isa 7:14, which was one of Luke's sources, renders part of the verse as: "... ἰδοὺ ἡ παρθένος ἐν γαστρὶ ἕξει καὶ τέξεται υἱόν." Gabriel translated and applied Isaiah's prophecy to Mary (see Luke 1:30–31 NASB). A close rendition provided by Luke says, "And behold, you will conceive in your womb and give birth to a son, and you shall name Him Jesus."

Luke depended on the LXX for an authoritative record of Jesus, for his proclamation as the Messiah throughout the Hebrew Scriptures. As spoken by Isaiah the prophet: "Therefore, the Lord Himself will give you a sign: Behold, the virgin will conceive and give birth to a son, and she will name Him Immanuel" (Isa 7:14 NASB). It was interpreted and defined by the Gospel writers Luke (1:26–35) and Matthew (1:22–23).

In Isaiah's prophecy the term הָמַלְעָה (ha'almá) in the context of Isa 7:14 does not mean young woman, as some have incorrectly assumed. The word הָמְלַע (alma) meaning virgin in Isa 7:14 was intertextually authoritatively ratified not only by Luke but by Matthew as well. In Luke 1:34 Mary said, "*I am a virgin.*" The angel Gabriel also confirmed as much (see Luke 1:35 and Matt 1:23); for Joseph also knew as much (see Matt 1:19–20).

---

45. Bousset, *Kyrios Christos*, 121–22, 128.

Géza Vermes stated that the Greek version of Genesis also uses three additional Hebrew words for virgin: *bethulah* (virgin), *Na'arah* (girl), and *almah* (young woman).[46] Nearly all English translations of Isa 7:14 use the English word "virgin," except for at least six of them that use the word "young woman" (e.g., GNT, JPS Tanakh 1917, NET, and NRSV). As an exegetical and hermeneutical principle of interpretation, the context will always render the correct meaning of the word. The word παρθένος is used by Matthew and Luke; that is, they render it as virgin (a female who has never had sexual intercourse).[47] Παρθένος, in Matthew and Luke, explains how Mary becomes pregnant without copulation. These writers render the birth of Christ a miracle.

The Hebrew term הָעַלְמָה (*alma*) is not translated "young woman" in Luke (1:27, 33) and Matthew (1:23). The scholars who make an argument for young woman instead of virgin likely take this assumption from one of the English translations mentioned earlier such as the GNT, JPS Tanakh 1917, NET, or NRSV, and not from the immediate context of the Hebrew text. An example from the NRSV renders Isa 7:14 the following way: "Therefore the Lord himself will give you a sign. Look, the young woman is with child and shall bear a son, and shall name him Immanuel." In the Old Testament, nearly all English translations except for the GNT, NET, YLT, NAB, NRSV, and JPS Tanakh translate the Hebrew term הָעַלְמָה (*alma*) in Isa 7:14 as "young woman." All other English translations apart from those six translate the word as "virgin." In the New Testament, the GNT appears to be the only English translation that translate the Hebrew term הָעַלְמָה (*alma*) in Isa 7:14 in the Septuagint as ἡ παρθένος (*parthenos*), as "young woman." Nearly all other English translations except for the GNT translate the word as "virgin." Luke used the same word from the LXX, τῆς παρθένου (*parthenou*), which is translated into English as "virgin." The translation will run into a problem if the meaning of the text is changed in the process of translating הָעַלְמָה

---

46. Vermes, *Jesus the Jew*, 215.

47. Παρθένος has a wide range of meanings in the Greek language such as maiden, girl, virgin, unmarried women who are not virgins, a virgin goddess, as a title of Athena at Athens, of Artemis, of an unnamed goddess, of the vestal virgins, the constellation Virgo, a young maiden, chaste, and an unmarried man. See Liddell et al., *Greek-English Lexicon*, 1339.

(*alma*) in Isa 7:14 as young woman, and not as virgin. This is also because a young woman is not necessarily a virgin, and a virgin is not necessarily a young woman. The Hebrew word used in Isa 7:14 is explicitly applied as virgin in the NT.

The first-century Hellenistic Jews and gentiles did not need to know Hebrew when a Greek version of the Hebrew Bible was comprehensible. Luke and other NT writers' treatment of Hebrew came from their reliance on the LXX.[48] Based on the text of 1:3, he seemingly believed it was his obligation to produce a written narrative concerning the things that they were believing.

> 1:3a It seemed fitting for me as well, having investigated everything carefully from the beginning . . . (NASB)
>
> 1:3a ἔδοξε κἀμοὶ παρηκολουθηκότι ἄνωθεν πᾶσιν ἀκριβῶς

Using the phrase "It seemed fitting to me" (ἔδοξε κἀμοὶ) indicates that Luke did not wish to criticize those who presented oral or written accounts before him.

The verb ἔδοξε(ν) is also used in Acts 15:22, 25, 28 for a conclusion reached by the Holy Spirit. He prepared himself to write an account by following everything with careful attention as suitable to/for a historian. When using the verb "followed" (παρηκολουθηκότι), it means that he brought himself abreast of all the events of which he is about to make a written record. By investigating "everything" (πᾶσιν), it referred to his sources used to build a written record of the narrative. It required him to go "back to the beginning" (ἄνωθεν), to the ministry of Zechariah, where the OT priests were continuing to burn incense in the temple. And finally, he investigated everything "carefully" (ἀκριβῶς).[49]

Plummer sees a frequent use of Hebraisms in the first two chapters of Luke, which indicate that a large amount of his material was originally in Aramaic.[50] Translating those Aramaic sources would have given him an opportunity to evince certain words, phrases, and constructions to enhance his narrative. If those materials were already

---

48. More discussion on this in chapter 5.
49. Garland, *Luke*, 51.
50. Plummer, *Critical and Exegetical Commentary*, xviii.

in Greek when Luke made use of them, then he could and did somewhat alter the wording of them.[51]

One problem, however, with the Aramaic assertion is the availability of those materials on the OT likely in existence to Luke apart from the Targums.[52] The OT was predominantly written in Hebrew apart from 268 verses that were written in Official or Imperial Aramaic, such as Dan 2:4b—7:28; Ezra 4:8–24; 5–6; 7:12–26. Both Hebrew and Aramaic belong to the same Semitic family of languages.[53] In *A Biblical Aramaic Reader*, Takamitsu Muraoka says that Gen 31:47 and Jer 10:11 were also written in Aramaic.[54]

The only evidential portions of the OT written in the Aramaic language at the time of the NT were more likely the Targums. However, a history of different Targum manuscripts was in existence, and the most literal was Targum *Onkelos*. It is a Targum composed during the first and second centuries AD by an elite priestly class of Judean Jews, and was later adopted and revised by Babylonian Jews.[55] With the exception of Targum manuscripts, there is not much to go on to support Plummer's argument for an Aramaic OT source for Luke (perhaps if one holds to an Aramaic Q, and then Q being a source for Luke).[56]

---

51. Plummer, *Critical and Exegetical Commentary*, xviii.

52. Matthew Black assumes because Jesus conversed with people in a Galilean dialect of Aramaic, he taught his audiences in a manner they best understood, Aramaic. At the heart of the Greek Gospels was a Palestinian Aramaic tradition rooted in the sayings and teachings of Christ. The tradition must have at one time been translated from Aramaic into Greek. Some, according to Black, also assumed the Gospel writers were their translators of the available Aramaic sources for their Gospels. It has also been assumed that they also made use of those early sources even if they did not personally translate them. But for Luke, this argument would assume that he also had a background in Hebrew or Syriac Aramaic, which cannot be proven. See Black, *Aramaic Approach*, 16.

53. Bromiley, *International Standard Bible Encyclopedia*, 657.

54. Muraoka, *Biblical Aramaic Reader*, 82; Howell, Review of *Biblical Aramaic Reader*, 137.

55. Some other manuscripts that have been discovered include Qumran manuscripts in part or in whole such as the Dead Sea Scrolls, apocryphal and pseudepigraphic writings, and copies of the Old Testament Scriptures.

56. Beattie and McNamara, *Aramaic Bible*, 245.

Israel Drazin asserts that an Aramaic translation of the OT existed around the beginning of the Common Era since fragments of it were found along with other early documents among the Dead Sea Scrolls (ca. 160 BC–AD 67) at Qumran, and before the Targum (meaning translation) Onkelos was composed. The name "Targum Onkelos" was derived from a man by the name of Onkelos and was given the name "The Translation of Onkelos." The rabbis of the Babylonian Talmud recognized this Onkelos translation as an authoritative translation of the Torah and Pentateuch into Aramaic. Rather than a mid-second century date for it, Drazin says it was not composed until around AD 400.[57]

Birth Narrative of the Church and Its Contribution to the Larger Narrative of Acts

In a similar way to ancient rhetoric, most ancient narratives could persuade. When reading or hearing a story, the reader may not realize they are being influenced by the author's narrative in the story.[58] Narratives do not always tell or are likely to hint at their indication of the purpose for which they are intended. Their alluring impact on audiences helps explain why narrative criticism focuses on literary structure and themes on persuasiveness and purpose.[59] Clouston sees that the text of the Acts of the Apostles is certainly a persuasive narrative.[60] Its story is not just historical but theological. The author is suggesting how the events being told should be interpreted as God's instructions and that a response is required on the part of the hearer and reader.[61]

The *ecclesia*, in this context, does not have a mission. It is the mission. It is God's mission to the world.[62] The first complete account

---

57. Drazin, *Maimonides*, 132.
58. Clouston, *How Ancient Narratives Persuade*, 2.
59. Clouston, *How Ancient Narratives Persuade*, 2.
60. Clouston, *How Ancient Narratives Persuade*, 2.
61. Clouston, *How Ancient Narratives Persuade*, 3.

62. James Littles sees God's call upon all believers in Christ as a *missiological eschatology*. It is what God intended for believers to do to minister to the world. That is, to go out into the entire world and make disciples of all people as commanded by Jesus in Matt 28:19. James Littles, lecture, "Mission of the Church," course at

given of God's mission to the world is Luke's volume 2 (the Acts of the Apostles).[63] Its origin is traced back through the Gospel of Matthew and Mark, which stood on the foundation of Peter's confession that "You [Jesus] are the Christ, the Son of the living God" (see Matt 16:16–18; Mark 8:29). Pentecost, from Acts 2:1, was one of the most important times in Israel's history, fifty days after the Passover. It was one of the three feasts at which all males were required to be present (see Exod 34:23).[64] The name used in the Pentateuch is πεντηκοστή (meaning fiftieth), but all three occurrences of the term in the NT (see Acts 2:1; 20:16; 1 Cor 16:8) refer to the OT Feast of Weeks.[65]

According to Acts chapter 2, the church originated on τὴν ἡμέραν τῆς Πεντηκοστῆς by anticipating the promise of the Father (Luke 24:49; Acts 1:8; cf. John 14:16–18).[66] It was signified by the coming of the Holy Spirit, demonstrating its first outpouring and infilling of believers gathered in an upper room in Jerusalem.[67] Luke bases the entire narrative of Acts on the Gospel (and its promises). All that the church was able to accomplish in Acts was only made possible by what Christ

---

Urshan Graduate School of Theology, 2009.

63. Though Jesus died for all mankind, his earthly ministry did not reach beyond the borders of Galilee and Judea. Jerusalem was the epicenter that he envisioned where the ministry of the church would expand to the entire world (see Matt 10:5–6).

64. The example is seen at the end of Paul's second missionary itinerary when he was in a hurry to get to Jerusalem before Pentecost (see Acts 20:16). The three required pilgrimage festivals were the Feast of Pentecost or Weeks (Shavuot), Feast of Tabernacles or Booths (Sukkot), and the Passover (Pesach).

65. Balz and Schneider, *Exegetical Dictionary of the New Testament*, 70.

66. The day of Pentecost (Acts 2:1) was meant to be a fulfillment of the OT ritual Feast of Weeks (Feast of the Firstfruits) or Tabernacles. The Scripture notes that it occurred fifty days after the Passover (Lev 23:15–16). John the Baptist called Jesus God's Lamb and Passover sacrifice for humanity (John 1:29–32). The day of Pentecost occurred fifty days after Jesus's resurrection.

67. Jesus prepared the disciples for this event before his departure (see John 14:16, 26; 15:26; 16:7, 13; Acts 1:7–9). It occurred with his outpouring of the Holy Spirit on the first believers fulfilling his words in Acts 1:8, saying, "But you shall receive power after that the Holy Ghost comes upon you, and you shall be witnesses for me first beginning at Jerusalem" (KJV). On the day of the new Pentecost, the church was established fulfilling Christ's promise in Matt 16:18, that he will build his church. It is an aspect of ministry that grows by making disciples of all gentiles (the nations) (cf. Matt 28:19) in the Acts of the Apostles.

accomplished and promised in the Gospel(s). It was important to Luke for the Gospel narrative to continue through volume 2, Acts.

Such traditions (continued set of beliefs and practices) that Theophilus learned are what Luke sought to place in an entire narrative format so there would not be any misunderstanding or confusion based on what he had already learned (been taught) from or by others. To this point, Koester makes a difference between traditions and narratives. For instance, Luke derived oral or written materials from traditions that were formed in the lives and experiences of the early Christian communities. Those traditions aided his ability to form narratives of the materials he possessed, which were mostly of the sayings tradition(s). Those traditions precisely or closely mirrored what Jesus said and those reported in the speech-acts before Luke becomes a personal eyewitness to those further events.[68]

The community Luke has in mind is derived from the term he uses in Acts 2:44, κοινά. All the believers were together and had everything in common (NIV). All the believers in a common fellowship shared all things among themselves. The coterie of believers existed in a community under a common and unified goal, and it was common for all to believe the same report. The community upheld a common fellowship among all members. Within this κοινά, all the traditions about the life, ministry, and deeds of Christ were able to flow without contention or dispute. It explains how Luke could look within this κοινά of believers to gather additional sources to develop his narratives regarding the traditions commonly held and believed among them.

A simplistic worldview regarding the term ἐκκλησία consists in two essences, spiritual and physical. The physical aspect represents something concrete such as the people or those who assemble in a common fellowship where Christ is said to be present (see Matt 18:20). The spiritual essence is also where Christ is present with no material embodiment with its members. In the spiritual essence of the ἐκκλησία all members have direct access to God (Heb 4:16), are the children of God (Gal 3:26), are all brothers and sisters in the body of Christ (Heb 10:19). John Sailhamer affirms that it is the name given to a spiritual body of believers united in Christ, where

---

68. Koester, *History and Literature*, 62.

Christ is the head and its life is found in the work and ministry of the Holy Spirit (cf. 1 Cor 12:13).[69]

In Acts, Luke does the same for the church as he does for Christ in the gospel. He provides a birth narrative by associating the day of Pentecost as the fulfillment of the OT *Shavuot*. The beginning, mission, and purpose are established to build his narrative audience from it. It takes place in the form of speeches. The narrative audience are the hearers, as presented within the world of the narrative.[70] The speeches indicate Luke's interest in the persuasion of his various narrative audiences.[71] In the final analysis, Clouston praises Acts, reckoning that it displays more evidence than the Third Gospel of being fashioned into a closely interconnected narrative.[72]

Scholarly Deduction: Luke as a Narrative Theologian

The reason it was important to discuss the three sets of birth narratives (i.e., John the Baptist, Jesus, and the church) in the previous two sections is for the sake and in support of the entire narratives running through Luke-Acts that hinge on their foundation. These events are necessary for Luke-Acts to work as continued running narratives. Luke has a similar idea with Acts as he did with the Gospel, by beginning with the birth of the church. From this premise, its members are equipped and begin making disciples of all the gentiles as Jesus commanded (see Matt 28:19).

In addition to serving as part of the narrative agenda that is seen in the way Luke-Acts is structured and written, the birth or infancy narratives also serve a theological purpose. I. Howard Marshall also notes a key point in how Luke 1–2 reflects a notable apotheosis in the OT and God's actions in *Septuagintal* terminology. But if these

---

69. Sailhamer, *Christian Theology*, 82. While being God's mission in the world, Christ is its head (Eph 5:23; Col 1:18), its life source (2 Cor 3:6), its sustainer (Rev 3:10; 22:9), and its leader (John 16:13; Rom 8:14), and he glorifies it (Rom 8:17, 30).

70. Clouston, *How Ancient Narratives Persuade*, 37.

71. Clouston, *How Ancient Narratives Persuade*, 127.

72. Clouston, *How Ancient Narratives Persuade*, 129.

narratives do not play a role in salvation, as mentioned by Marshall and others, it is an incorrect assumption.[73]

Luke's purpose in going into much detail was so Theophilus would know the certainty of the things that he had been taught (Luke 1:4). After all, the message of the angels to those that were in Bethlehem was "For there is born to you this day in the city of David a Savior, who is Christ the Lord" (cf. Luke 1:11). The infancy narrative of Christ was a message of salvation even before Jesus went to the cross. It is because the angels delivering the message spoke to install faith in Jesus to the world at his birth that he was Lord and Savior.

Even though John the Baptist was essential to the salvific ministry of Christ (see Isa 40:3; cf. Mal 3:1), it was also necessary for Jews to comprehend his role to signify the Messiah proclaimed in the prophets, as he was born in Bethlehem. It was, therefore, important to Theophilus that Luke purposely intended to provide such a detailed narrative of the birth of Christ. On the other hand, however, Marshall correctly points out that God had already begun his salvation action with the birth of John when considering the terminology in Zechariah's prophecy (Luke 1:67). His notion of how God visited his people and obtained redemption for them (Luke 1:68) is parsed out by the aorist tense, used to represent a prophetic perfect or indicate something God had done. Luke writes the infancy narratives in forms of theology.

To assume that Luke writes theology in a narrative is different from calling him a narrative theologian. Green uses both theology and narrative to deconstruct the Gospel of Luke. The same author of the Third Gospel writes the second volume in the same way. Both Luke and Acts contain groupings of smaller narratives, which Green uses to identify his theology. The author of Luke-Acts writes his theology in a style of narrative which he intended to be read like stories. They are groupings of stories about varying events which were reported.

Again, there is a difference between saying that Luke wrote his theology in a narrative versus Luke is a narrative theologian. In Acts alone, the main speeches amount to less than a quarter of the text (226

---

73. Marshall, *Luke*, 97.

out of 1,002 verses), and there are significant sections of narrative(s).[74] Such also appear as discourses. In the Gospel, there is no evidence that Luke was present, but he was made privy to many things that others heard Jesus say and teach. His statement in Acts 1:1–2a is clear, "Theophilus, I wrote about all that Jesus began to do and to teach until the day he was taken up to heaven."

At this point, it should not be a secret that Luke wanted to write theology in a narrative. The genre of Luke-Acts is treated different mostly because of their placement in the canon as the Gospel of John divides them. The Gospel of Luke reveals a narrative theology, and Acts reveals a narrative history. In *Narrative Theology and the Hermeneutical Virtues*, Jacob Goodson uses the term "narrative theology" interchangeably with "post-liberal theology."[75] But post-liberalism does not always have the same meaning as narrative theology. The reason, according to Goodson, that narrative theology has morphed into what some essentially consider as post-liberalism is because both critics and defenders of the term have worried too much about narrative and not too much about theology, whereas narrative since morphed into its own *ism*.[76]

Ronald Michener figures that there is not a straight way to define post-liberalism but this is more of a broad term. A negative label has been attached to narrative theology, which is not as bad as some have made it. If one could use a simple way of explaining it, it always stresses the narrative of Scripture along with the community of the church and its practices.[77] This is what Luke does in Luke-Acts, but it would be highly improper to use a modern term to describe Luke. He simply writes theology in the form of narrative where he is telling a story that he learned from others whom he interviewed to gather his data.

In an argument presented by John Frame, he uses narrative theology and post-liberalism synonymously and negatively.[78] Frame

74. Clouston, *How Ancient Narratives Persuade*, 128.
75. Goodson, *Narrative Theology*, 14.
76. Goodson, *Narrative Theology*, 14.
77. Michener, *Postliberal Theology*, 4.
78. See Frame, "Narrative Theology."

asserts that post-liberalism is a contemporary movement of relativism where it disconnects the truth portrayed in the narrative of Scripture from the eternal truth of Scripture, which is what shifted a complete focus to the narrative of Scripture itself.

The first misconception posed in this argument is misguided. Those who read Luke as a theologian writing in narrative form do not look to the author's cultural, societal, or historical context to retrieve knowledge and truth, they look to the text itself for that truth. The cultural, societal, and historical norms only aid the reader to understand the background of the text which thereby provides more detail to the author's intentions and purposes.

It is true that the Bible is written in many different genres, and a lot of it is presented in narrative as Scripture progresses through creation, the fall, Israel, redemption, the consummation of all things, etc. But narrative theology, according to Frame, seeks to avoid what he calls "the evangelical emphases on objective truth."[79] A denial of objective truth, according to Frame, seeks to adopt standards of truth and reasoning from the biblical narrative itself.[80] In contrast to Frame's thought process, objective truth is not based on an "evangelical emphasis," or the way that evangelicals define truth. A theological argument that states what is objectively true must come from the text and from what is directly expressed in Scripture, and not from any private interpretations of the biblical text.

However, others' views, such as Annette Thornburg's, are different from that of Frame. While Frame assumes narrative theology is the same as post-liberalism, Thornburg sees it simply as a way of finding the meaning in the author's story.[81] It is important that modern readers consider an author's background environment (cultural and sociological) that bear upon the text as crucial to acquiring meaning. Such influences upon the text are eyes into the first-century world that aids in understanding the reason and purpose behind the text in most

79. Frame, "Narrative Theology."

80. Frame, "Narrative Theology." Frame is a professor emeritus of systematic theology and philosophy at Reformed Theological Seminary. He condemns narrative theology, calling it post-liberalism, which rejects the objective truth of Scripture.

81. Thornburg, "Narrative's Revelatory Power," 2.

cases. The stories or narratives of Luke-Acts have a theological meaning behind them when they are instructions expected to be followed or practical applications that are intended to teach lessons.

It asks how such stories can continue to convey meaning and maintain their relevancy throughout each consecutive generation in time.[82] In addition, Leo Perdue sees narrative theology as a way that God reveals his will and activity through language within the setting of the story being told by the author.[83] And Grenz, Guretzki, and Nordling define it as a theological approach a storyteller uses to tell a story by providing a central motif for theological reflection.[84] Some also claim that the stories also reveal the writer's personal identity as they are joined with the transcendent story of the religious communities and ultimately with the overarching narrative of salvation history.[85]

Parsons and Pervo believe that literary critics appear to have often been concerned with the unity of the flow of the narrative (story) over the theology presented in the story itself.[86] Several scholars have also recently concluded that "Luke and Acts were intended to form one continuous unified narrative from the perspective of the newer narrative criticism."[87] The unity among the two volumes, according to Robert Tannehill, "is the result of a single author working within a persistent theological perspective, and thereby the unity is disclosed by a well-formed narrative on his part."[88]

In *Luke as Narrative Theologian*, Green elaborates on the views of other Luke-Acts scholars. These scholars felt a need to revisit this unity between the two, contesting that the gap should be closed between their division. For one thing, it serves no justice for the two being canonically divided between the Gospel of John. Perhaps if John

---

82. Thornburg, "Narrative's Revelatory Power," 2.
83. Perdue, "Theology, Old Testament."
84. Grenz, Guretzki, and Nordling, *Pocket Dictionary of Theological Terms*, 82.
85. Grenz, Guretzki, and Nordling, *Pocket Dictionary of Theological Terms*, 82.
86. Parsons and Pervo, *Rethinking the Unity*, 45.
87. Parsons and Pervo, *Rethinking the Unity*, 45.
88. Tannehill, *Narrative Unity of Luke-Acts*, 8; Parsons and Pervo, *Rethinking the Unity*, 45.

was placed in front of Luke in their canonical order, it would be easier to read from Luke into Acts.

A divide, however, contributes to their disunity, where the unsuspecting reader would not come to recognize how the two are connected. Twentieth-century studies, however, on the part of redaction critics often focused on Luke's Gospel regarding its relation with the Q hypothesis and the Synoptics, along with the placement of Luke among Matthew and Mark.[89] The studies that have focused on the Gospel in its relation to Acts or vice versa have done so without much consideration to their canonical location.[90]

Parsons and Pervo agree that some scholars affirm that the Third Gospel and Acts were intended to form one continuous, unified narrative, but from the perspective of the idea of new narrative criticism.[91] According to James Resseguie, "narrative criticism focuses on how biblical literature works as literature."[92] It gives a lot of focus and attention to the author's background and the background settings of the narrated events of the author.[93] The new narrative critics opposed this literary practice and insisted that the proper concern of literary analysis was the text itself and not the external events that surround it.[94]

In *The Narrative Unity of Luke-Acts*, Tannehill describes a narrative unity in terms of it being continuously developed and maintained as the author continues to tell the story. The unity presented in the narrative(s) should not be seen as a perfect unity, nor was Luke intending to bring unity between Luke and Acts, but he was simply telling a/the story. The continuous story from the Gospel into Acts is a continuous narrative in and of itself. Again, the present canonical order makes it difficult to read from the Gospel into Acts as a single narrative when John divides both volumes. If one reads

89. Green, *Luke as Narrative Theologian*, 4.
90. Green, *Luke as Narrative Theologian*, 4.
91. Parsons and Pervo, *Rethinking the Unity*, 45.
92. Resseguie, *Narrative Criticism of the New Testament*, 18. According to Resseguie, the now-coined "new criticism" developed out of narrative criticism between World Wars I and II and the Vietnam War.
93. Resseguie, *Narrative Criticism of the New Testament*, 21.
94. Resseguie, *Narrative Criticism of the New Testament*, 22.

the Gospel of Luke first then Acts second, episodes within the larger narrative continuously emerge from volume 1, with a continuous flow into volume 2 through the end of Acts.[95]

Joseph Tyson, according to the new criticism, agrees that the Third Gospel and Acts were written by one and the same author and that they were intended to be read consecutively. According to Tyson, both volumes were written in Greek and tell a single story that begins with Zechariah in Jerusalem and ends with Paul in Rome.[96] Luke's style of Greek in Luke-Acts says a lot about his acquaintance with the ways of writing narratives, whereas this awareness is seen in his use of the literary techniques that were available in the Hellenistic world of the first century.[97]

Ward Gasque agrees that Acts has been so much severed from the Gospel of Luke it is difficult to identify the connection between the two. And this is why he gives lots of his focus to Acts in *A History of the Interpretation of the Acts of the Apostles*. Even with this, however, he believed it was important in the development of his thesis to connect the Gospel with Acts. Regarding the new criticism, Gasque agrees that the Third Gospel and Acts are two volumes of a single work. As such, they must be considered together. According to Gasque, the author (Luke) is a theologian because questions regarding purpose, theology, speeches, and historical value cannot be rightly answered if both volumes are separated and not treated together.[98]

David Aune also believes that Luke's Gospel and Acts were originally a two-volume work written by a single author.[99] In chapter 3 of this book in the section on "The Separation of Luke and Acts," an analysis was completed of what contributed to the separation of the two volumes. Aune also adds points to how this happened, that the Gospel of Luke and Acts were separated in the early second

---

95. Tannehill, *Narrative Unity of Luke-Acts*, 8.

96. Parsons and Pervo, *Rethinking the Unity*, 45.

97. Tyson, *Death of Jesus*, ix–x; Parsons and Pervo, *Rethinking the Unity*, 45.

98. Gasque, *History of the Interpretation*, 309; Parsons and Pervo, *Rethinking the Unity*, 2–3.

99. Aune, *New Testament*, 77.

century.[100] The Gospel (within the Gospel genre) was/is within a group of other books known as the τό εὐαγγέλιον.

Luke was severed from Acts in the second century and combined with three other Gospels to form the *Tetrevangelium* (fourfold Gospel). There is only one gospel. Out of the four written canonical records, the four form one gospel. Or to express it another way using the words of Strauss, they are four portraits of the one Jesus.[101] Each of the four are unique and testify to the one gospel, the good news of salvation God has made available through the Messiah, Jesus Christ.[102]

The severing of both volumes warranted the conclusion that both were written on separate papyrus rolls (see the discussion in chapter 3 of this book in the section on "The Separation of Luke and Acts").[103] As it is with the other three written canonical Gospels, the four were considered as history and ancient biography (see the discussion in chapter 2 of this book in the section on "Analysis of Literary Genre of Luke-Acts in the New Testament Canon" for a thorough discussion on the literary genre of Luke-Acts).

Aune disagrees and sees the category of the Third Gospel as belonging with Acts, and neither can be forced into a biographical mode. In contrast to Aune's position on the biography consideration of the Third Gospel (and perhaps Acts), the point that is missed is that the Gospel resembles ancient biography and can indeed be compared to first-century Greco-Roman βίοι because it (they) reveals a biographical life story about Jesus.[104] A recognizable observation is not difficult to see specifically in Luke's narrative(s).

Robert Smith also considers the Third Gospel and Acts to be a unified whole and written from one and the same pen. As such,

---

100. Aune, *New Testament*, 77.

101. Strauss, *Four Portraits*, 24.

102. Strauss, *Four Portraits*, 24.

103. Aune also points out that it was common for ancient writers to publish a single book, separately. In cases such as this, it would not have been uncommon for Luke to do the same. See Aune, *New Testament*, 77.

104. Although Burridge does not equate any of the Gospels with a specific genre, he contends that they are written in the style of ancient βίοι (life, biography, life-story) as it appears in Greco-Roman style, and not in the way people judge it in contemporary writing biographic styles. See Burridge, *What Are the Gospels?*, 105.

one should not be studied in isolation of the other.[105] As is common among ancient writers before Luke and his contemporaries, he also dispenses rhetorical devices by employing discourses of narrative in speech acts. Most of Acts is written in the form of grouped narratives within the larger narrative of the entire volume. This, according to Smith, is theology, which makes this case by its continual confession of faith within the speeches and narratives required on the part of those who hear and read the message.[106]

Finally, Leander E. Keck and J. Louis Martyn state how it is generally accepted regarding Luke-Acts that both volumes have a single, common author, and that any conjectures that they do not belong together have not gained any large amount of contention or argument against this point of view. And because of the larger consensus to the two volumes that has put them forth as a single work, it should be accepted that the two belong together.[107] It is important as well as appropriate at this point to begin the discussion of the next chapter on Luke's literary and cultural context. The discussion rides on the back of Luke's presenting of this narrative and literary structure of Luke-Acts.

---

105. Smith, "Theology of Acts," 527–28; Parsons and Pervo, *Rethinking the Unity*, 2.

106. Smith, "Theology of Acts," 527–28.

107. Keck and Martyn, *Studies in Luke-Acts*, 18.

Chapter 5: Backgrounds—The Literary and Cultural Context of Luke-Acts

THE PRESENT CHAPTER MOVES from a narrative theological approach to Luke-Acts to a literary approach. The entire chapter deals specifically with backgrounds. The purpose is to present a historical background analysis of the era that contributed to the literary works of Luke the physician (and companion of Paul), and how those external elements within the first-century Roman Empire contributed to Luke-Acts. A study on historical backgrounds within, around, and outside the text of Luke-Acts discloses homogeneous writing trends during this period. The goal is a preemptive strategy to prevent arguments later.

It would be difficult or perhaps nearly impossible to analyze the background of the NT, in particular Luke-Acts, without homing in on some particulars of the Roman Empire. Presuming that the events reported in Luke-Acts (and the NT) took place within the event space of the first believers of *the way*, an examination of that history outside and around the text becomes an integral part of this research.[1] As

---

1. The term "Christian" is used three times in the NT: Acts 11:26, Acts 26:28, and 1 Pet 4:16. In Acts, the believers in Christ were known as followers of *the way*. It is not clear in Acts 11:26 if followers of *the way* were given this designation by their enemies, or if the saints in Antioch freely adopted the term to identify all believers of that movement. Because of its lack of use by Luke, it may imply that the first Christians never adopted the term early on among themselves until much later. The use of the term in Acts 25:28 is Agrippa's use in a negative context. Peter's use of the term (1 Pet 4:16) likely means that believers of *the way* later accepted it as a new connotation for their movement.

such, readers will appreciate those trends and gain a clearer understanding of the construction of Luke-Acts.

Real events occurring behind the text of Luke-Acts that contributed to their writing are oftentimes overlooked or deemed as unimportant. Those who may not be familiar with the way they were written, copied, and preserved through the ages can agree that those processes took place, that rightly juxtaposes Luke-Acts as it was to the first believers of *the way* to what it is today. The analysis fits into this book for its further need for developing the authenticity, authorship, and trust of the works handed down through history.

Luke is traditionally seen as the author, and his works can be regarded as ingenious. The current chapter agrees that this two-volume work was produced at a time when literature was manufactured and distributed by virtue of a ubiquitous physical infrastructure within that empire. And for the gospel of Jesus Christ, NT writers used that infrastructure for the dissemination of the message from Jerusalem, Samaria, Judea, and to the outermost reaches of the earth (see Acts 1:8). According to Luke 24:46–48, this is what Jesus intended. The message was first proclaimed orally. It then moved from an oral to a written record to maintain an accurate report of the message proclaimed by the apostles before they all left the scene.

An examination of literary issues is discussed at the beginning of the chapter, as it analyzes how writing functioned in Luke's first-century cultural context. It is important to examine literary functions in the first century to also demonstrate how Luke became the author of this extraordinary two-volume work. Again, it examines Luke's literary and cultural context, early writing in the first century (to include the method and surfaces used for writing), the manuscript tradition of Luke-Acts, the socio-environmental elements (historical-cultural, and social-scientific), Hellenistic rhetoric and oratory, and Lukan literary and rhetorical devices (including Luke's professional medical language and terminology).

To lead up to this point, and since this chapter deals with backgrounds, it is needful to backpedal before the birth of Christ when the Greco-Roman structures were being formed. The historical analysis in this chapter begins during the Second Temple period leading up to Jerusalem being absorbed into the Roman Empire.[2] Two additional areas of background analysis considered are what Craig Blomberg calls historical-cultural analysis and social-scientific criticism.[3]

The socio-environmental elements of Luke-Acts deal with background information behind those texts. According to Blomberg, historical-cultural analysis examines what was happening real-time in the contemporaneous world of the original author and the text such as authorship, date of writing, recipients of the message, and the historical events that led to the writing of a text in question.[4] Social-scientific analysis involves other parallel history at the same time of a text in question. It deals with cultural values, social relationships, religious and political systems, and other social events and patterns of behavior at the time of the author and his original audience.[5]

Bruce Malina also agrees how social-scientific criticism plays a role in the understanding of the ancient environment. Its goal is to find out what an initial audience understood when it heard someone read a given text audibly. It deals with the social systems and a recognition of the languages embedded in those systems.[6] Two of the social classes in that Roman society were the upper and lower classes. To comprehend the complex social experience resulting from different social layers of the world of early believers of *the way*, external and internal social minorities should be observed. Those external include the people coming into imperial Roman society from the outside: through channels of ethnic migration (immigrants), military campaigns (captives of war), and the slave market economy. Internal groups involve native peoples (e.g., Jews or gentiles).[7]

---

2. Jesus's arrival in Jerusalem for passion week, after the start of his three-year ministry that started in Galilee, was his goal in preparation for his crucifixion. Whereas Jerusalem (i.e., the temple) is the epicenter of the birth of Christianity, Rome is the epicenter of the Roman Empire. In the Gospel, Luke takes Jesus from Galilee to Jerusalem, and in Acts, he takes the church from Jerusalem to Rome. The history of Acts spans approximately thirty years. See Hays and Duvall, *Baker Illustrated Bible Handbook*, 695, 701.

3. Blomberg, *Handbook*, 66–67.

4. Blomberg, *Handbook*, 63, 66.

5. Blomberg, *Handbook*, 66.

6. Cromhout, Review of *Social World*, 191–96.

7. Berg, "Four Criteria," 6–27.

After decampment of Judah from Babylon and during the days of Ezra and Nehemiah, Jerusalem was returning to a monumental status. Its popularity in the world did not wane since the rebuilt temple in the sixth century.[8] More than four centuries later, the Romans laid siege to it for themselves. In 63 BC, it was incorporated into the Roman Empire.[9] After the birth of Christ, near the turn of the century, its popularity continued to heighten considerably as one of the world's foremost focal points of religious activity. The first century produced its share of Greek, Roman, Jewish, and Christian historians and writers; and other anonymous works on the NT became denoted apocryphal and pseudepigraphic.

After the heavenly ascension of Christ, there are four identifiable reasons among believers of *the way* explaining why Christ's second coming was not imminent as they likely assumed (refer to the responses to the four questions addressed at the beginning of chapter 3 concerning the delay of Christ's return). Luke wrote at a time when this hope was beginning to fade. He recognized the church was God's mission to the world which they had to settle down in. This is the reason Garland believes Luke was interested in a historical account of Christ and the church; beginning with the period of Israel from the OT, the period of Jesus's ministry in the center, and the period of the church.[10]

Additional clues behind a delayed παρουσία involved their treatment of Jesus's words literally, that he wanted the church to take the gospel beyond Jerusalem to the outermost reaches of the earth (see Luke 24:47; Acts 1:8; Matt 28:19). The church also appears to have developed an urgency in their witness from a sense that the apostles would soon die prior to Christ's return. An example provided by Luke is

---

8. Rodgers believes the empire was weakened over time by barbarians from without and Christians from within, as they encouraged soldiers to neglect their duties and become monks and priests. It essentially gave rise to the Byzantine Empire following its split between east and west by Constantine. See Rodgers, *Ancient Rome*, 250. According to Konstam and Keenan, the western part of the Roman Empire was sacked three times (AD 410, 455, and 475) in the fifth century, and it never recovered from the third devastation. See Konstam and Keenan, *Rome*, 18.

9. Ferguson, *Backgrounds of Early Christianity*, 411.

10. Garland, *Luke*, 36.

when Herod Agrippa killed the apostle James bar Zebedee and brother of John (see Acts 12:2). Agrippa then seized Peter after seeing how much his murder of James pleased the Jews (see Acts 12:3).[11] Yet, an additional emphasis evolved out of the rise of differing Christian factions and beliefs about Jesus and salvation. It was imperative for a permanent record to be written about what the church held to be true.

The rise of new Christian groups, beliefs, and teachings about Christ aided the church in recognizing the importance of writing Christian doctrine while the apostles were still living. The NT writers may not have thought they were writing Scripture, particularly works that would be placed on par with the OT. As *the way* started to evolve outside of Jerusalem, Samaria, and Judea, isolated sects that attached themselves to it were starting to form.[12] A permanent record of authoritative Christian doctrine was needed that plainly stated what the apostles taught and believed. In particular, the believers of *the way* needed a unified, authoritative, and sound message about the apostolic teachings believed and upheld in communities of all believers for those destined to be added to the church beyond Judea and Samaria.

It is reasonable to assume that writing in the first century was cumulative and fluid and that literacy was important to both reading and writing such works. Bart Ehrman is a modern, well-known voice on the NT who does not view the idea of high literacy favorably in the

---

11. Luke reported that the church prayed and Herod's desire to apprehend Peter was nullified by an angel that rescued him from impending death (cf. Acts 12:3–11).

12. Neander, *History of the Christian Religion*, 97. In addition were the Judaizers and the Ebionites. It is not certain who the Judaizers were Paul contended with in the regions of Galatia, but they were teaching a doctrine of circumcision for salvation that Paul called heresy. Following the Jerusalem council in Acts 15, he kicked off his writing of the Epistle to the Galatians. The Ebionites were seen as an offshoot Christian group and Judaism that rejected some of the essential doctrines taught by the apostles such as the virgin birth and the identity of Christ. It was stated that the Gospel of John was directed against their teachings, and both Paul and Luke had spoken against them. See Murray, *Dictionary of Early Christian Biography*, 283. In addition are false teachers that 2 Peter and Jude argued against, along with Paul in 2 Tim 2:18 and 1 Thess 2:2.

first century.¹³ According to Ehrman, only a few people could write.¹⁴ Ehrman argues the idea of widespread illiteracy among people as also a modern phenomenon. He believes that preindustrial societies did not have the incentive or means to provide mass literacy education for their children. And in classical antiquity people relied mostly on spoken words rather than written information, being that both Greece and Rome were oral cultures. Such a view, however, misses the mark of accuracy, which is explored in the next section.

The First-Century Literary and Cultural Context Contributing to Luke's Writing Style

Literacy and education are important considerations within a culture or society for the study of literary works within a specific period. According to the Education Policy and Data Center, both literacy level and educational attainment serve as indicators of the knowledge and skills that a population possesses.¹⁵ Scholars are split in their assessments of literacy levels within ancient societies. In addition to Ehrman, Moyer Hubbard also expressed a negative view of literacy rates among ancient people, specifically in the first century.

Craig Evans expressed the sentiment of some scholars that Jesus and his disciples could not read.¹⁶ Even though Evans does not agree or share this view, the thought of such reasoning is faulty and unsound.¹⁷ The sentiment is expressed despite Jesus's taking up a scroll

---

13. Ehrman does not look favorably upon literacy levels in the first-century Roman Empire. In fact, he charges between 85 to 90 percent of people during this era as being illiterate. For Ehrman, the people in this era were an oral culture, and therefore learning a trade to support their family took priority over pursuing further education above an elementary level, and over the importance of perfecting their skills in reading and writing. See Ehrman, *New Testament*, 74.

14. Ehrman, *New Testament*, 74.

15. Education Policy and Data Center, "Literacy and Educational Attainment," xx.

16. Evans does not ascribe to this view; he simply highlights the view that is held by critical scholars of the NT. Evans, *Jesus and His World*, 64; Andrews, *New Testament Documents*, 64.

17. Jesus was both human and divine. The thought that he was illiterate while on earth as a man does not make any sense, particularly in the way that people of

to read from the prophet Isaiah, or Peter reading from the scroll of the prophet Joel (see Luke 4:16; Acts 2:16). Moyer Hubbard holds the view that literacy and education in the ancient Mediterranean world were equivalent to education levels in some of the poorest countries in today's modern societies.[18]

In antiquity, most people outside the elite of society were obliged to pursue employment in place of further education. Some environmental, economic, and social conditions made (ancient) or make (modern) education difficult for many to pursue. Such external factors became a challenge for teens to choose between employment and education where employment was often chosen to provide or assist in providing for a household or family. The male youths had to learn and take on a trade from their father, or they would become an apprentice by way of a local tradesman.[19] An example in Scripture is where Jesus took on the trade of Joseph as a carpenter (see Matt 13:55; Mark 6:3). The girls, on the other hand, were taught to manage a household and entered marriage at a young age.[20]

Ehrman believes that only 10 to 15 percent of the population at the time of Socrates could read and write at an elementary level, in stark contrast to modern societies today.[21] While it was common for ancient writers to enlist the services of professional scribes or amanuenses, this alone does not prove it was always the case, or that it was done because the people were illiterate. Contrary to this view, the historical evidence points to a multifaceted, numerous number of writings among Romans, Jews, and Christ followers. Randolph Richards believes that a person's literacy in the first century was not determined by their ability to read but by the ability to write.[22]

Andrews believes that literacy today is defined as having the ability to read and write. In the Roman Empire, literacy was applied

---

faith view God. There is nothing in the kenosis (Phil 2:7) stating that Jesus debased himself of literacy. The same Jesus that created the universe (see Col 1:16–17; Heb 1:3) is the one who created all things.

18. Hubbard, *Christianity in the Greco-Roman World*, 74.
19. Hubbard, *Christianity in the Greco-Roman World*, 75.
20. Hubbard, *Christianity in the Greco-Roman World*, 75.
21. Ehrman, *New Testament*, 74.
22. Richards, *Paul*, 28; Andrews, *New Testament Documents*, 64.

to those having the ability to read, whereas the ability to write was not necessarily assumed.[23] As such, the measurement of literacy levels among people is a subjective term that should not be used generally or universally to categorize everyone in a particular time frame.[24] Organized systems for formalized education existed throughout the first century and were immersed in Hellenism.[25]

Hubbard believes that the Hellenization and Romanization of the ancient world were the keys to widespread educational models and systems that are depicted later in their ideal form for centers of universal learning.[26] The ancient world of Greece and Rome, however, specifically the Greeks, produced numerous libraries and centers of education, which makes it difficult to accede to the view of Ehrman and other modern scholars of an illiterate society.

William Barclay says when teachings of Christ went into the Greco-Roman world, it entered a world where books were familiar things and where the publishing of them to booksellers was considered big business.[27] It was during this era when Jesus came into the world (Gal 4:4). It was an era of a universal language (Koine Greek) and a sophisticated physical infrastructure (roads, postal systems, protection for traveling, etc.). It facilitated business, commerce, and communication between countries throughout the Mediterranean region and made it easier for the facilitation of the gospel.[28] It was a world where Christianity grew out of a melting pot of three primary languages, Aramaic, Greek, and Latin.[29] As the Gospel continued

23. Havelock, *Literate Revolution*, 41; Andrews, *New Testament Documents*, 63.

24. Andrews, *New Testament Documents*, 63.

25. Hadas, *Hellenistic Culture*, 59.

26. Hubbard, *Christianity in the Greco-Roman World*, 75.

27. Barclay and Bruce, *Making of the Bible*, 50; Patzia, *Making of the New Testament*, 47.

28. Patzia studied the work of Eldon Epp where he provided distances literature could or did travel throughout the Roman Empire and the amount of time it took for that literature to travel. According to Patzia, Epp provided the following figures: "Letters could travel some 800 miles in two months; or some 350 miles in thirty-six days, or 125 miles in three weeks; or some 400 miles in fourteen days, or 150 miles in four, six, or seven days; or fifteen miles in the same day." See Patzia, *Making of the New Testament*, 131.

29. When Jesus was being crucified on a Roman cross, Pontius Pilate hung up

to spread, the movement would later require translations of the NT into other languages.

Philo says that Jewish parents taught their children the law and how to read it.[30] Ferguson says that literacy became more general, and education was widespread, and that both abstract thought and practical intelligence were ingrained in a greater proportion of the population. Such philosophy coincided with the spread of Hellenism, so the level and extent of communication and intelligibility were important as well as significant for functional utilitarians.[31] And according to Andrews, the papyri evidence indicates that the literacy rate in the first century was high. It was more likely higher in this period than it was at any other time in history prior to the modern era.[32] As an international yet universal language, Koine Greek was the tool that later facilitated the books of the NT.[33]

Andrews states that some Bible scholars who comment on this subject are not familiar with the reading cultures of the first century. Many of them also ignore or are uninformed of the plethora or perhaps nimiety of evidence of a highly literate culture between the period of 50 BC and AD 325. While no numbers have been provided by Andrews, the overwhelming evidence of literacy even among Christians has proven to have been much higher than the general populations of people within the Roman Empire. Institutions for learning were in abundance, and the archaeological evidence, the papyri evidence, and the plethora and nimiety of literature that was produced in this period point to a literacy rate that appeared much higher than at any other time outside modern history.[34]

---

a sign above him that said, "This is Jesus, King of the Jews." According to John 19:20, the words were written in Aramaic, Greek, and Latin. And in Acts 22:2, Paul addressed the Sanhedrin in the Aramaic language. Some translations say it was Hebrew and others say Syriac, meaning that Aramaic, Hebrew, and Syriac are a part of the same family of languages.

30. Andrews, *New Testament Documents*, 67.

31. Ferguson, *Backgrounds of Early Christianity*, 14; Andrews, *New Testament Documents*, 76.

32. Andrews, *New Testament Documents*, 76.

33. Andrews, *New Testament Documents*, 76.

34. Andrews, *New Testament Documents*, 92–93.

It cannot be concluded from the evidence provided that the world around Luke was mostly an illiterate one. Nor can it be substantiated that Luke himself was not capable of accurately reporting events in his time, or that he was an amateur historian, as some scholars have suggested.[35] The NT does the best job of all ancient writings of the period in providing the modern world with the history of Jesus and early Christianity, with no exception to Luke. Martin Hengel identifies him as the most significant historian of the NT.[36] Robert Jamieson evaluates Luke's writing in an excellent classical style of Greek which comes to show that he was an educated Greek and traveled physician.[37] While he was a physician, it also shows that he had some form of secular education.

Hengel agrees that Greek education was firmly established even as far as Jerusalem and among Luke's contemporaries.[38] He possessed a great deal of formal rhetorical education.[39] Schnabel says the level of education demonstrated in his use of Greek suggests a high level of rhetorical, philosophical, and medical training compared to that of Galen of Pergamon.[40] Schnabel says Luke's Greek imitates that of the LXX in terms of quotations, allusions, and echoes and represents a living variety of biblical Greek even much wider than the LXX.[41] He belonged to a social context that gave him grounding in Jewish Greek literature that was available and limited to synagogues of diaspora communities. His education suggests his ability to engage in historical research and to write extensive biographical and historical monographs.[42]

---

35. Parsons and Pervo, *Rethinking the Unity*, 31.
36. Hengel, *Acts*, 51.
37. Jamieson, Fausset, and Brown, *Commentary Critical*, 95.
38. Hengel, *Acts*, 15.
39. Hengel, *Acts*, 48.
40. Schnabel, *Acts*, 25.
41. Schnabel, *Acts*, 25.
42. Schnabel, *Acts*, 25.

Writing in the First-Century Greco-Roman Empire

The LXX was the version of the OT used by the church and writers of the NT.[43] At least 80 percent of the quotes by the NT writers come from it.[44] It was common, but perhaps not quotidian, for writers to hire professionals to write their autographs or to copy an existing autograph to produce a manuscript.[45] The amanuensis was a profession for a reason. If he was fluent in reading and writing Hebrew and Aramaic, it was a benefit to the author if the scribe was also fluent in Greek and Latin.[46]

The assertion does not imply that the biblical author was not fluent or literate in those languages as well. But writing was tedious and time-consuming, and carefully done by hand. And mistakes with writing letters, words, and sentences were sometimes made, even by the professionals that were hired to perform the work. And not only were costs associated with the labor, but the author had to obtain the

---

43. Patzia highlights that the term OT was not used to define the Old Testament until the end of the second century AD. See Patzia, *Making of the New Testament*, 23–25.

44. The translation of the TaNaK into the Septuagint began in the third century BC as many people, specifically Jews, struggled to read and speak ancient Hebrew. Ptolemy II Philadelphus who desired to have the Hebrew Scriptures translated into a readable language for the great library in Alexandria recruited seventy-two Hebrew scholars (six from each tribe) to take part in the translation project. They were isolated on the island of Pharos to give strict attention to the project, which was then completed in seventy-two days. The first part was the Pentateuch, then followed by the Writings and Prophets. See Patzia, *Making of the New Testament*, 24.

45. Refer to Paul's use of Tertius in Rom 16:22 and Peter's use of Silvanus in 1 Pet 5:12. Andrews states that this first written autograph is also referred to as the first Authorized Text (Archetypal Manuscript), i.e., the text used to make other copies. See Andrews, *New Testament Documents*, 25.

46. The twenty-seven NT books that make up the canon were all written in Greek. Even with the Gospel of Matthew, there is not enough evidence to support an Aramaic Matthew as some scholars argue. Andrews argues for an original Gospel of Matthew written in Hebrew between AD 45–50 and translated into Greek shortly thereafter. See Andrews, *New Testament Documents*, 26. In addition, if a scribe was Jewish, he was more likely familiar with Aramaic, being that Hebrew has been the mother language of the Jews since Abraham. A scribe fluent in reading and writing Greek could pay huge dividends in writing down words spoken in any of the first-century languages.

materials needed to write down his words. These could be provided by a scribe that was hired to do the work for an author.

As seen in the way the several English translations use the theological term of "inspiration," it is given to the twenty-seven NT writings that intended to show God's involvement in them (see 2 Tim 2:16; cf. 2 Pet 1:21).[47] Luke-Acts are similar, and are included among those autographs said to have been inspired by God. As such, God did not choose to deliver those sacred writings through Tertius, Silvanus, or writers from the second and third centuries. He chose Matthew, Mark, John, Luke, Paul, Peter, James, and Jude.[48]

As far as the NT is concerned, Luke appears to be the only gentile writer. He was a coworker in the apostolic community especially seen in his close ties to Paul. There is no definitive evidence that anyone other than Luke the physician wrote the Third Gospel and Acts. The idea that Matthew and Luke used Q as a common source was a theory that originated in 1838, by Christian H. Weisse. He propagated that both Luke and Matthew independently employed the use of two sources, Mark's Gospel and a *logia* (sayings) source.[49]

When a biblical author wrote an autograph (Gal 6:11), the writing materials required to complete such a project were costly.[50] The dedication of a work or works to someone meant patronage in the

---

47. Luke and Mark are the only NT writers who are not clearly given the title apostles, although their works (or writings) and ministries were tied in association with the apostles of Christ. The following English translations say that God inspired the Scriptures: KJV, NKJV, NASB, CSB, HCSB, ASV, ERV, NET, and WBT. Other translations use the term "God-breathed" (θεόπνευστος) in a similar way that he breathed life into Adam during his creation (Gen 2:7). In 2 Pet 1:21, terms such as "carried along," "moved," "made to act," "compelled," "guided," or "under the influence" are used to describe God's involvement in the way the canonical books were written. To also describe inspiration, Cadbury uses the analogy of wind blowing on a flower or on leaves, causing them to move. Such a naïve conception is simple and highly overlooked. The doctrine of inspiration expressed a simple miracle in the ancient world. In the same way, biblical authorship was a superhuman function. According to Cadbury, either a poet or prophet was a person possessed, that is, inspired by the Holy Spirit. In this case, more than mere human genius marked the writing of Scripture. See Cadbury, *Making of Luke-Acts*, 12.

48. Andrews, *New Testament Documents*, 47.

49. Foster, "Q Source."

50. Hubbard, *Christianity in the Greco-Roman World*, 74.

Greco-Roman world of Luke's time. The dedication of Luke-Acts to Theophilus implied that he was a wealthy Christian who financed the publication and distribution of Luke's works.[51] The writing of shorter letters could have been affordable for most, but most of the NT documents were more expensive to write because of their length.[52] This is especially the case with volume 1 (Luke) and volume 2 (Acts) being that they are the longest writings in the NT.

As a result of the cost associated with producing copies of autographs or manuscripts altogether, some people preferred to hear the words orally. In ancient cultures, this kind of transmission is referred to as the living and abiding voice.[53] The written word, however, was more valuable in the long run because it kept the word pure. The written copies made it difficult to manipulate or corrupt. Even though attempts were always made on the latter two, written copies provided levels of safeguards for the protection of the author's original words.

Again, for an author to write an autograph, he had to purchase the materials (ink and a writing medium) and invest time in the project. And for Christian communities to reproduce copies of a work the size of Luke-Acts was costly because of their length.[54] It was quicker for someone to copy a small portion of Luke's writings rather than the entire book. But when it came to cost as a deciding factor, oral transmission had this advantage over the production of written copies of the texts.

In addition to the cost of making documents, a standard letter in Greek would have been written in *scriptio continua*, a style common in ancient Greek. The script style saved space in written texts because the text was written in all capital letters with no separation of words, sentences, paragraphs, and little to no punctuation.[55] Oral delivery

---

51. Fitzmyer, *Gospel According to Luke*, 300.

52. Green and McDonald, *World of the New Testament*, 361.

53. Bishop Papias of Hierapolis denoted how he did not seem particularly concerned about written testimony but preferred to hear it orally. The living source for Papias was the oral testimony of the apostles who heard, witnessed, and experienced Jesus. The story was told over and over until the oral tradition was nailed down completely and in memory. See Widengren, *Tradition*, 74.

54. Witherington, "Education," 189.

55. Witherington, "Education," 189–90.

required great memories. But the intended message could change as it was relayed from person to person before reaching its destination.

The length of a document posed a constraint for continued writing on the same scroll because the longer it was, the more expensive it was to produce. The length of the Gospel of Luke and Acts was calculated at approximately thirty-five feet. When unrolled, each volume individually filled an entire scroll. Aune noted the literary style of the Gospel and Acts are similar in terms of their vocabulary and theology.[56] When both volumes were pinned on separate scrolls, they became later severed into two separate books (as discussed in chapter 2), attributed to their scroll length. And, by the second century, Λουκᾶν εὐαγγέλιον was integrated into the fourfold Gospel collection, and Πράξεις surfaced as a separate work under the title the Acts of the Apostles.[57]

The term "book" used in Acts 1:1 refers to a papyrus roll.[58] It is a convention that was preserved from the Latin term *volumen* (meaning papyrus roll) as it came into English as volume (refer to Heb 10:17 where this term is also used in English translations).[59] The ancients used various kinds of writing surfaces for writing documents, messages, and books, such as stones, animal skins, and clay tablets. The papyrus roll, however, was one of the most common writing surfaces in the first century, along with parchment.

The scroll was a piece of writing that could be rolled; the term "roll" contained writings on papyrus, parchment, and any other piece of material that was able to be rolled and easily carried into a pouch. It is what Paul requested Timothy and Mark to bring with them on their way to Troas (see 2 Tim 4:13). The roll continued to be used toward the end of the first century until Christians started using the codex.[60]

---

56. Aune, *New Testament*, 17.

57. Patzia, *Making of the New Testament*, 90–91.

58. "In my former book [the Gospel of Luke], Theophilus, I wrote [past tense] . . ." (Acts 1:1 NIV). The New English Translation (NET) calls it "a former account." Luke's Gospel was a former account of Acts that was written on a prior scroll that was too large to continue Acts on the same scroll.

59. Aune, *New Testament*, 117.

60. Beal, *Dictionary of English Manuscript*, 369.

Greenlee believes it is unequivocally certain that all NT books were written on papyrus.⁶¹ The secular writers in Greco-Roman society preferred using the scroll-roll. Luke and the other NT writers appear to have done the same.⁶² When the book of Revelation was written toward the end of the century, the apostle John used his contemporary language to interpret βίβλος or βιβλίον as a roll-scroll with ink written on both sides.⁶³ In Rev 5:1, it was called an *opistrograph*—scroll. The identification of it was commonly denoted as a scroll that looked like those made from either parchment or papyrus.⁶⁴

Even though parchments were stronger and more durable than papyrus, the papyrus was cheaper, which is the reason it was preferred over the former.⁶⁵ The codex replaced the roll at the end of the first century or later. It allowed the attachment of pages from one side like a modern tablet.⁶⁶ Some of the earliest Christian manuscripts in existence were found on the codex, denoting a new transmission from scroll to the codex.⁶⁷

The scrolls like that of Luke and Acts were lengthy; in keeping with ancient practices of contemporary writers, those lengthy works would get published separately (published on separate scrolls).⁶⁸ Scholars believe Luke used the papyrus scroll-roll for this work. According to figures provided by Richards, an average length between thirty-two to thirty-five feet would have been enough for Luke's two volumes.⁶⁹

61. Greenlee, *Introduction*, 10.
62. Richards, "Reading, Writing, and Manuscripts," 364.
63. In Rev 1:1–4, the writer identifies himself as John the servant of Jesus Christ who was on the island of Patmos to receive the information about which he is writing. Gundry says that the book is dated during the reign of Domitian (AD 81–96). See Gundry, *Survey of the New Testament*, 507.
64. Greenlee, *Introduction*, 10.
65. Greenlee, *Introduction*, 10.
66. Richards, "Reading, Writing, and Manuscripts," 354–55.
67. Andrews, *New Testament Documents*, 88.
68. Based on the figures provided by Randolph Richards, he says that "papyrus rolls came in stock sizes with maximum lengths of 35 to 40 feet (an average thirty-foot roll could contain about 100 columns of writing with 30 to 40 lines per column and 20 letters per line). The dimensions of papyrus sheets varied considerably (8 to 12 inches high: 4⅓ and 9½ inches wide (cf. Pliny, *Natural History* 13.77–78)."
69. In chapter 3, it was explained that scroll or roll length is the reason that

The first-century writers always wanted book sizes mirrored equally so they could be evenly divided into halves.[70]

Table 1. Length of Luke and Acts[71]

Volume	Total Words	Total Stichoi
Luke	19,404	2,900
Acts	18,374	2,600

In contrast to Luke, the earliest manuscript type containing a portion of the Gospel of John is known as P[52]. It was written on papyrus and dates circa AD 125.[72] As with John, the original autographs of Luke-Acts have long perished. If believers of *the way* needed a copy of it, they would copy only a portion of it to suit their immediate purposes within their scattered congregations because of the time and expense involved in obtaining an entire copy.

To produce a copy of the Gospel and Acts, it required an equivalent of four thousand US dollars for each text in today's currency. It was beneficial in Luke's case, as seen in his dedication of both volumes to Theophilus, for the financial support provided to him to fund his lengthy project.[73] If a writing was too long to fit on the standard roll length, it was continued on a second scroll. This explains the reason Luke's two-volume work was written on separate scrolls.[74]

Latin was on its way to replacing Greek as the dominant language in the Roman Empire around AD 200. Later writers started using it in place of Greek. As the Gospel continued to spread, it also increased the demand for copies of manuscripts in languages other than Greek

---

Luke-Acts became separated into two separate books. A similar configuration followed throughout history until the time of canonization when all Luke and Acts were canonized as two separate books in addition to the other twenty-five.

70. Richards, "Reading, Writing, and Manuscripts," 364.
71. Aune, *New Testament*, 117.
72. Aland and Aland, *Text of the New Testament* (1987), 75–77.
73. Richards, "Reading, Writing, and Manuscripts," 364.
74. Richards, "Reading, Writing, and Manuscripts," 362.

and Latin.⁷⁵ The earliest manuscripts produced in Latin date to the fourth century.⁷⁶ The name given to their official copy of the NT was the Vulgate.⁷⁷ Around the eighth century, the *Byzantine* text prevailed as the official Greek version in the still Greek-speaking world. It is the text that became the basis of the Textus Receptus (or Received Text), as Desiderius Erasmus translated it.⁷⁸

The New Testament and Luke-Acts in the Early Manuscript Tradition

Christianity was birthed within a Jewish-Judaistic and Roman-Hellenistic environment in which Greco-Roman literature contributed to the construction of the NT. Luke and the other NT writers were familiar with the literary world in which they were seeking to share the Ευαγγέλιο του Ιησού Χριστού; its development from oral to written originated in a culture that used the linguistic forms and expression in everyday life.⁷⁹

A written letter was one of the highest achievements in communication to ensure that information was distributed throughout the empire securely and accurately. The Hellenistic world devolved its literary style upon Luke, Paul, and others.⁸⁰ Luke and Acts did not look the same in the first three centuries of Christianity as they existed in

---

75. Patzia, *Making of the New Testament*, 128.

76. Aland and Aland, *Text of the New Testament* (1987), 183.

77. Aland and Aland, *Text of the New Testament* (1987), 186.

78. Patzia says that Erasmus's text underwent five editions in 1516, 1519, 1522, 1527, and 1535. His third edition (1522) became the Received Text and was also the basis of the KJV. In addition, arguments were directed toward the quality of the Greek text behind the KJV, but as Patzia states this does not imply nor should anyone suggest that the KJV should not or cannot be God's word. However, since they were discovered, Alexandrinus, Sinaiticus, and Vaticanus were found to be much older and superior to the Received Text. It was then suggested that the Byzantine text was inferior to those three and that the Received Text did not represent a text that was closest to the original. See Patzia, *Making of the New Testament*, 135–36.

79. Patzia, *Making of the New Testament*, 33.

80. Patzia highlights that twenty-one of the twenty-seven NT books are in the form of letters. If a modern reader(s) can understand NT letters as Greco-Roman letters, it would provide a view into the world of the first-century Christians in the Roman Empire. See Patzia, *Making of the New Testament*, 33–34.

the fourth century and today.⁸¹ In the fourth century, the Acts of the Apostles became grouped with the General Epistles, and today Acts and the Third Gospel are separate books.⁸²

The original autograph of Luke-Acts was likely to be kept with the author and not a book distributor similar to a modern sense. Copies of the original were eventually widely circulated by a congregation or the province of its origin. As they began to be shared throughout a broad area by repeated copying, the close ties between those Christian communities would carry it between different areas where the process continuously repeated itself. And when another community desired a copy, additional copies of the original or an existing copy were made and multiplied.

The conscientious copier was meticulous in this task of copying the words believers of *the way* held in high regard. The promulgation of sacred and authoritative works (teachings believed and upheld in common among believers of *the way* about Christ) was not a swift and easy task in the absence of a scriptorium. Richards believes a community of believers could fund the expense for the composition of a text. Most importantly, they could also validate the document's authenticity and even the reason for its publication.⁸³ Luke dedicated the two-volume work to Theophilus as his benefactor, using the appellation κράτιστος. As the name implies, he was indeed God's friend for believing in the project and financing it for Luke for present and future generations.

Some scholars unsuitably assume all four canonical Gospels were written anonymously. It was often done to assign later dates to them. If the books were written by the same author bearing their names, it would mean that they were all written in the first century. Ehrman, for instance, argues for anonymous authorship of the four Gospels. He assumes each Gospel was written by educated Greek-speaking

---

81. In chapter 1 of this book, the analysis was made for the reason Luke-Acts did not fit on one single roll. Being that they are the longest works produced in the NT, they were too long according to the standard roll length for one roll, so Luke used a single roll for each volume.

82. Aland and Aland, *Text of the New Testament* (1989), 50. In addition, also compare P46 and Codex Bezae Cantabrigiensis.

83. Richards, "Reading, Writing, and Manuscripts," 364.

Christians near the end of the first century, and they got their data from oral tradition. Andrews disagrees with the sentiment and argues that each Gospel was written indeed by the author bearing each book's name and written in the first century.[84]

Andrews believes all NT books were written, edited, and published between AD 45–98.[85] If Andrews is correct in dating the original autographs, it is favorable to assume that the Gospels were written by the person bearing the book's name. Luke composed the longest and most literary Gospel among his contemporaries and connected it with the events in secular history under the reigns of Augustus and his successors. He does not mention his name in the Gospel or Acts.[86] By design, the Third Gospel bridges the last writing prophet, Malachi, whose final words proclaimed John the Baptist (Mal 4:5; cf. Matt 11:14). Acts ingeniously transitions from the earthly life and ministry of Jesus into the church and epistles.[87]

Luke's dependence on the LXX for the development of the Koine manuscript tradition meant that he was fluent in reading and writing in the Greek language. Such familiarity also included the social norms in which the church was immersed as full participants. The style used in writing documents or manuscripts was shaped by the writer's environment and culture. In another sense, modern writers are somewhat controlled by a specific set of protocols that assess a person's skill as a writer. This means that writing to both the writer and reader fits within a framework that is measured by the standard of that time.

Luke was substantively educated in a region of at least three language groups: Aramaic, Greek, and Latin (see John 19:20). His dependence on and use of the LXX was based on an older Greek culture dating back to the second century BC. Hellenism, as the Greeks conquered many people groups, including Jews and Romans, became the most prestigious influence on a person's thinking, lifestyle, and behavior (cf. 2 Cor 6:17). Writing in the early Roman Empire was influenced by Hellenism, whereas the rules of grammar were

---

84. Andrews, *New Testament Documents*, 27; Ehrman, *New Testament*, 70.
85. Andrews, *New Testament Documents*, 27.
86. Schaff, *History of the Christian Church*, 649.
87. Köstenberger and Patterson, *Invitation to Biblical Interpretation*, 108.

more subject to the linguistic protocols of that present culture for effective written communication.[88]

When the NT writers were writing their autographs, they would have been subject to the rules of Koine Greek, and not to similar styles persistent in the modern era. First-century writers would not have been expected to cite their sources or to guard against plagiarism. Writers were not subject to the rules of APA, MLA, Chicago, Turabian, or the SBL Handbook of Style. One of the prominent writing styles dating between 100 BC and AD 100 was the decorated rounded uncial.[89] The modification of the capital letters in words elicited an attractive look as the letters were rounded on the edges rather than squared.

The copied parts, portions, or sections of manuscripts produced fragments of small textual families like parent/child groupings. The child did not exist on its own but rather belonged to a larger grouping. The greater the distance among constituent scattered congregations, the more it brought about textual types that coexisted together.[90] The manuscript tradition developed into a living text unlike the text of the OT which was subject to strict Jewish control. As for the text of the NT, it continued as a living text for as long as it remained a manuscript tradition.[91] The three primary families or text types are the Alexandrian, Byzantine, and Western texts (and possibly the Caesarean as a later addition).[92]

---

88. In the first-century Roman Empire, Greek triumphed as the leading language of commerce. Everyone during this time spoke or had to speak Greek to communicate in business and society. The language itself is not dependent upon the ordering of words in a sentence as it is in the English language and others. Writing for Luke and the NT authors followed the conventions of that language. Common (*Koine*) Greek is an offshoot from Attic, and it is an inflected language where the voice or pitch is elevated or lowered based on word endings and functions.

89. Comfort and Barrett, *Text of the Earliest New Testament*, 1:17. Uncial letters are the modification of capital letters in which their curvy design takes the place of right angles. For example, the fifth letter in the Greek alphabet is E as a capital, and ε as an uncial. See Thompson, *Bible Illustrations*, 24.

90. Aland and Aland, *Text of the New Testament* (1989), 55–56.

91. Aland and Aland, *Text of the New Testament* (1989), 69.

92. Ellertson, "New Testament Manuscripts," 99.

Metzger believes that the Greek text of Acts that circulated among the first believers of *the way* was based on the Alexandrian and Western texts.[93] In comparison to the Alexandrian text, he says that the Western text is one-tenth longer. In addition, it is more picturesque and circumstantial, whereas the shorter text is generally more colorless and in places more obscure.[94] The Alexandrian text was considered the oldest and most faithful for preserving the original text. The Sinaiticus and Vaticanus, along with some significant papyri (Bodmer's P^{66} and P^{75}), contain this text type.

Some modern translations are represented by P^{75} (Bodmer XIV–XV).[95] The Western text was often found to contain the NT in both Greek and Latin. It is represented by Bezae and Claromontanus, whereas Bezae is the primary witness for the Western and contains the Gospels and Acts.[96] The listing is important to modern translations because they are manuscripts of the complete NT that likely survived to the modern era. The uncial-majuscule became a style in the fourth century having the rounded larger letter.[97]

Table 2. Four Great Uncials (Top to Bottom) Containing Luke and Acts[98]

Family and Tradition	Has Luke	Has Acts
Alexandrinus	Yes	Yes
Ephraemi Rescriptus	Yes	Yes
Sinaiticus	Yes	No
Vaticanus	Yes	Yes
Claromontanus (Codex Bezae)	Yes	No

---

93. Metzger, *Textual Commentary* (1994), 222.
94. Metzger, *Textual Commentary* (1971), 260.
95. Aland and Aland, *Text of the New Testament* (1989), 51.
96. Ellertson, "New Testament Manuscripts," 100.
97. Comfort and Barrett, *Text of the Earliest New Testament*, 1:17.
98. Patzia, *Making of the New Testament*, 156.

Pervo argues against the text of Luke-Acts claiming both are unreliable. He believes that the Gospel and Acts are corrupt, and Acts is more corrupt than the Gospel.[99] In furtherance of his argument against Acts, he thinks Acts was written circa 115 by an anonymous author that had a perspective on Ephesus and its general environs.[100] For Pervo, NA^{27}/UBS^4 is the earliest recoverable Greek text of Acts by its translators. He believes the Greek texts prior to NA^{27}/UBS^4 were lost and destroyed in AD 250.[101] And by extension, the original wording of Acts is irretrievable.

A little confusion arises in Pervo's argument about his 250 dating. If he is referring to the persecution of Christians under Diocletian, it was not until after the turn of the century that he ordered all scriptures to be destroyed. The exponential growth of copied manuscripts meant they were scattered over the Middle East well before this time. The severe persecution that Christians suffered under Diocletian during the fourth century was the great and last persecution. It was the most severe persecution Christians suffered in the Roman Empire (however, an argument can be made for the severe Neronic persecution in the first century as documented by Tacitus).

Michael Gaddis states in the year 303, Diocletian enforced policies that ordered all churches destroyed and all Christian scriptures burned, and Christians were dismissed and stripped of civil rights.[102] A lot of the Christian writings during Diocletian's reign between the third and fourth centuries were destroyed during that era and had to be replaced.[103] Comfort and Barrett place a juncture at AD 300 as a *terminus ad quem* because the production of manuscripts on the NT was disrupted.[104] When Christianity was welcomed throughout the empire under Constantine, the movement needed even more manuscripts. It gave rise to the need for a centralized place for copying

---

99. Pervo, *Acts*, 2. Along with Pervo, some textual critics criticize P^{75}, the Western text-type, along with the Sinaiticus and Vaticanus as faulty and corrupt.

100. Pervo, *Acts*, 5.

101. Aland et al., *Novum Testamentum*; and Aland et al., *Greek New Testament*.

102. Gaddis, *There Is No Crime*, 47.

103. Aland and Aland, *Text of the New Testament* (1989), 70.

104. Comfort and Barrett, *Text of the Earliest New Testament* (2001), 17.

manuscripts to support all the scattered congregations throughout the Roman Empire.[105]

Ironically, however, Pervo professes that Acts can be understood as a sequel to the Gospel, and that the canonical Luke represents the original form of the Gospel. He does not believe the author was Luke the physician who traveled with Paul. For Pervo, the Gospel and Acts were written anonymously but by the same author.[106] For Pervo, Luke does not require Acts because it is a complete story even for readers who are not familiar with any canonical Gospels.[107] He contend that Acts develops, fulfills, and plays upon the themes that are found in Luke and can both stand independently.[108]

Patrick Spencer dismantled similar arguments that persisted for some time that sought to dissolve the unity between Luke-Acts. In "The Unity of Luke-Acts: A Four-Bolted Hermeneutical Hinge," he posits that there exist four bolts that hold both volumes together: genre, narrative, theology, and reception history. And because these bolts remain firmly in place, the unity with both volumes is held together as a single, continuous hinge that remains unbroken.[109]

The Byzantine text-type (Majority Text) formed the basis for the Textus Receptus. The King James Version and a several other English translations were dependent upon it. According to Andrews, *The New Testament in the Original Greek*, also known as the Westcott and Hort text, was published in 1881 as the Greek-language version of the NT. The Nestle-Aland Greek NT, published in 1898, became a critical edition of the NT in its original Koine Greek and formed the basis for biblical criticism and most modern Bible translations.[110]

---

105. Aland and Aland, *Text of the New Testament* (1989), 70.

106. Pervo, *Acts*, 19.

107. For scholars to argue that a manuscript is corrupt is also like saying that it is unreliable. If Luke-Acts are unreliable then they are also untrustworthy in all their message presented to readers. The theological definition of canonicity is supposed to ensure that those books designated as *Sanctus Scriptura* are indeed sacred words given under God's help (2 Tim 3:16 and 2 Pet 1:21).

108. Pervo, *Acts*, 19.

109. Spencer, "Unity of Luke-Acts," 341–66; Garland, *Luke*, 28.

110. Andrews, *New Testament Documents*, 28.

From 1881 to today, hundreds of additional manuscripts have been discovered adding to extant copies in existence. With discoveries of early papyri dating decades to the originals, scholars might expect changes to both the WH and the NA[28] text. However, according to Andrews, the NA[28] is 99.5 percent identical to the WH Greek NT.[111] The abbreviation for papyrus, designated with a *siglum* (𝔓) and a number, plays special significance in the identification of manuscripts, especially in the third and fourth centuries.[112]

In *The Text of the Earliest New Testament Greek Manuscripts*, Comfort evaluated papyri 1 to 72 that all date between the late first through the late fourth centuries. Volume 2, *Papyrus 75 to 139*, includes uncials dating between the second to fourth centuries that are also evaluated.[113] Victor Martin dated P[75] to the early third century. It is also called the Bodmer XIV and XV papyrus and is one that stands out because it contains more of Luke and Acts in comparison to all the other Bodmer manuscripts.[114]

Comfort praises the copyist of P[75] that he was a professional Christian scribe, as the professionalism is displayed through his tight calligraphy and controlled copying.[115] The copyist also demonstrated a trait for making grammatical and stylistic improvements in keeping with the Alexandrian style and a tendency to shorten the text by dropping pronouns.[116] In P[75], Ευαγγέλιο κατά Λουκάν is at the end of Luke, and the Gospel of John begins on the same page.[117]

---

111. Andrews, *New Testament Documents*, 28.

112. Aland and Aland, *Text of the New Testament* (1989), 84.

113. Comfort and Barrett, *Text of the Earliest New Testament*, 2:10.

114. The Papyrus Bodmer XIV and XV contains Luke 3:8–22; 3:33—4:2; 4:34—5:10; 5:37—6:4; 6:10—7:32, 35-39, 41-43; 7:46—9:2; 9:4—17:15; 17:19—18:18; 22:4—4:53. It does not include 7:53—8:11. See Comfort and Barrett, *Text of the Earliest New Testament*, 2:11.

115. Comfort, *Text of the Earliest New Testament*, 2:12.

116. Comfort, *Text of the Earliest New Testament*, 2:15.

117. According to Comfort's findings, P[75] contains large parts of the Gospel of Luke, from Luke 3 to John 15. Comfort and Barrett, *Text of the Earliest New Testament*, 1:11.

Papyrus P¹²⁷, also referred to as P. Oxyrhynchus 4968, contains a large part of Acts and dates to the middle of the fourth century.¹¹⁸ Comfort highlights that many of these Bodmer manuscripts predate the Vaticanus, Sinaiticus, Alexandrinus, and Ephraemi Rescriptus by about two hundred years and contain about two-thirds of the NT.¹¹⁹ The Bodmer grouping has three important manuscript types, P⁶⁶, P⁷⁷, and P⁷⁵, and in contrast to Martin's dating, they are dated to the late second century. Papyrus P⁷⁵ contains nearly all of Luke's Gospel except for the birth narratives of John and Jesus. It begins in verse 18 where John is baptizing Jews in the Jordan River.¹²⁰

The early Alexandrian manuscripts display salient harmony with the later Alexandrian, Vaticanus, and Sinaiticus, which are two witnesses to it.¹²¹ According to Comfort and Barrett, the Alexandrian text in manuscripts is seen as the best text among trained scribes in the Greco-Roman world. Their work shows that they were well educated and talented for producing such accurate copies of manuscripts, as the later Alexandrian reflects great resemblance to the proto-Alexandrian text types.¹²² It is also called the Neutral text by Westcott and Hort and has been usually considered to be the best text, the most faithful in preserving the original. The text is shorter

---

118. Oxyrhynchus 4968 contains Acts 10:32–35, 40–45; 11:2–5, 30; 12:1–3, 5, 7–9; 15:29–31, 35–36, 38; 41; 16:1–4, 13–40; 17:1–10. See Comfort, *Text of the Earliest New Testament*, 2:186.

119. According to Comfort, these manuscripts provide a direct and most important witness of the autographs. See Comfort and Barrett, *Text of the Earliest New Testament*, 1:10.

120. "And with many other words John exhorted the people and proclaimed the good news to them" (Luke 3:18 NIV). See Comfort and Barrett, *Text of the Earliest New Testament*, 1:11.

121. Comfort makes the following assessment. He highlights among the early manuscripts of the NT, the foremost of the early Alexandrian manuscripts are listed as follows: "Gospels: P¹, P⁴/P⁶⁴/P⁶⁷, P⁵, P²⁸, P³⁵, P³⁹, P⁶⁶ᶜ, P⁷¹, P⁷⁵, P⁷⁷, P⁹⁰, P⁹⁵, P¹⁰¹, P¹⁰³, P¹⁰⁴, P¹⁰⁶, P¹⁰⁷, P¹⁰⁸, P¹¹⁹, P¹²⁰, P¹³⁴. Acts: P⁴⁵, P⁵³, P⁹¹, P⁰¹⁸⁹. The most reliable texts are: P¹, P⁴/P⁶⁴/P⁶⁷, P²³, P²⁷, P³⁰, P³², P³⁵, P³⁹, P⁴⁹/P⁶⁵, P⁷⁰, P⁷⁵, P⁸⁶, P⁸⁷, P⁹⁰, P⁹¹, P¹⁰⁰, P¹⁰¹, P¹⁰⁴, P¹⁰⁶, P¹⁰⁸, P¹¹¹, P¹¹⁴, and P¹¹⁵." See Comfort and Barrett, *Text of the Earliest New Testament*, 1:19–20.

122. According to the findings of Comfort and Barrett, "there is a high percentage of textual agreement between the early papyri themselves. The Bodmer P⁴ and P⁷⁵ show a high percentage of agreement in Luke." See Comfort and Barrett, *Text of the Earliest New Testament*, 1:18.

than others and does not display an extent of grammatical and stylistic polishing reminiscent of the Byzantine.[123]

Carol Ellertson says that the Western text is traced back to the second century and was used by Marcion, Tatian, Irenaeus, Tertullian, and Cyprian, and is represented by the manuscripts of Bezae (Gospels and Acts), *Claromontanus* (Pauline Epistles and Mark 1:1–5:30), and *Washingtonianus*.[124] Its textual readings, according to Ellertson, have a fondness for paraphrases. It is a text type that could potentially move Acts away from the original text coherent with the Gospel of Luke based on scribal word choices, the inducement of clauses, and whole sentences freely modified, omitted, or inserted. Ellertson believes the motives appear to have been a desire for harmonization, while at other times an enrichment of the narrative by the inclusion of traditional or apocryphal material.[125]

For Ellertson, what baffles some textual scholars is finding where Luke's Gospel ends. There, and in a few other places in the NT, some Western witnesses omit words and passages that are present in other forms of text, particularly the Alexandrian text.[126] Metzger believes some of the problems raised by the Western text of Acts is that it is 10 percent longer than the form that is commonly regarded to be the text of its original. This introduces more space for variant readings in Acts than any other book in the NT.[127]

Historical-Cultural, Social-Scientific, and Socio-Environmental Elements

Within a given passage, there are immediate, literary, and historical sub- or inter-contexts that aid in determining meaning. Womble

---

123. Ellertson, "New Testament Manuscripts," 101.

124. Ellertson, "New Testament Manuscripts," 101.

125. Ellertson, "New Testament Manuscripts," 101.

126. "In Luke 23:53, the Western text adds 'twenty men could not move the stone.' And in 22:19–20 the reference to 'the cup after supper' and to Christ's sweat as 'great drops of blood' in Luke 22:44 are also omitted. In 23:34, it does not have Christ's prayer on the cross, 'Father, forgive them . . . .'" Ellertson, "New Testament Manuscripts," 101.

127. Metzger, *Textual Commentary* (1994), xix–xx.

states how the study of the literary context, literary forms (genre), and backgrounds (historical, cultural, geographical, authorship) are important keys to understanding the message of a given author.[128] The socio-environmental contextual elements before and after Jesus make the historical context to understand the world in which Luke wrote his two-volume work, Luke-Acts.

In the historical context, the way the NT books are ordered is not chronological based on the time they were written. The Gospels represent the first coming of Jesus, and Revelation is about his second coming. The Gospel to the Jews, Matthew, is ordered first in modern Bibles and Revelation is placed at the end. The authors who wrote the Bible were writing to small communities of people who believed in Jesus Christ as their Savior, which was the story proclaimed by the people who saw, knew, and experienced him personally. For this reason, a disregard (or rejection) of the historical context and setting in which the texts were written would contribute greatly to the misunderstanding and misinterpretation of a two-millennia-old group of ancient texts.[129]

The books of the New Testament emerged within the historical context shaped by an era, environment, and society that was largely hostile to the movement that actively sought to convert outsiders to faith and salvation in the Christ they proclaimed. The historical contexts of Jesus's birth and ministry only spanned within the regions of Galilee, Samaria, Judea, the Decapolis, Perea, and Phoenicia.[130] Second, the beginning Christian movement emerged out of Judaism into its own entity.[131] It reached outside the regions Jesus visited beginning with the call of Barnabas and Saul of Tarsus, and then with others.

Borg emphasizes Roman imperial theology to understand the NT setting within the context of the Roman Empire before and after Jesus's messianic ministry. He states that Rome legitimated its rule by religion and politics amplified during the reign of Augustus. After the issuance of the *Pax Romana* that proclaimed the end of all wars,

---

128. Womble, *Bringing the Depths*, 12–13.
129. Borg, *Evolution of the Word*, 5.
130. Borg, *Evolution of the Word*, 6.
131. Borg, *Evolution of the Word*, 8–9.

Octavian was typified as someone highly respected.[132] He changed his name to Augustus, meaning *the one who is to be revered and worshiped*. The subjects predisposed him as one having a miraculous birth perpetrated as *good news* to the world.

Jews and Christians felt differently about a deity than gentiles. The former held to strict monotheism and believed that the one true God revealed in the OT Scripture was the only divine being. According to Luke, the angel Gabriel said Christ would be called the Son of (God) the Most High or Highest (Luke 1:32). To many of the Roman minds, the title *son of god* carried the notion of an imperial cult.[133] Before the death of Julius Caesar, Octavian deified him.[134] The influence of the emperor upon religion and politics overlapped, whereas Caesar's elevation to divine status brought about emperor worship within the empire.[135]

The worship of rulers was not original to Romans. It was a common cult among gentile nations of the world. *Divus* came to be identified with a deified emperor whereas *deus* was a divine entity. The imperial cult within the empire encouraged the magnification of the emperor as the one who stood for Rome and the empire. It moved to building alters to *Roma et Augustus* on conquered people groups. Emperor worship was also a political tool for recruiting people into the empire.[136]

The additional mixture of divine titles that surfaced among emperors was god, son of god, god manifested, epiphany, lord, savior, savior of the world, and *imperator*.[137] The subjects heralded them as gods and divine beings in the empire and outside of the city of Rome.[138] The angel Gabriel and the NT writers entered a conflict with the imperial cult by reserving all these titles only for Christ himself.

---

132. Borg, *Evolution of the Word*, 9–10.
133. Fay, *Father, Son and Spirit*, 281.
134. Fay, "Greco-Roman Concepts of Deity," 18.
135. Fay, "Greco-Roman Concepts of Deity," 16–18.
136. Fay, "Greco-Roman Concepts of Deity," 17.
137. Fay, "Greco-Roman Concepts of Deity," 20.
138. Fay, "Greco-Roman Concepts of Deity," 23.

His followers worshiped him as God (see Matt 2:11; 14:33; 28:9, 17; Luke 24:52; John 9:38; 20:28; Heb 1:6; Rev 1:17; 22:3).

Paul the apostle conferred that this was the specific timing God had chosen for Christ to come into the world to begin his redemptive work (see Gal 4:4; Eph 1:10). The stumbling block for both unbelieving Jews and gentiles was Christ (see 1 Cor 1:23). His followers promulgated him and his message as the only way to salvation. For the followers of Christ, he was the new Moses whom they had to turn to for redemption and salvation (see Acts 3:22–23). And for the gentiles, it meant that Christ alone was divine and not Caesar. As such, Jesus alone was worthy of worship. Gabriel's announcement that Jesus will be called the Son of God (see Luke 1:32) essentially gets to the heart of Luke's theology.

The number of Christ's followers continued to increase despite the persecution and martyrdom directed at the infant church. Those who rejected Christ viewed his followers in a negative way. Because of much misunderstanding of the movement, the pagans forged rumors that the Christians were perpetrators of *a new and wicked superstition*.[139] At the beginning of the second century, the Roman writer Tacitus referred to Christians as people hated for working abominations and promoting a deadly, dangerous superstition. He defamed Nero with suspicion of starting a fire that burned part of Rome in AD 64; a fire that Nero falsely blamed on the Christians for a crime that he committed.[140]

The term used by Suetonius and Tacitus to characterize Christians in the first century is "superstitious." It was a difficult world for them in the first three centuries. The Christians were simply doing what Jesus commanded them to do, but to obey him was a crime even punishable by death. Luke-Acts, however, were written in an empire extremely hostile to the message of Christ and the way of his followers. If Luke's Gospel was written from Caesarea in AD 58, and Acts was written from Achaia in AD 63, then both volumes would have been written during the Neronic persecutions, and before the death of Paul.[141] Such perse-

---

139. Hurtado, *Destroyer of the gods*, 4.
140. Tacitus, *Annals* 15.44.2–5; Hurtado, *Destroyer of the gods*, 21.
141. Unger, *New Unger's Bible Handbook*, 420, 464, 496.

cutions continued through the first three centuries until Christianity was legalized in AD 313 by Constantine.[142]

At the turn of the century, the Roman writer Pliny (the younger) wrote an assessment to Trajan about how he regarded and treated Christians. He was perplexed regarding the nature of the crimes reported against them. He said the Christians conducted gatherings on a fixed day to cite hymns to Christ as to a god. They made vows and oaths to walk uprightly and to share in ordinary harmless food. Despite the accusations, he responded based on actions their accusers leveled against them. Even though no one found any indication of crimes with which they were charged, they were still being condemned for holding to an adverse position contrary to society.[143]

The Christians were accused and charged of committing to and promoting *a perverse and extravagant superstition*. But for Pliny, he was fearful of something else. He was afraid that the spread of Christianity would ravage the revenues of their temples, "which were almost deserted anyway," and destroy the celebrations of the traditional rites of their gods.[144] The Christians were sought out and tortured for information, demanding that they apostatize their faith. If they refused, they were given over for execution.[145]

Pliny's report to Trajan noted that those accused were given three opportunities to recant their position as Christians. The accusers learned that those who were truly Christians refused to renounce their position despite the threats against their lives. Even when their execution was ordered, the people who were truly Christians were made known by their refusal to denounce their faith publicly. The litmus test (so to speak) to prove the matter was to "recite a prayer

---

142. John Eadie says that Christianity received a *de facto toleration* in 312 as it became universally recognized, officially in an Edict of Toleration issued by Constantine and Licinius, which also became the Edict of Milan. Although some scholars argue that there was no such thing as an Edict of Milan, a ratification of the decree was published by the eastern Emperor Galerius that legalized Christianity. See Eadie, *Conversion of Constantine*, 2–3.

143. Pliny the Younger, *Epistles* 10.96.5–6; Hurtado, *Destroyer of the gods*, 22–24.

144. Pliny, *Epistles* 10.96.5–6; Hurtado, *Destroyer of the gods*, 22–24.

145. Hurtado, *Destroyer of the gods*, 22–24.

to the gods and worship them, to make supplication to the image of the emperor with incense and wine, and to curse Christ." According to Pliny, these things genuine Christians would never do if they were truly Christians.[146] The Christians who recanted their position were released following a public demonstration of these spectacles.

As seen, the NT authors were both products of their time as well as counter-cultural. Luke, therefore, would have had to tailor his writing in a way that it could minister to more than one culture with relevancy.[147] The environment of Luke was certainly a barrier and had a bearing on his writing style, as well as the audience whom he was seeking to reach. Writing from a gentile background not embedded in Judaism, he had to transcend ethnic boundaries without abandoning a Judaistic awareness and patrimony into a message of Christ that involved world evangelism.

His writing to a contemporary audience eventually spanned time and cultural boundaries and became relevant to every generation transcending beyond his first intended audience. His Christ-centered message to reach a multicultural audience introduced a counter-cultural message in an empire that was opposed to it. His use of ancient rhetoric, which was prominent in Greek writers, was clever. And his use of it was his way of selling his message to the world by this art of persuasion.

Ancient Rhetoric and Hellenistic Oratory, Lukan Literary and Rhetorical Devices

Greek rhetoric played an influence on the literary writing styles of the NT writers.[148] It includes assonance (e.g., Matt 6:10; 2 Cor

146. Pliny, *Epistles* 10.96.5–6; Hurtado, *Destroyer of the gods*, 22–24.

147. It is highly probable that all first-century Jews understood specific provisions within the law of Moses regarding circumcision, food laws, and idolatry. But a non-Jewish, objective approach to Scripture had to be declared when James and the apostles saw it necessary to make provisions for the new gentile converts who placed faith in Christ so as not to burden them down with Mosaic stipulations familiar in Jewish tradition and culture (Acts 15:19–21).

148. Rhetoric was widely used throughout the ancient world in speeches and writing whereas its intended purpose was to persuade an audience to the speaker's or writer's point of view. It is often solicited on a persuasion and response technique,

3:17), alliteration (e.g., 1 Thess 1:2; Heb 1:1), rhythm (e.g., Matt 26:41), rhyme (e.g., John 1:1), and the use of rhetoric as is also seen throughout Luke-Acts. The awareness of biblical rhetoric reflects a considerable knowledge of Hellenistic literacy of general Greco-Roman influence and culture.[149]

Jerome Neyrey believes, specifically, that Luke's writing style reveals an education akin to someone having a high status. It reveals his training and ability to write adult prose based on preliminary exercises learned from rhetorical handbooks called *progymnasmata*.[150] A genre called *encomium* is what he used to compose his narrative about Jesus. It endeavored to bring honor and praise to a figure using topics related to origin, nurture, and training, accomplishments, and noble death.[151] Luke was not simply another writer in the past. He was erudite in his time.

Luke's skill in the idiomatic expressions of elegant Greek demonstrates how familiar the Koine style was to the NT writers when

---

in a similar fashion to a sermon in modern times. See Patzia, *Making of the New Testament*, 33; James Herrick traces rhetoric back to an orator named Empedocles in the fifth century BC on the island of Sicily. In addition to being an orator, he was also known as a poet, magician, and physician who possessed a legendary speaking ability. According to Herrick, it systematically originated as a discipline in the fifth century in Syracuse, Sicily, by another orator named Corax. His style was adopted and eventually spread to other Greek city-states by others. The Sophists would soon construct courses in rhetoric. See Herrick, *History and Theory*, 34. In contrast to Herrick, David Sansone traces it back to Aristotle where he says, "it was invented by Sicilian Greeks in the fifth century BC and it flourished after it was brought to Athens." This view is inconclusive when Sansone highlights Aristotle as referring to rhetoric in his lost works, implying that it was already in use before him. See Sansone, *Greek Drama*, 5; furthermore, Sansone highlights how Aristotle spoke of a Sophist named Empedocles as the one who invented rhetoric. See Sansone, *Greek Drama*, 5–6. It eventually made it into schools, becoming part of elementary, secondary, and tertiary education throughout the Mediterranean world. See Witherington, "Education," 191. In the first century AD, rhetoric was widely and commonly used in the education system and letter writing. See Aune, *New Testament*, 70–71; Porter and Olbricht say that most rhetorical studies of the NT have been identified as rhetorical units with variable lengths but consisting of discourse, an identifiable beginning, middle, and ending. See Porter and Olbricht, "Rhetoric and the New Testament," 91.

149. Witherington, "Education," 189–90.
150. Neyrey, *Encomium for Jesus*, 1–2; Dennert, "Encomium for Jesus," 156–57.
151. Dennert, "Encomium for Jesus," 156–57.

they read the OT.[152] Luke's style was influenced by an Antiochene theology. This was a designation associated with the church at Antioch. It emphasized the literal and historical sense of the text, along with the literal and complete humanity of Christ. Great care was taken to not ignore the divine and human nature or to allow one to overwhelm the other. In this understanding, Christ was simultaneously and completely divine and human. It is a theology that differed from the later Nestorianism.[153]

Luke's formal dedications of the Gospel and Acts to someone were not prototypical. It was an ancient style accustomed in the Hellenistic world.[154] The preface to the Gospel was written in an excellent classical style. Leon Morris notes that verse 5 through the end of chapter 2 resembles a strong Hebrew flavor where scholars conclude that the material came from an original Hebrew translation.[155] However, there is not much to go on regarding this hypothesis unless it references part of an unknown Q source that was perhaps written in Aramaic.[156]

Since Luke, as well as his counterparts, used the Septuagint (unless they read in Hebrew), Hellenistic Greek would not have been a weak point for any of them. According to Morris, he uses 266 words (other than proper names) that are not found in any other place in the NT. Including his quotes that are from the LXX, his use of vocabulary sometimes contains Hebraisms or Aramaisms and at times is more Semitic in contrast to others.[157]

Along with Andrews and others, Steven Waterhouse also believes the four Gospels are the product of the authors that give the books' names who were the first-hand eyewitness to Christ and his

---

152. Cross and Livingstone, *Oxford Dictionary of the Christian Church*, 1005.

153. Nestorius taught that the incarnate Christ was two separate persons, one human and one divine. See Cross and Livingstone, *Oxford Dictionary of the Christian Church*, 78–79.

154. Ferguson, *Backgrounds of Early Christianity*, 132.

155. Morris, *Luke*, 29.

156. Refer to chapter 4, in the section "Birth Narratives in Luke's Gospel and Their Aim to His Larger Gospel Narrative" for this complete discussion about a supposed Aramaic copy of a portion of Luke.

157. Morris, *Luke*, 29–30.

ministry.¹⁵⁸ And not only were they written by Matthew, Mark, Luke, and John, but they were all written between AD 50 and 60 in contrast to the views of those who call them anonymous.¹⁵⁹ According to Acts 5:42, Luke claimed that the church continued teaching the gospel of Christ without ceasing. When it happened that all the apostles died, the church continued to teach Christ, and a writing called the Didache appeared, which was used to instruct new converts to *the way* based on the teaching of the Twelve.¹⁶⁰

No amount of credible evidence has been produced to credit authorship of Luke-Acts to an anonymous writer or to any person other than Luke called the beloved physician (Col 4:14; Phil 24; 2 Tim 4:11). The anti-Marcionite prologue to the Third Gospel designates Luke as the author, and states that he was a doctor from Antioch who wrote it from Achaia (Greece), and died at the age of eighty-four. The Muratorian Canon designates Luke as the author of the Third Gospel, adding that he was a doctor and companion of Paul.¹⁶¹

> The third book of the Gospel is according to Luke. Luke the physician, when Paul had taken him with him after the ascension of Christ, as one skilled in writing, wrote from a report in his own name, though he did not himself see the Lord in the flesh (Muratorian Canon, Rome, A.D. 170–180).¹⁶²

Irenaeus recorded in AD 170–180, conferring authorship to Luke and stating he was the companion of Paul and with Luke's Gospel preached by him.¹⁶³

A notion to this view is that Paul referred to Luke's Gospel as his gospel (Rom 16:15). In 1 Cor 15:1–4, Paul's gospel was scriptural, and according to the tradition that Christians had already believed and received (1 Cor 11:23).¹⁶⁴ As companion volumes, Luke's presence is felt in the Acts travel narratives when the author begins using the

---

158. Waterhouse, *Jesus and History*, 65.
159. Waterhouse, *Jesus and History*, 65.
160. Schmidt, *How Christianity Changed the World*, 171.
161. Waterhouse, *Jesus and History*, 35.
162. Waterhouse, *Jesus and History*, 35.
163. Irenaeus, "Against Heresies" 3.1.1 (see also 3.11.8–9 and 3.14.1).
164. Waterhouse, *Jesus and History*, 67.

plural pronoun "we," proving to the fact that he was with Paul (Acts 16:10–17; 20:5—21:18, and 27:1—29:16).¹⁶⁵

In these "we" sections, Waterhouse eliminates all of Paul's traveling companions, which include Silas, Timothy, Sopater, Aristarchus, Secundus, Gaius, Tychicus, and Trophimus. His early coworkers Barnabas, John-Mark, and Silas are excluded as well.¹⁶⁶ Through these processes of elimination, Luke is the voice referring to himself, Paul, and others that were with them, on their second missionary itinerary after the Jerusalem council. The internal evidence as quoted by early church fathers claims Acts was written in the first-person by its author, Luke the physician.¹⁶⁷

Πράξεις was not (is not) intended to be a dossier of Paul. Luke was interested in only recording the progress of the gospel.¹⁶⁸ The Gospel of Πράξεις essentially extends the Gospel from Luke to Acts, making it a continuous story, not a separate book or a different one. It is the same story that Luke started in the dedication of volume 1 to Theophilus. Paul sometimes used the term εὐαγγέλιον in a possessive sense. He sometimes said κατὰ εὐαγγέλιον in Rom 2:16, 16:25, and 2 Tim 2:8. He then followed it up with "to the Jew first, and also to the Greek," referencing the point that it first came to the Jews as a nation. After the Jews as a nation rejected it, the gospel then went to the gentiles. Τὸ κατὰ Λουκᾶν εὐαγγέλιον or κατὰ Λουκᾶν is the Gospel used by Paul.¹⁶⁹

Many tête-à-têtes took place around and outside the text of Scripture that it would be nearly impossible for textual critics to reconstruct. It is precisely where Luke found himself. He conducted private interviews with those who knew Jesus personally to gather data for writing the Gospel and the first half of Acts. The biblical writers only disclosed the data they intended their readers to know to not overwhelm. They wrote to capture the attention of readers and to keep

---

165. Waterhouse, *Jesus and History*, 36.
166. Waterhouse, *Jesus and History*, 36.
167. Waterhouse, *Jesus and History*, 43.
168. Garland, *Luke*, 32.
169. Jerome, "Lives of Illustrious Men," 363–64.

their attention on what was needful. The ancient practice of rhetoric is on full display in Luke's Hellenistic writing.

According to Aune, historians were trained in rhetoric, not historiography. Aune believes that Luke was an amateur historian well-trained in Greek rhetoric.[170] One criticism of this point is placed on the assumption that Luke was also not trained in historiography. In contrast to Aune's perspective, there is not any evidence to accuse Luke of being an amateur. A writer was either supported regularly or paid a lump sum by a sponsor. If a work was constructed through independent means the writer would gain financial support within a community or from a wealthy patron who would join as a backer of the project. Luke's patron of course was Theophilus (Luke 1:3; Acts 1:1).[171]

Both Luke and Acts contain rhetorical devices such as travel narratives and speech acts, as will be discussed in the next chapter. An additional rhetorical device is Luke's medical language. By use of his rhetorical skills, he adapts a specific kind of history as a unique literary technique for apprising the origins and development of Christianity.[172] In volume 2, Luke's "we" sections are full of medical terminology to also lend credence to his authorship and credence as a physician.[173]

In the Gospel, he particularized terms in contrast to Matthew and Mark. When they only spoke of a fever, Luke particularized it as a high fever (see Luke 4:38; cf. Matt 8:14; Mark 1:30). Similarly, when others spoke of a person having leprosy, Luke identified the condition as being full of leprosy, diagnosing it as an advanced case (5:12). Whereas Mark only tells the story regarding the woman with the hemorrhage, Luke gets into specifics saying that she was the subject of much bleeding (see Mark 5:26; cf. Luke 8:43).[174]

---

170. Aune, *New Testament*, 77.

171. There is lots of scholarly consensus that Theophilus played a role in financing Luke's scrolls because both are the longest in the NT. See Hays and Duvall, *Baker Illustrated Bible Handbook*, 604.

172. Aune says Luke uses an ancient practice of general history as his unique literary vehicle for telling the story of the church. In contrast to this view, the story of the church is a unique yet specific history within a general historical era. Aune, *New Testament*, 77.

173. Julicher, *Introduction to the New Testament*, 447.

174. Morris, *Luke*, 20.

Finally, when Jesus prayed in the garden of Gethsemane, Matthew simply tells what Jesus said, that his soul was overwhelmed with sorrow to the point of death (Matt 26:38). Mark, on the other hand, says Jesus was deeply distressed and troubled (Mark 14:33). Luke identifies the dilemma as anguish and that his sweat looked like drops of blood falling to the ground (Luke 22:44). Out of the three accounts, only Luke identifies the agony, the bloody sweat, and the appearance of an angel that helped him beyond a medical condition.[175]

The discussion at hand was not intended to be an exhaustive discourse about Luke's professional or medical language throughout Luke-Acts. It is significant, however, to the discussion of authorship. Many of the words throughout Luke-Acts are in line with professional terminology from the ancient medical world, and they disclose the fact that Luke the physician had his hand involved in the authorship of both volumes. In his letter to the Colossians, Paul expressed him in the phrase, "Our dear friend Luke, the doctor" (Col 4:14 NIV). As Luke was a trained physician, it leads to the fact that Luke was more specific in naming specific physical ailments dealt with by Christ and the church, more so than other writers who were not of his profession.

In addition, Luke was able to take his professional knowledge and write through theological and historical discourse in basic terms about what Christ and the church were doing through the supernatural activity of the Holy Spirit. Cadbury highlighted that W. K. Hobart listed more than four hundred terms only found in Luke-Acts that are absent in all other books in the NT. These terms are only used in Luke's writings, and they parallel the writings of Hippocrates, Aretaeus, Dioscorides, and Galen, whom he regarded as technical in terms of medicine.[176]

At the time the Gospel and Acts were written, the present nomenclature was a latter designation. According to Cadbury, a book (or books) that survived without an author's name or designated title took

---

175. Unger, *New Unger's Bible Dictionary*, 383.

176. Hobart, *Medical Language of St. Luke*, xxxii–xxxiii; Cadbury, "Lexical Notes," 190–209.

on a later or a newly adopted name.[177] In association with the internal content, it is not difficult to see that the Third Gospel was part of the gospel genre and Acts was a fleeting history of the church at a specific time. The Gospel preceded John's and was integrated into the fourfold Gospel collection, whereas Acts preceded the Epistles. Based on all the evidence presented up to this point, Luke the physician and companion of the apostle Paul wrote the two volumes Luke-Acts.[178]

The author who named the text or his title given to the work(s) was likely lost because it was either not in the text, and possibly written on a separate tag, or on the back of the roll. In such cases, the name and/or title were guessed for them. In order to emphasize the historical unity of the two volumes addressed to Theophilus, the convention Luke-Acts is justifiable in the way OT books were viewed that also belonged together.[179] For example, 1 and 2 Samuel is 1 Kingdoms, and 1 and 2 Kings is 2 Kingdoms, and 1 and 2 Chronicles was perhaps a continuation of the same story for the Second Temple period. Cadbury says if this same nomenclature was applied to Luke-Acts, they could be *Ad Theophilum* 1 and *Ad Theophilum* 2, respectively.[180]

Cadbury highlight four factors that aid in determining authorship. These are based on accessible materials, conventional media of thought and expression, the author's individuality, and his conscious purpose.[181] The accessibility of materials is seen in the way the author came by his material. It is based on whether he was a direct eyewitness to events being reported or if he got the information from someone else. If the material is limited to the testimony of others, his indirect testimony is based on his ability to remember

---

177. Cadbury, *Making of Luke-Acts*, 10–11.

178. Cadbury, *Making of Luke-Acts*, 348; Patzia, *Making of the New Testament*, 90–91. The Western text-type (Codex Bezae) preserves the order of the two apostles (Matthew and John), followed by the two apostolic companions (Luke and Mark). According to Parsons, here is where Luke and Acts could easily have been placed together, but the Western text (Codex *Claromontanus*) places Mark between them. In *Claromontanus*, Luke is placed last among the Gospels, and Acts is placed after the Pauline Epistles. On the other hand, Bodmer P[74] (which includes the four Gospels and Acts) places Acts with the General Epistles. See Parsons, *Reading Acts*, 21.

179. Cadbury, *Making of Luke-Acts*, 10–11.

180. Cadbury, *Making of Luke-Acts*, 13.

181. Cadbury, *Making of Luke-Acts*, 15.

those events reported to him. If the events are based on his direct observation, his reporting of them is also subject to his own ability to remember them as they happened.

The conventional media of thought and expression is based upon the language used in his present historic setting. Three primary languages in the first century were Aramaic, Latin, and Greek, as far as it being expressed by Pontius Pilate (see John 19:20). It is less likely that everyone was fluent in Aramaic and Latin, and highly likely that everyone spoke and wrote publicly in Greek. Being that Greek was the universal language in the Roman Empire, it was incumbent upon the biblical writers to write their messages in this language recognizable to the majority.

Third is the author's individuality. According to Cadbury, the author's interests, tastes, prejudices, and mannerisms of speech may crop up simply because he is human. To this point, Cadbury believes that no writer can completely obliterate himself. Finally, his conscious purpose, according to Cadbury, cannot be entirely omitted from the calculation. To any writer, the possibility to paint a compelling story that suits his own agenda always exists.

Cadbury identifies these factors as necessary in the process of seeing how Luke-Acts was written. Luke's writings were given inspiration by the Holy Spirit, but Luke was also human. In the process, he was not a robot run by a program, but led and influenced. The Holy Spirit permitted Luke's genuine humanness in the process of his work. Luke, however, was not writing from a pagan perspective, but from the perspective of a man whose life was changed by Christ. Also, in the process, he was guided or carried along as a piece of dust is guided by the wind. People of faith mostly accept the simple example of biblical inspiration.

For some scholars, inspiration is not cut and dry, or a rightly settled issue. Additional questions at the forefront have to do with motive and purpose. Cadbury asks if Luke's emphasis is a result of the proportion of his sources or his own treatment of the information. And if the author chose to make omissions to his material because he does not know, because he does not care, or if it was based on his deliberate suppression of information, are fair questions.[182]

The entire chapter specifically covered backgrounds. The research on this subject further examined the *Coherent Chiastic Oeuvre in the Unity of Luke-Acts: Two Volumes Conjoined as a Single Book*. A historical background analysis was done of the era that contributed to the literary works of Luke the physician and companion of Paul, and how those external elements within the first-century Roman Empire contributed to his writing of the two-volume work. The analysis, as it was worked into this chapter, was intended to further develop the authenticity, authorship, and trust in Luke's works that have been handed down through the ages.

In the next chapter, the discussion of Luke's literary rhetoric will continue by unfolding small grouped literary structures of material as themes within travel narratives. The Gospel therefore becomes Luke's bridge from the OT prophet Malachi into the NT church. Even as the prophet foretold a literal visit of YHWH to the temple (Mal 3:1), Ananias foretold Paul's visit to Rome (Acts 9:15–16). The Gospel develops and builds upon this narrative as Luke moves Jesus's ministry forward from Galilee to the Temple Mount.

At the beginning of Acts, that continuing narrative is formed around the beginning and development of the church with the apostles, and the deacons, Stephen (Acts 6–7) and Philip (Acts 8), as it continues branching outwardly in Samaria and Judea (see Acts 1:8). While the latter part of Acts is not a dossier of Paul, he enters the scene and develops an understanding of the Lord's plan for the church when he cleverly made his appeal to Caesar to hear his case in Rome (see Acts 22:14; 25:11). These themes within the travel narratives are Luke's literary design and structure for taking Jesus and the good news of Christ from Galilee to Rome.

---

182. Cadbury, *Making of Luke-Acts*, 13–17.

Chapter 6: Exploration of the Themes of the Lukan Travel Narratives from Galilee to Rome

A HISTORICAL BACKGROUND INSIDE, around, and outside the text of Luke-Acts was explored in the previous chapter to examine how both volumes were written in conjunction with writing in the first century. A background study in the literary and cultural context of Luke the physician was examined for the first three centuries of Christianity to understand the bearing of Hellenistic historiography on the shaping of Luke and the NT. The current chapter continues the thesis that argues for the momentousness of reading both volumes as a single story to fully understand the author's meaning of Luke-Acts as it was understood by his first-century audience.[1] Based on all the evidence presented up to this point, Luke intended Luke-Acts as a single unity and not as two separate yet independent books as they exist today.

Again, all prior arguments directed at dissolving their unity will do so by unfastening the four bolts (genre, narrative, theology, and reception history) that hold them together.[2] As long as these

---

1. Garland, *Luke*, 28.

2. Spencer's hermeneutical hinge is important for interpreting Luke in his original context. The removal of the hyphen between Luke and Acts fixed by Cadbury in the 1920s aids in disunifying and severing the two volumes that has been common among readers and some scholars. Spencer demonstrates their unity remains in place if the four bolts remain in place that hinge them together, hermeneutically. See Spencer, "Unity of Luke-Acts," 341; Green, *Luke as Narrative Theologian*, 3.

remain firmly in place, the unity of the volumes fastens it as a single, continuous hinge that remains unbroken from its single story.³ Any understanding of Luke-Acts should be read today as it was read and understood by the author's original audience and treated to avoid postulating modern inferences and judgments into the text that would be far from original.

The narrative features in this bolted unity stitch the two volumes together (chapter 8 will examine how the ascension narratives in Luke and Acts become the nucleus that contains a primary but main chiasm that stitches together both volumes as one book). Spencer refers to Simeon's prophecy in Luke 2:25–35 to demonstrate how it was used to extend salvation to the gentiles through Jesus the Messiah.⁴ However, the fulfillment of Simeon's prophecy does not come to fruition until Paul enters the scene in Acts (cf. Rom 11:13; Gal 2:7–8).⁵ Prior to the last two verses at the end of volume 2, Luke connects it to Simeon's prophecy regarding the work Jesus completed in volume 1. The Acts 28:28 verse essentially forms an *inclusio* with Simeon's prophecy.⁶

Johnson postulates that any discussion of the development of Luke's themes must take into account his two-volume work so as not to view them independently of each other.⁷ In as much as Acts continues the story of the gospel, it also provides Luke's authoritative commentary on the first volume.⁸ The current chapter, therefore, moves into an exploration of the themes and travel narratives of Christ, and how Luke wrote his Gospel by plotting Jesus's divine

---

3. Spencer, "Unity of Luke-Acts," 347; Green, *Luke*, 28.

4. Spencer, "Unity of Luke-Acts," 341–66.

5. At the time of Paul's conversion in Damascus to *the way*, he was given his purpose through Ananias, and his mission was mainly to the gentiles (see Acts 9; cf. Gal 2:7–8). According to Acts 11:25–26, Barnabas recruited Paul and brought him to Antioch to help him.

6. Spencer, "Unity of Luke-Acts," 353; Garland, *Luke*, 30. "For mine eyes have seen thy salvation, which thou hast prepared before the face of all people; a light to lighten the gentiles, and the glory of thy people Israel" (Luke 2:30–32 KJV); cf. Acts 28:28, "Be it known therefore unto you, that the salvation of God is sent unto the Gentiles, and that they will hear it" (KJV).

7. Johnson, *Gospel of Luke*, 1; Garland, *Luke*, 28.

8. Johnson, *Gospel of Luke*, 28.

circuit from Galilee to Jerusalem whereas the circuit continues in Acts from Jerusalem to Rome.

Themes are identified in both volumes as divulging major points of a story, and then repeating and fulfilling them. It implies that themes are found in major forms with the mission of Jesus in the Gospel and are reached in minor forms in Acts. They are larger versions in the Gospel and smaller versions that are repeated in Acts. Essentially, the Gospel of Luke appears moving toward what the gospel is (the starting of the gospel), whereas Acts is moving toward the spread of it.

In as much as this chapter continues to examine Luke's rhetorical thought in the form of what modern writers call themes, travel narratives are also motifs given to highlight major points in the story that the author deems only important to what he desires his readers to know.[9] In the collection of discourses in the Gospel, the author writes in a way that intends to highlight Jesus's goal in his earthly ministry as a continual progression toward the temple.[10] In the first century, Jerusalem was a major epicenter of religious and divine activity in the world, as one of Luke's clearest passages demonstrating this progression is the highlighted salient point of Luke 9:51, "When the days drew near for him to be taken up, he set his face to go to Jerusalem" (ESV).[11]

The themes within the travel narratives are based on the author's coherent structure and design and are essentially rhetorical devices as commonly used in ancient writing. Luke's desire to take Jesus and the gospel from Galilee to the outermost reaches of the earth (Acts 1:8), considering God's salvation history, contributed to his purpose

---

9. As is the case with any serious writer, Luke presumes to write down what he wants his readers to know.

10. See Fay, "Narrative Function of the Temple," 255–70.

11. Jesus did not reveal his purpose in going to Jerusalem from the onset. As his disciples continued with him, the revelation of his crucifixion became much clearer (see Luke 24:44, 46–47; cf. Mark 9:31–32; Matt 27:63; John 2:19). Jesus's face (πρόσωπον) being set like flint to go to Jerusalem to complete his mission implied that nothing could stand in his way nor stop him. He had already determined to complete his mission regardless of the reality of his suffering.

for writing an orderly account of the traditions held among the early Christian community (see Luke 1:1, 3).[12]

Some additional ideas present themselves that Luke also sought to accomplish.[13] These are seen as literary connection points between both volumes and within the travel narratives between Galilee and Rome. Whereas Jerusalem is the centerpiece, from it, Luke's readers reminisce back into the past while meditating on what Jesus started. And from there, or Galilee, readers cogitate forward into the future about the salvific work Jesus accomplished at Jerusalem. Luke wanted to demonstrate how Jesus was always progressing forward to Jerusalem during his earthly messianic ministry and forward from Jerusalem to Rome as the gospel continued to extend by the church.

The epicenter is what this book calls the melting pot of Judaism where God's program transitioned from Levitical priestly temple service to Christ service.[14] The focal point in God's redemption plan passed from the temporal antitypes in Moses to their greater, completed fulfillment in Christ. The apostles were thereby made extensions of Christ's earthly ministry in their announcement of the εὐαγγέλιον first to the Jews and then to the gentiles.

After much persecution, and the Jews' rejection of the gospel, Saul of Tarsus was called and compelled to ministry to the gentiles (Gal 2:7; also Acts chapters 13–28). Several events transpire when Jesus arrives at the epicenter. He first cleanses the temple. He is then arrested and placed on trial before Jewish authorities, Herod, and

---

12. Luke extended God's salvation history from the OT, from his Gospel, and then into Acts. The gospel first came to the Jews with Jesus as Israel's promised Messiah. Upon their rejection of him as a nation, the message was taken to the gentiles. Still in Luke's purview, Acts 1:8 (cf. Luke 24:47) becomes the contour to which Acts is written. Acts take the Third Gospel from Jerusalem into the gentile world. Rome, the capital of the empire, was in Luke's purview and, after Paul landed there, Luke stopped writing. Even after Paul's ministry was over the gospel continued to spread to the outermost reaches by later generations of Christians. See O'Day and Petersen, *Theological Bible Commentary*, 326–29; Schnabel, *Acts*, 1062.

13. See chapter 3 in the section "What Was Luke Intending" for a full discourse on his intentions and purpose of writing Luke-Acts.

14. An epicenter is a focal or central point of something. See Guralnik, *Webster's New World College Dictionary*, 456. As it is used in the context of this book, and in the case of God's activity among the Jews, it is Jerusalem. The epicenter is where Solomon built the First Temple.

Pontius Pilate. He is then crucified and raised, and he ascends into heaven. The first members of the church receive the Holy Spirit on the day of Pentecost, and they begin the Christian witness to the unbelieving Jews and then seek to convert the gentiles to *the way*.[15]

Another purpose Luke was seeking to accomplish was his desire to fill a void among new gentile converts to Christianity. He wrote Acts as a continuation of the gospel narrative and to document the practical work of the Holy Spirit in and among Christians as it continued to extend beyond Jerusalem.[16] Acts begins with the ascension of Christ from the same account in the former treatise.[17] Luke explains that he wrote about all Jesus began to do and teach until the day he was taken up to heaven. In Acts 1:1, the previous scroll is said to reveal all that Jesus began to do and teach before his ascension. Acts makes known the works of Christ through the church as the Holy Spirit leads them.[18]

Luke's two volumes provide a complete account of the beginnings of the life and works of Christ and Christianity. In his birth narrative, Luke takes Jesus's genealogy back to Adam, who is called the son of God and the origin of humanity.[19] For Paul, Christ is this

---

15. Another rhetorical device used by Luke in Acts involves the Christian witness by Philip the Evangelist in Samaria where his witness of Christ is backed up by a miraculous event. Then Judea, where Saul of Tarsus enters the scene as the greatest persecutor of the church. The gospel message continues branching outwardly to Judea and continues toward Rome.

16. Acts continues the narrative of the gospel and highlights the outpouring of the Holy Spirit at Jerusalem, the works of the apostles and deacons, the subsequent development of the early church, and the spread of the gospel of Christ from Jerusalem to Rome. Even as the gentile world had oral discourses of the gospel, the Holy Spirit moved Luke to write a complete narrative while the apostles were still alive to preserve the authoritative witness (Luke 1:3–4).

17. Whereas Acts is the present scroll, Luke's Gospel is his former scroll. Some translations use a treatise or book to identify a previous scroll written containing the gospel.

18. Verse 1:8, in Acts, provides Luke's theological and geographical map of the entire volume. In Jerusalem (chapters 1–7), in Samaria and Judea (chapters 8–12), and unto the outermost reaches of the earth (chapters 13–28).

19. Luke says that Adam was the son of God (see Luke 3:38). The Gospel of Matthew is predominantly a Jewish Gospel. When Luke's birth narrative of Jesus is compared to that of Matthew's, unlike Luke, Matthew begins Jesus's genealogy with Abraham as the distinct originator of the Jewish race.

new, howbeit, last Adam (e.g., 1 Cor 15:45), and there is no failure in him. Whereas the first Adam is the source of humanity, Christ is the source of a new life beyond the natural state of creation and the Savior for all descendants of Adam.

In the first scroll, Luke explains those instructions Jesus gave to his apostles through the Holy Spirit following his resurrection (Luke 24:15–49; cf. Acts 1:1–2). The role of the Holy Spirit is highlighted and distinctly emphasized as the promise of the Father promised by Jesus (John 14:16–18; Luke 24:49; Acts 1:4). Luke shows that the church or *ecclesia* continued to grow and expand despite its rejection and persecution by unbelievers. The *ecclesia*, for Luke, is God's living organism empowered by and through the Spirit. Therefore, the Holy Spirit is never absent in the text. Those faithful to Christ proclaimed the gospel and continued the ministry from Jerusalem.

Luke's Big Idea: Theme of Salvation History

John Sailhamer expresses the importance of finding an author's big idea as it is key to discovering the author's intent.[20] Even as the Pentateuch had its place within the context of the author's big idea, so does Luke-Acts in the context of its author. The meaning of the whole aids in seeing and understanding the importance and meaning of each of the parts.[21] The pivotal notion in determining the big idea in any biblical text is conveyed by what is there in the text or exegesis.[22]

The sum of all the parts composes the whole. A group of disjointed unrelated or related discourses lacks aim and focus and presents a breakdown in communication of the main idea. As in the case of any ancient writer who conveys their message in a full discourse, so is Luke. Luke's big idea in the purpose of Luke-Acts contains a primary theme grounded in the salvation history of God that extended to mankind through Jesus Christ. For Luke, the events he reported

---

20. Sailhamer, *Meaning of the Pentateuch*, 20.
21. Sailhamer, *Meaning of the Pentateuch*, 20.
22. Sailhamer, *Meaning of the Pentateuch*, 29.

did not just happen through mere coincidence. They were divinely ordered and directed through the Holy Spirit.[23]

Luke presents John's long birth narrative as reminiscent of the OT prophet Samuel.[24] His mother, Elisabeth, was suffering a similar anguish as Samuel's mother, Hannah. Both were unable to conceive a child (1 Sam 1:2; cf. Luke 1:7) and were disparaged before God at the tabernacle and temple (1 Sam 1:10-11; cf. Luke 1:13). Luke's devotion to and focus on John the Baptist was intended to demonstrate a transition from that OT era of the prophets to a new era of fulfillment in Jesus. Samuel was the first of the prophets after Moses. In like manner, John was the last of the prophets before Jesus (Luke 16:16). Luke was attempting to solidify Jesus as the new Moses but also one who was greater than him. Luke used John to demonstrate the era of OT prophetic ministry ended with him and transitioned to Jesus.

Similar characteristics exist among Samuel, John, and Jesus. The first two contained similarities related to a Nazarite vow (see 1 Sam 1:11; Luke 1:15). For Jesus, Simeon proclaimed that he would be a light to the gentiles (see Luke 2:32; cf. Isa 42:6). Brakke affirms that this context is the style of speeches in Greek reminiscent of the LXX.[25] As such, they allude to and draw their language from numerous biblical passages such as the praises from Mary (Luke 1:46-55), Zechariah (Luke 1:68-79), and Simeon (Luke 2:29-32), and sound like a character from the OT that indeed belongs to the time of the prophets. In the final analysis, they are transitional because of mixing OT with the new Gospel of Luke.[26]

Again, Simeon said that Jesus was the fulfillment of Isaiah's prophecy, a (the) light to the gentiles (see Luke 2:32; cf. Isa 42:6). In volume 2, Luke deals holistically with the gentile church from the concept developed by Jesus as he transmitted the extension of

---

23. Brakke, *Understanding the New Testament*, 101.

24. Freed believes the OT narratives of the births of Isaac, Samuel, and Samson served as Luke's basis for the births of both John and Jesus. In addition, the narrative of Elkanah, Hannah, and Samuel was one model used by Luke for his construction of the birth narratives of John and Jesus. See Freed, *Stories of Jesus' Birth*, 87.

25. Brakke, *Understanding the New Testament*, 101.

26. Brakke, *Understanding the New Testament*, 101.

his mission to them.[27] Unlike Matthew, who focused on the Jewish ancestry of Jesus beginning with Abraham (Matt 1:2–18), Luke-Acts brings together the story of Israel and the story of all children of Adam. The salvation intrinsic in Christ is not only for the Jew but for the world. For Luke, this had been based on God's providential plan and will in accordance with the narratives that unfold in volume 1 extending through volume 2.[28]

For Luke, the transition in the Gospel narrative from John the Baptist becomes a new era from the old tradition under Moses into the new reality in Christ. In this sense, Jesus stands between the period of Israel and the period of the church as a hinge to both entities. Luke narrates the third period as an era of the church in volume 2 or Acts. In accordance with his big idea, God has done something new through Jesus (gospel), and the church (Acts).[29] It is as Paul would later call it a mystery that was hidden from all ages and has been revealed by Christ to his saints (Eph 5:2; Col 1:26–29).

Jerusalem and Rome in Luke's Thematic Design of the Gospel and Acts

The gospel of Christ first came to the Jews (see Matt 10:5–6). Paul often uses this refrain in his epistles during his discussions of the gospel of Christ by emphasizing it as a gospel "to the Jew first, and also to the Greek."[30] It came to Jerusalem, the capital of Judaism, where many Jews rejected it, resulting in an opportunity opening to the gentiles who Paul said would hear it (see Acts 28:28). Rome was the city of the gentile world and Jerusalem was the center of Judaism

---

27. Refer to Luke 2:31–32; 4:23–27; 7:1–10; 8:26–39; 9:52–56; 10:33–37; 17:11–19; 24:46–47. See O'Day and Petersen, *Theological Bible Commentary*, 327.

28. Refer to Luke 7:30; 22:22, 42; Acts 2:23; 4:38; 5:38; 13:36. See O'Day and Petersen, *Theological Bible Commentary*, 327.

29. O'Day and Petersen, *Theological Bible Commentary*, 327.

30. The rejection of the gospel of Christ by the Jews as a nation allowed the opportunity for the gentiles to be made partakers of the kingdom alongside the Jewish remnant that received Christ (cf. Acts 13:46; 28:28). Paul emphasizes this in at least two of his epistles with the phrase "to the Jew first, and also to the Greek." See Rom 1:16; 2:9–10; 1 Cor 9:20.

and of the Jewish world. The church's center of activity after Pentecost began moving away from Jerusalem (its focal or central point) beginning with Paul and Barnabas, and Antioch (in Syria) thereby became the new epicenter of Christianity.[31]

The narrative of the Gospel of Luke goes toward Jerusalem and the narrative of Acts goes away from Jerusalem toward Rome. The Gospel of Luke describes the historical development of the gospel that started in Galilee and concluded in Jerusalem. Luke continued this narrative in his second volume by describing the historical development of the gospel in Jerusalem and ending in Rome. In Acts, Luke connects David as a prophet who spoke of Christ.

In the Old and NT, Jerusalem was connected to David's capture of it and was the site of the temple as a permanent architectural component of God's activity on earth. Jerusalem itself had worldwide significance, largely because of the temple where its primary religion centered around Judaism. A vast majority of all adherents to this religion lived in the diaspora and had long since adopted the language and culture of their various places of residence outside Palestine. When Hellenism affected Jerusalem, the Greek language was as much at home among Jews as Aramaic.[32]

Rome had conquered the land of the Jews, including many gentile lands, by the first century, and it was the seat of Caesar. Jerusalem and Rome became the two focal points where the religion invented by Christ clashed with the imperial religion of Rome. Jerusalem was God's holy city and Rome was the capital of the imperial cult, the capital of paganism where polytheism was promoted.[33] The gospel taught that Jesus alone was and is divine, and it had to be proclaimed at Rome in direct conflict with the throne of imperial theology.

---

31. Garland, *Luke* 38.

32. Koester, *History and Literature*, 97.

33. See Pss 132:13–14; 137:5–6; 2 Chr 6:6; Isa 4:3–4; Joel 3:17; Zech 8:3; see also Ferrero and Tridimas, "Divine Competition," 143–66.

Subversive Movement and Progression Toward Jerusalem

Jerusalem was part of God's plan when David captured it from the Jebusites (see 2 Sam 5:7). When David became king over all twelve tribes, he moved the headquarters from Hebron and made Jerusalem (see 2 Sam 5:4–10) the capital or center of God's activity in the world.[34] Jerusalem became the headquarters of Judaism. It remained the center of the Jews' religion (referenced this way by Paul in Gal 1:14) during the time of Jesus and progressed this way throughout the first century, perhaps until the temple was destroyed in AD 70 by the Romans. The Sadducees disappeared as a religious party, and so did the Pharisees, eventually giving rise to the new movement, rabbinic Judaism.[35]

God was emphasizing something new from at least two aspects. In keeping with Mal 3:1, the prophet told the Jews that the Lord whom they were seeking would suddenly come to that temple. Jesus's first recorded visit to Jerusalem was denoted in Joseph and Mary's keeping of the law of Moses (Luke 2:22–24; cf. Lev 12; Exod 13:11–16). A second occurrence was based on the divine choosing of it as the place where Christ would proclaim his final message prior to his crucifixion.

Each of the four canonical Gospel writers record a different number of times Jesus was physically in Jerusalem. The mentions are based on each writer's individual purpose and intention for telling their version of the story. For example, Matthew and Mark list only one occurrence of Jesus being in Jerusalem. It only occurred during his triumphal entry (Matt 21:1–11; Mark 11:1–11). Both Luke and John list four occurrences. For Luke, these are his presentation (2:22), his observance of the Feast of Tabernacles at the age of twelve (2:41–44), the beginning of his ministry (4:9), and the triumphal entry (19:28–44). John has him visiting for the Passover (2:13—4:3), the

---

34. According to Mic 4, Jerusalem is the place that the law and the word of the Lord will go out from; and the Lord will rule from it. In Christ's millennial reign on earth (Rev 19:11—20:10), he will come to rule from it. The nations will worship in Jerusalem before the Lord, he will settle all disputes, and all judgments and verdicts will be decided and rendered by him. Jerusalem is the only place on earth the Lord has chosen for this destiny.

35. Neusner and Chilton, *In Quest of the Historical Pharisees*, 139, 386.

Feast of the Jews (5:1–47), Tabernacles and Dedication (7:14—10:39), and the triumphant entry (12:12–19).

Jerusalem itself was significant to Judaism as the location where the Israelites would continuously appear before the Lord and observe three feasts a year: the Feasts of Unleavened Bread, Harvest, and Ingathering (see Exod 23:14–19). The Jews were required to make pilgrimages to Jerusalem once a year. Jesus progressed toward Jerusalem knowing that it was the place where he was to be crucified (see Luke 9:51). He determined that this was the purpose for his coming into the world, and he was set on completing his mission.[36]

Subversive Movement and Progression Toward Rome

In Acts, Luke continues the narrative of Christ in the Gospel by outlining its progression away from the Jewish homeland into gentile regions. The progression of the gospel in Acts goes from Jerusalem to Rome. The latter was important in the role of the church because of its sin and idolatry; therefore, Christ wanted the gospel to be taken right to the doorsteps of the city of Rome. The Roman Empire was the material entity that God used to prepare the world for the crucifixion of Christ, and he used this entity to aid the spreading of the gospel message beyond Jerusalem. The Romans built the infrastructure and provided a level of security and made traveling conducive for traveling disciples.

The issuance of the *Pax Romana* (including the *Pax Deorum*) implemented years of peace throughout the empire. Travelers could move around in peace. Merchants who settled in faraway places established trading posts throughout the Mediterranean world. The scattered differing people groups from one end of the empire to the other brought their favored gods and built shrines to them. The acceptance of polytheism widened the range of cults in many places and provided

---

36. New Testament passages demonstrating Jesus knowing his purpose and destiny: Matt 16:21; 12:40; 17:12, 22; 27:63; Mark 8:31; 9:12, 31; 10:33–34, 45; Luke 9:22, 44; 17:25; 18:31–33; 4:7; John 3:14, 16–17; 12:23, 34.

upstarts that also made converts in new lands through marriage, slavery, and sanctioned deities.[37]

The significance of Rome in God's plan equally corresponded with his plan for the gentiles. Rome was the capital city of the empire and the seat of Caesar. He was one of the monarchs on earth to whom Paul was chosen to proclaim the name of Christ before gentiles and their kings. According to Acts 9:15, it was obvious that the gospel of Christ was destined to come to this capital city of the empire, proclaiming that Jesus Christ was the Savior of mankind and that his death on the cross served this purpose. In Gal 4:4, Paul wrote that it was at this specific time in history that God chose the salvation of humanity. After some time in Rome, however, Paul (along with Peter) was martyred.

In the Hebrew Scripture, God told Israel that he was the one and only God. He said he was a jealous God, and commanded them to not have any other gods besides him (see Exod 20:3). Gentiles in the Roman Empire stood up a plurality of gods and goddesses and worshiped them in the place of Israel's God in the OT, in addition to having the city of Rome personified as the main deity. Rome elevated numerous alluring temples in the city.[38]

The public and social life of people centered on them with celebrations, entertainments, banquets, dinner parties, special speakers, concerts, and the like.[39] In addition to the emperor's claims to deity, this was a matter the Lord God would not gloss over nor ignore. The capital gentile city was an emerging hotbed for Paul to take the witness of Christ to the doorsteps of the emperor and declare Christ as the blessed and only Potentate, the King of kings and Lord of lords (cf. Acts 9:15 and 1 Tim 6:15).

Christians did not attack the structure directly because it would simply have meant suicide for the young movement. It was attacked indirectly through code words such as Peter's use of the term "Babylon" for Rome or, if it led to no other alternative, being placed on trial. Disciples indirectly attacked it through their preaching and

---

37. Ferrero and Tridimas, "Divine Competition," 150–51.
38. Westfall, "Roman Religions."
39. Westfall, "Roman Religions."

teaching of counter-cultural messages. They proclaimed Christ's message based on his holiness in contrast to the worldly behavior of sinners. Rather than verbally refuting the practices, they simply proclaimed the words of Christ and preached against sin, that it was contrary to God's nature and that he would return not only to judge it but to condemn all who reject him and his reign.

Conceptualization of the imperial cult also meant that being a friend of Caesar signified an individual was also aligned with Rome. And being aligned with Rome was conceptualized as being a friend of Caesar. It meant adopting the ways and lifestyles of its culture, even the worshiping of Roman gods. Christians were ridiculed by the societal perceived populace as enemies of Rome for their rejection of the conceptualization.[40] The point of view for Christians was expressed by their rejection of the emperor cult leading to punishment.[41] Luke appears to have been concerned with forging a bridge between Jerusalem (the place where the church began) and Rome (the center of the empire).[42]

John's attitude was a communal replacement of the prototypical empire and its evil order by God's kingdom as the gospel extended to the gentiles.[43] For John, the book of Revelation embodied all that was wrong with Rome and the present world.[44] The prophet, writing during the pinnacle of the Roman Empire at the time of Domitian, according to Leonard Thompson, rejected its public institutions by giving them a negative force attached to evil, demonic powers.[45] In contrast to Caesar's view of a divine being, Jesus as described by John in Revelation proclaims him to be the almighty (see Rev 1:8), which confuted all claims of the Roman emperors.[46]

Jesus was offended at the Jews for the lack of consciousness of their idolatry. According to Meyer, the Tyrian shekel was likely the coin

---

40. Lyle et al., "Lexham Figurative Language."
41. White et al., "Christianity," 950.
42. Balz and Schneider, *Exegetical Dictionary of the New Testament*, 216–17.
43. Zeichmann, "Roman Empire."
44. Zeichmann, "Roman Empire."
45. Thompson, *Book of Revelation*, 177.
46. Zeichmann, "Roman Empire."

referenced in the NT in terms of dealing with taxes and Scripture money.⁴⁷ The collectors in Capernaum questioned Peter about Jesus paying the two-drachma temple tax. It was equal to half the sanctuary shekel to cover the tax. The Roman *stater* was equal to four drachmas, which Jesus told Peter would be enough to pay the tax for them both (see Matt 17:24–27). The Roman *stater* bore the εἰκών of Caesar. When Jesus overturned the tables of money exchangers, he was expressing outrage at the temple's desecration by the Jews. Specifically, money bearing the image of a deity in the temple likely portrayed rejection of a form of graven images condemned in the past (see Exod 20:3–4).⁴⁸

Jerusalem was small compared with the empire's vastness. For monetary efficiency, the Romans minted coins in various places for the efficient dissimulation of them from one end of the empire to the other. The Jews also used Roman money. The *fiscus Judaicus* implemented by the Romans following the temple's destruction redirected the annual Jewish half-shekel tax from the Jewish temple to the temple of Jupiter in Rome. It was mulcted to mock and humiliate the Jews with an explicit declaration that Jupiter (Acts 14:12) had defeated YHWH.⁴⁹

In the OT, YHWH sent Moses to טַלֵּמ (*mélet*, deliver) Israel from the bondage of Egypt (see Exod 7:1–5) and challenged their deities (see Exod 12:12).⁵⁰ In the NT, the man Christ Jesus is the prophet like Moses, who came into the world to σώσει (rescue, deliver) people from their sins (Matt 1:18; also cf. Acts 3:22 and Deut 18:15). When the Jews rejected Christ and his message as a nation, he sent Paul to the gentiles who would hear the message. Acts became the continuation of the gospel that would go to the capital of the empire to challenge Caesar with the message of Christ. While not exhaustive, these issues are what led to Jesus's continued progression toward Rome. In

---

47. Meyer, "Coinage in Biblical Times."

48. Meyer, "Coinage in Biblical Times."

49. Meyer, "Coinage in Biblical Times"; Dio, *Roman History* 66.7.2; Josephus, *Jewish War* 7.6.6.

50. By the hand of Moses and Aaron, God sent ten plagues upon Egypt: Exod 7:19–20 (first, blood); 8:1–3 (second, frogs), 16–17 (third, lice), 20–23 (fourth, swarms of flies); 9:1–4 (fifth, disease), 8–11 (sixth, boils), 22–25 (seventh, hail); 10:12–15 (eighth, locusts), 21–23 (ninth, darkness); 11:4–6 (tenth, death).

Acts, Luke was expressing how the church was taking the gospel of Christ to the headquarters of sin and idolatry.

Travel Narratives Through Luke-Acts

The circuit that traces Jesus's movement from Galilee to Jerusalem is known as travel narratives. Luke uses his Gospel to outline this journey from Nazareth to Jerusalem, and in Acts, from Jerusalem to Rome. Luke constructs the circuit used by Jesus from the beginning to the end of his earthly ministry. The travel narrative of Christ resides between Luke 9:51—19:48. The Galilean section of the Gospel (3:1—9:50) is primarily oriented around the establishment of Jesus's messianic ministry adjacent to his forerunner (Isa 57:14; Mal 3:1; Matt 11:10; Mark 1:2; John 1:23-29).[51] Three primary junction points in setting out his structure are Galilee, Jerusalem, and Rome. He constructs this movement from Galilee to Jerusalem in the Gospel, and from Jerusalem to Rome in Acts.

The first introductory episode in the travel narrative to Jerusalem (9:51-53) describes Jesus moving toward his purpose of coming into the world; it makes clear the veritable journey and the disabusing of his colloquy of revelation.[52] The impending journey will make a stop in Jerusalem and head toward Rome. In the process of time, however, the disciples come to understand and learn what it really means to be a disciple and follower of Christ even to the point of suffering rejection and losing their lives (9:57-62). Jesus expresses what it means to be his disciple. The way of a transgressor is hard (Prov 13:15) but not for the disciple. The disciple is to believe in Jesus as the Christ, to follow him wholeheartedly, and to obey his words.[53]

Luke turns back to the subject of Christ's mission in 10:1-6 and reconnects it again with Jesus's journey to Jerusalem.[54] Once the mission is grasped by the disciples, Jesus must strengthen them to continue their faith. The account parallels with Paul and Barnabas

---

51. Green, *Gospel of Luke*, 394.
52. Refer to Luke 12:49-50; 13:31-33; 17:25; 18:31-34.
53. Gill, "Observations on the Lukan Travel Narrative," 199-221.
54. Gill, "Observations on the Lukan Travel Narrative," 199-221.

in the Acts narratives that, after they had proclaimed the gospel in every city, they returned to their previous evangelistic grounds to strengthen the disciples and to encourage them to continue in the faith, saying, "It is through many tribulations that we must enter the kingdom of God" (Acts 14:22 NASB).

In chapters 9 through 19, Jesus travels through Samaria toward Jerusalem.[55] Regarding the separate regions in his travel itinerary, Conzelmann identifies that Samaria and Peraea are missing.[56] Luke also does not take Jesus into Phoenicia and the Decapolis. He stays within Galilee and Judea. For Luke, people came to Jesus from regions where Luke did not physically take him.[57] One exception for the Decapolis is Gadara. He calls this "the region of the Gerasenes across the lake from Galilee" (8:26). He mentions this one episode to highlight Jesus's power and authority over demons, and as a sign that he was the Messiah (see 8:26–39).[58]

In John's Gospel, he includes a chunk of information at this juncture (4:4–52) that Luke either skips over or omits. In 4:4, John emphasized, "But He needed to go through Samaria" (NIV). It was clearly a reverse trip from Judea back to Galilee. Luke, however, does not take Jesus's journey through Samaria. He says Jesus only sent messengers ahead of him to prepare them for his coming. The Samaritans rejected him when they thought he was heading to Jerusalem.[59] As a result, Luke says that he and his disciples then went to another village (see 9:52–56).

All the events from Luke chapter 18 through the first seven chapters of Acts are set in Jerusalem as the *Sitz im Leben* for Luke's volumes 1 and 2. In the remainder of volume 2, the gospel continued to spread

---

55. Conzelmann documents that Jesus's journey from Galilee to Jerusalem recorded by Luke in the Third Gospel extends from 9:51—19:27. See Conzelmann, *Theology of St. Luke*, 60.

56. Conzelmann, *Theology of St. Luke*, 18.

57. Conzelmann, *Theology of St. Luke*, 31.

58. After driving out demons, Jesus told the man, in verse 39, to return home and publish what God has done for him.

59. John 4:3 says that Jesus "left Judea and went back once more to Galilee" (NIV). If the Samaritans supposed he was going up to Jerusalem, they were mistaken because Jerusalem was in the opposite direction.

away from Jerusalem.⁶⁰ Luke surfaces as a direct eyewitness to those events he is reporting.⁶¹ He writes in the third person outside of these sections assuming that he was not a direct eyewitness to the accounts; rather, the events in the life of Jesus are a testimony based on actual eyewitnesses who were likely with him from the beginning to the end of his ministry (Acts 1:21–22).⁶²

Alan Thompson identifies a particular narrative unit in the section of 18:9—19:10, which is important for several reasons. Rather than documenting a copious collection of events in Jesus's life and ministry, it places an emphasis on the kingdom of God.⁶³ It is the concluding section of the long journey (9:51—19:27) before his arrival in Jerusalem. The kingdom section, according to Thompson, includes two parables (regarding a Pharisee and a tax collector), emphasis on children who were brought to Jesus, a rich ruler, the prognostication of Jesus's death and resurrection, a blind beggar who was healed by Jesus, and an interaction with a tax collector named Zacchaeus. The importance of this section between the end of the journey and the crucifixion stresses the importance of entrance into God's kingdom.⁶⁴

Luke does something unique between both volumes. As the day drew near to the time of Jesus's passion, Luke centralizes the setting of all activity in the last seven chapters of the Gospel and the first seven chapters of Acts in the region of Judea, more specifically in Jerusalem. The unique literary feature ties volume 1 and volume 2

---

60. Brakke, *Understanding the New Testament*, 110.

61. For the "we" sections in Acts, see, e.g., Acts 16:10–17; 20:5—21:18; 27:1—28:16. Padilla says the use of αὐτόπται in Luke 1:2, the first-person pronouns in the prologue "of the events that have been fulfilled among us" (Luke 1:1), "just as they were handed down to us" (Luke 1:2), "it seemed to me" (Luke 1:3); in addition to the "we" passages from Acts indict Luke as participating in dissection, examination, and exploration. See Padilla, *Acts of the Apostles*, 73.

62. Both the Gospel and Acts are a collection of speech-acts where Luke recorded what others said and did. Jesus is the predominant speaker in the Gospels, whereas in Acts speech-acts are recorded from Peter (2:1–41), from Stephen (Acts 7:1–53), at Cornelius's home (Acts 10:34–48), at Athens (Acts 17:16–31), and before Agrippa (Acts 26:1–32). Although additional voices are present, the former is what Padilla says are the main theological speeches. See Padilla, *Acts of the Apostles*, 152.

63. Thompson, *Acts of the Risen Lord Jesus*, 41.

64. Thompson, *Acts of the Risen Lord Jesus*, 41.

together as the same continuous story. It, howbeit, is unique to Luke among the Gospel writers. In contrast, Matthew says that Jesus met the eleven apostles outside of Judea in Galilee after his resurrection (see Matt 28:16–17). While Mark does not report a post-resurrection location, John also says Jesus met the eleven in Galilee, at the Sea of Tiberius (see John 21:1).

It is not until chapter 8 of volume 2 that Luke moves the apostles from Jerusalem to Samaria. He intended volume 1 to advance from Galilee to Jerusalem, the center of Judaism (headquarters of the Jewish religious system) without taking Jesus through Samaria. Volume 2 was intended to go from Jerusalem to Rome, the center of the imperial cult (headquarters of the Roman religious system). Below is an outline providing the circuit used by Luke to trace the spread of the gospel based on Luke 9:51—19:48 and Acts 1:8:

Table 3. Regional Travel Circuits in Luke's Volume 1 (9:51—19:48)

Unnamed Region	Luke 9:51	Samaritan Village
Judea	Luke 10:38	Bethany
Samaria and Galilee (passed by)	Luke 17:11	Samaritan Village
Judea (Jordan Valley)	Luke 18:25	Near Herodian Jericho
Judea (Jordan Valley)	Luke 19:1	Herodian Jericho
Judea	Luke 19:29	Bethphage and Bethany
Judea	Luke 24:13	Road to Emmaus
Judea	Luke 18–24	Jerusalem

Table 4. Regional Travel Circuits in Luke's Volume 2 (1:1—12:25)

Judea	Acts 1–7	Jerusalem
Samaria	Acts 8:4, 14	City of Samaria
Unnamed Region	Acts 8:40	Azotus, Caesarea Maritima
Syria	Acts 9	Damascus

Judea	Acts 10	Caesarea Maritima, Joppa
Judea	Acts 10–12	Jerusalem
Syria	Acts 13:1–4	Antioch

Table 5. Regional Travel Circuits in Luke's Volume 2 (13–28)

Region	Passage	Places
Galatia	Acts 13–14	Seleucia, Cyprus, Salamis, Paphos, Perga in Pamphylia, Antioch in Pisidia, Salamis, Iconium, Lystra, Derbe, Lycaonia, Attalia
Judea	Acts 15	Jerusalem
Macedonia	Acts 16:1—17:14	Troas, Samothrace, Neopolis, Philippi, Amphipolis, Apollonia, Thessalonica, Berea
Greece	Acts 17:15—18:17	Athens, Corinth, Cenchreae, Achaia
Syria/Judea	Acts 18:18	Caesarea, Jerusalem, Antioch
Galatia/Phrygia	Acts 18:23–28	Galatia
Turkey (modern)	Acts 19	Ephesus
Macedonia/Greece/Turkey (modern)	Acts 20:1—21:14	Asos, Mitylene, Chios, Samos, Miletus, Ephesus, Achaia, Troas, Ephesus, Cos, Rhodes, Patara, Phoenicia, Cyprus, Tyre, Ptolemais
Judea	Acts 21:15—26:30	Jerusalem, Caesarea
Journey to Italy	Acts 27–28	Sidon, Crete, Cauda, across the Adriatic Sea, Malta, Rome

Theological Parallels and Thematic Connections Between Luke-Acts

Garland believes in the importance of reading Luke-Acts as a single story. It is imperative to do so because Acts contains the story of the gospel, and it provides the author's authoritative commentary on it.[65] Reading both volumes as a single story prevents individual narrative proof-texting as it has been done for ages. When both volumes were pinned on separate scrolls because of their length, they were separated into two separate books.

The separation led to centuries-old ideas of reading and interpreting both volumes independently of each other.[66] The reading of both volumes collectively is necessary for the proper interpretation of Luke's entire message when both volumes take into account their isolationism. Even though Pervo makes a correct assertion that Acts develops, fulfills, and plays upon the themes found in the Gospel, it is inaccurate to assume that they both can stand independently and on their own.[67]

In addition, any discussion of the author's purpose or the development of the themes must take into account the entire two-volume work. Luke's book contains fifty-two chapters and covers roughly ninety-seven years.[68] Luke's work is the longest single piece of literature in the New Testament.[69] It is a single story that spans from the OT priest Zechariah to Paul's arrival in Rome where he waits for Nero to hear his case (see Acts 25:7–12; 28:16). Using the form of a historical monograph, he pens his message in terms of a salvation history of the Jews and of the world.[70]

---

65. Garland, *Luke*, 28.

66. Patzia, *Making of the New Testament*, 90–91.

67. Pervo, *Acts*, 19.

68. Garland, *Luke*, 28. The structure and design of the Bible into chapters and verses is a modern formulation that was not original to Luke or to any of the biblical writers. The present system of chapter divisions was done in the thirteenth century and verses in the sixteenth century. See Biblica, *New Testament*, v.

69. Brakke, *Understanding the New Testament*, 97.

70. The gospel first came to the Jews. After the Jews, it then went to the gentiles, where Paul says the gentiles were grafted into God's plan and kingdom (see Rom 11:11–31). Conzelmann, *Theology of St. Luke*, 26.

In Luke's prologue to the Gospel, he emphasizes "τῶν πεπληροφορημένων ἐν ἡμῖν πραγμάτων" (Luke 1:1b). "The things" the author is discussing implies a completed action regarding "the things" he is indeed reporting to his readers. It is not something that is to come about at a future time, but those things have already been fulfilled. Luke was writing about the past. It is through this work of Christ that Luke builds his story by dividing salvation history into three periods that specify three distinct eras. That is the time of Israel, the time of Jesus, and the time of the church.[71]

The first era extends from the time of Israel in the OT to the time of Luke's narrative of John the Baptist.[72] The time of Israel began with God's calling of Abraham (see Gen 12:1–3). Matthew's writing of a Jewish Gospel did this by starting Jesus's genealogy with Abraham (see Matt 1:1). Luke expressed his own sentiment on this transition in 16:16, stating that the Law of Moses, the Prophets, and the Writings were in effect until the time of John the Baptist. Since John, the gospel is now proclaimed to everyone.

The OT ministry (Law, Prophets, and Writings) looked forward to Jesus (Luke 24:44) and the apostles looked back to Jesus (Luke 24:48) as they spread the message of salvation to the world; these same unique ideas run through both Luke and Acts. The first era was the Law, Prophets, and Writings. The prophets were the voices of YHWH that were enforcing the covenant between God and Israel. The ministry of the prophets spanned from Samuel to John the Baptist, where Luke demonstrated the transition from John to Jesus.[73]

John the Baptist completed the era of the prophets as the second phase transitioned to Jesus with his messianic ministry of redemption and salvation. When John baptized Jesus in the Jordan, Luke's intention was to make it clear that the time of the OT ministry was culminating with the time of Jesus. The time of the prophets had ended when Herod Antipas cast John into prison and killed him (Luke 3:20). From Jesus,

---

71. O'Day and Petersen, *Theological Bible Commentary*, 327; Fitzmyer, *Luke the Theologian* (1989), 175.

72. O'Day and Petersen, *Theological Bible Commentary*, 327.

73. It is not clear why Luke did not capture the words of John the Baptist in his discourse as John did: "ἐκεῖνον δεῖ αὐξάνειν, ἐμὲ δὲ ἐλαττοῦσθαι" (John 3:30 NA[28]).

the era of the church began with the apostles, where the apostles in Acts became an extension of Christ's earthly ministry to proclaim what they saw and heard about Jesus (see Luke 24:46–48).

During Jesus's early ministry in Galilee, his conflict was primarily with the religious leaders (Pharisees) and the teachers of the law (scribes).[74] The Pharisees sought to undermine his ministry as a prophet because he was from Galilee despite his birth in Bethlehem that fulfilled Mic 5:2. Jesus was reared in Nazareth, Galilee (see Luke 4:16). The negative portrayal of Galilee by the Pharisees in the Gospels was likely a result of the following reasons. A long resentment of the region settled in because it was known for having gentiles. One part was of the Jews, and the other was of the gentiles.

The residents of the region were negatively stereotyped for illiteracy due to their neglect of studying their language along with their errors in grammar and their mispronunciation of words. The stigma made Galileans recognizable by their dialect and tone as seen in Peter's identification by the damsel during Jesus's arrest (Mark 14:70).[75] The Pharisees assumed that God did not appoint prophets from out of this region. They so despised Jesus that they indignantly berated Nicodemus for attempting to defend him (John 7:51 GNT).

Sarcastically, they jeered at Nicodemus with the words, "Are you also from Galilee?" In such rage of apparent ignorance, they also exclaimed, "Study the Scriptures and you will learn that no prophet ever comes from Galilee" (see John 7:52–53 GNT). Contrary to this misconception on their part, both Jonah and Nahum were prophets and they were from Galilee. According to 2 Kgs 14:25, Jonah was from Gath Hepher, Galilee, and Nahum was from the small village of Elkosh in Galilee (also refer to Nah 1:1).[76]

In Luke's theological theme of salvation history through Jesus Christ, several themes join both volumes and point to the author's obvious intention that both be read as one book. These themes that flow between Luke-Acts reveal a single author, whereas Acts can be read without realizing a break in the flow of the narrative at the end

74. Strauss, *Jesus Behaving Badly*, 42.
75. Unger, *New Unger's Bible Dictionary*, 452–53.
76. Feinberg, *Minor Prophets*, 133, 188.

of the Gospel. The central theme is God's purpose to bring salvation to all people through the life and mission of Jesus by the message of his followers.[77]

Various theological themes and parallel accounts run together throughout the Third Gospel and Acts making thematic connections and stitching together both volumes.[78] Such demonstrates the literary unity between both volumes and uniquely reveals a single author. The parallel accounts and contextual similarities run within Luke-Acts but were never intended to prove they were written by the same author, but their similarity is evident in being written by the same singular author. Such are also seen as prototypes from the life of Jesus in the Third Gospel and are repeated and/or amplified in Acts with reference to episodes involving the apostles, deacons, and others mentioned by name in Luke's second narrative.[79]

In addition to Luke's literary unity, he reiterates his primary theological ideas of how God's salvation history continues from the ministry of Jesus (Gospel) to the ministry of the apostles (Acts).[80] For example, just as Jesus heals the lame man in the Gospels, so does Peter heal the lame man in Acts (Luke 5:17–24; cf. Acts 3:1–11).[81] The lameness in both cases implies that the man was unable to walk because of physical paralysis. In the Gospel account, the people carried the man to Jesus. In the Acts account, the people carried the man to the beautiful gate. In both cases, the onlookers were amazed at the events that transpired before their eyes.

In the case of Jesus, the miracle was intended to increase faith in the observers as a sign that he was the Messiah who was able to forgive sins. In Acts, the miracle was also intended to increase faith in the onlookers as well as to point them to Jesus who could heal them and forgive their sins. The Acts account opened the door for the apostles to proclaim Jesus was the Messiah and the prophet

---

77. Schnabel, *Acts*, 26.
78. Brakke, *Understanding the New Testament*, 100.
79. Edwards, "Parallels and Patterns," 485–501.
80. Brakke, *Understanding the New Testament*, 100.
81. Refer to Matt 9:1–8; Mark 2:1–12; and John 5:8–9.

spoken of by Moses (Deut 18:15).[82] In John's quotation of Jesus, he said, "the one who accuses you is Moses, in whom you have put your hope" (5:45 NASB). It calls attention to the Israelites who would disobey the words of Moses, "I will punish anyone who refuses to obey him" (Deut 18:19b GNT).

Luke's two-volume work takes the time of Israel's prophets to John the Baptist at the beginning of the Gospel. Luke-Acts extends the time of Jesus to the time of the church, beginning with the apostles. In the Gospel, Luke reported on stories he learned from those who were with Jesus throughout his ministry and who knew him personally. In Acts, he composes stories in mostly in the form of speech-acts because he was not personally present to eyewitness those events. He narrates Peter and the other apostles, who share in the prophetic power of Jesus and the earlier prophets.[83]

Literary

Literalism is a way of maintaining strict adherence to the exact word meanings, interpretation, and translation of a biblical author's message. It, however, has a weakness. If meaning is left up to the interpreter, it is then possible to draw more than one interpretation of the text as it is often done today.[84] On the other hand, literary exactness leaves little to no room for personal biases, assumptions, or allusions; careful exegesis is involved in determining the author's original meaning.

Many of the parallel accounts between Luke-Acts contain similarities to parallelism as they resemble common literary rhetorical devices like the way they are structured in the OT and in ancient writing. They contain contextual similarities, also seen as chunks of similar information used by the author when he is often writing on the same subject as his story progresses. While literary criticism focuses on the final form of the text, it ignores how the text was developed to

---

82. Brakke, *Understanding the New Testament*, 97–102.
83. Brakke, *Understanding the New Testament*, 100.
84. Grenz, Guretzki, and Nordling, *Pocket Dictionary of Theological Terms*, 73.

reach its final or current state.⁸⁵ It also does not care how it came into being what it is but how it exists in its final form.⁸⁶

The collection of grouped narratives throughout Luke-Acts coheres into a unified, complete story. When taking into account, the juxtaposition of the prologues of both volumes is Luke's literary statement, and the final form of the dedication sets the path for the rest of the content for both volumes. His dedication to Theophilus is a powerful inclusion of gentiles in God's plan of salvation through Christ. It insists that a "friend of God" is an all-inclusive meaning and regardless of a person's background or racial ethnicity and that they are equally made participants in God's kingdom.

Regarding all the types of literature in antiquity, the kind that belongs to Luke-Acts is closely associated with Greco-Roman historical biography.⁸⁷ The life of the founder of the Christian community followed by narratives about his successors are all selected in one complete work.⁸⁸ Examples of literary themes containing thematic parallels are seen in the author's preface to Theophilus in Luke 1:1–4 and Acts 1:1–5. In addition, a final conveyance of the Scripture being fulfilled at the end of volumes 1 and 2 (Luke 24:45–47; Acts 28:23–28) is not uncommon in the apparent mindset and writing style of a single author.⁸⁹

Messianic Prophet

When Jesus entered the synagogue at the start of his messianic ministry, he stood up and read from the Isaiah scroll. At the conclusion of Isa 61:1–2a (Jesus only quoted the first part of verse 2 because the day of God's vengeance had not yet arrived), he declared that this Scripture had been fulfilled in their hearing. In doing so, he was proclaiming himself as Isaiah's messianic prophet fulfilling this OT prophecy.

---

85. Powell, *What Is Narrative Criticism?*, 7.

86. Powell, *What Is Narrative Criticism?*, 6–7.

87. See Burridge, *What Are the Gospels?*, 105; Pitts, *History, Biography, and the Genre*, 1–2.

88. Talbert, *Reading Luke*, 3.

89. Powell, *Introducing the New Testament*, 202–3.

The Jewish unbelievers believed Isaiah's prophecy, but they did not want to accept it for Jesus as the Messiah.[90]

In the Acts version of Ps 2:1–3, Peter identified it as a messianic prophecy pertaining to Jesus. In Acts 4:16–27, the Jewish leaders who persecuted the apostles noted an undeniable miracle was done in Jesus's name, to the point they forbade the apostles from speaking or teaching in it. The undeniable work that only God could perform was evidently performed by the power associated with the name Jesus.

In addition, Peter correlated Acts 2:14–40 as the fulfillment of Joel's prophecy.[91] The significance was based on Jesus's promise in Luke 24:49, which he called the promise of the Father. An important point in this verse is a recognition of Jesus's authority. He used the first-person nominative singular pronoun ἐγὼ to identify that he and not someone else was sending the Holy Spirit to indwell his followers. Luke assured his readers that Jesus was directing the events of Pentecost as well as being the fulfiller of the prophecy.

Travel

In the Gospel, Luke proclaims Jesus's missionary journey to the gentiles (10:1–12). He also does so in Acts by proclaiming the apostles' mission to the gentiles (13:1—19:20). Such connections and parallel structure are common in Luke-Acts as themes often repeat themselves. In addition, Jesus's travel itinerary in the Gospel is set from Galilee to Jerusalem (9:51—19:28).[92] And also in Acts, Paul's travel itinerary is set from Jerusalem to Rome, revealing a parallel structure that began in the Third Gospel.

Throughout Jesus's messianic ministry, he was always on the move. Luke's statement the "foxes have dens and birds have nests but the son of man has no place to lay his head" (Luke 9:58; cf. Matt 8:20) specifically supports this idea. It is also evident that the Lord did not intend the apostles to be permanent residents in Jerusalem. The reference has a contextual similarity with the Babel narrative of

90. Brakke, *Understanding the New Testament*, 100.
91. Powell, *Introducing the New Testament*, 202–3.
92. Powell, *Introducing the New Testament*, 202–3.

Gen 11:7. The unified language of all the world was confounded and the Lord scattered all of them throughout the face of the earth (see Gen 11:9b NIV).[93]

Rather than the languages confusing the early believers in Acts, they unified them (Acts 2:44; cf. Luke 29:49; Acts 1:8). And after the Holy Spirit fell upon them in the upper room, the Lord had a mind to move them to take their message to the world outside of Jerusalem, beginning in Acts 8. By this, it is evident that the message of the Gospel was intended to be spread outside the confines of Israel. In 1 Cor 3:10, Paul calls Jesus the chief apostle who laid the foundation of the church (cf. Heb 3:1; 1 Pet 5:4). He physically starts in Galilee and stops at Jerusalem. The apostles under Christ were travelers who built their message and work on Jesus's foundation. They started in Jerusalem, and Luke's canonical written account ends when Paul reaches Rome.

Role of the Holy Spirit

Luke regards the Holy Spirit as indispensably significant between the Gospel and Acts. Jesus described the beginning sign to his messianic ministry by announcing that the Spirit of the Lord was upon him (Luke 4:18a). The significance of the ministry of the church was the sign of their reception of the Holy Spirit. The same parallel regarding the work of the Spirit connects the Gospel and Acts. Luke demonstrates the role of the Holy Spirit in Acts as relevant and necessary for ministry.

In addition to the beginning of the Gospel, the Holy Spirit descends upon Mary and the Messiah is born. And at the beginning of Acts, the Holy Spirit descends on the disciples and the church is born.[94] The parallel structure is not coincidental. Luke remarks on another example in the act of prayer between Jesus in the Gospel and the apostles in Acts. In the Gospel, the Spirit descends on Jesus as he prays (3:21–22), and in Acts, the Spirit aids the apostles as they pray (2:1; 6:6; 12:5–7).[95]

93. Keener, *Acts*, 843.
94. Brakke, *Understanding the New Testament*, 100.
95. Powell, *Introducing the New Testament*, 202–3.

Persecution

Jesus and his followers suffered persecution from Jews and gentiles. Dicken analyzes the Herodian dynasty and forms a composite character of Herod throughout Luke-Acts.[96] This is done by compiling the four Herodian rulers (Herod the Great, Herod Archelaus, Herod Antipas, and Agrippa I) into the term "Herod" as a composite character.[97] The Herodian dynasty was active against God's servants in the Gospel and Acts and lasted nearly a century and a half, from Herod's appointment as governor in Galilee in 47 BC to the death of Agrippa II in AD 100.[98] These individuals imitated the same spirit in their persecution of God's people from Jesus in his infancy to Paul's voyage to Rome. At this time Agrippa II had succeeded Agrippa I.

The Gospel and Acts exemplify symmetry in their parallel accounts of the persecution of God's servants. For instance, Antipas puts John the Baptist in prison and kills him with the sword (Luke 9:9; cf. Mark 6:27–29). Agrippa puts James and Peter in prison and kills James with the sword and proceeds to kill Peter (Acts 12:1–3). In the Gospel, the Jewish religious leaders attack Jesus (Luke 5:29–6:11) and attack the apostles (Acts 4:1–8:3).

In addition, Jesus is seized by an angry mob (Luke 22:54); an angry mob also seizes Paul (Acts 21:30). One of the servants to Caiaphas slaps Jesus in the face (Luke 22:63–64); the same happens to Paul (Acts 23:2). While Jesus is rejected by the Jewish leadership establishment (Luke 23:18), Paul is also rejected by the establishment (Acts 21:36). In the Gospel, Jesus is tried four times and declared innocent three times (Luke 22:66—23:13), In Acts, Paul is tried four times and declared innocent three times (Acts 23:1—26:32).[99]

---

96. Dicken, *Herod as a Composite Character*, 45; Gelb, *Herod the Great*, 9–10.
97. Dicken, *Herod as a Composite Character*, 45.
98. Gelb, *Herod the Great*, 9–10.
99. Powell, *Introducing the New Testament*, 202–3.

Ministry (John the Baptist, Jesus, and the Church)

The ministry of Jesus began with a transition from John the Baptist (see Mal 3:1; cf. Isa 40:3, Mark 1:3; John 1:19–26). According to Luke, Jesus began his ministry in Galilee.[100] Koester suggests that many of the places where Jesus was active are uncertain because some of the places named in the tradition may be cities and towns where his disciples were also successful.[101] At least three of the Hellenistic cities cited by Koester, Caesarea, Sepphoris, and Tiberias, are missing in the tradition, whereas locations such as Caesarea Philippi, Gadara, and the Sea of Galilee are occasionally mentioned.[102]

According to Luke 4:20, the signification of the messianic ministry was Jesus's proclamation to the fulfillment of Isa 61:1–3, which he quoted in the synagogue in Nazareth (cf. Luke 4:18–19). He began his statement by saying Πνεῦμα Κυρίου ἐπ' ἐμέ. According to Luke, when his messianic ministry was rejected in Nazareth, he relocated to Capernaum, Galilee, and taught the people. In Capernaum, he began healing the sick and afflicted and driving out devils. The works affirmed those who believed that Jesus was the Messiah as proclaimed by the prophets.

Brakke and others call a directed speech occurring at the beginning of a movement an inaugural sermon.[103] Two are cited in the Gospel and Acts. For example, when Jesus entered the synagogue in Nazareth, he delivered his first sermon signifying the start of his messianic ministry. Likewise, Peter delivered the first ecclesiastical sermon on the day of Pentecost. Both sermons share important themes that reoccur throughout Luke-Acts.

In the Gospel, Jesus opens his sermon with a passage from the prophet Isaiah about God's time of deliverance and healing to all who were troubled by Satan. In Acts, Peter opens with a passage from the

---

100. The signification of Jesus as the Messiah was his baptism by John in the Jordan. After being forty days in the wilderness, he returned to his hometown in Nazareth, Galilee, in the power of the Spirit. Luke makes it clear that this was the beginning of Jesus's ministry.

101. Koester, *History and Literature*, 80.

102. Koester, *History and Literature*, 80.

103. O'Day and Petersen, *Theological Bible Commentary*, 329, 366.

prophet Joel about God pouring out his Holy Spirit. In the Gospel, Luke highlights that Jesus began his ministry. In Acts, he denotes that the apostles began their ministry in the absence of Jesus on earth. And throughout Luke-Acts, the author places a special emphasis on the Holy Spirit as the one who moves characters and events.[104]

Healing

Luke records at least fourteen instances of healing that took place in the Gospel. Acts, however, is uncertain because of the specificity of many more miracles that took place and were not recorded.[105] John is the only Gospel writer who speaks on this account that Jesus did many other things that were not recorded, and if they were all written down the whole world would not be able to contain all the books that would have been written of them (John 21:25).

According to Acts 2:43, the apostles did many signs and wonders. Through the ministry of Stephen, God worked great wonders and signs among the people (6:8). And while multitudes of believers were added to the Lord the people brought the sick into the streets and laid them on beds and couches so that the shadow of Peter passing by healed them (5:14–16). Such parallel accounts exist between Luke and Acts regarding Jesus's healing of the sick and lame, as does the ministry of the church throughout Acts.

The work of the Holy Spirit in the life of Jesus's disciples resolved to a single, common goal of testifying to and developing Jesus subjectively and objectively in and through his followers (John 15:26). He commissioned them to preach God's kingdom realm with the power to heal the sick to demonstrate God's kingdom had arrived (see Luke 9:2). The gifts and miracles were by the work of the Spirit through the apostles. Luke says in 9:6 of his Gospel that they departed and went through the towns preaching the gospel and healing everywhere. Luke shows how this mission that started in the Gospel continued through Acts. In Acts, Peter is then a recast of Jesus, and Paul is a recast of Peter.[106] The miracles done by the apostles were

---

104. Brakke, *Understanding the New Testament*, 101.

105. Refer to Luke 4:38–39; 40–41; 5:12–16, 17–26; 6:6–11; 7:1–10; 8:42–48; 9:11, 37–43; 13:10–17; 14:1–6; 17:11–19; 18:35–43; 22:50–51.

106. Ron C. Fay, personal email communication, September 23, 2023.

intended as signs pointing to Jesus as Lord and Christ (Messiah) calling people to faith and repentance.[107]

Prayer

Jesus taught the importance of prayer as communion with God. He demonstrated it as a practical trait in the lifestyle of human beings to be in fellowship with God. In the garden of Gethsemane, Luke's version was the spectacle of agony in Jesus's appearance as if he was sweating drops of blood while he was praying (see Luke 22:44). He taught his disciples to pray to avoid entering Satan's temptation (22:46). In Acts, the Christians all joined together constantly in prayer along with the women and Mary the mother of Jesus, and with his brothers (Acts 1:14). They were in an upper room in Jerusalem and the Holy Spirit descended upon them while they were praying (cf. Acts 2:1–4). Furthermore, the church prayed for Peter, and God sent an angel that delivered him from Herod and his persecutors (Acts 12:4).

Paul made prayer a significant part of his ministry realizing that his connection to Jesus was the only way of accomplishing his mission. In the Gospel, Jesus devoted the temple as a house of prayer that should not be defiled by materialism and idolatry (Luke 19:45–48).[108] In Acts, Paul is seen as a person devoted to the temple as a place of prayer (see Acts 21:26). Another parallel is seen in the act of the breaking of bread. In the Gospel, Jesus breaks bread and gives thanks (see Luke 22:19), and in Acts Paul also practiced breaking bread and giving thanks as an act of faith, surrender, thanks, and worship (see Acts 27:35).[109]

The last supper with Jesus and his disciples likely resembled the upper room in Acts 2:1 on the day of Pentecost. The community was never devoid of prayer in any of these instances. Following Jesus's example in the Third Gospel, Paul would later admonish the Thessalonians

---

107. Hays and Duvall, *Baker Illustrated Bible Handbook*, 711.

108. See the earlier discussion in the section titled "Subversive Movement and Progression Toward Rome" where Jesus drove the merchandisers out of his Father's house of prayer (i.e., the temple) where the materialistic money changers were marketing coins bearing the image of the self-exalted god, Caesar, in the place of offering up prayers to the Lord God (Luke 1:10; cf. Acts 3:1).

109. Powell, *Introducing the New Testament*, 202–3.

to pray without ceasing (see 1 Thess 5:17). Prayer is reiterated throughout the Gospels and Acts as Luke continuously purports its necessity. It was not a NT origin but had its beginnings in the OT. There was a set hour of prayer for the Jews at the temple (see Acts 3:1). It is how Luke opens his Gospel, with Zechariah burning incense in the temple while the people stood outside praying (see Luke 1:8–10).

Rejection and Acceptance

The Gospels open with the rejection of Jesus, his mission, and his disciples by the Jewish leadership establishment. Luke adds his perspective to the discussion by showing how Jesus was received by some as well as rejected by others. The Gospel and Acts demonstrate parallels in this respect. Jesus was the Jewish Messiah sent to the Jewish nation, yet their rejection of him and his mission diverted his mission away from the Jews to the gentiles (Acts 14:46).

Paul emphasized a similar point in this fashion by rebuking them for their unbelief in Christ. In Acts 13, he said it was because the Jews rejected the word of God that they turned to the gentiles who would indeed hear the message (Acts 28:28). The gentiles rejoiced and the angry Jews drove Paul and Barnabas out of the region. Similar themes repeat themselves throughout Acts corresponding to the Jews who rejected Christ and his message throughout the Gospel.[110]

Not all Jews rejected the gospel message. Nicodemus and Joseph of Arimathea were some among the Sanhedrin who believed in Jesus and his message (John 3:2; 19:38). In the Gospel, the centurion invites Jesus to his house (see Luke 7:1–10), while a similar event occurs in Acts 10:1–23. In the Gospel, Jesus is received favorably (Luke 19:37; 23:47), and in Acts, Paul was received favorably (Acts 21:17–20; 27:43).[111]

"To the Jew first" was Paul's emphasis of implying the Jews having the first opportunity among all the nations for salvation. Jesus and the apostles charged them as guilty of rejecting God's plan and being unworthy of eternal life (cf. Luke 4:23–31; Acts 3:15; 13:46). In Acts, Luke writes his entire account unfavorably toward the Jews. While the

110. Brakke, *Understanding the New Testament*, 101.
111. Powell, *Introducing the New Testament*, 202–3.

Gospels (Luke in particular) come to the Jews, Acts moves away from them to the gentiles. It began with Phillip to Samaria (see Acts 8:5, 14), Peter to Judea (see Acts 10:17–24), and Paul to the outermost reaches of the earth beginning in Syria (see Acts 11:25–28).

Just as Jesus did in the Gospel (Matt 23:24), Paul also accused the Jews of being blind (see Rom 11:25). Between the first and second centuries, the grandson of Rabbi Gamaliel, Gamaliel II (ca. AD 80–120), used eighteen benedictions cursing Christians. He said to "let the Nazarenes and the heretics perish as in a moment, let them be blotted out of the book of the living, and let them not be written with the righteous."[112] The move by Gamaliel II effectively excommunicated Christians from synagogues which all but formalized the break between the religion of the Jews and Christianity."[113]

Wealth

The NT does not always look favorably on wealth. Regarding what Jesus called unrighteous mammon (see Luke 16:9), Paul called filthy lucre (see Titus 1:11; 1 Tim 3:3, 8). Jesus also said the condition of a person's heart is identified by what is dearest to them. In other words, where your treasure is, so is your heart (Matt 6:21). Luke inserts two parallel scenes in Luke and Acts. In the Gospel, Jesus said he came to deliver the good news to the poor (see Luke 4:18). Peter and the apostles have grown sensitive to Jesus's teaching on this subject with a heart of supporting the poor and those in need of material substance. Peter concludes his sermon by challenging those added to the faith to share in their earthly possessions.[114]

Endings

Luke concludes both volumes with a trial scene. Garland highlights that the last 23 percent of the Gospel (see Luke 19:28—24:53) deals with the arrest, trial, death, resurrection, and ascension of Jesus. It is not by accident for the same author to reciprocate a similar ending

---

112. Ferguson, *Backgrounds of Early Christianity*, 491.
113. Ferguson, *Backgrounds of Early Christianity*, 491.
114. Brakke, *Understanding the New Testament*, 104.

in his second volume. He concludes the last 24 percent of Acts by dealing with trial scenes from the ministry of Paul. They deal with his arrest, trials, and arrival in Rome.[115] In addition, Jesus appears on trial before the Jewish council and Pontius Pilate toward the end of the Gospel. In Paul's trial scene toward the end of Acts, he appears before the Jewish council and the Roman procurators Antonius Felix and Porcius Festus.[116]

Implications and Takeaways

The current chapter continued the support and defense for Luke's two volume work, Luke-Acts. It examined how the author originally intended both volumes to be read as a single story to fully grasp and understand its message. It explored primary themes and travel narratives in the way Luke presented his story to describe the beginning of the movement and its development throughout Acts. The progression of the gospel message in Luke's structure and design of both volumes presented Jesus Christ as the originator of the movement he started in Nazareth, Galilee. These are what Luke presented as travel narratives. In the furtherance of Luke's structure and design, his goal was to take Christ and his gospel from Galilee to Rome.

The next chapter zooms in specifically on connecting Luke-Acts together in the ascension narrative at the end of the Third Gospel and the beginning of Acts. The primary term is ἀναβαίνω meaning "I go up." The chapter is intended to juxtapose ἀναβαίνω in the ascension narratives in Luke 24:50–53 and Acts 1:1–11. In addition to ἀναβαίνω, additional Greek terms in these passages are examined. Finally, this chapter examines the use of the term in the LXX and NT, its use in antiquity and in Greco-Roman culture and society, and its use as divine ascension terminology among Jews, Christians, and gentiles.

115. Garland, *Luke*, 28.
116. Brakke, *Understanding the New Testament*, 100.

Chapter 7: Juxtaposition of Ascension Narratives in Luke 24 and Acts 1 and Introduction to Chiasmus

ACTS CONTINUES THE STORY of the Third Gospel and provides Luke's authoritative comprehensive commentary.[1] Acts intentionally and uniformly repeats similar themes and motifs seen in the Gospel.[2] Regarding the latter, it proclaims all that Jesus did and taught in the ministry of the apostles. In Acts, the disciples followed Christ's example in ministry, but proclaimed the gospel as the Holy Spirit empowered them. In doing so, whether intentionally or unintentionally, Luke shows a continuation in the narrative that ended in the Gospel as it continues through Acts (cf. John 20:21).

Pervo asserts that Acts develops, fulfills, and plays upon the themes found in the Gospel and that both Luke and Acts can stand independently on their own.[3] Kummel, on the other hand, says that Acts cannot stand on its own detached from the Gospel.[4] In Luke's dedications to Theophilus, he shows that Acts constitutes the carrying forward of the gospel message proclaimed by Christ in the Gospel of Luke. Both belong together as part of a complete historical work.[5]

---

1. Garland, *Luke*, 28.
2. Woolsey, *End of Luke's Gospel*, 593, 599.
3. Pervo, *Acts*, 19.
4. Kummel, *Introduction to the New Testament*, 156.
5. Kummel, *Introduction to the New Testament*, 156.

If Luke had not written a Gospel, Acts, as it begins in chapter 1, would not have a clear aim. A different message presented by Matthew, Mark, and John at the end of their Gospels would not transition well with "In my former scroll, Theophilus, I wrote about all that Jesus began to do and to teach . . . ." Without Luke's Gospel, there would be a lot of confusion surrounding Theophilus and confusion over the previous scroll it is referencing in support of the statements he is making. If the start of Acts was in chapter 2, "When the day of Pentecost came, they were all together in one place . . . ," a transition from the other three Gospels would be much smoother without Luke. With chapter 1, any transition into Acts is not likely to flow smoothly apart from Luke.

Juxtapositional Analysis of Ascension Narratives in Luke and Acts

The ascension narratives at the end of the Gospel and beginning of Acts were not two events but one event that separated Jesus's physical imminence in the world, from the world, and ushered in God's incomprehensible ontological spiritual essence in a new way. The events in the life and ministry of Christ from his birth through his ascension are all connected to the Holy Spirit. In Luke's telling of those events, he taught how ministry in the lives of Jesus's followers must also be completely dependent upon the Holy Spirit.

The consummation of the Gospel pointed to several important yet critical events. It signaled the close of Jesus's life on earth vindicating his claims as the Messiah in a glorified exaltation and the move toward the established kingdom of heaven as it now extended to earth in the church.[6] It was an attempt to define the relation between Jesus the Messiah dying on the cross and the risen Lord who appeared to the apostles and ascended to heaven.[7] Some interpolation theories have been posed suggesting that someone other than Luke wrote the narratives of Christ's ascension.

---

6. Woolsey, *End of Luke's Gospel*, 594.
7. Foakes-Jackson, *Beginnings of Christianity*, 16, 139.

Amos Wilder assumes that Luke 24:50-53 was intended to be a summary of Acts 1:1-11 by an anonymous author other than Luke that was added to the end of the Gospel and to the beginning of Acts when both were separated from each other.[8] Hans Conzelmann assumes that Luke 24:50-53 is not original to the Gospel, but the original account of the ascension is in Acts 1; whereas the longer ending is found in most MSS it is an interpolation, yet an addition by someone other than Luke.[9]

Henk Jan de Jonge assumes the ascension in Luke 24:50-53 and Acts 1:2-11 were two separate events. He follows others that also assume the ascension and resurrection took place on the same day and not within a forty-day interval as stated in Acts 1:3 (being seen of them forty days) as represented by the Western textual reading of Luke 24:51, and by Tertullian, Cyprian, Lactantius, Chrysostom, and others. And because de Jonge assumes that Luke 24:50-53 and Acts 1:2-11 are not the same event, he assumes interpolation by means of a Western text editor that was introduced to the end of the Gospel and at the beginning of Acts when both were split into two separate books, based on the timetable on what he assumes as two separate events.[10]

A proposed or suggested solution for harmonizing both ascension narratives is weakened by assuming that they were or are two separate events written by an anonymous author, with no justifiable proof for the conjecture. Nor should the narratives be counted as interpolations by some unknown writers during the process of the books' canonization when they were added to the canon as separate books, as it is assumed by Kummel.[11]

Acts or volume 2 was written on a separate scroll because the first scroll containing the Gospel was too long to continue writing, and then Acts became the second volume (see chapter 5). It was not mandatory for Luke to begin writing Acts using the exact wording of the ascension narrative contained in volume 1 when he started writing Acts on the second scroll. The perspective also takes it for

---

8. Wilder, "Variant Traditions," 311; Parsons, "Text of Acts 1:2," 61.
9. Conzelmann, *Theology of St. Luke*, 94; Parsons, "Text of Acts 1:2," 61.
10. De Jonge, "Chronology of the Ascension," 151-71.
11. Kummel, *Introduction to the New Testament*, 157.

granted that he may not have had a copy of the Gospel in hand when he started writing Acts.

The data regarding the ascension presented by Paul to the Corinthians most likely came from those who were present at Christ's ascension. It cannot be supported by any evidence that he was an eyewitness to the ascension, notwithstanding that he was an enemy of Christ until his conversion (Acts 9:5; 26:14). While Luke does not provide the numbers, Paul says that Jesus appeared to James and five hundred additional disciples after his resurrection, likely referring to those who were eyewitnesses of his ascension to heaven (see 1 Cor 15:5).[12]

Luke and Acts are stitched together as a continuing story by the ascension narratives between them. It is unclear why the Gospel of John was placed between them, but if John was placed before the Gospel of Luke the continuing narrative of Luke-Acts would likely be more noticeable. These narratives that flow through Luke 24:45–51 and Acts 1:6–11 are the thread that stitches them together as one book. In both volumes, Jesus is seen standing on the Mount of Olives giving his final speech to all the disciples who remained with him up to the time of the ascension (cf. 1 Cor 15:6).

The promise of the Holy Spirit continued as the principal subject of Jesus's final words with the disciples before his arrest in the garden of Gethsemane and were continually repeated after the resurrection as "the promise of the Father" (see 24:49; Acts 1:4).[13] Luke 24:6 through the end of the chapter implies continued correspondence between Jesus and his apostles until they arrived at the Mount of Olives. In the Gospel of Luke, the location is called "in the vicinity of Bethany" (see 24:50).

Luke does not say the ascension took place in Bethany but in the vicinity of it. The place that the NIV and the NASB calls Bethany in John 1:28, the KJV and NKJV calls Bethabara. According to John 11:18, Bethany or Bethabara was approximately two miles from Jerusalem. While landmarks and geographical areas often change over time, it proves likely that the vicinity of Bethany included the Mount

---

12. Woolsey, *End of Luke's Gospel*, 596, 598.
13. Woolsey, *End of Luke's Gospel*, 602.

of Olives at the time of Jesus's ascension. The play on words would not have been confusing to the original audience because they were familiar with the geography as with any other village, town, or region. In Acts 1:12, he returns to what Theophilus expected, calling it the Mount of Olives (Luke 24:50; cf. Acts 1:12).[14]

Regarding this location of the ascension, the Gospel assumes it occurred in Bethany's vicinity (an area in the vicinity of Bethany or Bethabara) on the same day of the resurrection (24:50), whereas Acts says it was on the Mount of Olives forty days after the resurrection (1:3, 12).[15] According to Luke 24:33, the disciples are in a house in Jerusalem where Jesus enters in among them (24:36). In Acts 1:12 the ascension takes place outside in the open on the Mount of Olives without any change in location. This makes any hypothesis of an interpolation of Acts 1:3–14, or a part of it, highly unlikely.[16]

Regarding the time of the ascension, some assume Luke was not clear when it took place following the resurrection and that he made a mistake on the timing of the event, which he sought to correct in Acts. Such arguments are replete with some theological problems. For example, if Luke's research contained inaccuracies, so would the Gospel and Acts have inaccuracies in the stories they report. Mistakes and inaccuracies would bring into question the trustworthiness of Luke's Gospel as a message for faith, hope, and salvation in Christ, which is said to have been written under the inspiration of the Holy Spirit (see 2 Tim 3:16; cf. 2 Pet 1:20–21).

In the Gospel, Jesus led the apostles out of Jerusalem as far as Bethany (see Luke 24:50). And while he was blessing them, he departed from them and was taken up into heaven. According to verse 52, it is noted that after they worshiped Jesus, they all went back into Jerusalem to the temple. In Acts, he adds that it was forty days after the crucifixion (see Acts 1:3). At the close of volume 1, Luke summarizes the joyous occasion between Jesus and his apostles with fellowship and eating, reciprocating this event he started with them before his arrest and crucifixion.

14. Woolsey, *End of Luke's Gospel*, 603.
15. Kummel, *Introduction to the New Testament*, 157.
16. Kummel, *Introduction to the New Testament*, 158.

Shortly after the resurrection, and though many speculations have often been suggested, not too much of a time span between the resurrection and ascension have been provided by the Gospel writers. Luke does this in his second volume, saying, "For forty days after his death he appeared to them many times in ways that proved beyond doubt that he was alive" (Acts 1:3 GNT). The assertion leaves only one of two options that are possible. The first option is that he ascended to heaven immediately after the resurrection and then made scattered appearances to his disciples. The second option is that he remained on earth and ascended to heaven on the fortieth day after the crucifixion.

A possible reason Luke introduced the forty days in Acts 1:3 was a desire to connect it with the OT Passover and Feast of Weeks.[17] The Gospel writers portrayed Jesus as the Lamb of God, that he was the perfect, ultimate sacrifice for humanity according to God. And being that the OT Feast of Weeks occurred on the fiftieth day after the Passover, the day of Pentecost in the NT occurred fifty days after the crucifixion. Luke was therefore declaring the fulfillment of the OT Passover and Feast of Weeks with Jesus's crucifixion on Calvary and the outpouring of the Holy Spirit on the day of Pentecost (Acts 2:1; 2:2–4; cf. Mark 1:8).[18]

The resurrection narrative is an accurate timeline to measuring all events leading up to the ascension. On that day, Luke's Gospel record that Jesus went to Emmaus with two disciples and stayed with them overnight. The account implies that he spent some time on earth before ascending to heaven (Luke 24:29). It also gives credence to Luke's account of the forty days in Acts. Some difficulties are

---

17. A reading of Lev 23:15–22 reveals a timeline between the preparation, the Passover, the Sabbath, and Firstfruits. Leviticus 23:15–16 says, "You shall also count for yourselves from the day after the Sabbath, from the day when you brought in the sheaf of the wave offering; there shall be seven complete Sabbaths. You shall count fifty days to the day after the seventh Sabbath; then you shall present a new grain offering to the Lord" (NASB). Each of the Gospels states that the OT day of preparation of the Passover was the organization of the plans for Jesus's crucifixion and the next day was the Sabbath (see Matt 26:17–29; 27:62; Mark 14:12–25; 15:42; Luke 22:7–20; 23:54; John 13:1–10; 19:14, 31, 42). It is likely that Jesus was crucified on the Friday following the Thursday preparation, Sabbath was observed on Saturday, and the resurrection was on Sunday. See Marie, *Law Fulfilled*, 90.

18. Woolsey, *End of Luke's Gospels*, 593.

presented in harmonizing the two accounts of the ascension at the end of Luke and beginning of Acts.

The post-resurrection scene told from John's (20:19–23) and Luke's (24:30–32) point of view are connected yet told differently from each writer's perspective of the event. While John does not name the specific location, he says they were inside a house, and Luke says it was in a village called Emmaus. In the final analysis, it is a fair peroration to conclude that they were in a house in the village Emmaus near Jerusalem.

Those who contend Luke had made a mistake regarding the time of the ascension from the time of the resurrection assume he would have corrected his mistake in Acts. The assumption, however, leads to additional historical and theological problems such as the facts of the historicity of Luke's Gospel. It would also introduce a conflict-based concern regarding the testimony of the events obtained from witnesses who claimed to have been eyewitness of the actual events.

Regarding the first argument about Luke's potential unintentional error in the timeline he reported on the ascension at the end of the Gospel, some insisted that if Luke had become more aware of the timing after he finished pinning the account at the end of the Gospel, he would have been seemingly chagrined for misstating this very important portion of history and would have sought to reconcile it in his second volume.[19]

Luke indeed referred to his Gospel in a way that put his stamp of truth on it. He said volume 1 contains the account of the works and words of Jesus until the day, after giving instructions to his apostles, he was taken up into heaven (Acts 1:1–2). And then comes a statement of what he did and how long he stayed on earth in a visible form. Luke identified the two accounts and made no explanations for the wording. Any theory assuming Luke made a statement in the Gospel that he felt he had to retract and correct in volume 2 would be merely suppositional as there is no sufficient evidence to support such a claim.[20]

The time frames given in Acts carry literal and symbolic significance. For example, the author notes a forty-day period between

19. Woolsey, *End of Luke's Gospel*, 598.
20. Woolsey, *End of Luke's Gospel*, 598.

Jesus's resurrection and ascension (Acts 1:3), the arrival of the Holy Spirit at Pentecost fifty days after Easter (Acts 2:1), and the three years Paul spent in Ephesus (Acts 20:31). These time frames provide not only literary and narrative sensitivity but also a sense of historical reality as they also have symbolic significance.

The forty-day period between the resurrection and ascension echoes other significant forty-day periods in the Bible, such as the forty days of rain during Noah's flood (Gen 7:12), Moses's forty days on Mount Sinai (Exod 24:18), and Jesus's own forty days in the wilderness (Luke 4:2). The forty days in the Acts version of the ascension narrative links to such earlier episodes, suggesting a pattern of divine action while underscoring their significance.

Moreover, the timing of the Holy Spirit's arrival at Pentecost also bears theological significance. Pentecost, originally a Jewish festival held fifty days after Passover, celebrates the giving of the law at Sinai.[21] By linking the advent of the Holy Spirit to this festival, Luke suggests a parallel between the giving of the law and the gift of the Spirit, emphasizing the new covenant established through the prophet like Moses (Deut 18:15–19; cf. Acts 3:22), the Lord Jesus Christ.

Ascension Language in Greco-Roman Thought

The worldview of God or gods consisting of a plurality of deities was contrasted and clashed with the idea of a single deity of monotheistic Jews and Christians as they taught it. A theology of God promoted by Christians in the early Roman Empire was unwonted. Hurtado stated how Christianity in the eyes of many people in the first three centuries of its existence was odd, bizarre, and in some ways dangerous to their accepted standard of religion.[22] Roman writers such as Tacitus and Pliny antagonized Christianity as a perverse superstition.[23]

Paul's correspondence with his Jewish brethren and those of the pagan world presented common sets of facts, cultural and religious norms with which they were familiar. Even as he perceived

21. Wheeler, *God's Word Unfolded*, 108.
22. Hurtado, *Destroyer of the gods*, 1–2.
23. Hurtado, *Destroyer of the gods*, 1–2.

the message of Christ as a stumbling block to Jews, the message of the cross did not force him to forsake his own distinct Jewishness. Such interactions with Jews and gentiles alike centered his thoughts on God as holistically, ontologically One as he explained God's effect on his readers with Christ at the center of his messages (e.g., Acts 17:22–32). He assumed his readers would have a familiarity with the God of Israel (Acts 17:23), yet he did not hesitate to clarify and correct the many misperceptions of God in Christ based upon the culture of the day (e.g., Rom 1:18–23).[24]

When he wrote to the Corinthians in Greece, he perceived the message they preached of Christ was simply "foolishness to gentiles" (see 1 Cor 1:23); as for Paul, Jesus Christ was a divine being in human flesh who died and rose again. The gentiles had no outlet of declaring anyone rising from the dead, particularly after physical death. Crucifixion was a punishment for those condemned of committing major crimes in society as they were given over to capital punishment.

Views on the afterlife varied from those taught in Christianity, which indeed promised life after death in an unending eternity with God.[25] As a whole, religion in the Greco-Roman world was concerned with creedal beliefs about gods, but with cultic acts that demonstrated devotion to them by offerings of food, prayers before long journeys, animal sacrifices in pagan temples or at festivals, which were all designed to court the benevolence and benefaction of their prestigiously exalted deity.[26]

Christians living in Roman society demonstrated a similar devotion to Christ. Unlike many gentiles, they rejected polytheism and promoted monotheism, liberation from sin by Christ's crucifixion, eternal life in Christ, and a belief in Christ that he alone was divine. Natural inclinations to abandon all ingrained traditions and turn to Christ emphasized struggles among gentiles coming into Christianity, particularly with the concept of a single deity, as to be a disciple, Christ expected his followers to abandon all for him (Luke 9:23–24; 14:26–27; Mark 8:34–35; Matt 16:24; 19:27–29).

24. Fay, "Greco-Roman Concepts of Deity," 51.
25. Wright and Bird, *New Testament in Its World*, 153.
26. Wright and Bird, *New Testament in Its World*, 153.

Parallels (literary connections, see chapter 6) exist between the ascension narratives of Jesus in the NT and those of Greco-Roman figures. Jesus's resurrection was necessary for his ascension that followed the crucifixion. Ascension stories among gentiles presumptuously sparked curiosity among Luke's gentile readers as to how these connections were made in the Lukan narrative of Christ (see chapter 5).[27] Some Samaritans did not believe in the resurrection of the dead, often aligning themselves with some Jews in this respect (Acts 23:8).[28]

Unlike the Jewish Sadducees who denied the resurrection of the body, it was ambiguous for gentiles to believe in such an event as imagined in the myths. In the tale of Alcestis, she is rescued in death by Hercules. In death she fights physically with θάνατος, beats him, and is restored back to life to her husband, Admetus. Alcestis returned from θάνατος to life, paralleling John's story of Lazarus (see John 11:38–44) where she would later die again.[29]

The first century produced numerous gentile writers of their own having a theology from the perspectives of their many religions. It, however, is not evident that Luke borrowed in any way from Greco-Roman literature to narrate the Christ event at the end of the Gospel and the beginning of Acts. It is also important to understand the term "ascension" in a literary and religious backdrop of the Greco-Roman world, rather than in modern connotations, essentially because the NT is a product of that world. In a Greco-Roman idea of a person ascending to heaven, the indication is that the person was divine or immortal. In essence, the person had undergone an ἀποθέωσις. The

---

27. Brasfield, "Jesus, Ascension of." Chapter 4 of this book, under the section "Birth Narratives in Luke's Gospel and Their Aim to His Larger Gospel Narrative," highlighted myths that existed surrounding the Roman and Greek gods, that those deities produced children in supernatural ways, which rendered those children with superpowers. As such, Luke wanted to convince the gentile convert Theophilus that the tales of the Roman and Greek gods were simply myths and that Jesus's birth was not a myth. Whereas, Luke's interest was in writing about the miraculous birth of Christ and the miracles performed by the apostles as genuine and real. Such conclusions regarding truth are another reason Luke took such interest in Paul's ministry, and he did not want these stories to sound like myths to Theophilus as seen in Greco-Roman literature.

28. Vinzent, *Christ's Resurrection in Early Christianity*, 41.

29. Wright and Bird, *New Testament in Its World*, 273.

concept in ancient mythology was applied to figures like Zeus or Heracles, or in Hebrew thought to Enoch, Moses, and Elijah.[30]

Known as son of Zeus to Greeks, Heracles (as known to Romans) is one the most popular hero figures from Greco-Roman history, who presents a parallel to the ascension of Christ.[31] In the case of Heracles or Hercules, it was thought he had become divine when he was thought to have ascended, but it is not a true comparison to Christ. In biblical thought, Jesus did not become divine when he ascended. He ascended because he was divine.

An additional usage of a Greco-Roman ascension (and apotheosis in gentile thought) with an idea of paralleling the ascension of Christ was the Roman imperial cult between the time of Julius Caesar (ca. 100–44 BC) to the end of the first century AD.[32] The cult erroneously labeled emperors and some of their family members as gods and assigned places for them in the heavens, but they were not officially worshiped in Rome during Caesar's lifetime.[33] During the Roman occupation of Jerusalem (and Palestine), Herod renovated the Jewish temple in the Second Temple period. He boasted about it being a gift to the Jews and for the glory of the God of Israel. But as a demonstration of Roman supremacy over the Jews, Caesar placed a golden eagle over its eastern gate, as it was later torn down.[34]

The stories about the ascensions of people are sometimes called translation stories because they represent people that were taken to another realm of existence without experiencing a physical death. A

---

30. Brasfield, "Jesus, Ascension of."

31. Brasfield, "Jesus, Ascension of."

32. Julius Caesar helped to move the government of Rome from republic to empire in the first century before Christ. Julius is his family name and Caesar identified the family to which he belonged. All Roman emperors after Julius adopted the name Caesar as a title like that of the pharaohs of Egypt. Garbarino, "Julius Caesar." Fay says that "the Imperial Cult was not strictly about magnifying the emperor as ruler as it was much about magnifying him as the one who stands for Rome and the Empire." Fay believes this could be disputed in the cases of Nero and Domitian. It would also include Caligula, who almost started a civil war by ordering his image to be installed in the Jewish temple in Jerusalem. See Fay, "Greco-Roman Concepts of Deity," 65.

33. Garbarino, "Julius Caesar"; Lipka, *Roman Gods*, 131–32.

34. Hatina, "Palestine," 479.

human translation experience, however, does not require physical death with the person undergoing the event. For instance, Moses died prior to his being physically translated to heaven (Deut 34:5–7; Luke 9:30–31; Matt 17:2–4). The Greek stories also depict humans, such as Heracles, who physically died before being taken to another place of existence.[35]

In non-biblical literature, worthy persons are brought into the company of the gods, but in biblical literature, they are brought into the direct presence of God. Even though the Bible makes it clear that Jesus was the only human being who lived on earth to never commit any sin (2 Cor 5:21; 1 John 3:5), he died a physical death before he ascended into heaven. From the creation to the present age, the Bible identifies only two people who ascended to heaven without dying, Enoch (Gen 5:24) and Elijah (2 Kgs 2:11–12).

An example in Roman literature was Romulus, the twin brother of Remus, the founder of what became Rome. In book 1 of *The History of Rome*, Titus Livius (Livy) purported an account of Romulus who underwent an apotheosis by ascending into heaven in a thunderstorm.[36] The event proposed that no one was able to find his body, which some invented as background similarities with stories told of Christ in the Gospels of Jesus's post-resurrection empty tomb (e.g., Mark 16:6; Matt 28:6). As the story goes, Romulus was inspecting his army near the swamp of Capra at Campus Martius. Suddenly, there was a storm with loud claps of thunder that enveloped him in a cloud so thick that he was hidden from their sight. During the postmortem review of the soldiers, they saw that his royal seat was empty and later heralded Romulus as divine.[37]

Heracles is another example as purported by the Greek historian Diodorus. In the *Library of History*, he delineates Heracles as an ancient hero (viz. legendary hero) who underwent an apotheosis.[38] During his despondency, he inquired of Apollo how he could be healed of his

---

35. Brasfield, "Jesus, Ascension of."

36. Rodgers, *Ancient Rome*, 22; Livy, *History of Rome*, 57–61; Dodson and Smith, *Exploring Biblical Backgrounds*, 217.

37. Livy, *History of Rome*, 57–61.

38. Diodorus, *Library of History*, 465–67 and 4.1.1–4.39.1.

malady. His wife, Deianira, was in anguish as she blamed herself for his condition to the point that she committed suicide by hanging. Apollos instructed Heracles to build a suttee and carry his military gear with him to Mount Oeta, and the rest would be left up to Zeus.

Heracles, having abandoned all hope, placed himself onto the suttee as instructions were given to light it. Philoctetes, the only bystander demonstrating courage, lit it. In the process, lightning fell from the sky and completely consumed it, reminiscent of Elijah's experience with the Lord on Mount Carmel (1 Kgs 18:38–39). In the aftereffect, Heracles was nowhere to be found, whereby the people concluded he had ascended into the presence of the gods.[39]

Christ's Ascension Circumjacent to Hebrew Thought and Literature

Ascension stories among the Jews should have gracefully prepared them for expectation of the ascension of Christ, by realizing such an event as not unusual.[40] The gentiles accepting Christ and entering the church would have also been prepared having nostalgic recollections of events in written and oral stories of the past. In Greek traditions, stories were about ancient Greek heroes who were said to have ascended to heaven after they died and would become divine. In contrast, ascension stories among the Jews were mostly about humans ascending to heaven without dying.

While continuing the narrative of these stories, Luke and his contemporaries sought to vindicate Jesus that he was precisely who he claimed and that he literally died for all the sins of humanity, and that he underwent a physical resurrection and a physical ascension to heaven. Additional ascension stories that were told about angels descending and ascending were not unique events NT writers noted as movements. The religion of the Jews also told about divine wisdom ascending and descending, but it was not in a narrative context

---

39. Diodorus, *Library of History* 4.1.1–4.39.1. Also refer to 1 Cor 8:5–6 regarding Paul's view of monotheism.

40. Keener, *IVP Bible Background Commentary*, 587.

because wisdom was personified as a metaphor and not a historical person (e.g., Prov 8:22–31).⁴¹

In contrast to Greco-Roman thought regarding apotheosis, the NT writers did not teach that Jesus underwent one. Rather, Jesus was already divine before he became human. More specifically, Jesus was God who became a man (e.g., John 1:1, 14), meaning that he was divine without having to ascend to any status or position. Even as ascension stories exist in Hebrew thought and literature, the Jewish leadership in the first century was divided about specific theological points. The Sadducees, in contrast to the Pharisees, denied basic theological points of the supernatural.

The Jewish people were familiar with stories surrounding Enoch, Moses, and Elijah. Enoch's disappearance from earth is simply stated as "God took him [ויקח אתו אלהים] away" in Gen 5:24 (NIV) implying that he was taken into God's presence in heaven (also see Sirach 44:16 and 49:14). According to Heb 11:5, "Enoch was taken up so that he would not see death and he was not found because God took him up" (NASB). Some English translations bold this phrase to highlight this important point. Another term used in Heb 11:5 says that Enoch was translated, or that God translated (μεταθέσεως) Enoch.

The Greek term μεταθέσεως as it is used to describe what happened to Enoch means that he was instantly changed and transferred from one place to another. The OT pseudepigraphic book 2 Enoch is an account detailing Gen 5:21–24, but more than that, it was written as an amplification of Gen 5:21–32, as it covers the events from the life of Enoch to the onset of the flood of Noah's day.⁴² It begins by describing how God took him from earth to heaven to show him his eternal kingdom and all the glory of it.⁴³ Enoch did not experience a physical death because God took him from the earth (Heb 11:5).

---

41. Keener, *IVP Bible Background Commentary*, 587.

42. Charlesworth, *Old Testament Pseudepigrapha*, 91.

43. The OT pseudepigraphic book 2 Enoch tells how "the Lord took him, a wise man and a great artisan, away to heaven so that he might see the highest realms and the wisest and great and inconceivable and unchanging kingdom of God almighty, and of the most marvelous and glorious and shining and many-eyed station of the LORD's servants, and the LORD's immovable throne, and the ranks and organization of the bodiless armies, and of the indescribable composition of the multitude

The New Testament places significant emphasis on Moses and Elijah, portraying them in a manner that suggests a parallel to the ascension of Jesus and the eschatological vision of the church's rapture as described by Paul in 1 Thess 4:16–17. Both figures "appeared in glorious splendor, talking with Jesus" (as rendered in the NIV) on the Mount of Tabor, an event commonly referred to as the Transfiguration. During this momentous occasion, they conversed with Jesus about the impending crucifixion that he was about to accomplish—or would soon fulfill—at Jerusalem (Luke 9:30–31; cf. Mark 9:4; Matt 17:3). This appearance not only affirms their continued existence in the divine realm but also serves as a theological bridge between the Old Testament prophetic tradition and the NT revelation of Christ's redemptive mission.

In 1 Thess 4:14–18, Paul identifies one church yet two events that will happen in the future involving those in Christ who have died and those in Christ who are still alive at the time of his coming. The dead in Christ will rise from the grave, and those who are still alive on earth at the time will be ἁρπαγησόμεθα in the clouds.[44] In such an aspect, Moses died and was taken to heaven, and Elijah did not die and was taken to heaven. The attestation is also seen with both Moses and Elijah talking to Jesus about his death, making ascension a possibility for everyone who places faith in him for salvation.

In the OT pseudepigraphic book called the Assumption (or Testament) of Moses, Jude quotes a conversation between Satan and the archangel Michael about Moses. To prevent Michael from taking Moses, Satan brings a charge of murder against Moses. Rather than Michael bringing a railing acquisition against Satan (see Jude 1:9) for inspiring the serpent to tempt Adam and Eve, Michael appealed to the Lord's authority and sovereignty over heaven, earth, and mankind as the one who created them all.[45]

---

of elements, singing of the army of the cherubim, and the light without measure, to be an eyewitness" (verse 1a). See Charlesworth, *Old Testament Pseudepigrapha*, 102.

44. Nearly all English translations use the terms "caught up" or "caught away," denoting an English word meaning rapture.

45. In 1:9, the KJV's translation of Jude says during this dispute between Michael and Satan, the archangel "did not bring against Satan a railing accusation."

Josephus wrote that at the end of Moses's life, the elders of Israel, Eleazar, the high priest, and Joshua, their commander, went with him to the place where he was to depart this life. While Moses was still speaking to Eleazar and Joshua and embracing them, a cloud came over him, and he disappeared. The reason, Josephus says, it was written in the holy books (Deut 34) that Moses died is that the writer was concerned that the people would say that Moses went to God on account of any extraordinary virtue he possessed of his own accord.[46]

The Hebrew verb חקל used regarding Elijah in 2 Kgs 9 is alluded to in Gen 24 of Enoch. It means to take, and according to Alexander, it was used this way in rabbinic exegesis to show that both Enoch and Elijah were translated and departed from earth the same way.[47] Just as it was with Moses, Elijah's body was nowhere to be found. The writer of 2 Kings says that there was a manifestation of chariots of fire that carried Elijah away to heaven, but not too much detail is given about Jesus's ascension other than in the *Epistle of the Apostles*, where Jesus gives details of his departure from earth.

The apostles asked Jesus when he would depart to heaven. He responded that the praise of his Father would first be perfected in him, and after that, he would go home and abide with his Father, and then all things would be accomplished which he told them about concerning himself.[48] And just as he raised the dead back to life, he likewise will be raised from the dead and taken up into the highest heaven.[49]

After Jesus finished his discourse with the apostles, suddenly there was thunder, lightning, and an earthquake; the heavens were parted asunder, and he was taken up and enveloped in a light, bright cloud that appeared in sight of the spectators. Then were the voices of

---

The account in the Assumption of Moses says Michael accused Satan of working deception against Adam and Even in the garden of Eden. But reading the GNT rendering of the verse gives a different understanding. It says that "Michael did not dare condemn the Devil with insulting words" so there is no contradiction between Jude and the Assumption of Moses. Moreover, this appears to be the source Jude is quoting for his text. Charles, *Assumption of Moses*, 106.

46. Josephus, *Complete Works of Josephus*, 119, 164–66; Josephus, *Jewish Antiquities* 4.320–326; Dodson and Smith, *Exploring Biblical Backgrounds*, 216.

47. Alexander, "New Translation and Introduction," 246.

48. James, "Epistle of the Apostles," 497.

49. James, "Epistle of the Apostles," 493.

many angels rejoicing and singing the praises, "Gather us, O Priest, unto the light of the majesty." And as they drew closer unto the firmament his voice was heard saying "Depart hence in peace."[50]

Christ's Ascension Circumjacent to New Testament Thought and Literature

The ascension of Christ is not narrated in the NT, except for Luke-Acts and in the Gospel of Mark. His disciples were witnesses of his ministry, crucifixion, resurrection, and ascension. Luke was implicit in stating this as obvious to gentile converts to Christianity, as many of them possessed a Weltanschauung in their cultural beliefs and practices. Even as Jews had a unique culture based on their own set of religious beliefs and practices, so did gentiles.

It was not uncommon among gentiles, and those converted to Christ, to believe if anyone famous ascends, he or she would undergo an apotheosis, that is, to ascend and then become divine. "In *Quaestiones et Solutiones in Exodum* (QE 2.40), Philo indicates a holy soul is divinized by not ascending to the air or to heaven (which is) higher than all but to (a region) above the heavens. And beyond the world, there is no place but God."[51] Luke, and other NT writers, taught the opposite of many religious beliefs from Greco-Roman culture, even from that of some Jews like Philo. The two parent cultures stood and were held in contradistinction of this point that Jesus did not become divine when he ascended. Rather, he ascended because he was divine.

Many people talk about Jesus's crucifixion and resurrection in the forefront as if those two are the most important events in the history of God's plan in the world. The ascension is also on par with those two events and is equally important. The apostle Paul placed emphasis on the ascension saying, "When he ascended up on high, he led captivity captive" (Eph 4:8; cf. Ps 68:18). The hermeneutical problem introduced in reconciling Paul's application of Ps 68 to Christ is

---

50. James, "Epistle of the Apostles," 503.
51. Penner, "Philo's Eschatology," 391.

resolved with an understanding of the psalm's typological expectation and its redemptive-historical fulfilment in Christ.[52]

In Greever's interpretation of the Psalm describing the captives YHWH takes away, it is likely referring to human enemies from the conquered nations. He likewise sees Eph 4:8 as applying to evil principalities and powers.[53] This does not appear to be the case, as those referenced in 4:8 appear as human captives Christ is leading out of captivity. It sounds more like a hymn song and chant of victory, whereas human captives would indeed be the focal point of the passage.

The apocryphal Gospel of Nicodemus (Acts of Pilate) alludes to describing these captives as saints from the OT era that were held captive in death (died prior to Christ's crucifixion), that they long awaited deliverance.[54] To the latter, it made Matt 28:52–53 a reality, implying how his resurrection guaranteed the resurrection of everyone who preceded and followed him.[55] In this perspective, saints held captive by death were led to heaven by Jesus after completion of his work on the cross on their behalf.[56]

Paul's use of Christ ascending on high is an obvious reference to his ascension into heaven. In *A Handbook on the Acts of the Apostles*, Newman and Nida point out Luke's use of the verb "he

52. Greever, "Typological Expectation," 253–79.

53. Greever, "Typological Expectation," 254.

54. Hone, *Lost Books of the Bible*, 83–89.

55. According to Matt 27:52–53, when Jesus rose from the dead, it made the resurrection of all human beings a reality for all who died before and after him. Upon Jesus's resurrection, Matthew says the graves were opened. Many saints who had died were raised back to life as they came out of their graves after the resurrection and went into Jerusalem and appeared to many people.

56. The ESV says, "When he ascended on high, he led a host of captives"; however, it is still not that clear who the captives are unless it is a universal statement designating everyone he has led out of sin when he died on the cross. The cluster of verses in 4:8–14 is together and they interpret themselves based on the keywords: ascended, captivity, captives, gifts, and descended. The gifts are revealed in 4:11. He descended by coming to earth to release sinners from the power of darkness and Satan's kingdom, thereby transferring them into his kingdom (Eph 1:20–22; 2:5–6; cf. Col 1:16). He also went (descended) to paradise after he died on the cross (Luke 23:42–43) which, before the crucifixion, it was visible from the torment side of hell (and vice versa) before his ascension (Luke 16:19–31). In the process, he released all captives who had died before his crucifixion and those who were still alive on earth. The message implies that when he ascended to heaven in Luke 24:51 and Acts 1:9, he led a host of captives like a train (so to speak) with him to heaven; those who had already died ascended with him.

was taken up" (Luke 24:51). Many English translations add "heaven" to this verb to make explicit for the reader what was evident in his mind and thoughts.[57] Explicitly, nearly all English translations add "heaven," where some say he was "taken up to heaven" and others say he was "carried up to heaven."

Luke is the only Gospel writer who narrates the ascension of Christ. Mark only alludes to the ascension in one verse: "After the Lord Jesus had spoken to them, he was taken up into heaven and he sat at the right hand of God" (16:19 NIV).[58] Perhaps, Luke desired to write an orderly account of the things that happened among them, so Theophilus and all the lovers of God would know for certainty the things they have been taught. Luke details more about the ascension than any NT writer, while it is more assumed in Paul rather than explained (e.g., Phil 2:9, 4:8, 9; 1 Tim 3:16).[59]

Among the three events, crucifixion, resurrection, and ascension, the ascension appears as the least discussed in the NT. Entire chapters in the Gospels are given to the former two, but the latter is only discussed by Luke and more than any other writer. The first impression is likely that there was not much to be said about it. However, it would seem odd for NT writers to seem to skip over it being that it was widely discussed in Greco-Roman literature.

In describing ascensions into heaven, the terms used in English translations are often "carried up" (Luke 24:51) and "taken up" (Acts 1:9) when used of Jesus, and "taken up" when used of Elijah (see 2 Kgs 2:1, 11). English translations of Luke-Acts do not use the terms "ascend" or "ascension" to describe the Christ event. It is used twice, however, in Acts: 2:34 (about David) and 25:1 (about Festus coming from Caesarea and going to Jerusalem). Arie Zwiep contends that

---

57. Newman and Nida, *Handbook on the Acts of the Apostles*, 13.

58. Some scholars argue that the long ending of Mark's Gospel was added by a redactor. Not all Greek manuscripts carry the long ending of Mark (16:9–20), as do modern translations of that Gospel. Those critical of the long ending note these verses as missing from both the Codex Vaticanus (B) and Codex Sinaiticus (א), although nearly all other manuscript traditions contain them. However, nearly all English translations include vv. 9–20, but in many Bibles, these verses are bracketed, indicating the question as to their originality of the original ending to Mark.

59. Fitzmyer contends that the ascension of Christ is only alluded to in NT writings outside of Luke and Mark such as Romans, Ephesians, John, and Hebrews. See Fitzmyer, "Ascension of Christ and Pentecost," 409.

Luke uses the cognate verb ἀναλαμβάνομαι in Acts 1:2, 11, and 22 which are also the ascension terms used in the standard LXX for Elijah's ascension.[60] In contrast, another use of take or taken up common in Acts is ἀνελήμφθη (1:2, "was taken up"), ἀναλημφθείς (1:11, "has been taken"), ἀνελήμφθη (1:22, "was taken up").

The clause in Luke 24:51 εἰς οὐρανόν has various meanings depending on the context when and where it is used. Unlike the NKJV, in Acts 1:10–11, the NIV uses "sky" twice in the verse, whereas the clauses "looking intently up into the sky" (v. 10), "looking into the sky" (v. 11a), and "into heaven" (v. 11b) all translate the same expression, literally "into heaven." In 2 Cor 12:2, Paul called the heavenly abode beyond the sky "paradise." It was a literal place where he was caught up (raptured) and while there, heard inexpressible things, things that no one is allowed to utter (2 Cor 12:4).

The term οὐρανόν as it is used in nearly every instance in the NT regarding heaven could refer to the location of God's throne, or merely to the sky above the earth's atmosphere.[61] One distinct difference is that the sky is physical to the earth and heaven is spiritual to the abode of God. When used with the Acts 1:2 version of the ascension, ἧς ἡμέρας ἀνελήμφθη designates a location beyond earth's atmosphere, i.e., the literal heavenly throne of God.

Table 6. Westcott-Hort's alignment with P⁷⁵

Bodmer 𝔓⁷⁵ Text	και εγενετο εν τω ευλογειν αυτον αυτους διεστη απ αυτων και ανεφερετο εις τον ουρανον[62]
Westcott-Hort Greek Text	καὶ ἐγένετο ἐν τῷ εὐλογεῖν αὐτὸν αὐτοὺς διέστη ἀπ' αὐτῶν [καὶ ἀνεφέρετο εἰς τὸν οὐρανόν][63]

---

60. Zwiep, *Ascension of the Messiah*, 84.
61. Newman and Nida, *Handbook on the Acts of the Apostles*, 20–21.
62. Comfort and Barrett, *Text of the Earliest New Testament*, 2:75.
63. Westcott and Hort, *New Testament*, 186.

Table 7. Westcott-Hort's Alignment with the Byzantine Text-Type

Byzantine/Majority Text	και ανεφερετο εις τον ουρανον[64]
Westcott and Hort Greek Text	[καὶ ἀνεφέρετο εἰς τὸν οὐρανόν][65]

Bodmer P[75] agrees with the Greek text of Westcott and Hort on Luke 24:51, and the Majority Text also agrees with the Greek text of Westcott and Hort. When both Luke 24:51 and Acts 1:2 say Jesus was taken into heaven many languages have no distinction between the physical sky and the abode of God. When there is no distinction in terminology, it is quite unnecessary to try to translate οὐρανός always as the literal place God is enthroned.[66]

The term "ascended" is used twice by Paul in Eph 4:8, 9, as Paul explains what Christ had already done for believers. It is also used in the Gospel of John and Revelation. In John 20:17, the term "ascended" is in the past tense and again "ascending" is in the present active. In the book of Revelation, verse 8:4 describes the "prayers of the saints" as they ascended to God out of the angel's hand, and in 11:12, of the two witnesses ascending upward to heaven in a cloud. The final reference to the term "ascended" as how it is used in John 3:13 becomes rather confusing when seen in the perspectives of Enoch, Elijah, and perhaps Moses going upward to heaven.[67]

Another English term also used to describe Jesus's transition from earth to heaven is "assumption." However, the *ascension of Christ* has become the traditional way of referring to the event.[68] Uniquely to the term that is not used in Luke-Acts is John's reference to God's two witnesses. They follow a similar pattern as Christ in persecution. They are killed in the same city as was Christ, resurrected, and ascend to heaven in a cloud, while their enemies look on.

---

64. Comfort and Barrett, *Text of the Earliest New Testament*, 2:75.
65. Westcott and Hort, *New Testament*, 186.
66. Newman and Nida, *Handbook on the Acts of the Apostles*, 20–21.
67. "No man hath ascended up to heaven, but he that came down from heaven, [even] the Son of man which is in heaven" (John 3:13 KJV).
68. Brasfield, "Jesus, Ascension of."

Reminiscent of this ascension, the disciples of Christ looked on as he ascended to heaven in a cloud.[69]

Idiosyncratic Locution of Christ's Ascension Reminiscent of Luke-Acts

There has been much debate about Luke's apparent usage of the clause "into heaven" in recent scholarship. Some arguments ensued insisting that the clause is missing in some salient manuscripts containing Luke's Gospel, and it is therefore unlikely that it was original to him.[70] Amos Wilder argued that the omission by the Western text happened because of a desire to minimize the difficulty presented in Acts 1:3 regarding the amount of time Luke said was forty days.[71]

Sinaiticus provides an additional witness to the NT. It is said that in 1844 the German scholar Constantin von Tischendorf obtained it from monks at St. Catherine's Monastery, Mount Sinai.[72] Tischendorf had come to believe that four scribes originally produced it wherewith he labeled them scribe A, B, C, and D.[73] After further reinvestigation conducted by textual critics Milne and Skeat, the conclusion was that only three scribes were responsible for the copying. Comfort affirms that Milne and Skeat's research demonstrated that scribe D of Sinaiticus was likely the same person as scribe A of the Vaticanus.[74] Accordingly, scribe D was not as careful because of omissions of the ascension in the Gospel and Acts.[75]

Fitzmyer conceded that the clause exists in most MSS but confessed that it is missing in Sinaiticus and Bezae. Westcott and Hort suggested the longer reading to the critical apparatus beginning in the 1881 publication of a critical edition of the Greek NT, and others followed by either bracketing or omitting the clause in other modern

69. Brasfield, "Jesus, Ascension of."
70. Parsons, "Text of Acts 1:2," 409; Brasfield, "Jesus, Ascension of."
71. Wilder, "Variant Traditions," 311.
72. Comfort, *Encountering the Manuscripts*, 77.
73. Comfort, *Encountering the Manuscripts*, 78.
74. Comfort, *Encountering the Manuscripts*, 78.
75. Comfort, *Encountering the Manuscripts*, 106.

critical editions.[76] Modern translations of Luke's Gospel represented by P[75] (Bodmer XIV–XV) contain the clause in addition to *lectio difficilior*, which prefers the longer rendering in the verse.[77]

Metzger concedes how the longer reading is preferred based on rhythmic readings requiring it, such as the opening reference in Acts 1:1. And the omission in Sinaiticus and Bezae was due to an accidental scribal oversight or a deliberate removal to relieve the apparent contradiction between Luke and Acts; and based on an earlier argument that appears to place the ascension late Easter night in the Gospel and forty days after Passover in Acts.[78] Either way, the Acts account (1:1) refers to the Gospel of Luke where he wrote all about what Jesus taught and did up to the day he literally ascended up to heaven.

The ascension of Christ serves as an irregularly haphazard transition between both volumes, Luke-Acts, yet it connects both together and those to the same author. Acts picks up where the ascension narrative in the Gospel leaves off, yet both narratives overlap, and Acts retells it in a different way. Acts 1:3–5 repeats Luke 24:49 by retelling Jesus's command to the disciples to remain in Jerusalem until they receive the Holy Spirit. After the resurrection, Jesus presented himself alive for forty days, which seemingly placed the Acts version of the ascension much later than it appears in the Gospel. To harmonize the two apparent differences, it is conceivable to take the Acts version as being further expressed rather than seeing it as a mistake or contradiction.[79]

Several arguments have been elicited to reconcile the case of Luke's forty days in Acts and its lack of support in the Gospel. Luke's focus in the Gospel is on Jesus's human origin, his ministry, death, resurrection, and ascension. Jesus's focus in Acts begins with the apostles who already know the former and are perhaps the source of Luke's dossier.[80] Even though the ascension connects both volumes,

76. Fitzmyer, "Ascension of Christ and Pentecost," 409; Brasfield, "Jesus, Ascension of."

77. Parsons, "Text of Acts 1:2," 58.

78. Metzger, *Textual Commentary* (1994), 162–63; Brasfield, "Jesus, Ascension of."

79. Brasfield, "Jesus, Ascension of."

80. O'Day and Petersen, *Theological Bible Commentary*, 325.

his focus shifts specifically from Jesus's earthly ministry to the ministry of the apostles.

The ascension narratives in the Gospel and in Acts differ because both narratives contain a direct dialogue between Jesus and the Eleven in Acts (1:1–9) where Luke likely records these as speeches. For Zwiep, Jesus is the new Elijah in Acts 1, as confirmed by the parallels between Acts 1:6–14a and 2 Kgs 2; whereas he did not intend to portray Christ as the new Elijah in Luke 24:50–53, but as the new high priest of a new covenant for everyone that comes to him by faith.[81] Zwiep identifies no parallels to Luke's forty days in Acts in any Hellenistic ascension stories, but rightly so, because he presents only Jesus as divine, and sets him apart from all other ascension stories.[82]

The OT Pentecost was fifty days after Passover. Luke demonstrated how Jesus fulfilled both. He was God's Passover Lamb that delivers people from spiritual death, reminiscent of the blood placed over the door before the exodus, preventing the destroyer from entering (see Exod 12:13–28). It would make sense that Luke connected both events with Jesus's crucifixion in the Gospel and with Pentecost in Acts. To fulfill Pentecost would imply that the disciples waited in the upper room for ten days after the ascension until they were filled with the Holy Spirit, and indirectly implying the day of Pentecost stated in Acts 2:1 occurred exactly fifty days after the crucifixion (cf. Acts 1:3).[83]

Keener highlights how Luke 24:36–53 is recapitulated in Acts 1:1–14, as the points previously cast are repeated but in greater

81. Zwiep, *Ascension of the Messiah*, 32–33.

82. Zwiep, *Ascension of the Messiah*, 97. In biblical numerology, a continual series and accomplishment of forty days is recited throughout the Bible and is not unusual for Luke in Acts. For example, Noah (Gen 7:4), Joseph (Gen 50:3), Moses (Exod 7:7; 24:18; Deut 34:7; Acts 7:23), spying Canaan (Num 13:25), Goliath (1 Sam 17:16), Elijah (1 Kgs 19:8), Ezekiel (Ezek 4:6), Nineveh (Jonah 3:4), and Jesus (Luke 4:2; Matt 4:2). The collective similarity of numbers throughout the Bible reveals God working in time and working according to a divine plan and pattern to accomplish his purposes. Also see Brasfield, "Jesus, Ascension of."

83. The Bible has proven that God works his plans on earth by human calendars. Luke uses real numbers as markers to count the NT fulfillment of the OT Passover and Pentecost. But to connect the outpouring of the Holy Spirit with the day of Pentecost, the 120 disciples had to wait in the upper room for ten days to make the math work. Based on Luke's forty days in Acts 1:3, ten days after Jesus's ascension would place the day of Pentecost fifty days after the crucifixion.

detail.[84] In Hellenistic writing, it was common for historians to arrange and/or rearrange material in their own words, or perhaps to paraphrase themes in two-volume works. As Luke's theme of Jesus's ascension is told at the end of the first volume, it has been reiterated at the beginning of the second. In such cases, modern readers become aware of the different wording existing between the two volumes of the same work as a variation that was common in ancient writing for the sake of readability.[85]

The ascension theme at the end of Luke's Gospel was retold at the beginning of Acts but in more detail to suit his specific purpose.[86] Reading Luke-Acts, modern readers would notice the differences in wording when comparing both volumes. Ancient writers used such a style for the sake of readability, which should not been seen as simply an accidental oversight or the work of a later redactor. For Keener, it would be a mistake for modern readers to interpret such differences as an accidental oversight, mistake, error, or inaccuracy, and for them to read their modern expectations of verbatim quotation into ancient works that writers and readers in Luke's day did not do themselves.[87]

Luke ends his Gospel with the prompt ascension narrative to present it as the final step in several key points of Jesus's earthly existence, for as much as the ascension is a closure, it is also a beginning. In the second volume, it becomes the opening scene that connects the Holy Spirit to the ascension of Christ and to the apostolic ministry and progression of the Gospel. Whereas Jesus was the main figure in the entire first volume, Luke is intent on making the Holy Spirit the main figure for the entire second volume.[88]

---

84. Keener, *IVP Bible Background Commentary*, 585.

85. Keener, *IVP Bible Background Commentary*, 585.

86. The ascension narrative at the end of Luke's volume 1 and at the beginning of volume 2 is understood as God's shifting to the next phase in kingdom work. At the end of Jesus's earthly ministry, and the beginning of the ministry of his apostles, was God's transition to the practical ministry of the church; where Jesus was no longer present on earth in physical form, the church became Christ's representatives and ambassadors to carry out Christ's task of discipleship (Matt 28:19).

87. Keener, *IVP Bible Background Commentary*, 585.

88. Brasfield, "Jesus, Ascension of."

Idiosyncratic Locution and Terminology Reminiscent of Luke-Acts

The word "ascension" has different meanings based on the way it appears in different passages of Scripture. The context where the word appears will always reveal the correct meaning behind the author's intent of using the specific word to express the point being made as it is used in a passage. It follows that this word does not always have the same meaning on every occasion when used in and outside of the Bible. Fuhr and Köstenberger identify this as a contextual principle.[89] Some terms used in the NT and LXX that describe ascension are as follows:

Βαθμ- from the root βαθμ(-ός), was a structured rest for the feet that marked a stage in ascending (going up) or descending (going down) to the high place of a monarch.[90] When used as βῆμα, again it identified a dais or platform steps that assisted in walking upward to a throne.[91] A step does not necessarily have to equate to a *dais* of a high person or monarch. But βαθμός is usually associated with steps used for going up to something.

ἐλεημο- from the root ἐλεημοσύν(-η), identifies alms as they went upward to God in heaven, and those memorial acts (alms, prayers, praises, etc.) as they go up to or before God and are remembered by him (Acts 10:4).[92] Ἐλεημοσύνη involves pity or an act of kindness on behalf of the giver. People render things to God and they go up to him in heaven (e.g., Acts 10:4). The word can be translated as ascended to God in heaven.

ἀναβαίν- from the root ἀναβαίν(-ω), implies an upward motion as going up, to ascend. As a verb (-ω), it means "I go up [into heaven]," εἰς (τοὺς) οὐρανούς or εἰς οὐρανόν. In addition, he [Jesus] "was taken up" (ascended) "into Heaven" in Acts 1:2, specified when the text is

---

89. Fuhr and Köstenberger, *Inductive Bible Study*, 23.
90. BDAG 162.
91. BDAG 175.
92. BDAG 316.

translated from ἀνελήμφθη,⁹³ in contrast to ἀνεφέρ(-ετο) as in Luke 24:51, meaning "[Jesus] was carried up [into heaven]."⁹⁴

ἐπήρθ- from the root ἐπήρθ(-η), as it is used in Acts 1:9 is literally in the sense that "he [Jesus] was taken up." Furthermore, it means in context that Jesus is taken up to heaven (see Luke 24:50–53; Mark 16:19–20; Acts 1:9–11). Furthermore, Jesus was taken up to heaven (Luke 24:51), departed from them (Luke 24:51), and was "taken up from you into heaven" (Acts 1:11). πορευ- from the root πορευ(-ομένου), as in Acts 1:10 means "as he was going." And ἀναλημφθ with -εἰς is "having been taken up." The root ἀνάληψη and "going up" or "an ascent" from the root ἀνάβαση are also terms translated from ascension.⁹⁵

λαμβάν- from the root λαμβάν(-εται), slightly changes the meaning as "to take" or "to take up."⁹⁶ Several words are translated from the root that specifies a specific ending. Λαμβάνω, for example, becomes a verb meaning "I take or receive from someone else." When used with -εται, the meaning slightly changes whereas the context reveals the author's meaning of the term. Λαμβάνεται, when used to describe the ascension of Christ, would imply that someone was to take up Jesus to heaven. It would not fit the context because Jesus simply ascended with no mention of his being assisted by anyone else.

In the *Inductive Study Bible*, Fuhr and Köstenberger say, "the text of any portion of Scripture must always be understood within the confines of its historical-cultural, literary, and theological-canonical context."⁹⁷ This would affirm that words at the time of the author carried different meanings based on history and culture during the time the author lived who wrote it. One problem with the term "ascension" is that the word is not used in modern English translations of Luke 24 and Acts 1, but rather is translated "carried up" or "taken up."

In the context of Jesus either being taken up to heaven or his going up to heaven in Luke 24:51 and Acts 1:1–2, 8–10, the term used in every instance of heaven is οὐρανόν. In Luke 24:51, Jesus was

93. BDAG 58.
94. BDAG 58.
95. BDAG 58.
96. BDAG 1038.
97. Fuhr and Köstenberger, *Inductive Bible Study*, 23.

carried up to heaven. As it is used in the Gospel, ἀνεφέρετο οὐρανόν is the exact wording that is also used in Acts 1:1–2. Most English translations switch the wording in Acts 1: 8–10 to "taken up" and "going up," yet different Greek words are used to describe it. For example, Acts 1:9 (ἐπήρθη) and 1:10 (πορευομένου) both mean "he [Jesus] was taken up," whereas the direct object again is οὐρανόν. Another different yet synonymous term used in verse 9 is πορευομένου (as was going up). Finally, ἀναλημφθεὶς in verse 11 means having been taken up is a completed action.

Takeaways and Moving Forward

Leading up to this point, chapter 6 investigated the travel narratives and major themes within Luke-Acts. Ascension terms, their use in biblical and extrabiblical writings, and in classical and Greco-Roman literature were examined in this chapter. Chapter 8 further explores the connection between Luke 24:45–51 and Acts 1:6–11 as the main or primary chiasm between Luke and Acts that conjoins both volumes.

Using John H. Sailhamer's expression of two garments being sewn together at the seams, Luke-Acts is stitched together at a seam, in a similar fashion to two pieces of a quilt being sewn together at the ends of their edges, making the quilt one garment. When considering how two quilts (or two garments) are stitched or sewn together to make one garment, chapter 8 will use this same analogy to sew together both volumes, thus making one book as the author intended.

Furthermore, this example of sewing and stitching garments together is metaphoric as well as practical. For instance, the left quilt piece is the ascension narrative in the Gospel of Luke, and the right quilt piece is the ascension narrative in the Acts of the Apostles. The ascension is the thread that holds together the two narratives, and the Holy Spirit is the needle. The use of chiasmic concepts in the construction of Luke-Acts aids in determining the key points of a given passage, which, in some occasions (but not always), are revealed in the middle of the chiasm.

The concept was seen in chapter 4 where Luke placed Christ's arrival at the epicenter, the temple in Jerusalem. In the fulfillment of Malachi's prophecy (3:1) that the Lord would come to the temple, the prophet did not say the Lord would come to it to be condemned by his people and crucified. But it did indeed happen (cf. John 1:11), as Luke's Gospel becomes a transition from the last OT writing prophet, Malachi.

Luke 9:51 is a primary verse that helps understand Jesus's desire. He set his face like flint toward Jerusalem to be crucified. As he continued pressing forward to accomplish his mission, there was nothing on earth that could deter or stop him. The Gospel comes into the chiasm by bringing Jesus from Galilee to Jerusalem, and Acts goes out of the chiasm by going outwardly from Jerusalem to Rome. The ascension of Christ demonstrates how the chiasm helps us understand Luke's intentions.

Preliminary Survey of Chiasmus

In biblical studies, the modern era of scholarship has seen an awareness of a chiastic arrangement in the study and composition of ancient writings. It is inverted parallelism as generally seen in the study of ancient prose and poetry. In a chiasm, the second part of the passage is inverted and balanced against the first part.[98] John Breck says it exists in a rhetorical form where key words and concepts are constructed in synonymous, antithetical, or inverted parallelism about a central theme.[99]

Chiasmus structures were used widely in the prose of ancient Semites and had originated in their poetic literature.[100] They are also seen in the Hebrew poetry of the OT in parallelism, which is the relation between lines in a message consisting of but not limited to rhyme, assonance, repetition, and refrains in the written or spoken message. It is such that the entire message is structured based on the terms of a chiasmus. It is important to see the importance of the

---

98. Welch, *Chiasmus in Antiquity*, 9–10.
99. Breck, *Shape of Biblical Language*, 21.
100. Breck, *Shape of Biblical Language*, 21.

chiasmus to recognize the central theme of the passage that seeks to prevent readers from distorting it.[101]

The interpretation of Scripture requires the readers to detect as well as recognize the chiastic patterns that exist in specific passages containing them.[102] Unlike today's rules and principles of writing, the Bible is a combination of ancient and Hellenistic writing that is much different from modern style and rules of grammar today. The Scriptures, therefore, should not be read in a modern context for interpretation and understanding. The chiastic structures in biblical passages also contains strophes of at least three lines that are arranged about a pivot or conceptual center, such as: A:B:B′:A′ or A:B:C:C′:B′:A′ and etc.[103]

First Example

    A—Jerusalem (Luke 19:28—24:12)

        B—Ascension (Luke 24:50-53)

        B′—Ascension (Acts 1:1-11)

    A′—Jerusalem (Acts 1:12—8:3)

Second Example

    A—Jerusalem (Luke 19:28—24:12)

        B—Ascension (Luke 24:50-53)

             C—Jerusalem (Luke 24:33-53)

             C′—Jerusalem (Acts 1:1-5)

        B′—Ascension (Acts 1:6-11)

    A′—Jerusalem (Acts 1:12—8:3)

In addition to the main chiasm (Christ's ascension), there are other chiasms such as a beginning, middle, and ending or main (primary) chiasm. The main chiasm is also a rhetorical literary device as

---

101. Breck, *Shape of Biblical Language*, 17–20.

102. Breck, *Shape of Biblical Language*, 17–20.

103. Breck, *Shape of Biblical Language*, 33.

it is used to understand how both volumes are connected. The note on the importance of forming chiasms in chapter 8 makes the analytical work of chiasms a focus of this book. Finally, the forming and development of a chiasm between Luke-Acts is important to the thesis of this book because it finally proves the case of this argument and finally conjoin volumes 1 and 2 together as one book.

Chapter 8: Stitching Luke and Acts Together at the Seams

IN BOTH ANCIENT AND modern eras, the concept of sewing and stitching is common. Just as the careful interlacing of threads binds disparate pieces of fabric into a coherent whole, so too can the art of narrative stitching bind together related or unrelated events, characters, and themes into a unified literary tapestry. When authors sew together stories, characters, or themes, they essentially craft connections, interweave backgrounds, and bind beginnings to endings.

In this pursuit to understand the unity between Luke and Acts through the metaphor of sewing and stitching, the significance of tangible practices in ancient societies aids in this understanding. The symbolism associated with sewing and stitching signifies unity and cohesion.[1] Delicate narratives used with correlations can bridge gaps in time, space, and perspective, while constructing seamless transitions and enhancing the cohesiveness of stories.[2]

Sewing and Stitching in Literature

Sewing, as in literature, explains nothing is arbitrary because each stitch, like each word, is chosen with intent, placed with purpose, and executed with care. It mirrors the meticulousness with which the biblical authors threaded together their narratives. The literary

---

1. Barber, *Prehistoric Textiles*, 53.
2. Clayton, *Penelopean Poetics*, 34.

metaphor goes back to the ancient practice of the craft of storytelling itself. It underscores the beauty of interconnection and intertextuality in the art of weaving multiple threads into a unified whole, constructing the skillful balance between individual components and overarching narratives, by merging disparate pieces into a unified, coherent whole with intent and purpose.

In the composition of large works like Luke-Acts, where Luke's narratives, themes, and sections are sewn or stitched together to construct a complete and interconnected literary quilt, each stitch is likened to a careful, thoughtful analysis and interpretation of a text, bringing together many literary elements.[3] Sewing and stitching in Luke's literary design structure is the process of contextualizing individual narratives within the broader biblical narrative where common themes are identified and different parts of the text are balanced.[4] It suggests an active, intentional effort on his part to construct a seamless narrative where each element is carefully positioned to the others.[5]

Like the intricate patterns of a quilt, Luke's narratives are woven with myriad threads of history, theology, prophecy, speech-acts, testimony, rhetoric, narrative, and literary criticism. Therefore, Luke and Acts are like two individual fabric pieces, each unique in design, texture, and color as they exist in two volumes. When they are joined, they form a unified, cohesive whole.[6] Classical texts are filled with references to sewing and stitching, including weaving as metaphors for fate, destiny, and the intricate designs of life. Using textual analysis, scholars unstitch texts to understand their components, only then to restitch them to explore how the parts coalesce into a larger unified narrative.[7]

Additional examples are seen in classical works such as Homer's *Odyssey*, for instance, which features Penelope weaving and unweaving a burial shroud, which is a literary motif representing hope,

---

3. Fuhr and Köstenberger, *Inductive Bible Study*, 23.
4. Stephens and McCallum, *Retelling Stories*, 30, 56, 85.
5. Rhoads et al., *Mark as Story*, 63.
6. Stephens and McCallum, *Retelling Stories*, 34; Barthes and Marshall, "Textual Analysis," 143, 163.
7. Stephens and McCallum, *Retelling Stories*, 1–11.

deception, and the passage of time.⁸ In Shakespeare's tragedies, the interconnectedness of events and the inevitable convergence of paths can be likened to the act of sewing, where each stitch is deliberate and foretells the unfolding of the narrative.⁹

The physical and literary practice of sewing and stitching is intrinsic to human civilization since ancient times when the Lord used animal hides to stitch together clothing for Adam and Eve (Gen 3:21).¹⁰ The quilt also has long been an object rich in cultural, historical, and metaphorical significance.¹¹ Proverbs 10:12 says: "Hatred starts fights, but love pulls a quilt over the bickering" (MSG). The writer is not referring to a literal physical quilt, but the power of love. Just as a quilt serves as a wall for privacy and protects the body from the cold, love is like a quilt that protects one from hatred.

Another with specific theological connotations is where the psalmist, in 139:13, says, "For you created my inmost being; you knit me together in my mother's womb" (NIV). The metaphor of God as a weaver or seamstress knitting together a human being in the womb expresses the intimate involvement of the divine in the creation and sustenance of life. It also signifies repair and restoration. The act of mending a torn garment by sewing it back together is a potent symbol of healing and stitching (cf. Jer 14:19; Col 2:2).

Such processes mirror the way stories of old are sewn together to form a cohesive whole. Each thread, like each event in a narrative, has its place and purpose as constructed by the author. The quality of the thread and the stitchwork, like the integrity of a narrative and its elements, contribute to the overall strength and appeal of the final product. As disparate pieces of fabric were joined together to form a coherent whole, so too were the pieces of a story stitched together to construct a unified narrative.

Such varying threads resonate in the context of forming other narratives from parables, teachings, and historical events, as they are carefully woven together to form the tapestry of sacred texts.

8. Clayton, *Penelopean Poetics*, 34.
9. Stephens and McCallum, *Retelling Stories*, 255–59.
10. Barber, *Prehistoric Textiles*, 23, 51, 79.
11. Shaw, *Quilts*, 158.

When applied to the context of Luke and Acts, it serves as a powerful metaphor for the intricate narrative construction and unity that bind his two volumes together. By appreciating this metaphor, readers gain a deeper understanding of the thoughtful structuring of the Lukan corpus and its overarching themes of unity, continuity, and divine orchestration.

The Metaphor of the Quilt: Luke, Acts, and the Ascension Narratives

The ascension narratives at the end of the Gospel and the beginning of Acts serve as two quilt pieces, and the ascension is the thread down the seam connecting them into a unified narrative that is more than just its parts. It is through this process of stitching that the unity between them is illuminated. The two texts, read independently, offer unique insights into the life of Christ and the life of the early church. When read together, and when the seam between them is carefully examined, the two volumes reveal a coherent, interconnected narrative that extends from the earthly ministry of Christ to the apostles in Acts uniquely stitched together by Christ's ascension.

The metaphor of sewing and stitching in Luke's narrative in the ministry of Christ and the nascent church elicits correlated symbolism worthy of examination and offers varied insights into the socio-cultural and religious fabric of ancient societies. They were not merely utilitarian tasks but also carried profound symbolic meanings, exploring a metaphor of sewing and stitching with new relevance.[12] Luke skillfully weaves together multiple narrative threads whose the metaphoric use is a compelling way to understand his narrative strategy. Like the seamstress, he stitches together the narratives of Jesus and the early church into a coherent unified whole, making the two inseparable pieces become one story. In a sense, he acts as a spiritual seamstress, stitching together diverse strands of narrative and tradition into a single tapestry.

Understanding this ancient practice and its symbolic relevance aids readers in appreciating the intricate narrative tapestry Luke

---

12. Barber, *Prehistoric Textiles*, 376.

constructs with his two volumes. His theological vision is akin to the making of a woven garment, a unity formed from diverse strands, held together by the needle of the Holy Spirit. The approach provides a robust, interconnected view of Jesus's ministry and the church's mission as the Holy Spirit empowers it.

The unity of Luke-Acts has been obscured by traditionally segmenting them into separate books as they exist today. It is clearer when the seam joining them is visible, whereas the depth of Luke's narrative is disclosed.[13] Stitching, then, becomes a central metaphor in the exploration of the unity of Luke-Acts. Like a careful hand guiding the needle and thread through fabric, he demonstrates a meticulous approach to sewing these two distinct volumes together.

F. J. Foakes-Jackson argues against this concept of a seam between the ending of Luke's Gospel and the beginning of Acts except that which is provided by the divisions into two books by the editor.[14] In addition, Rowe is also against the proposition of Luke-Acts being a single work on the basis that there is no hermeneutical practice that has been exhibited that Luke-Acts existed as one work in two volumes. On his basis of reception history, Rowe argues that no ancient author nor any NT manuscript in existence states a unity of Luke-Acts or even hints at this unity by placing Acts directly next to the Gospel of Luke.[15]

In contrast to Foakes-Jackson's view, this book and chapter argue an opposite approach to Luke-Acts, that there is indeed a seam where both volumes are joined together by the ascension of Christ. In contrast to Rowe's position, there is essentially no evidence to conclude that Luke and Acts were originally placed between the Gospel of John at their inception; but the opposite is true because the NT canon was

---

13. Foakes-Jackson is conflicted in his statement regarding the opening chapters of Acts as a continuation of the early tradition. He asks if it is a continuation of the traditions within the early community or a compilation of scattered accounts penned together from other oral sources. These are fair questions as well as contradictory if he concludes that the ascension narrative, Judas's replacement of Matthias in Acts, and the outpouring of the Holy Spirit at Pentecost are indeed regarded as continuing the tradition where Luke left off in the Gospel. See Foakes-Jackson, *Beginnings of Christianity* 2:138–39.

14. Foakes-Jackson, *Beginnings of Christianity*, 2:138–39.

15. Rowe, "Literary Unity," 449–57; Green, "Luke-Acts," 106.

not finalized until the fourth century.[16] They argue from such perspectives while appearing to pass over Luke's evidential preface that calls Luke's Gospel a former account of Acts (Acts 1:1a).

Green also identifies a problem in Rowe's argument. He says that Rowe has no grounds to claim that reading Luke-Acts together is to interpret their literary unity historically, essentially based on the premise of there being minimal evidence regarding how Luke and Acts were received by their first audiences, and that there is minimal evidence of how they were read in the second century.[17] "Reception history" has to do with the way Luke-Acts was received and read by the early church. It is one of the bolts in Spencer's four-bolted hermeneutical hinge that hold together their unity. The argument in this book is not for the way Luke-Acts was received and read, but what Luke intended on conjoining them.[18]

For Green, three internal aspects cementing the literary unity of Luke-Acts are based on their canonical, authorial, and theological unity.[19] Their canonical unity holds no disagreement for how both must be read as a narrative representation of their historical events. Second, their authorial or any disunity cannot be made apart from the question of narrative unity. And third, their theological unity is identified by the theological tensions within both volumes.[20]

Finally, the unity of both volumes is also sewn together by the two ascension narratives. In comparing the opening of Acts 1:1, it has similarity to other ancient texts when considering how they also contain examples of multi-volume works that are linked by a recapitulatory sentence at the beginning of their successive volumes. The literary relations between the two versions of the ascension story are how the story is presented in the text as it exists today.[21]

16. Metzger, *Canon of the New Testament*, 238.
17. Green, "Luke-Acts," 107.
18. Spencer, "Unity of Luke-Acts," 346–47.
19. Green, "Luke-Acts," 107.
20. Green, "Luke-Acts," 112–13.
21. For example, in reciting the recapitulatory statement used in Acts 1:1, Alexander cites the commentary of Apollonius of Citium on the Hippocratic De Articulos existing in three volumes. Alexander states that "the five volumes of Artemidorus Daldianus's Oneirocritica, and the writings of Theophrastus that are

While leading up to this point, now it becomes clearer how sewing and stitching goes beyond a simple metaphor. It serves as a hermeneutical tool that allows for a detailed examination of the needle (Holy Spirit), thread (ascension of Christ), and quilt pieces (ascension narratives) conjoining these two volumes. The contextual principle in the art of stitching also refers to contextualizing individual narratives within the broader biblical narrative, identifying common themes, and exploring connections between different parts of the text.[22]

Luke's Gospel is the first fabric piece. It presents a richly textured account of the life, teachings, crucifixion, resurrection, and ascension of Christ. Acts is the second fabric piece that charts the ministry of the apostles and the early days of the Christian church. It is a complementary narrative account of the gospel, and it provides a treatment of discipleship that reflects the life and teachings of Christ that are presented in the first piece.[23]

Before Jesus's ascension, he assured his apostles of the coming Holy Spirit, effectively passing the mantle of ministry to them and, by extension, to the church (Luke 24:45–49; Acts 1:1). Several terms (see chapter 7) used in both narratives translating ascension are ἀνεφέρετο (Luke 24:51), ἀνελήμφθη (Acts 1:2), ἐπήρθη (Acts 1:9), πορευομένου (Acts 1:10), and ἀναλημφθεὶς (Acts 1:11).

A possessive verb not listed but used to represent this approach from Christ's perspective meaning "I go up" is ἀναβαίνω. It is the same term John uses in 20:17: "I ascend unto my Father, and your Father; and *to* my God, and your God" (KJV). It is not only a transition but also a profound theological statement that marks the completion of Christ's earthly ministry, the beginning of his intercessory role in heaven (Heb 4:15; 7:25), and his forever reign as King of kings and Lord of lords (Rev 17:14).

The ascension narratives weaved the earthly life and teachings of Jesus to a lived-out practical expression and mission of his

---

linked by recapitulatory words describing a previous treatise as parts of a single work." See Alexander, *Acts in Its Ancient Literary Context*, 25.

22. Rhoads et al., *Mark as Story*, 73; Stephens and McCallum, *Retelling Stories*, 163.

23. Fitzmyer, *Luke the Theologian* (2004), 118.

followers, thereby making the ascension narrative a single cohesive chronicle.[24] Luke's meticulous narrative techniques, when viewed through the lens of this quilting metaphor, highlight his intention for readers to perceive and appreciate the Gospel and Acts as two pieces of a unified tapestry.[25]

Chiasmas: Establishing Connections and Unity Between Different Parts of a Text

Chiasmus is a rhetorical or literary figure in which words, grammatical constructions, or concepts are repeated in reverse order, in the same or a modified form.[26] A rhetorical device is quite often used in literature and particularly in biblical texts. Figures of speech quite often involve the repetition of concepts and ideas in reverse sequential order such as A:B:B′:A′ etc., thereby constructing a mirror image or crossing-over structure.[27]

Consider Luke 9:48: "For he who is least among you all is the one who is great" (ESV). Here, the structure can be laid out as:

A—least among you all
   B—is
   B′—is
A′—great

The example is a relatively simple instance, whereas a chiasm can often extend beyond the length of a single sentence, as seen in the prologue of John's Gospel (1:1–18). The structure envelops paragraphs, chapters, and perhaps even entire books where entire passages are shaped into intricate mirrored structures. They serve more than just aesthetic or stylistic appearances in texts, but underscore key themes that draw attention to the centrality of the message and balance the

---

24. Tannehill, *Narrative Unity of Luke-Acts*, 283–84.
25. Tannehill, *Narrative Unity of Luke-Acts*, 8.
26. Roisman, *Sophocles' Electra*, 23.
27. Thomson, *Chiasmus in the Pauline Letters*, 25.

interconnections within the different parts of the text while reinforcing the unity and coherence of the passage.[28]

One portion of Jesus's Sermon on the Mount contains a set of Beatitudes (Luke 6:20–26; cf. Matt 5:3–12). Each of the three sections (6:20–26, 27–36, and 37–49) presents a chiastic arrangement of his teaching. The first section addresses two types of people, the poor and the rich.[29] It centers on God's blessings flanked by promises and rewards. A second arrangement begins with a group of woe articles to those who choose wealth over Christ, flanked by the result of their choices (those who do not live by faith in Christ). Consider the first section, for instance: "Looking at his disciples, he said,"

> A—Blessed are you who are poor (Luke 6:20b)
> > B—for yours is the kingdom of God (20c)
> > > C—Blessed are you who hunger now (21a)
> > > > D—for you will be satisfied (21b)
> > > > > E—Blessed are you who weep now (21c)
> > > > > > F—for you will laugh (21d)
> > > > > > > G—Blessed is the persecuted for Christ's sake (22a)
> > > > > > > > H—Rejoice for your great reward in heaven (23a)
> > > > > > > > H'—But woe to you who are rich (24a)
> > > > > > > G'—for you have already received your comfort (24b)
> > > > > > F'—Woe to you who are well-fed now (25a)
> > > > > E'—for you will go hungry (25b)
> > > > D'—Woe to you who laugh now (25c)
> > > C'—for you will mourn and weep (25d)
> > B'—Woe to you when everyone speaks well of you (26a)
> A'—for that is how their ancestors treated the false prophets (26b)

28. Thomson, *Chiasmus in the Pauline Letters*, 25.
29. Garland, *Luke*, 271.

The literary arrangement above emphasizes the centrality of righteousness and unrighteousness. God's promises of blessings are imputed to those who place faith in Christ and his teachings, mirrored by blessings imparted to those who endure persecution on account of their faith, underscoring the unity and cohesiveness of the message. Those who do not live by faith in Christ are warned only to later reap a bitter end.

Returning to the metaphor of the quilt, a chiasm can be viewed as an additional form of stitching.[30] The meticulous crafting of these chiastic structures by Luke constructs a unifying literary and theological pattern that fosters an intricate connection and interdependence between Luke's volumes 1 and 2. A notable instance linking them can also be found in the treatment of the themes of Jerusalem, the Holy Spirit, and witnessing.

The final witness of Christ to the disciples and his ascension, followed by the descent of the Holy Spirit and the expansion of the Christian witness in Acts, all take place in Jerusalem. His ascension serves as a vital literary and theological tool in biblical texts, particularly in Luke-Acts. It is a rhetorical device, like the stitches in a quilt, that connects and unifies the narratives, emphasizing key themes, central messages, and the overall cohesion of the texts.

Metaphorical Analogy of Sewing and Stitching in the Unity of Luke and Acts

The same author wrote Luke and Acts to present a comprehensive narrative of the messianic life and ministry of the Lord Jesus Christ and the subsequent establishment and expansion of his church. To appreciate the intricate interconnectedness between them, the metaphor of sewing and stitching has been used to encapsulate the unity of the author's narrative beautifully and the purpose that ties both volumes together. While Luke ends with the ascension of Jesus, Acts picks up the narrative thread right there, with the apostles witnessing it.

Such a deliberate overlap stitches the two volumes together, ensuring that the reader understands them as two parts of a single

---

30. Thomson, *Chiasmus in the Pauline Letters*, 25.

narrative tapestry.[31] Like the process of stitching, which unites individual pieces of fabric into a coherent whole, Luke-Acts presents the life of Jesus and the story of the early church as interconnected pieces of the same narrative garment. The actions of Jesus and the apostles, the teachings of Christ, and the spread of Jesus's teachings through the church are all stitched together, forming a beautiful tapestry that portrays God's salvific plan unfolding through history.

The Thread of Christ's Ascension: Luke's former treatise was successful in taking Jesus from Galilee to Jerusalem. His second treatise achieves the same success in taking Jesus from Jerusalem to the capital of the empire, the doorstep of Caesar. It was important from this aspect for both narratives to join for Theophilus, similarly as thread holds together two separate garment pieces making them one. In like manner, Luke's intention for the Gospel and Acts to Theophilus (and for his readers) must grasp the entirety of Luke's two-volume narrative so that he (they) would know "the full truth about everything" (or the complete story), a story that started in Galilee and ended in Rome.[32]

The Acts narrative picks up at the end of the Gospel and ends with Paul under house arrest in Rome, "preaching the Kingdom of God and teaching about the Lord Jesus Christ" (Acts 28:31). Luke's unbroken hinge in reconciling the Luke-Acts ascension narratives presents a thorough account of the truth he received, making it easy to recognize counterfeits and alternatives to the beliefs upheld within the community of believers. Luke's thorough account would have made alternative accounts noticeable to readers.[33] The two ascension narratives (Luke 24:45–51; Acts 1:6–11) stitch both volumes together down their seams and join them together.

The Needle of the Holy Spirit: Just as thread holds together two separate pieces of fabric in a sewn garment, the Holy Spirit serves as

---

31. Tannehill, *Narrative Unity of Luke-Acts*, 231.

32. It is likely that many other existing accounts (see Luke 1:1) contained inefficiencies whereas God moved (inspired) Luke to write a detailed account by his direction.

33. The four Gospel accounts differ in many places because each writer gives an independent witness from his perspective on the events he is reporting. The uniqueness of the four Gospels is that not one of them contradicts the other, and they all harmonize together as the canonized fourfold Gospel.

the unifying needle that stitches together Luke and Acts. The Holy Spirit is integral to both volumes, guiding, empowering, and directing the actions of key characters. In the Gospel, the Holy Spirit descends on Jesus during his baptism, marking the commencement of his public ministry (Luke 3:22; Acts 10:38). In Acts, the Holy Spirit is poured out on the disciples at Pentecost, signaling the beginning ministry of the church (Acts 2:4).

The Holy Spirit's presence and activity link the earthly messianic ministry of Jesus and the mission of the church, serving as the divine needle that stitches together the book of Luke and Acts. The continuity of the Spirit's work underscores the theological unity of purpose between Jesus and the church, as the same Spirit empowered both to bring about God's kingdom on earth (Acts 10:38; cf. 1:8).[34]

Christ brought in the kingdom by his faithfulness and obedience to his Father, and the church participates in God's work of discipleship by proclaiming it through Jesus Christ, as his ambassadors (see 2 Cor 5:20). In addition to the twelve apostles to whom Jesus appointed the mission of the gospel message, it is likely that the total number was eighty-two (Luke 10:1). In addition, Paul says that more than five hundred disciples saw Jesus alive after his resurrection (1 Cor 15:6). Jesus ordained them to bring his word to all ἔθνος (gentiles). By Christ's appointment of them as his ambassadors and direct representatives, God guaranteed the accuracy and success of their mission through the Holy Spirit.[35]

The ascension of Christ and the descension of the Holy Spirit is a pivotal point captured only by John (16:7) that speaks to this regard. For the Holy Spirit to descend, Jesus first had to ascend, therefore making the ascension between Luke and Acts crucial and a critical link for both volumes to connect. The Holy Spirit is completely prevalent

---

34. God divested himself of some attributes in the incarnation such as omnipresence, omniscience, and omnipotence. As a human being, Jesus was limited to only one location at a time. According to Mark 13:32, he stated some things he did not know in his earthly form as a human being (he relied completely on the Father to reveal things to him). John 5:17 notes that Jesus works as the Father works, and on his own, he could do nothing even though he was God manifested in human existence (cf. 1 Tim 3:16).

35. Moseley, *Biographies of Jesus' Apostles*, 13.

and active throughout Luke and Acts, but one pivotal point how Luke connects him is Luke 24:49 and Acts 2:1–4.

The ascension is connected to the crucifixion and resurrection. Did Jesus's "promise of the Father" include the soteriological requirement proclaimed by Peter in Acts 2:38, or was it merely for the sake of being witnesses as seen in Acts 1:8? Being that the ascension, now the descension of the Holy Spirit as well, is connected to soteriology, as proclaimed by Peter in Acts 2:38, the necessity of his followers being baptized by the Holy Spirit appears to also have soteriological aspects tied to it (Luke 3:16; cf. Mark 1:8 and Matt 3:11).[36]

John's Gospel adamantly defends the idea that the Holy Spirit in the lives of Jesus's followers goes beyond the role of simply making them witnesses of Christ. As stated, the Holy Spirit will lead his disciples into all truth and righteousness (see John 16:13–15). The pivotal role of the Holy Spirit connects the Gospel and Acts. The helper would also teach them all things and bring all things Jesus taught them to their remembrance (cf. John 14:26). By having this connection, they were able to author and write the NT.[37]

Mending and Restoration—Sewing up the Old and the New: Another significant aspect of sewing and stitching is the mending of what is torn or broken. The metaphor of mending has great relevance from the view of Luke's vision of God's salvation history. He presents Jesus as the one who has come to mend the broken relationship between God and humanity, offering forgiveness and reconciliation through his sacrificial death and resurrection (see 2 Cor 5:18–20).

In Acts, the church carries forward this mission of mending, reaching out to both Jews and gentiles with the message of God's forgiveness in Christ. In this sense, Luke-Acts narrates the story of God's grand mending project, sewing together the old covenant and the new, the Jews and the gentiles, under the salvific work of Christ and the mission of the church. God's "salvation history" of the Jews (OT)

---

36. The baptism of the Holy Spirit runs prevalent throughout Acts and throughout all the Gospels.

37. Moseley, *Biographies of Jesus' Apostles*, 13.

and gentiles (NT) is Luke's big idea and theme that was pointed out in chapter 6 of this book and is precisely what Luke intended.[38]

The act of mending and restoration further underscores the unity of both volumes, though dealing with different historical periods participating in the same narrative of reconciliation and restoration initiated by God. The analogy of sewing and stitching provides a rich insightful metaphor to understand the united interconnectedness between Luke and Acts. Just as sewing and stitching bring together separate pieces of fabric into a coherent, functional garment, so Luke-Acts unifies diverse narrative threads into a cohesive image of God's salvation of the Jews and gentiles.[39]

The Ascension in Luke—The Pinnacle of Christ's Mission: The ascension narratives play a pivotal role in bridging the narrative gap between the Gospel and Acts by sewing or stitching together these two unique pieces of Luke's literary tapestry. By situating the ascension narratives within the context of these two volumes, the author strategically underscores the unity and continuity in his grand theological exposition.

In the Gospel of Luke, the ascension narrative comes at the end, not signifying the end of the book, but acting as the climax of Jesus's life and ministry. It is not just an isolated event, but the fulfillment of his mission on earth and the validation of his messianic claims. The ascension signifies his glorification, marking the completion of his earthly mission and paving the way for the inauguration of his church's mission (Luke 24:50–53). This is in addition to the theological plot Luke shares across both volumes.[40]

While standing on the Mount of Olives, Jesus gives his disciples final instructions, commissioning them as witnesses to his ministry, crucifixion, and resurrection, and promising them the Holy Spirit.

---

38. See chapter 6 in the section "Theological Parallels and Thematic Connections Between Luke-Acts" for a full discussion of how the first era of God's salvation history extended from the time of Israel in the OT to the time of Luke's narrative of John the Baptist, and essentially that John was the last of the OT prophets (see Luke 16:16).

39. Tannehill, *Narrative Unity of Luke-Acts*, xiii; Dunn, *Baptism in the Holy Spirit*, xiv–xv.

40. O'Day and Petersen, *Theological Bible Commentary*, 326.

The ascension, therefore, not only marks the end of his physical presence on earth but also becomes the transition to his replacement in the lives of his followers by the Holy Spirit. Such a grand finale in the Gospel is not merely an end but an essential transition.

The Ascension in Acts—The Genesis of the Church's Mission: While moving to Acts, the ascension is set at the outset (Acts 1:1–11), signifying a fresh beginning of God's salvation history.[41] Just as Jesus's birth takes place at the beginning of the Gospel, the birth of the church takes place at the beginning of Acts. The ascension at the Mount of Olives as confirmed by the two witnesses in Acts is the place in the Acts narrative where Jesus ascended and will also return (see Zech 14:4).[42]

The ascension, as it introduces Acts, marks the commencement of the church's mission. Significantly, it occurred in Jerusalem, the city where Jesus was crucified and resurrected, and where the Holy Spirit descended on the apostles and infilled them. Luke's geographical thread in his travel narratives (see chapter 6) links the crucifixion, resurrection, ascension, and Pentecost, establishing a narrative continuity from Luke to Acts.

The Ascension as the Stitching Thread: In the literary tapestry of Luke and Acts, the ascension narratives operate as the essential thread, stitching or connecting the two volumes into a coherent seamless whole. They form a unique narrative overlap between the two parts, indicating that Luke and Acts are part of a single, continuous story rather than two isolated ones. The ascension narratives mark the point of transition. It is the end of Jesus's earthly ministry in the Gospel and the start of the church's mission in Acts.[43]

---

41. The proclamation of the gospel in Acts begins moving away from the Jews in Jerusalem (Acts 1–7), who were rejecting it, to the gentiles.

42. Zechariah's proclamation of the Lord's return to the Mount of Olives is eschatological if a great battle is taking place preceding it. In Rev 16:16, John calls this the battle of Armageddon. Jesus's descent upon the Mount is where he last ascended from earth. The two men in Acts 1:11 confirm Christ's return to earth in the same manner he ascended. Zechariah's prophecy in 14:4 is an overview of the cataclysmic events that will happen in the last days that will accompany Jesus's physical return to Zion to put an end to unrighteousness and to inaugurate his holy reign in the millennium (see Rev 20:4–7). See Klein, *Zechariah*, 403.

43. O'Day and Petersen, *Theological Bible Commentary*, 327.

In this stitching metaphor, the ascension narratives hold the same crucial function. Just as a thread ties two or more fabric pieces together into a functional whole, the ascension narratives connect the narratives of Jesus's life and the nascent church, ensuring they are read and interpreted as an interconnected whole. The thread just being a functional element carries aesthetic significance. When carefully chosen, it can enhance the overall design and beauty of each stitched piece.

Similarly, the ascension narratives significantly contribute to the overall theological unity of Luke-Acts. In addition to the Third Gospel, which brings the OT story of Israel into the NT, Acts brings in Jesus and the church, there is salvation for all the world, and everything unfolds in the narrative under God's providential plan and will.[44] They highlight the handover of Jesus's proclamation of God's kingdom to the church under the guidance of the Holy Spirit, reinforcing the unity of purpose across these two narratives.

In essence, the ascension narratives serve as a powerful literary tool, skillfully employed by the author of Luke-Acts, to illustrate the continuity in God's salvific plan from Jesus's earthly messianic ministry to the church's earthly mission.[45] The repetition of the ascension, first as the denouement to the Gospel and then as the inception in Acts, is the stitch that secures the two volumes together, allowing them to function as a coherent, unified whole.

By utilizing the ascension narratives as the thread, Luke demonstrates his intricate narrative craftsmanship, knitting together his comprehensive account of Jesus's life and the inception of the Christian church. Luke's ingenious strategy encourages readers to approach the Gospel and Acts as a continuous narrative of God's salvation history rather than some disjointed standalone stories with a non-interconnected theological-historical narration of events.[46]

The role of the ascension narratives in Luke-Acts goes beyond merely documenting a theological and significant set of events in Christian history. Acting as the thread that stitches together the two

---

44. O'Day and Petersen, *Theological Bible Commentary*, 327.
45. Sleeman, *Geography and the Ascension Narrative*, 5.
46. O'Day and Petersen, *Theological Bible Commentary*, 326–27.

volumes, they illustrate the continuity of divine action from the life of Jesus to the early church, while underscoring the transition of the divine mission from the Messiah to his followers.[47] The development in understanding as much allows readers to fully appreciate the literary and theological unity in Luke-Acts, beautifully crafted in the metaphor of a meticulously stitched garment.

Luke's Use of Chiastic Structures as Rhetorical Devices and a Detailed Exploration of Some Chiastic Structures Present in Luke and Acts

As a skilled literary craftsman, Luke uses a variety of narrative techniques to shape his storytelling. One technique that prominently stands out in both the Gospel and Acts is chiasmus, which is a rhetorical device that structures ideas or phrases in a mirrored or reversed sequence.[48] The following section delves into the exploration of some chiastic structures present in Luke and Acts and their implications for interpretation.

Chiastic Structures in Luke and Acts: Some studies identify various chiastic patterns in Luke and Acts. The following does explore a few examples:

1. The Gospel of Luke: Some propose that Luke's entire Gospel can be seen as one grand chiastic structure. The key pivot point is Luke 9:51, "When the days drew near for him to be taken up, he set his face to go to Jerusalem" (ESV). Here, the journey to Jerusalem marks a significant turning point in the Gospel, with events and themes before and after this point mirroring each other in various ways.[49]

2. The Parable of the Good Samaritan (Luke 10:30–37): The well-known parable also exhibits a chiastic structure, centering around the compassion and action of the Samaritan. The structure can be outlined as follows:

---

47. Sleeman, *Geography and the Ascension Narrative*, 3.
48. Roisman, *Sophocles' Electra*, 23.
49. Murai, "Database System."

A—Man falls among robbers (v. 30),

    B—Both priest and Levite pass by (vv. 31–32),

        C—The traveling Samaritan sees and comes to his aid (v. 34)

        C′—The Samaritan takes action and continues care (v. 35),

    B′—Unlike those nearby, the neighbor was one rejected by Jews (v. 35),

A′—Jesus's command to go and do likewise (vv. 36–37).

3. Peter's Denial and Restoration (Luke 22:31–34, 54–62): Here, the predictions and outcomes of Peter's denial of Jesus form a chiastic pattern.[50]

A—Prediction of denial (22:31–34),

    B—Peter follows at a distance (22:54),

        C—Peter denies Jesus (22:57–59),

        C′—The rooster crows, and Jesus turns and looks at Peter (22:60–61),

    B′—Peter remembered Jesus's words (22:61),

A′—Peter weeps bitterly (22:62).

4. The Acts of the Apostles: It is also suggested that the Acts of the Apostles exhibit an overarching chiastic structure with the pivot point being Acts 15, the Jerusalem council; whereas the following examples elicit sort of a mirrored structure.[51]

A—The mission to the Jews in Jerusalem (chapters 1–7),

    B—The expansion of the mission (chapters 8–12),

    B′—The mission to the gentiles (chapters 13–21),

A′—And the journey to Rome (chapters 22–28).

---

50. Murai, "Database System."
51. Murai, "Database System."

Some also propose that Luke-Acts is itself organized in a chiastic arrangement. The correspondence of this chiasm is primarily based on a correspondence of the geographical setting in the travel narrative that began in Galilee and ended in Rome.⁵²

The Gospel of Luke

    A—Rome
        B—Jesus in Galilee
            C—Samaria-Judea
                D—Jerusalem

The Acts of the Apostles

                D′—Jerusalem
            C′—Judea-Samaria
        B′—Apostles in Asia-Minor
    A′—Rome⁵³

Significance of Chiastic Structures: Chiastic structures are not merely ornamental; they serve key functions in biblical texts such as:

1. Highlighting of Central Themes: The central point of a chiasm often carries significant weight, highlighting the main theme or message of the passage.

2. Linking of Ideas: They help connect related ideas and themes across different parts of a text.

3. Guiding Interpretation: The mirrored structures provide clues for interpreting passages, as parallel elements often illuminate each other.⁵⁴

Finally, the use of chiastic structures in Luke-Acts is an example of the author's sophisticated literary craftsmanship. Recognizing these

---

52. Louden, "Chiastic Arrangement," 138–39.
53. Louden, "Chiastic Arrangement," 138–19.
54. Welch, *Chiasmus in Antiquity*, 15, 259.

structures aids in appreciating the intricate composition of these texts and guides a reader's interpretation by illuminating connections and themes that might otherwise remain obscured or unnoticed. Using parallelism, balance, and particularly chiasmus is the awareness of a sophisticated literary technician.[55]

Front, Middle, and Back Chiasms, with Emphasis on the Back (or Primary) Chiasm

The front, middle, and back chiastic structures are recognized within the texts of Luke and Acts. It is essential to remember that the recognition of chiasmus requires a degree of interpretive sensitivity. Most of the focus here is particularly on the back or primary chiasm, which is often deemed the most critical and intricate for leading into the primary chiasm for this chapter that becomes the pivot or role to providing a smooth transition from the Gospel of Luke into the Acts of the Apostles, known as volume 1 and volume 2.

The Front Chiasm: The front chiasm generally covers the introductory sections of a narrative that sets the stage for the events to follow. Consider the following example as seen in the opening of both volumes:

A— Having a perfect understanding of all things from the beginning (Luke 1:3a)

    B—To write to you in order, most excellent Theophilus (Luke 1:3b)

    B'—The former treatise have I made, O Theophilus (Acts 1:1)

A'—All that Jesus began both to do and teach (Acts 1:3c)

The chiasm constructs a balanced symmetrical arrangement that emphasizes key points, elucidates cohesion, and underscores the unity of the text.[56]

---

55. Welch, *Chiasmus in Antiquity*, 199.

56. In the Gospel of Luke, the front chiasm can also be observed in the birth narratives of John the Baptist and Jesus (Luke 1–2). The births of these key figures, framed in a parallel yet contrasting manner, provide a counterbalance to the events that would transpire later. The scenes match each other in terms of the angelic

The Middle Chiasm: The middle chiasm often encapsulates the pivotal events or turning points of a narrative. In the Gospel of Luke, an instance of a middle chiasm can be identified in Jesus's journey to Jerusalem, while leaving Galilee, which begins in Luke 9:51 and concludes in Luke 19:48 (see the section in chapter 6 "Travel Narratives Through Luke-Acts"). In this section on the middle chiasm, a range of events, teachings, and encounters are arranged in a mirrored sequence around the central theme of discipleship and Jesus's messianic mission to the temple and then his crucifixion.[57]

The Back Chiasm: The back chiasm is the primary chiasm and is often seen as the most crucial and comprehensive in connecting the two volumes and spans the entire ascension narrative(s). The chiasm is the central pivot. Here, the actual description of Jesus's rapture is brief and concise and almost reflects a hymnal structure (*parallelismus membrorum*, chiasms).[58] Consider another example as seen in the opening of both volumes:

---

announcement, parents' responses, births, and prophetic rejoicing. The mirroring structure serves to underscore the distinct roles that John and Jesus will play in God's salvation history.

57. Jesus was not shy about his destiny in which the crucifixion became the most important event in his life and ministry. It is because it was the only plan by which God could save humanity from being lost forever. The canonical Gospels Matthew and Mark captured this notion when Jesus said, "Just as the Son of Man did not come to be served, but to serve, and to give his life as a ransom for many" (Matt 20:28; Mark 10:45) While defending his messianic ministry, he said, "You say that I am a king. The reason I was born and came into the world is to testify to the truth. Everyone on the side of truth listens to me" (John 18:37 NIV). The truth Jesus refers to is the OT prophecies that proclaimed him as the Messiah. The Messiah came into the world to be crucified and to die for the sins of all humanity.

58. Zwiep, *Ascension of the Messiah*, 18.

The Ascension—Luke 24:45–51

   A—The disciples' understanding opened to understand the Scriptures (24:45)

     B—Jesus express that the OT predicts his suffering and resurrection (24:46)

       C—Preach repentance and remission of sins from Jerusalem to all nations (24:47)

         D—Disciples made eyewitnesses of all Jesus accomplished on earth (24:48)

           E—Jesus's command to wait in Jerusalem for the Holy Spirit (24:49)

              F—Jesus led the disciples to a designated place and blessed them (24:50)

                 G—He blessed them and was carried up into heaven (24:51)

The Ascension—Acts 1:6–11

                 G'—The disciples ask Jesus if he would restore Israel's kingdom (1:6)

              F'—Jesus said the times or seasons are all determined by his Father (1:7)

            E'—Jesus reiterates they would receive the promise of the Father (1:8a)

         D'—Disciples commissioned to preach Jesus from Jerusalem to all nations (1:8b)

       C'—While commissioning them, he was lifted in a cloud from their sight (1:9)

     B'—As he was ascending upward, two men stood among them in white robes (1:10)

   A'—Jesus's second return to earth foretold as the same way he goes to heaven (1:11)

When reading the two ascension narratives in Luke and Acts, an acknowledgment of the chiastic structure presented above means that the reader must consider the context of the surrounding verses as well as the context of the matched verses from the chiasm. Again, Luke places more emphasis on the ascension than any other canonical Gospel writer. The given chiasm contains seven sets of pairs in its structure. While highlighting Luke's literary structure and design, the Gospel primarily focuses on Jesus and his messianic ministry. In Acts, Luke intentionally constructs a seamless transition from the ministry of Christ to that of the apostles, stitched together by these two narratives seen in the chiasm.

In the Gospel, Jesus is the speaker and his speeches continue through Acts 1:1, where he gives instructions to the apostles, thereby setting the stage for the events that follow. Acts begin with a prologue like the Gospel, but it contains more introductory material that demonstrates how the volume picks up from the "former account" (NKJV's rendition); whereas this former account (volume 1) continues through the latter account (volume 2). Again, Luke continued writing volume 2 on a new scroll because the Gospel that was written on a previous scroll was too long to continue writing Acts on that same scroll. If the additional introductory material did not exist on the second scroll, the ascension narrative would naturally pick up in verse 1:6 of Acts.

Being the same event, Luke builds upon the Gospel narrative in Acts with this added detail, while he takes this opportunity to expand upon the latter events in the Gospel's version of it. In Acts 1:1, he tells how he wrote about "ὁ Ἰησοῦς ποιεῖν τε καὶ διδάσκειν" until the day Jesus was taken up to heaven. The phrase appears to be a little confusing because his apparent reference to Luke 24, following the resurrection, does not appear to relay "all that Jesus began to do and to teach." Jesus did a lot of things following his resurrection according to John 21:25, while John stated if the things Jesus did after his resurrection were written down, he supposed that the whole world would not be able to contain all the books that would be written of those things.

For whatever reason, Luke does not chronicle any great amount of detail from this statement he makes in Acts. In his latter or second treatise, he simply tells Theophilus that he had previously written about all that Jesus had done and taught until the day he ascended. To avoid any incorrect assumptions that would attempt to charge Luke with dishonesty or inaccuracy, a simpler way to resolve the apparent discrepancy would be to take his statement as a reference to the entire Gospel, rather than looking at it as a statement for a specific set of deeds done by Christ after his resurrection. Even though John said he did many things after his resurrection, Luke did not state them as he mentions in 1:1 of Acts.

Luke 24:45 (A) mirrors Acts 1:11 (A'): It is obvious to the reader that the Acts version contains more detail than the Gospel's version. In Luke 24:45, Jesus is the primary speaker, and it begins with what he was saying and doing; he opened their minds to enable them to comprehend all the events associated with his claims as Messiah and the OT Scripture that testified about him and all those things. He was present in the Gospel as a teacher and instructor to those who were present, even as the two strangers in Acts were present to the people to instruct them in the present and on things to come. In Acts 1:11, the two men (i.e., angels) are the primary speakers, and it ends with what they were saying and doing. The two angels were proclaiming to the spectators about things to come: the events surrounding Jesus's ascension, his future return, and that he will return to earth the same way he is going up to heaven.

Luke 24:46 (B) mirrors Acts 1:10 (B'): In Luke 24:46, Jesus reiterated the importance of his suffering as necessary to bring in the new covenant purchased by his blood during crucifixion (Matt 26:28; Heb 9:15–28). As God's sacrifice for sins, he did not offer the blood of any other but his blood to wash away sins. It was the task of the high priest as seen in the Mosaic law. In Acts 1:10, the prognostication of the two observable witnesses whom the Galileans did not seem to notice is to what Luke brings attention. Their appearance "in white apparel" signified a priestly ministry as seen in Lev 16:4. It also signified the beginning of Jesus's role as a heavenly high priest (see Heb 4:14–16). The white apparel worn by the angels mirrored the *bigdei ha-bad* (white linen apparel) worn by the levitical high priest on Yom

Kippur to atone for all the sins of the people.[59] The visual act by the angels pointed to Christ's ascended priestly role where he makes the garments of believers white in his blood.[60]

Luke 24:47 (C) mirrors Acts 1:9 (C'): In Luke 24:47, Jesus commands that the gospel of repentance and remission of sins be preached beginning at Jerusalem and extending to all the nations. In Acts 1:9, he commissions them to do the same before being lifted in a cloud from their sight. Jesus conferred authority upon his disciples. By the Spirit's enabling, the disciples are equipped to complete his commands in Luke 24:47. His being lifted in a cloud draws a similar picture of Elijah's ascension and his cloak falling to Elisha (2 Kgs 2:13). Elisha took up the cloak and continued in the prophetic anointing by dividing the water with it. Those observing the scene said, "The spirit of Elijah is resting on Elisha" (2 Kgs 2:14). In like manner, the Holy Spirit rested upon Jesus's followers allowing the continuation of his anointing for the task of discipleship. Christians were able to perform miracles with Christ's anointing upon them through the Holy Spirit.

Luke 24:48 (D) mirrors Acts 1:8b (D'): In Luke 24:48, Jesus had eyewitnesses, those he had chosen to be with him from the time he walked among them beginning from John's baptism to the time of his ascension (Acts 1:21–22). The disciples were directly taught by Jesus and learned directly from him to bear witness to his messiahship. The disciples were able to testify to Christ based on eyewitness testimony alone. They were commanded to preach about what they had seen about Jesus, that he is the Messiah. As such, in Acts 1:8b, Jesus commissioned and sent them to proclaim the gospel to the world. In Luke 24:48, the disciples witnessed the works of Jesus, which they were empowered to replicate in the Father's timing.

Luke 24:49 (E) mirrors Acts 1:8a (E'): In Luke 24:49, it is documented as the place of Jesus's choosing to pour out the blessing. And while he was blessing them, he departed from them and was taken up

---

59. Norris, *Unravelling the Family History of Jesus*, 166.

60. In the book of Revelation, the white garments given by Jesus to believers represented the righteousness of Christ bestowed upon them. In Isa 61:10, it was a figurative speech of salvation. In Acts 1:10, the spectators appeared more concerned with Jesus's ascending than the two prophetic angelic signs demonstrated next to them.

into heaven. Acts 1:8a is made possible by the disciples receiving the Holy Spirit. The sign of the NT age rests on the fact that his followers received the indwelling Holy Spirit, which fulfills the promise Jesus made to them.[61] Again, in Luke 24:49, he conferred "the promise of the Father" upon them in the place of his choosing, as he blessed them to receive it, fulfilled in Acts 2:1–4. The times and seasons of future events are all determined by his Father, and in Acts 1:8a, he reiterated to the disciples that they will receive the promise of the Father (Holy Spirit) to enable them to proclaim the message.

Luke 24:50 (F) mirrors Acts 1:7 (F'): In Luke 24:50, Jesus led them out to the Mount of Olives in the vicinity of Bethany, and "εὐλογεῖν αὐτὸν αὐτούς." The Gospel records this as Jesus's final act before he ascended. The blessing Jesus bestows upon them is the same as his breathing on them in John 20:22 and telling them to receive the Holy Spirit. Because times are under his Father's authority, he did not give them the specific date the promise would be fulfilled. Based on God's work in the past, they could have understood the time was near based on OT shadows of fulfillments. Christ was God's Passover Lamb (see John 1:29–34), and the Pentecost occurred fifty days after the Passover. In this way, the math could have been done for them to see when the promised fulfilment was going to take place.

Luke 24:51 (G) mirrors Acts 1:6 (G'): Acts 1:6 is a natural beginning of the ascension narrative in Luke's volume 2. It begins with a question posed to Jesus by his disciples. Verse 1:6 is symmetrical with Jesus blessing them before his ascension, and is confirmed in Luke 24:51 as preparation of his disciples to receive the Holy Spirit on the day of Pentecost (see Acts 2:1–4). John 20:21 and 23 are symmetrical, where Jesus blesses them with his authority. The direct commissioning of his disciples is also reflected in Acts 1:8, where he tells them that they will receive δύναμιν when the Holy Ghost comes upon them at the appointed place and time.[62] Acts 1:6 implies that Israel must suffer before it is restored to the former days of David and Solomon. It is not

---

61. O'Day and Petersen, *Theological Bible Commentary*, 366.

62. According to Luke 24:52–53, the disciples went back to Jerusalem to the temple praising God. It is a similar event following the ascension recorded in Acts 1:12, because after the ascension Luke says they went back to Jerusalem and spent all their time in the temple giving thanks to God.

a settled matter until the end of times, the time of the gentiles, a time that points to Christ's future return to earth seemingly referred to by the two angels in 1:10–11 in response to the question posed by the disciples in v. 1:8.[63] Jesus did not reveal the timing of his second coming, but the angels confirmed that he will come again, and at that time it would include the restoration of Israel as a kingdom.[64]

Resolving Discrepancies over the Word "Ascension": Two terms used in place of the term "ascension" occur in Luke 24:51 and Acts 1:11. Luke 24:51 says Jesus was taken up and Acts 1:11 says he was "carried up" (see the full discussion in chapter 7 in the section "Idiosyncratic Locution and Terminology Reminiscent of Luke-Acts"). The wording between the two narratives is not a contradiction in the text. Both terms accurately describe the ascension, and they do not change the meaning of the verse.[65]

---

63. The "Times of the Gentiles" was a result of Israel's failure under the Palestinian covenant (Deut 28:64) to obey YHWH, which resulted in judgment by the nations. Expressed by Daniel (2:36–44) and specifically by Jesus (Luke 21:24), it will not be completed until the second advent of Christ (Matt 24:29–30). Verse 1:8 was seemingly conferred by the two angels in Acts 1:10–11, where the gentile world power structures and those that oppose Christ's reign and rule will be destroyed at his second coming. Daniel symbolizes Christ as the stone in Daniel's vision, "cut out without hands" and returning to earth as "King of kings and Lord of lords" (Rev 17:14). See Unger, *New Unger's Bible Dictionary*, 728, 915, 1473.

64. The gospel of Jesus is preached to all nations by the indwelling Holy Spirit, who is also the orchestrator of present and future events. He expressed the OT predicted his suffering and resurrection on the third day. The apostles witnessed this and took note and assumed that Jesus's time of suffering was completed. In the same thought, they asked Jesus—now—if it was a time that he would restore Israel as its kingdom. A kingdom requires a king. It is the domain or dominion of a monarch. Jesus fulfilled the prophecy of Israel/Judah as the king who inherited David's throne (see Luke 1:32). Surprisingly, those posing the question to Jesus did not understand this at the time. Israel is restored as a monarchy when Jesus sits on David's throne in the millennium. Jesus replied that history had not yet been written and that such things they were asking him to do were governed by his Father. History or prophetic history was determined by God when the apostles received prophetic revelation regarding the future reign of Christ and when John wrote the book of Revelation outlining the future.

65. The original NT documents perished a long time ago. It happens as with other ancient documents due to the climate and the papyrus and vellum bearing the writing, which fell apart. The process of copying ancient texts by hand had to be completed for the preservation of those texts. It is estimated that roughly six thousand extant MSS of the NT have been preserved and are still in existence today.

Zwiep noticed how Luke used the cognate verb ἀναλαμβάνομαι in Acts 1:2, 11, and 22 the same way it was used in the standard LXX version of Elijah's ascension.[66] In contrast, another use of terms "to take" or "was taken [up]" that is also common in Acts is ἀνελήμφθη (1:2, was taken up), ἀναλημφθεὶς (1:11, has been taken), ἀνελήμφθη (1:22, was taken up). The words at the time of the author were synonyms based on the history and culture during the time the author lived. Words evolve similarly to languages, as new ones are invented and old ones die.

The English term "ascension" is not used this way in modern English translations of Luke 24 and Acts 1 but is translated as "carried up" or "taken up." In the context of Jesus ascending to heaven, the term describing heaven in Luke 24:51 and Acts 1:1–2, 8–10 is οὐρανόν. In Luke 24:51, when Jesus "ἀνεφέρετο εἰς τὸν οὐρανόν," it is the same wording also used in Acts 1:1–2 to express the action. To use the word "ascension" in place of "carried up" or "taken up" does not and will not change the meaning or anything in the text, like the way the word "rapture" is also used to express being "caught up" in the NT.

Most, if not all, English translations switch the wording in Acts 1: 8–10 from "going up" to "taken up," derived from ἐπήρθη (1:9) and πορευομένου (1:10), where both terms denote a fact that Jesus "was taken up" to οὐρανόν. Note that the term used in verse 9 is πορευομένου and is used to denote an observable fact about the event "as was going up." Finally, the term used to denote a completed action is ἀναλημφθεὶς in verse 11, denoting a fact in the present tense of "having been taken up." It implies additional actions that are to follow.

Papyrus was the bearer of the earliest NT texts. It was the writing material from which the word "paper" was later derived and was the most common material used for the transmission of writing. The Bible today is closed to anyone who is not committed to God. When putting together the Greek MSS from which today's Bible was produced, some in whole and others in part, enough information is given for anyone to know what was said by the original author of any book in the Bible. A letter or word here or there does not make or break an entire writing or document. If one manuscript says "Christ Jesus" and another one says "Jesus Christ," or one says "God" and another one says "he," it becomes a matter of semantics and does not support a falsity of an ideal of corruption during the copying process of these MSS.

66. Zwiep, *Ascension of the Messiah*, 84.

Additional Emphasis on the Back (Primary) Chiasm: In the Gospel of Luke, it could be suggested that a back chiasm could consist of the resurrection and ascension of Jesus (Luke 24:1–53). The events preceding and following this turning point mirror each other in several ways. For instance, the ministry of John the Baptist, which prepares the way for Jesus (Luke 3:1–20), is paralleled by the ministry of the apostles, who carry forward Jesus's mission (Acts 1:1–11). Similarly, the ministry of Jesus in Galilee (Luke 4:14–9:50) finds a counterpart in the spread of the gospel in Jerusalem and Judea (Acts 1:12–8:3).

The back or primary chiasm deserves special attention because it encapsulates the entire narrative framework that Luke intends to present. The central pivot is the resurrection and ascension of Jesus, which marks a radical shift from Jesus's earthly ministry to the church's mission. The transition, however, is not a rupture but a continuation of the work Jesus started in Galilee. The apostles, empowered by the Holy Spirit, carried forward the message "repentance and remission of sins should be preached in his name among all nations [ἔθνος]" (Luke 24:47), "extending it to the ends of the earth" (cf. Acts 1:8).

The understanding of this primary chiasm helps readers appreciate the unity and coherence of Luke's two-volume work. It underscores the continuity between the Gospel and Acts, suggesting that they should not be read in isolation but as integrated parts of a unified narrative. The ascension of Jesus serves as a thread, stitching together these two parts into a single, seamless exceptional garment.

The exploration of the chiastic structures throughout Luke and Acts, particularly the primary chiasm, significantly enriches the reading and interpretation of these texts. It enables discernment of the intricate narrative design, interconnected themes, and overarching message the author is conveying. They echo ancient literary techniques of rhetoric whereby Luke's application of such technique signals a conscious and deliberate effort on his part to present his two-volume work as a unified composition.

Role of Chiastic Structures in Establishing Unity Between Luke-Acts

While it is acknowledged that both volumes are penned by the same author (discussed in chapter 5), the understanding of their unity goes far beyond simply acknowledging the same hand on the pen behind them. Their unity is the product of a well-formed narrative and is maintained because the scenes and characters contribute to the author's larger story, which determines the significance of each part.[67] Through this use of chiastic structures, the significant insight gained into how they intricately connect and convey a singular coherent narrative thread further cements their unity.

First, the chiastic structures play a key role in linking the themes and narratives of Luke and Acts. By presenting parallel and mirrored events, characters, and messages across the two interconnected scrolls, Luke effectively interweaves them into a harmonious whole. Parallel themes not only unify the two volumes but also highlight the continuity of God's salvific work from the time of Jesus to the early Christian apostolic mission.

Second, the central pivot of the primary chiasm, the ascension of Jesus, represents a critical turning point in the narrative as a necessary event for the reign of Christ and the future resurrection and ascension of his followers. Rather than presenting a rupture, however, the chiastic structure emphasizes that the work of Jesus is seamlessly continued by his followers under the guidance of the Holy Spirit. The apostles, then, are not initiating a new movement; they are extending and taking the ministry of Christ to the ends of the earth as he instructed.

Third, the chiastic structures lend a sense of coherence and symmetry to the overall narrative of Luke-Acts. The use of chiasm helps to structure the narrative in a manner that is not linear but circular, with the beginning mirroring the end. The symmetry underscores the unity between the two volumes and reinforces the cyclic nature of God's salvation history, which Luke depicted from

---

67. Tannehill, *Narrative Unity of Luke-Acts*, xiii.

the announcement of Jesus's birth to the proclamation of his Gospel message of Christ to the world.

Finally, the author's chiastic structure(s) portray the connection between individual events and the broader narrative. Each story, character, and element of teaching, no matter how small, is not isolated but integrated into the larger narrative framework. The interconnectedness contributes to the unity and cohesiveness of Luke-Acts, highlighting the interconnected fabric of God's unfolding plan from the Jews extending to the gentiles.

Understanding Luke's Intention and Purpose in Using Chiastic Structure

Luke's meticulous application of the chiastic structure throughout Luke-Acts is not an accidental or mere artistic embellishment. It serves critical theological, pedagogical, and literary purposes. By scrutinizing these purposes, one can unravel his intention behind employing such a complex structural framework. Mirrored patterns and paralleled sequences of the ascension across the two volumes exhibit an overarching symmetry, underlining divine orchestration in the unfolding connectedness across the two narratives.

By structuring his narrative chiasmatically, he draws attention to this critical event, while emphasizing its significance in the Christian faith. The employment of the chiastic structure also serves a multi-fold purpose: theological, pedagogical, and literary. By weaving this complex pattern throughout his two-volume work, he can convey God's grand narrative of salvation, facilitate understanding and memorization of his narrative, and present a coherent, balanced, and aesthetically pleasing narrative.

Theologically, Luke's juxtaposition of the Luke-Acts ascension narratives is the smooth transitional pivotal point of Luke's primary chiasm. By positioning the ascension at the core of this chiastic structure, he underscores the centrality of these events to Christian belief. Moreover, it suggests that the mission of the early church is not an isolated event but a continuation of Jesus's ministry, revealing God's seamless plan of salvation.

Pedagogically, the chiastic structure aids in memory retention and comprehension. It was a vital function in an oral culture where written texts were scarce and most learning was transmitted orally. Repetition, parallelism, and patterns, such as the chiastic structure, would have made the narrative more memorable and easier to comprehend for the original audience. By structuring his narrative in a chiastic fashion, Luke was making his message more accessible to his audience, thus enhancing the dissemination of the Gospel.

Literarily, the chiastic structure of the many narratives lends a sense of order, coherence, and balance to the ascension narrative of Luke-Acts.[68] Each story, character, and teaching, no matter how seemingly insignificant, contributes to the broader narrative. The chiastic framework allows Luke to present a complex, multifaceted narrative with multiple characters, locations, and themes in a coherent, organized manner. The coherence and order not only enhance the aesthetic quality of the Luke-Acts ascension narrative but also attest to his skills as an author, historian, and theologian.

Finally, for Luke, the ascension becomes the central eschatological event for giving meaning to the whole of God's salvation history.[69] It is because Jesus is the embodiment of truth and his words are truth. He made promises that cannot be broken or left unfulfilled. The apostle John in his Gospel captured his words about the importance of his ascension. According to John, Jesus said, "This is why I am going away. The Holy Spirit cannot come to help you until I leave. But after I am gone, I will send the Spirit to you" (CEV). In Luke-Acts, Jesus continued reiterating this event as "the promise of the Father" (Luke 24:49; Acts 1:4).

Jesus's crucifixion, resurrection, and ascension are all connected. The use of the chiastic structure(s) throughout Luke-Acts, specifically regarding the two ascension narratives (e.g., Luke 24:45–51 and Acts 1:6–11), enables him to highlight the key themes and messages. Hence, Luke's chiastic structures are more than stylistic features for the sake of Hellenistic eloquence. They are also rhetorical

---

68. Bovon, *Luke the Theologian*, 515.
69. Bovon, *Luke the Theologian*, 82.

devices used to convey his message and achieve his purpose as a theologian and historian.

The Significance of the Ascension Narratives as a Bridge of Two Volumes

A robust examination of Luke's objective underscores his brilliance as an author, historian, and theologian and brings the church closer to understanding it. The λόγοι (Luke 1:4) beginning in the Gospel prologue suggests a kerygmatic schema of the later christological speeches in Acts where the salvation messages are conveyed. It is also to say that the objective was to confirm the Christian message of Christ.[70] This intentional structuring not only reinforces the unity between Luke's Gospel and Acts but also highlights his commitment to presenting a coherent and compelling narrative that affirms the fulfillment of God's redemptive plan in Christ.

By employing chiastic structures, Luke demonstrates his intention to write a detailed, organized, and coherent record ("an orderly account," Luke 1:3) of the major events and teachings that underpin Christian belief. Such structure(s) rhetorically influences the overall understanding of Luke and Acts. It serves to highlight key theological themes, unify the narrative, encourage deeper engagement with the text, facilitate oral transmission, and enhance the literary appeal of the work. It aids his audiences to gain a more profound appreciation of the narrative artistry and the in-depth nature of the theological message of salvation in Christ.

The ascension narratives, located at the juxtaposition of Luke's Gospel and the outset of Acts, possess paramount significance in NT scholarship. Not merely recounting Christ's departure, they bear dense symbolic, theological, and narrative weight. This is an exposition that endeavors to elucidate the significance of these narratives, positing them as the cohesive elements interlinking the Gospel and Acts, thus ensuring an uninterrupted narrative flow within the Lukan corpus.

---

70. Bovon, *Luke the Theologian*, 36.

1. Theological Resonance: Foremost, the ascension stands as a testament to Jesus's divinity and his earthly mission. It celebrates his victory over mortality and his esteemed position "on the right hand of God" (Acts 7:55) becoming a concrete realization of OT prophecies and a testament to his messianic role.[71]

2. Focus on the Holy Spirit: After the ascension, the descent of the Holy Spirit takes precedence in the experiences of the early Christian community. The ascension set the stage for Pentecost, allowing for the advent of the promised advocate, the Holy Spirit, ensuring Jesus's disciples receive the guidance and empowerment necessary to pursue the Great Commission.[72]

3. Linking the Two Texts: The ascension narratives act as the pivotal juncture connecting the Gospel and Acts. Luke's Gospel captures Jesus's terrestrial endeavors, while Acts maps out the formative years of the church. Through the lens of the ascension, it is perceived not as a culmination but as a shift from Jesus's teachings to the church's expansive mission.

4. Anchoring Apostolic Legitimacy: The ascension reinforces the apostles' credibility as they were Jesus's firsthand witnesses. Their proximity to his final teachings and his ascension equips them with unparalleled authority within the budding Christian community, marking them as bona fide witnesses of Christ.[73]

5. The Anticipation of Christ's Second Coming: The ascension introduces an eschatological perspective. The apostles, who observed Jesus's ascent, were assured of his promised return (Acts 1:10–11), instilling hope and anchoring Christian eschatological beliefs helping to guide their witness and warning others regarding things to come.[74]

6. Blueprint for Universal Evangelism: Following Christ's ascension, his instructions to his disciples were to wait in Jerusalem until they received the Holy Spirit, which validated personal

---

71. Johnson, *Luke*, 128–29.
72. Bovon, "Reception and Use," 391.
73. Keener, *Acts*, 17.
74. O'Toole, *Luke's Presentation of Jesus*, 132.

salvation and capacitated edification. It signaled and substantiated the divine call to global evangelistic mission destined to span from Jerusalem to the ends of the earth (Luke 24:47; cf. Acts 1:8b).

7. An Invitation to Action: Far from it being a passive spectacle, the ascension mandated the observers. The apostles, while witnesses of the miracle, were also entrusted and commissioned with a mission. The commissioning, bolstered by the impending Holy Spirit's power, beckoned Christians throughout generations to propagate Christ's commands of preaching repentance and remission of sins in his name actively (acclimated with teachings of love, redemption, and reconciliation).

8. The Balancing Point of Belief: The resurrection heralds Jesus's conquest over sin, death, and the grave, as it emphasizes his divinity. It becomes the axis upon which all Christian doctrine (all that are indeed based on NT doctrine) hinges, as they harmonize the intricate tenets of Christology.

9. Harmonization: All NT Scriptures harmonize, where there is no confusion nor contradiction in all that it says. The ascension narratives in the Gospel and Acts balance, depicting a single author whose text is an original scroll linking the ascension from the resurrection to the outpouring of the Holy Spirit. The chiasmus structure connects both volumes of Luke-Acts as a single book.

The Ascension—Luke 24:45–51

> A—The disciples' understanding opened to understand the Scriptures (24:45)
>> B—Jesus express that the OT predicts his suffering and resurrection (24:46)
>>> C—Preach repentance and remission of sins from Jerusalem to all nations (24:47)
>>>> D—Disciples made eyewitnesses of all Jesus accomplished on earth (24:48)

> E—Jesus's command to wait in Jerusalem for the Holy Spirit (24:49)
>
> F—Jesus led the disciples to a designated place and blessed them (24:50)
>
> G—He blessed them and was carried up into heaven (24:51)

The Ascension—Acts 1:6–11

> G'—The disciples ask Jesus if he would restore Israel's kingdom (1:6)
>
> F'—Jesus said the times or seasons are all determined by his Father (1:7)
>
> E'—Jesus reiterates they would receive the promise of the Father (1:8a)
>
> D'—Disciples commissioned to preach Jesus from Jerusalem to all nations (1:8b)
>
> C'—While commissioning them, he was lifted in a cloud from their sight (1:9)
>
> B'—As he was ascending upward, two men stood among them in white robes (1:10)
>
> A'—Jesus's second return to earth foretold as the same way he goes to heaven (1:11)

In essence, the ascension narratives, although occasionally eclipsed by other pivotal events in the NT, operate as a conduit of theology and mission bridging Luke and Acts, called Luke-Acts. They elucidate the smooth transition from Christ's ministry to the church's burgeoning mission, underpinned by the Holy Spirit's guidance. By appreciating the ascension's centrality, a comprehensive grasp of Lukan theology unfolds, highlighting God's master plan for humanity, initiated by Jesus and perpetuated by his disciples.

Shared Themes and Purpose of the Ascension Narratives

The ascension narratives, as presented in Luke-Acts, having both scrolls penned by the same author, are not mere historical records of an event. They are layered with theological, eschatological, and missiological significance. Revisiting these narratives is crucial in comprehending their shared themes and the overarching purpose they serve in the Christian narrative. Both narratives underscore Jesus's divinity and his unique status as God.[75]

The act of ascending to heaven, particularly in Luke's portrayal of Christ, reaffirms his divine origin and the fulfillment of his mission on earth.[76] Christ's ascent, as observed by his followers, was not only a testament to his overcoming death but also a reaffirmation of his exalted status. It vindicated him of the last words of the onlookers, "If you are king of the Jews, save yourself" (see Luke 23:37).[77] The final analysis of the NT proved that he had no desideratum of being saved whereas all others now look to him for the same.

The narratives, particularly in Acts, emphasize the promise of the Holy Spirit's imminent arrival. Jesus instructs his disciples to "stay in the city [Jerusalem] until you are clothed with power from on high" (Luke 24:49 NASB), while assuring them that they would be baptized with the Holy Spirit (see Acts 1:5).[78] The pneumatological promise underscored the shift from Jesus's earthly ministry to the Spirit-led movement of the church.

The ascension in both narratives is intrinsically linked to the mission Jesus entrusted to his followers, as in Luke he declares that the disciples are essentially "witnesses of these things" (see Luke 24:48), while in Acts, he asserts they will be his "witnesses in Jerusalem, in all Judea and Samaria, and to the ends of the earth" (see Acts 1:8). The ascension, therefore, is not an endpoint but a launchpad for global evangelism with eschatological undertones, that he is coming back to

---

75. Gallagher and Hertig, *Mission in Acts*, 319–20.
76. Gallagher and Hertig, *Mission in Acts*, 319.
77. O'Toole, *Luke's Presentation of Jesus*, 60.
78. Dunn, *Baptism in the Holy Spirit*, 100.

earth a second time but not as Isaiah's suffering servant (Isa 53) but as King, Lord, and Judge (see Rev 17:14).[79]

The eschatological promise proclaimed in the Christian witness is pivotal in shaping Christian expectation and hope. It is plausible for the ascension narratives as they are strategically positioned at the end of Luke and the beginning of Acts. The strategic placement of the narratives not only demonstrates continuity between Jesus's life and the early church's acts but also signifies that the church's mission is a direct continuation of Jesus's work.[80]

The ascension lends greater weight to the apostles' teachings and missionary endeavors in Acts. It serves as a transition from Jesus's earthly ministry to his heavenly intercession. As Heb 7:25 states, Jesus "always lives to make intercession" for believers. The two narratives, hence, transition Jesus from being a physical, tangible presence on earth to a mediating figure in the heavenly realms as the greatest high priest who abides forever.[81]

Finally, the two ascension narratives serve more than a historical function; they are thematic bridges that connect pivotal theological, eschatological, and missional concepts, reinforcing the unity and purpose of Luke-Acts as a singular, continuous narrative. By revisiting these narratives, one can grasp the intricate design of Lukan theology, which emphasizes continuity, promise, and mission, culminating in the person and work of Jesus and continuing through the Spirit-led church. Moreover, these ascension accounts function as a literary and theological hinge, demonstrating how Jesus's departure is not an ending but rather a transition that inaugurates the church's global mission, empowered by the Holy Spirit and rooted in divine commission.

Understanding the Ascension Narratives as the Seam and Thread That Unite Luke-Acts

The textual composition of Luke-Acts is a testament to the literary finesse of the author. Though nuanced in their narratives, they are

79. Gallagher and Hertig, *Mission in Acts*, 12.
80. Gallagher and Hertig, *Mission in Acts*, 316.
81. Crump, *Jesus the Intercessor*, 177, 199.

interconnected by an essential thread: the ascension of Christ. Much like the role of a meticulous stitch in a garment, the ascension acts as a bond, the thread that sews or stitches together the two garment pieces down the seam to make the two one, ensuring continuity while accentuating the individuality of each tome.[82] It involves the following.

1. Crafting Continuity: By situating the ascension at the end of the Gospel and the outset of Acts, the ascension's pivotal role as a connector is illuminated. As a thread melds fabric pieces, the ascension narratives render the progression between the books fluid. They uphold the storyline, bridging Jesus's teachings in Luke to the endeavors of the apostles in the nascent church era.[83]

2. Bridging Themes: Beyond mere linkages, the ascension serves as a thematic corridor. Luke's rendition encapsulates Jesus's terrestrial mission, asserting his divinity and realizing ancient predictions. Conversely, in Acts, it heralds the Holy Spirit's arrival and the genesis of the church's crusade. Its dual functionality fosters themes such as divine realization, the Spirit's promise, and the universal missionary call.[84]

3. Marking Shifts: Every stitch delineates a shift in the material. In parallel, the ascension denotes a shift in divine orchestration.[85] Luke orbits around Jesus by focusing on early portions of his life, ministry, death, and resurrection. Acts pivots toward the Holy Spirit, fortifying the apostles and pioneering new disciples. The ascension underscores this transition, tracing the journey from Christ's endeavors to the Spirit's undertakings.

4. Celebrating Unity Amid Distinctiveness: A meticulously sewn stitch preserves the essence of each cloth slice while integrating them. Similarly, the ascension narratives permit Luke and Acts to retain their distinctiveness yet underscore their literal relationship. While the Gospel is more christological-soteriological, Acts extends to more to a christological, pneumatological,

---

82. Schweizer, *Good News According to Luke*, 94.
83. Johnson, *Luke*, 27–28.
84. Lorenzen, *Resurrection and Discipleship*, 164.
85. Barrett, *God's Word Alone*, 245.

soteriological, ecclesiological, eschatological, missiological discussion.[86] The ascension is where these systematic theological trajectories converge, underscoring the synergy between Christ's redemptive acts and the church's vision.

5. Inviting Contemplation: A stitch also beckons introspection, allowing the beholder to admire the entirety of the garment. Within the Lukan framework, the ascension catalyzes reflection. It stimulates a retrospective assessment of Jesus's journey and kindles eagerness for the ensuing church saga.[87]

6. Affirming Apostolic Legitimacy: The ascension as witnessed by the apostles, portrayed in both texts, solidifies their mandate. The thread weaves their intimate encounters with Jesus into their Spirit-driven endeavors, augmenting the credibility of their missions.[88]

Mirroring the quintessential role of a thread in fusing fabric, the ascension narratives are paramount in discerning the synergy and rhythm between the Gospel and Acts. The stitches amalgamate the poignant stories of Christ's liberation and the church's genesis, bestowing readers with a symphonic, incessant narrative of God's blueprint for humankind. In this coherent literary and theological tapestry, the ascension functions as both a climactic resolution and an inaugural commission, ensuring that the reader perceives not a disjointed account, but a divinely orchestrated continuum of redemption and mission.

The Chiastic Structure and Ascension Narratives of Sewing Luke-Acts as a Single Book

The Third Gospel and Acts emerge within the rich spectrum of biblical literature as intricately interwoven components, reflecting Luke's profound oeuvre of literary and theological cohesion. A rigorous analysis delineates not just a continuous narrative but an intricate

---

86. Neyrey, *Passion According to Luke*, 14–15; Green and McKnight, *Dictionary of Jesus*, 50.

87. Fitzmyer, *Luke the Theologian* (2004), 62.

88. Dunn, *Acts of the Apostles*, 14.

structural design underscoring their unity. The chiastic design and the central role of the ascension narratives illuminate this interconnectedness. This deliberate composition reinforces Luke's theological vision, demonstrating how divine sovereignty orchestrates the transition from Jesus's earthly ministry to the Spirit-empowered mission of the early church.[89]

The chiastic structure, characterized by its mirroring and focal emphasis, transcends mere literary ornamentation. In the context of Luke-Acts, it provides a schematic, guiding readers through the sequential narratives of Jesus's ministry and the nascent church's mission.[90] The strategic literary choice fosters linkage among distinct textual segments, thereby amplifying their thematic resonance. Notably, the foundational, intermediate, and concluding chiasms serve as textual pillars, drawing parallels and accentuating the overarching themes of divine fulfillment, salvation, and global evangelism.

Concurrently, the ascension narratives function as a lynchpin, coherently binding Luke-Acts as a single book. Situated at this critical juncture, these accounts provide both narrative closure and inauguration.[91] Again, they mark the zenith of Jesus's terrestrial mission, simultaneously signaling the advent of the Holy Spirit's dispensation. Consequently, the ascension is not an isolated event but a bridge linking Christ's redemptive endeavors with apostolic pursuits of salvation history.

Emphasizing the ascension narratives further reinforces the perception of Luke-Acts as harmonized chronicles rather than disparate accounts. Collectively, they offer a holistic portrayal of God's salvific enterprise, spanning from the annunciation to the gospel's proliferation across the Roman Empire. The narrative continuum, accentuated by the dual presence of the ascension, underscores the authorial intention of presenting a consolidated account.[92]

To culminate, a synchronized reading of Luke-Acts unveils a meticulously crafted literary and theological tapestry. The chiastic

---

89. Zwiep, *Ascension of the Messiah*, 103–6.
90. Parsons and Pervo, *Rethinking the Unity*, 23.
91. Bovon, *Luke the Theologian*, 558.
92. Parsons and Pervo, *Rethinking the Unity*, 23.

configurations and the ascension narratives are instrumental in maintaining this cohesion. Contemporary readership, upon discerning this unified construct, gains deeper insights into the Lukan corpus, recognizing the profound synergy between Christ's mission and the church's genesis; though articulated as distinct volumes as they exist in the canon today, they reverberate in unison, echoing God's perpetual love and divine design for humankind.

Chapter 9: Climactic Denouement of Christ's Ascension in the Coherent Narrative of Luke-Acts

THE ASCENSION OF JESUS Christ from earth to heaven stands as a pivotal moment in Christianity, marking the transition from his earthly ministry to his exalted reign. Luke records this event twice—first in his Gospel (Luke 24:50–53) and again in Acts (Acts 1:6–11)—not as mere repetition, but as a deliberate literary and theological device that unifies both volumes into a cohesive narrative. Through this chiastic structure, Luke underscores that Jesus's departure is not the conclusion of his mission but the catalyst for a new phase, where his disciples, empowered by the Holy Spirit, will carry forward his work.

Together, Luke's two volumes provide a comprehensive historical account of Jesus's life, teachings, and miracles, along with the rise and expansion of early Christianity. Luke carefully structures these narratives to construct an uninterrupted transition from Jesus's ascension to the disciples' mission. This deliberate symmetry positions the ascension as both the climax of Jesus's earthly ministry and the launching point for the apostolic mission, now carried out through the enabling of the Holy Spirit's power.[1]

This study explored the chiastic structure within Jesus's ascension narratives, analyzing both their literary design and theological significance. Recognizing how Luke employs this technique enhances the reader's understanding of the unity between Luke and Acts, as well

---

1. Shin, "Narrative Development," 203–30.

as the ascension's central role in the broader salvation narrative. As the pivotal bridge between the two volumes, the ascension shapes the trajectory of the early church while highlighting key themes such as divine calling, prophetic fulfillment, and the work of the Holy Spirit.

My Contributions

This section distinctly underscores my contribution by framing the ascension narrative within the metaphor of stitching, illustrating the intricate unity between Luke and Acts. To fully grasp its nuance and depth, one must look beyond the simple act of threading a needle through fabric. In literary contexts, stitching and sewing transcend their practical functions, serving as rich metaphors that convey deeper theological and structural meaning. Just as the careful interlacing of threads binds disparate pieces of fabric into a cohesive whole, so too does the art of narrative stitching weave together seemingly distinct events, characters, and themes into a unified theological tapestry.

Within this study, the concept of stitching serves as a central metaphor in demonstrating the literary and theological unity of Luke-Acts. The ascension of Christ—occurring in Jerusalem—functions as the thread that binds the two volumes into a single, continuous narrative, while the Holy Spirit, like a guiding needle, enacts this divine union. The chiastic structure of Luke-Acts further reinforces this unity, revealing the intentional parallelism that frames the ascension as the hinge between the Gospel and Acts.

Luke 24 and Acts 1 form a literary seam, where the ascension is not merely a transitional event but the pivotal moment that stitches the two works together into a single, cohesive composition. In this metaphorical framework, the Holy Spirit, as the needle, guides the ascension (the thread) through the fabric of Luke-Acts, binding them together as a masterfully woven theological and literary opus. Luke-Acts stands as a *magnum opus*, not only because of its scope but because of its deliberate narrative craftsmanship and theological intent.[2]

A key contribution of this study is demonstrating how the ascension serves as the chiastic hinge that unifies Luke and Acts, establishing

---

2. Comfort, *Encountering the Manuscripts*, 15.

their cohesion as a single literary and theological work. This perspective challenges conventional views that regard Luke and Acts as separate books, instead emphasizing Luke's intentional narrative design, where the ascension operates as both a structural turning point and a theological climax.[3] Identifying the ascension as the chiastic hinge underscores Luke-Acts as a cohesive and intentional work, where Jesus's earthly ministry transitions harmoniously into the church's Spirit-empowered mission. Rather than merely concluding Jesus's story, the ascension serves as a pivotal turning point, reinforcing Luke's overarching narrative structure and theological vision.[4] This approach moves beyond viewing them as separate works and instead highlights Luke's deliberate narrative and theological cohesion.

Recognized as both a unified narrative and a distinct two-volume work, Luke-Acts should be read as a continuous story while also being presented as separate books in modern versions of the Bible. By drawing on historical, literary, and theological evidence, objections to viewing Luke-Acts as a unified narrative can be set aside. Rather than emphasizing their separation, analyzing the continuity between the two volumes reveals the ascension of Jesus as a pivotal event that transitions the narrative from the third Gospel to the book of Acts.

Additionally, this contribution lies in demonstrating that the ascension serves as the pivotal structural key connecting the Gospel with Acts, thereby affirming the literary unity of the two volumes. This approach moves beyond viewing Luke and Acts as merely two orderly historical accounts, emphasizing instead the deliberate narrative and thematic connections that Luke establishes.[5] While some might reduce the ascension to a transitional genre within Luke's narrative, this work underscore its dual function: it both concludes Jesus's mission in the Gospel of Luke and inaugurates the church's mission in Acts. It is a perspective that reveals what readers can recognize as a continuous narrative with the ascension acting as the essential hinge that unifies the two volumes.

---

3. Shin, "Narrative Development," 206.
4. Shin, "Narrative Development," 210.
5. Tannehill, *Narrative Unity of Luke-Acts*, 6.

The final contribution conjectures how the ascension, as both a literary and theological seam, demonstrates how Luke-Acts forms a cohesive narrative. This perspective reveals: (1) the continuity between Jesus's story in Luke and the church's mission in Acts, (2) the extension of Jesus's ministry through the Spirit empowering his followers, (3) the geographical shift from Jerusalem to a global mission, and (4) the authority to minister in Jesus's name is granted to the apostles.[6]

Arguments for Objections

One of the primary arguments scholars make against viewing Luke and Acts as a single, unified work is their division within the biblical canon. As the books were incorporated into the New Testament, they were arranged separately—Luke among the Gospels and Acts following John—rather than being preserved as a continuous narrative. This canonical separation contributed to the perception that they are independent works rather than two volumes of the same account.

Additionally, scholars argue that Luke and Acts exhibit distinct literary genres, further reinforcing their perceived division. While the Gospel of Luke follows the conventions of ancient Greco-Roman biography, focusing on the life, teachings, death, and resurrection of Jesus, Acts aligns more closely with historical and historiographical writing, chronicling the development of the early church and the spread of the gospel. This distinction in genre, coupled with their physical separation in the canon, has led some to treat them as independent compositions rather than two interwoven parts of a single literary and theological project.

Gospel Versus Acts: Within the differing literary categories of the NT includes the Synoptic Gospels, the Gospel of John, Acts of the Apostles, the Epistles, and the book of Revelation. The divisions seem more due to later theological and editorial considerations rather than the outline intended by the authors. The first advocates and compilers of the NT preferred the four Gospels and canonized the Scriptures

---

6. Green, *Luke as Narrative Theologian*, 346.

in a way that focused on the church's life, teachings, and institution.[7] Thus, although Luke-Acts appear as two discrete books in modern practice, this should not rule out their literary cohesiveness.

Biography Versus Historiography: One of the difficulties mentioned here is related to the differences in the type of literature of the two treatises (Luke 1:3; Acts 1:1). Again, for Burridge, the Gospels that include Luke are genre-less, which all can be compared to first-century Greco-Roman βίοι (i.e., life, biography, life-story).[8] Acts, on the other hand, adheres to that pattern of a Hellenistic historical monograph in the Jewish tradition. Although these terms did not exist in antiquity, it is essentially a modern label for Acts as Padilla suggests.[9] As such, some critics have noted that this genre change proves two different projects.

Nevertheless, ancient authors who operated when literature was still developing employed different literary devices depending on the shifts in its subject matter. The prologues of both volumes (Luke 1:1–4; Acts 1:1–2) uphold the idea of a two-part historical work and give the impression that Luke always intended it as such. Also, the change in tone signifies the move from Jesus's ministry to the church and the world rather than essentially switching authors.

Additional Arguments for Objections

Three additional arguments against Luke's literary unity are thematic and theological differences, the presence of two separate dedications to Theophilus, and the lack of direct manuscript evidence supporting a single work. Thematically, the Gospel focuses on Jesus's earthly ministry, while Acts shifts to the expansion of the early church and the work of the Holy Spirit, leading some scholars to view them as distinct theological compositions.

Additionally, the fact that both treatises begin with separate dedications to Theophilus suggests to some scholars that Luke may have intended them as independent works rather than a single

---

7. Shin, "Narrative Development," 214.
8. Burridge, *What Are the Gospels?*, 105.
9. Padilla, *Acts of the Apostles*, 61.

continuous narrative. Furthermore, no ancient manuscript has been found that presents Luke and Acts as a single, uninterrupted text, raising questions about whether they were ever conceived as one unified literary piece. These factors have contributed to the ongoing debate over whether Luke and Acts should be read as a singular composition or as two separate but related works.

Thematic and Theological Differences: Perceived thematic and theological considerations pose questions regarding the unity of Luke-Acts in the mind of some scholars. While the Gospel concentrates on the ministry of Jesus Christ, Acts is about the church's growth through the operation of the Holy Spirit. Also, Shin argues that Luke 24:50–53 and Acts 1:6–11 have differences in the kind of descriptions given on the ascension of Jesus.[10] However, the variations serve to enforce the chiastic structure of the single event. In addition, some themes for inclusion of the gentiles in Acts are already present in the Gospel, though in a progressing rather than stagnating sense. And discussions of impartiality in the Gospel (Luke 4:25–27; 13:29) sets the scene for the inclusive mission to the gentiles in Acts.

The Address to Theophilus: Two Separate Dedications? Another instance involves the reference to Theophilus. Critics noted that if Acts was initially intended to be the sequel to the Gospel, there would be no need for a second prologue. But, since many works in antiquity consisted of multiple parts, individual prologues were sometimes repeated to help the reader get their bearings especially if the texts were read consecutively.[11] Thus, Luke begins volume 2 by referring to a "former treatise" (Acts 1:1), supporting the tradition that Acts is the sequel of Luke.

Consider the apocryphal book of Baruch to which the opening of Luke-Acts can be compared. Baruch exhibits stylistic and structural choices that distinguish it as a unique work while also drawing from other biblical texts. Baruch acts as a recorder of events handed down to him from Jeremiah, and Luke does the same in his two-volume account.[12] Authors such as Josephus in *Against*

---

10. Shin, "Narrative Development," 205.
11. Shin, "Narrative Development," 213.
12. Adams, *Studies on Baruch*, 2, 61–62.

Apion and Thucydides in *History of the Peloponnesian War* produced works suggesting that the stylistic and structural choices observed in Baruch were not merely a result of differing modes of origin but a deliberate literary device employed by its authors. Given the sophistication of historical and theological writings during that period, it is reasonable to argue that their composition aligns with a broader tradition of consciously crafted narratives rather than being an outlier in literary development. The presence of similar literary techniques in other contemporary works further supports the idea that these methods were intentionally adopted rather than arising from a fundamentally different approach to writing.

No Direct Manuscript Evidence of a Single Work: This is based on the primary argument scholars use for suggesting Luke-Acts were not originally cohesive because of their lack of early manuscript support and evidence.[13] In early MS copying, however, the placement of MSS by genre rather than by author usually led to the placement of Luke with the other Gospels and placement of Acts along with the apostolic letters. Some ancient large-scale works, including Josephus's *Jewish War*, were divided into separate volumes even if these works were designed as single compositions. Schnabel believes that the physical division of Luke-Acts was practical and theological rather than the result of Luke's intent.[14]

Final Takeaway: Luke-Acts as a Unified Yet Distinctive Work: In conclusion, though Luke and Acts are two different works in modern versions of the Bible, they complement each other in the evolution from Jesus's ministry to the establishment of the first Christian congregations. The ascension symbolically becomes the main connecting link between the two volumes rather than the dividing line. It becomes proper to therefore maintain that Luke-Acts constitutes a complete single literary work that should be compared to multi-volume histories in the Greco-Roman world.

---

13. Shin, "Narrative Development," 221.
14. Schnabel, *Acts*, 39.

Reestablishing the Original Points of the Argument

Luke's accounts of Christ's ascension (Luke 24:50–53 and Acts 1:6–11) should not be seen as disparate but as parallel and structurally arranged in a chiasm that conjoins two narratives of a single continuous story. The ascension narratives assimilate the figure of Jesus with the role of the first Christians to establish a parallel that emphasizes the continuity of the mission of salvation in the kingdom of God. This repetition reveals the theological significance of presenting the ascension twice—as the removal of Jesus's physical presence and God's spiritual manifestation in and through the church.[15]

Such repetition is not merely accidental but serves a deliberate purpose in highlighting the transition of authority and divine presence from Jesus to the apostles. By emphasizing this shift, the narrative underscores the continuation of God's mission through the disciples, who are now empowered to carry forward the teachings and works of Christ. This intentional literary and theological design reinforces the idea that Jesus's departure is not an end but a transformation of leadership, ensuring that his divine presence remains active through the apostolic mission.

The goal of this study was not to debate the existence of chiasms or to argue for their presence in Luke and Acts. Instead, it seeks to acknowledge their presence in Luke-Acts and specifically highlight the chiastic structure surrounding the ascension of Jesus Christ. By doing so, it demonstrates how Luke intentionally uses this literary device to unify his two volumes, encouraging readers to interpret them as a single, continuous narrative rather than separate works. Building upon the previous chapter, Luke introduces his chiastic presentation of the ascension in two instances:

Luke 24:45–51 (ending the Gospel)

Acts 1:6–11 (beginning Acts)

The two accounts of the ascension are not redundant but complementary, forming a chiastic transition that structurally links Luke-Acts as a single literary unit. Again, building upon the previous

---

15. Wright, *Surprised by Hope*, 111–15.

chapter, the chiastic structure that frames the conclusion of Luke's Gospel (Luke 24:45–51) and the opening of Acts (Acts 1:6–11) not only highlights the pivotal role of the ascension but can also and even allow for a refined yet expansive interpretation. While the arrangement can be distilled to its essential elements for clarity, its implications can also extend beyond the ascension itself, encompassing broader theological and narrative continuities that unify Luke-Acts as a single cohesive work as follows:

Luke 24:44–53 (ending the Gospel)

Acts 1:4–14 (beginning Acts)

The sequence begins with (A) Jesus instructing his disciples (Luke 24:44–49), where he opens their minds to understand the Scriptures and prepares them for their role of world evangelism. It is followed by (B) his ascension from Bethany (Luke 24:50–53), during which he blesses them before being taken up.[16] (C) The disciples worship and return to Jerusalem with great joy (Luke 24:52–53), engaging in worship and anticipating what is to come (C'). The movement is mirrored in Acts, where the disciples remain in Jerusalem (Acts 1:4–5), waiting for the fulfillment of the promise—the coming of the Holy Spirit.[17] (B') The ascension is then retold, this time from the Mount of Olives (Acts 1:6–11), with angels interpreting the event and affirming Jesus's return. (A') And the disciples prepare for their mission (Acts 1:12–14) through unified prayer.[18] This carefully structured parallelism reinforces the ascension's pivotal role as both the conclusion of Jesus's ministry and the inauguration of the church's Spirit-empowered mission.

Again, Luke's recounting of the ascension in both his Gospel (Luke 24:45–51) and Acts (Acts 1:6–11) is not merely a repetition but a deliberate literary strategy. By employing a chiastic structure, he creates thematic and structural symmetry between the two volumes, reinforcing their unity as a single, continuous narrative. The ascension serves as a pivotal moment, marking a transition in the

16. Shin, "Narrative Development," 213.
17. Shin, "Narrative Development," 219.
18. Shin, "Narrative Development," 221.

story by highlighting Jesus's commissioning of his disciples, signifying his impending departure, and preparing the disciples for the coming of the Holy Spirit. This dual presentation underscores the ascension's theological and narrative significance, positioning it as the hinge that connects Jesus's earthly ministry with the Spirit-empowered mission of the early church.

The sequence of events surrounding the ascension follows a deliberate structure in both Luke and Acts, reinforcing the continuity and theological depth of Luke-Acts. In Luke's Gospel, the progression begins with Jesus opening the minds of his disciples to understand the Scriptures (Luke 24:44-49), followed by his ascension from Bethany as he blesses them (Luke 24:50-53), and concluding with the disciples returning to Jerusalem in joyful anticipation of the Holy Spirit (Luke 24:52-53).

Acts, however, presents a reversed sequence: the disciples remain in Jerusalem, waiting for the promised Holy Spirit (Acts 1:4-5), Jesus is then taken up from the Mount of Olives while angels interpret the event (Acts 1:6-11), and finally, the disciples devote themselves to prayer and preparation for their mission (Acts 1:12-14). This literary parallelism emphasizes the ascension as the climactic fulfillment of Jesus's earthly ministry while simultaneously inaugurating the church's mission. By structuring these narratives with careful symmetry, Luke strengthens the theological and historical framework that unites his two volumes into a cohesive whole.

This structural design not only enhances the literary cohesion of Luke-Acts but also highlights its central themes.[19] Structurally, it underlines how the disciples moved from listening to Jesus's teachings and seeing him ascend to heaven to their formation for a Spirit-filled mission.[20] The deliberate structure underscores the transition of the disciples from being recipients of Jesus's teachings and eyewitnesses to his ascension to becoming Spirit-empowered leaders prepared for their mission. This deliberate narrative progression reinforces the theological significance of the ascension as the pivotal moment bridging Jesus's ministry and the church's expansion.

19. Litwak, *Echoes of Scripture*, 20.
20. Pettis, "Ascension," 147-48.

The presence of angels at the ascension (B′) mirrors Jesus's blessing at Bethany (B), signifying divine approval and the continuity of God's plan. Additionally, Jerusalem plays a crucial role in this structural arrangement.[21] The shifting locations of the disciples—moving between the interior and exterior of Jerusalem (C, C′)—underscore the city's theological and geographical significance as the starting point for the spread of the gospel. This movement aligns with Jesus's directive in Luke 24:47, where he proclaims that repentance and forgiveness of sins must be preached in his name to all nations, beginning in Jerusalem. Thus, Luke's use of a chiastic framework reinforces the overarching narrative, linking Jesus's ministry to the apostles' mission, which extends from Jerusalem to the ends of the earth.

Luke's chiastic structure reinforces the continuity between God's redemptive plan in the Old Testament and the gospel message of Jesus Christ in the New Testament. By remaining in Jerusalem as instructed, the disciples align themselves with Israel's tradition as the people entrusted with the divine word. Just as the prophets once called Israel to prepare for God's redemptive acts, the apostles in Acts are positioned in Jerusalem, where they receive the Holy Spirit. This moment signifies the inauguration of a new phase in God's salvific plan, marking the transition from Israel's prophetic tradition to the Spirit-empowered mission of the church.

Luke's emphasis on theological continuity aligns with his concern for gentile inclusion, demonstrating that the gospel, which began in Israel, is now poised to extend to the gentiles. This expansion fulfills God's covenant with Abraham, in which he promised that all nations would be blessed through his offspring (Gen 12:1–3; 22:18).[22] Luke reinforces this theme through parallel motifs, particularly the necessity of waiting for the Spirit's empowerment before bearing witness to the gentiles.

The contrast between the disciples' emotions before and after the ascension further highlights this transformation—while they were filled with despair following Jesus's crucifixion, their return to Jerusalem after his ascension is marked by joy and expectation. This

---

21. Pettis, "Ascension," 148.
22. Kiley, *Reading Between the Letters*, 47–48.

shift is vital to Luke's depiction of the early church, underscoring that the apostles' mission is not a human initiative but a divinely ordained continuation of God's redemptive plan.

The structural design of Luke-Acts reinforces both Jesus's physical departure and his enduring presence among his followers. Just as the angelic references in section A reaffirm the central message of Acts, the blessing in B′ provides reassurance that Jesus remains spiritually present even as he ascends. The angels' testimony in Acts 1:11 declares that Christ will return in the same manner as he departed, while Luke's Gospel concludes with the apostles worshiping in the temple—an act signifying their faith in the ongoing work that Jesus initiated. Thus, the ascension is not merely a departure but an enthronement, marking Christ's exaltation and ensuring the church's continuation under divine guidance.

Luke ensures that the readers understand the continuity of Jesus's ministry and the church's obligation. The disciples are not abandoned but are divinely appointed to carry forward his teachings, empowered and guided by the Holy Spirit. This continuity is reinforced through the chiastic structure, which highlights God's ongoing work and the expansion of salvation—from its beginnings in Jerusalem to its reach to the uttermost part of the world (across the entire world).

Reaffirming the Significance of the Ascension Across Two Volumes

A crucial question to consider is the significance of the ascension within the broader framework of God's divine plan for creation. The ascension is not merely a concluding event in Jesus's earthly ministry but serves as a pivotal moment that reinforces God's overarching purpose for humanity and the world. It marks the transition from Jesus's physical presence among his disciples to his exaltation at the right hand of God, signifying the completion of his redemptive work and the inauguration of a new era led by the Holy Spirit. This event bridges the gap between the earthly and the heavenly, affirming Christ's divine authority and foreshadowing his return.

Furthermore, the ascension plays a critical role in fulfilling biblical prophecy, demonstrating God's sovereign plan throughout history. It also establishes the foundation for the church's mission (until the return of Christ), as his first departure ushered in the empowerment of his followers to continue his work. In this way, the ascension is not an isolated event but an essential component of God's grand design, ensuring the spread of the Gospel, the growth of the church, the establishment of the kingdom of God, and the ultimate fulfillment of his kingdom purposes.

Theological Significance of the Chiastic Structure: The chiastic structure within these passages serves to bridge meaning, interpretation, and theology in both a logical and overarching sense. At the heart of this structure lies Jesus's ascension (B, B'), marking the pivotal transition from his earthly ministry to his heavenly enthronement.[23] The shift is crucial for the unfolding of God's plan through the church, as the ascension not only brings Jesus's mission to its fulfillment but also inaugurates the work of the Holy Spirit, who will empower and guide the disciples in their divine calling.

The dual narration of the ascension in Luke and Acts serves a significant purpose, offering complementary perspectives that contribute to a broader theological message. In the Gospel, it is the climactic conclusion of Jesus's earthly ministry, signifying the fulfillment of his mission of the salvific work for which he was entrusted. After having accomplished all that was entrusted to him, he returns to his Father. In this transition, he sends the Holy Spirit to indwell his followers to proclaim his message of the kingdom of God.

Jesus's ascension in Acts serve as the foundation for the church's apostolic mission, shifting the focus to Christ's ongoing work through the Holy Spirit and the apostles. This transition highlights that while Jesus is no longer physically present, his influence and authority continue to operate through them. When viewed alongside the account in the Gospel, the ascension narratives present an unbroken continuity between Jesus's earthly ministry and his enduring presence within the church. The chiastic structure further reinforces this theological connection, emphasizing that both Jesus's time on

---

23. Giacobbe, *Luke the Chronicler*, 155.

earth and his exaltation in heaven are integral components of the overarching narrative of salvation history.

The Ascension in Luke: Culmination and Worship: In the Gospel of Luke, the ascension serves as the culmination of Jesus's life, crucifixion, death, and resurrection, conferring and imparting salvation and eternal life to all people who places faith in him. In the last verses in the Gospel and the first verses in Acts, he is depicted physically ascending into the sky while bestowing a blessing upon his disciples. This is an act reminiscent of the priestly blessings in the Old Testament. This imagery aligns with his role as the ultimate high priest, as described in Heb 4:14–16, emphasizing his continued intercession on behalf of humanity. Through his ascension, Jesus assumes his position as the mediator between God and humanity, ensuring the ongoing fulfillment of his redemptive work.

Equally important is the reaction of Jesus's disciples to his ascension event. As the entire host of heaven observed, Jesus was lifted up and eventually hidden from sight. Rather than responding with sorrow or despair, the disciples returned to Jerusalem "with great joy" and were "continually in the temple, blessing God" (Luke 24:52–53). Their elation reflects their deep reverence for Jesus's glorification and their unwavering faith in his promises. Instead of mourning his departure, they perceived it as a transformative moment—one that signified not an absence, but a new form of presence in the Holy Spirit ensuring that his guidance and power would remain with them in a different yet equally profound manner.[24]

Luke's second volume, Acts, emphasizes that worship at the temple among the early Christian community reflected the appropriate response to divine revelation. It was marked by gratitude, reverence, and anticipation of a second return to earth (Acts 1:10–11). Their devotion not only demonstrated their faith but also set in place a precedent for the church's posture of worship, dependence, and readiness for God's ongoing work. Through this portrayal, Luke reinforces that the ascension is not a conclusion but rather the prelude to the church's emergence and the unfolding of God's redemptive mission throughout the world.

---

24. Kiley, *Reading Between the Letters*, 76.

The Ascension in Acts: Commission and Empowerment: In Acts, the ascension marks a decisive transition from Jesus's direct ministry to the apostolic mission, the establishment of the church, and the spread of the gospel. While the Gospel presents the ascension as the climactic conclusion, culminating in worship and joy, Acts portrays it as the starting point of a new era, characterized by commissioning and the promise of divine empowerment. This contrast underscores the ascension's dual function: as both the fulfillment of Jesus's earthly work and the launching of the disciples' Spirit-led mission.

The depiction of Jesus's ascension in Acts 1:9–11 also serves a pivotal transition, shifting the narrative focus from his earthly ministry to the entrusting of the world's mission to his disciples. The mission involves their preaching repentance and remission of sins in his name among all nations, beginning at Jerusalem (Luke 24:47; Acts 1:8). This commissioning provides a foundational blueprint for the expansion of Christianity, emphasizing that the work of Jesus continues through his apostles. Their mission to proclaim salvation to all nations underscores the ascension's role as both a conclusion and an inauguration, ensuring the gospel's reach far beyond its origins.

Acts 1:10–11 introduces two angels, infusing the ascension with eschatological significance. Their message offers both reassurance and a prophetic declaration: "This Jesus, who was taken up from you into heaven, will come in the same way as you saw him go into heaven" (Acts 1:11 ESV). The statement affirms the certainty of his second coming, framing the ascension not as a permanent departure but as a necessary phase in God's redemptive plan for creation.[25] Rather than signifying final separation, it establishes a period of active mission. The angel's words redirect the disciples' focus from gazing at the heavens to engaging in their calling of spreading the gospel message to the ends of the earth in anticipation of Jesus's promised return.

And finally, it highlights the essential role of the Holy Spirit's empowerment of believers in which Jesus instructs them to remain in Jerusalem and wait for the "promise of the Father" (Luke 24:49; Acts 1:4), "the baptism of the Holy Spirit" (Matt 3:11; Mark 1:8). This moment was critical, as the apostles required divine guidance, wisdom,

---

25. MacArthur, *Second Coming*, 12, 199.

and authority to fulfill their mission effectively. Their waiting was not a passive delay but a necessary preparation for the transformative event of Pentecost. Rather than Luke signaling an end, it became a pause in the narrative that served as a pivotal transition ensuring that the disciples are/were spiritually equipped for the task ahead.

The Disciples' Return to Jerusalem: Obedience and Continuity: The disciples' return to Jerusalem (C, C'), as seen in both the Gospel and in Acts, demonstrates their obedience to Jesus's command and their readiness for the coming of the Holy Spirit at Pentecost. In the Gospel account, their return was marked by joy (Luke 24:52), having recognized the fulfillment of Jesus's promises and eagerly anticipating the outpouring of the Spirit. Their willingness to remain in the city, in accordance with Jewish law, signified their trust in God's unfolding plan of redemption.

In Acts, however, their return took on an additional dimension—it was not only an expression of joy but also an act of preparation for their impending mission. The disciples are portrayed as gathered in prayer and expectation, actively positioning themselves to receive the Holy Spirit.[26] This return to Jerusalem serves as a theological symbol of their faithfulness, their readiness to embrace the next phase of God's redemptive work, and their commitment to the mission that lay ahead of them.

This missional framework encapsulates the central theological theme of Luke-Acts: the expansion of God's kingdom through the church. After Pentecost, the church becomes the primary instrument for carrying out God's redemptive plan, empowered by the Holy Spirit to continue and extend the work of Jesus. This continuity reinforces the idea that the church is not a separate entity but the living expression of Christ's ongoing mission on earth. Through his blessing and commissioning, Jesus reaffirms the disciples' calling, emphasizing their responsibility to remain faithful and dependent on the Spirit to fulfill their divine mandate.

The Ascension as a Pivotal Event in Salvation History: The ascension in the lens of salvation history serves as a pivotal event maintaining the theological and narrative continuity between Jesus's earthly

---

26. Green, *Luke as Narrative Theologian*, 17.

ministry and the global spread of Christianity. It marks the transition from what has been fulfilled to what is yet to come in God's redemptive plan. This moment affirms Christ's resurrection and his divine authority as Lord over creation, as emphasized in Phil 2:9–11, where Paul declares his exaltation above all. Furthermore, it assures believers that Jesus continues to intercede for them and remains present through the Holy Spirit, their παράκλητος, guiding them on earth. It keeps the continuity of the plan of salvation emphasized by God.

Pentecost is directly linked to the ascension, as Jesus, after ascending to heaven, sends the Holy Spirit to empower the apostles for their mission. The ascension thus prepares the way for the Spirit to dwell in believers, guiding them as they continue Jesus's work. This event fosters hope among the disciples and early Christians, reinforcing an eschatological expectation that history is moving toward the ultimate realization of the dominion of the divine reign.

The ascension, therefore, cannot be conceived merely as the passing to a new stage in salvation history but also as the church's mission continues to be a part of God's purpose for the world. It gives direction and motive, as those who are saved are commanded to spread the message of the kingdom of God and prepare for the second coming of Christ. It offers apostolic exegesis in light of the church's place in the world, its vocation, and the hope that powers it as it fulfills its task of preaching the gospel.

Using the ascension, Luke-Acts paints a systematic view of salvation history in which Christ remains king, the apostles are commissioned, and the church is given hope in the second coming of Christ. Liturgically it bridges the past and the future, keeping the church in the present moment conscious of God's ongoing saving work and pointing it toward the coming of the kingdom of God. Hence, the ascension is not only a point in time but a continuous process defining the existence and purpose of the church in history.

The Ascension as the Centerpiece of Luke-Acts: In Luke's narrative, the ascension aligns with Jesus's teachings about his departure, referred to in Greek as *exodos* (ἔξοδος), as seen in Luke 9:51 and 18:31–33. These earlier references establish that his ascension is not a random occurrence but a fulfillment of Scripture, marking a pivotal transition in his earthly manifestation. His physical departure signifies a movement from an embodied presence to a transcendent one through the Holy Spirit. This shift is essential for the progression of the divine plan, as the coming of the Holy Spirit at Pentecost empowers the apostles and the early church to carry forward God's will.

It serves as the definitive moment of authority transfer to the apostles, paralleling the ascent of Elijah and the subsequent passing of his mantle to Elisha (2 Kgs 2:9–12). Just as Elisha inherited Elijah's prophetic mission, the apostles assume their commission through Christ's ascension, signifying the completion of his earthly ministry and the delegation of his authority to them. The angelic proclamation that Jesus would return in the same manner as his ascension underscores the eschatological dimension of this event. This assurance of Christ's second coming not only reinforces the theological significance of the event but also instills a sense of hope and urgency within the early Christian community, compelling them to advance the mission as part of an unfolding divine plan.

Luke-Acts exhibits a grand chiastic structure that unifies both volumes under the overarching theme of salvation history. This structural design is evident in the Gospel, where the narrative begins in the temple (Luke 1:5–25) and concludes in the temple (Luke 24:53), while Acts commences in Jerusalem (Acts 1:4) and culminates in Rome (Acts 28:30–31). The literary arrangement not only underscores the geographical expansion of the gospel—from its origins within the Jewish community in Jerusalem to its establishment among the gentiles in Rome—but also reflects a theological progression. The movement from Jewry particularity of Jesus's ministry to the universal scope of the early church encapsulates Luke's central theological vision: the extension of salvation beyond ethnic and national boundaries, affirming the gospel's accessibility to all people, regardless of location and/or heritage.

It notably occupies a pivotal position within the overarching chiastic structure of Luke-Acts, serving as the crucial hinge that links the two volumes. The central event illustrates a harmonious continuity of God's redemptive plan from the Gospel through Acts. The structural and theological unity of the ascension underscores that Luke-Acts should not be treated as two independent compositions but rather as a single, cohesive narrative that charts the progression of salvation history throughout the entire Bible. Luke's theological aim is clear: salvation history advances through the church's mission, guided by his exaltation and the indwelling Holy Spirit. The chiastic structure of Luke-Acts underscores their narrative cohesion, illustrating a unified account of God's redemptive plan for all humanity.

By depicting the disciples as continuing Christ's work through the Holy Spirit, the ascension functions as the structural and theological seam that unites Luke-Acts as a cohesive narrative.[27] It is not an ending but a turning point, reinforcing Luke's structural and theological design. It refutes the separation of Luke and Acts, highlighting their chiastic unity. As a literary hinge, the ascension links the conclusion of Luke with the beginning of Acts, marking the shift from Christ's direct ministry to the church's mission. Just as Jesus was exalted, the church, despite their suffering, will also triumph (Acts 28:30–31).[28]

The upward movement of the ascension establishes a structural and thematic symmetry, linking Jesus's journey to Jerusalem with the church's subsequent mission to Rome. This deliberate parallelism underscores Luke's chiastic design, where the trajectory of Jesus's ministry finds its continuation in the apostolic mission. The use of chiasmus between Jesus's earthly actions and the church's expanding mandate demonstrates that Acts does not function as an independent narrative but rather as the continuation of his work, now carried out through the empowerment of the Holy Spirit. This structural cohesion further reinforces the literary unity, positioning it as the pivotal transition that bridges Jesus's mission with the church's global commission.

The Ascension as the Chiastic Stitch of Luke-Acts: The chiastic structure of Luke-Acts reinforces the unity of the two volumes, emphasizing thematic and theological continuity. Luke begins and ends in the temple, highlighting the divine presence within sacred spaces (Luke 1:5–25; 24:53). Similarly, Acts mirrors this structure, opening in Jerusalem, the birthplace of the early church (Acts 1:4), and concluding in Rome, symbolizing the Gospel's expansion to the

---

27. DelHousaye, *Fourfold Gospel*, 41.
28. Green, *Luke as Narrative Theologian*, 119.

wider world (Acts 28:30–31). This deliberate literary design underscores the progression of salvation history from its Jewish origins to its universal mission.

The continuity between the two volumes is evident through their thematic and structural parallels. Both begin with divine intervention: Luke opens with angelic announcements and miraculous conceptions, while Acts begins with the descent of the Holy Spirit with tongues of fire at Pentecost.[29] God's sovereign control is affirmed in Luke through the disciples' joyful return to Jerusalem (Luke 24:53) and in Acts through Paul's persistent evangelism in Rome (Acts 28:30–31). Key themes such as prophetic fulfillment, the central role of the Holy Spirit, and the inclusion of the gentiles further reinforce their unity, demonstrating the harmonious progression of salvation history from Jesus's ministry to the early church.

Luke employs chiastic structures, parallel narratives, and recurring theological motifs, aligning with the Greco-Roman tradition of multi-volume works that unify their sections through literary patterns.[30] Although Luke-Acts is rendered in two volumes, it functions as a single, continuous account of salvation history. The ascension serves as the pivotal moment in this narrative framework, both concluding Jesus's earthly mission and inaugurating the church's Spirit-empowered mission to the world.

Literary Techniques Employed in Greco-Roman Rhetoric

First-century biblical writers were heavily influenced by Greco-Roman rhetoric and Jewish traditions, shaping both their oral and written expression. They employed structural techniques such as parallelism (synonymous, antithetical, and synthetic) to organize ideas, inclusio to frame passages for thematic unity, and amplification to reinforce key points through repetition and elaboration. Persuasion was achieved through classical rhetorical appeals. Additionally, they utilized midrashic interpretation to expand on scriptural texts, diatribe to create

---

29. Green, *Luke as Narrative Theologian*, 145.
30. Corbett, *Classical Rhetoric for the Modern Student*, 301.

rhetorical dialogue, hyperbole for dramatic emphasis, and chiasmus (ABBA structure) to enhance coherence and memorability.

The ascension functions as a pivotal rhetorical device shaping Luke's narrative structure, theological argumentation, and interaction with Jewish and Greco-Roman traditions of divine enthronement. It carries significant implications for Christology and eschatology while grounding itself within the historical context of first-century thought. Structurally, it serves as the central hinge in the chiastic design of Luke-Acts. Theologically, it affirms Jesus's exaltation, divine authority, and the transition to a Spirit-empowered church. Historically, it engages with Jewish and Greco-Roman concepts of apotheosis and divine enthronement, reinforcing its broader cultural resonance.

The rhetoric of the first century is particularly compelling, as it influenced early Christian writings, Roman political discourse, and philosophical arguments. Rooted in both Greco-Roman rhetorical traditions and Jewish interpretive methods, first-century communication relied on a range of sophisticated techniques in both oral and written forms. Key among these techniques were the following.

Repetition or Expansion: This provided ways to restate or expand the points being made or discussed in the text. Classical rhetorical appeals—ethos (credibility), pathos (emotional appeal), and logos (logical reasoning)—were fundamental to persuasion.[31] Additionally, Jewish interpretative traditions, such as midrashic exegesis, played a crucial role in scriptural interpretation and hermeneutics. The diatribe, a rhetorical style characterized by raising objections and providing counterarguments, was frequently utilized by the apostle Paul in his letters. Lastly, hyperbole, a technique of deliberate exaggeration, was often employed in moral and apocalyptic contexts to emphasize the gravity of a message and capture the audience's attention.

Summarizing a Previous Narrative: In their endeavor to abridge narratives, first-century writers employed specific techniques to redo focal ideas using as few words as possible. Paraphrasing involved summarizing content concisely without unnecessary details.[32] Recapitulation reiterated earlier points within the same work, often with

---

31. Corbett, *Classical Rhetoric for the Modern Student*, 35, 459.
32. Corbett, *Classical Rhetoric for the Modern Student*, 605.

added explanation or elaboration. Simplification, through omission, excluded fewer essential elements to maintain focus on the most relevant aspects of the narrative.

Metalepsis: Fables often employed metalepsis, referencing an earlier story without retelling it, relying on the audience's familiarity with the original narrative. Augustine utilized prolepsis to anticipate key themes from prior works and integrate them into the current discourse.[33] Writers also practiced paraphrastic summarizing, restating content with slight variations in wording or tone. Additionally, allusion and echoes subtly incorporated phrases or themes from previous texts without explicit attribution, prompting the audience to recognize their origins.

Luke's Rhetorical Techniques in the Ascension Narrative in Luke-Acts

Again, classical rhetorical appeals, as identified by Aristotle, encompass ethos (credibility), pathos (emotional appeal), and logos (logical reasoning). Luke skillfully weaves these elements into his narrative, enhancing its persuasive impact within its historical and cultural context. He employs rhetorical questions to provoke reflection and reinforce key themes. In the ascension accounts, various rhetorical strategies highlight theological and eschatological dimensions. Notably, parallelism and contrast shape the narrative: Luke 24 concludes with the glorification of Christ, while the first chapter of Acts (Acts 1) shifts focus to apostolic mission and eschatological anticipation.

Luke-Acts exemplifies the sophisticated rhetorical conventions of the first century, demonstrating cohesion, strategic arrangement, and adherence to historiographic norms. A defining feature of this rhetorical design is the inclusion of speeches, which function as persuasive instruments within Acts.[34] Notably, some speeches align with classical rhetorical forms, such as Peter's Pentecost sermon and Paul's Areopagus address. Additionally, Luke employs an imitative parallelism between the two volumes, exemplified by Jesus's journey to

33. Parsons, *Study of the Vocabulary*, 189.
34. Corbett, *Classical Rhetoric for the Modern Student*, 624.

Jerusalem in the Gospel and Paul's journey to Rome in Acts, reinforcing the narrative and theological unity of Luke-Acts.

Luke conforms to Greco-Roman historiographical conventions, particularly in his emphasis on eyewitness testimony. His prologue (Luke 1:1-4) follows the historiographic style of writers like Thucydides, who prioritized meticulous research and reliable sources.[35] A notable example of Luke's use of double commissions within his two-volume work is the ascension of Christ, which appears in a condensed form at the end of the Gospel (Luke 24:50-53) and in a more detailed account at the beginning of Acts (Acts 1:6-11). This dual presentation serves both as a literary device to reiterate key themes at the outset of each volume and as a structural link binding Luke and Acts into a unified narrative.

Luke employs a chiastic structure to frame his narrative, linking Jesus's birth with his ascension (Luke 3:22; 24:51), while Acts introduces the coming of the Holy Spirit. His emphasis on eyewitness verification in accordance with Greco-Roman historiographical practices mentioned earlier, where credible testimonies were essential for establishing historical authority.[36] Additionally, the ascension scene reflects broader Greco-Roman literary themes, particularly the apotheosis of deified leaders such as Romulus, reinforcing its significance within both Jewish and Hellenistic thought.

Nevertheless, unlike these legendary accounts, Jesus does not simply vanish or ascend into the heavens without purpose; rather, he commissions his followers as witnesses, emphasizing both the continuity of his mission and the transition to the apostolic era. This deliberate act reinforces the ongoing work of salvation through the church. The intertextual connections highlight the theological depth of Acts 1:9, particularly through the imagery of the cloud. This motif echoes Dan 7:13, where the Son of Man comes with the clouds of heaven, signifying divine authority, and Exod 40:34, where the cloud represents God's presence in the tabernacle. These references underscore both Jesus's divinity and the fulfillment of biblical prophecy, situating the ascension within the broader narrative of redemptive history.

35. Peters, *Luke Among the Ancient Historians*, 67.
36. Peters, *Luke Among the Ancient Historians*, 194.

Conclusion

THIS BOOK EXAMINED THE *Coherent Chiastic Oeuvre in the Unity of Luke-Acts: Two Volumes Conjoined as a Single Book*, by demonstrating that the author intended both volumes to be read as a single book. Luke and Acts continue God's story of salvation history from the OT into the NT. Called Luke-Acts, it is a continuous story about God's salvation history that began with the Jews in the OT and continued through John the Baptist, Jesus, and the apostles, extending through the *ecclesia*. Volume 1 was seen as bringing the Jews into Christ, while volume 2 continued the story through Christ to the gentiles, bringing them to Christ. Both volumes were written in Hellenistic contemporaneous retrospection by the same author.

The coherent structure and design of Luke-Acts is often missed or insufficiently grasped when reading Luke and Acts. Both have been widely and traditionally recognized as two independent separate works. The book proved an opposite view that Luke, the companion of the apostle Paul, the same individual Paul in Col 4:4 called "the beloved physician," wrote both volumes. The book calls Luke's Gospel volume 1, and it calls Acts volume 2. It is so because both volumes were intended by the author, Luke, to be read as a single book and story with no break in the narrative between the last chapter of volume 1 and the first chapter of volume 2.

It has also been proven that Luke was responsible for writing both ascension narratives in both volumes, as they were not the result of anonymous interpolations as some people assumed. If Luke was not the author of both volumes, or if the two ascension narratives were merely interpolations of anonymous authors pretending to be Luke, the ascension narratives themselves would do less than connecting both volumes together. The Holy Spirit inspired Luke's autographs and not just some or most of it. If inspiration is either marred or taken away, these works would only and merely be the works of a man and thereby possess no divine authority at all. Luke and Acts, or Luke-Acts, however, is more than a human contrivance. They are also part of God's inspired revelation to humanity, and useful for teaching the truth, rebuking error, correcting faults, and giving instruction for right living (see 2 Tim 3:16).

In addition to these facts, there was no intention to attach new genres to the Gospel or to Acts. Luke's Gospel still belongs within the gospel genre (while each still has unique sub-genres), and Acts still belongs to the genre style with the appearance of a work of history. As such, this book was not intended to coin any sort of new genre, but it examined this area to explain such; it did, however, address the way these works are read, which is literary-theological-historical-narrative, whereas the Gospel also adds a biographical element of the life of Christ.

It was also examined how both volumes of Luke's work are connected, and how they were written as a single book before their separation into separate books in the second century. Before their acceptance into the canon as separate works, Luke intended his readers to read them as a continuous story. Luke and Acts contain many chiasms from a couple of verses to paragraphs and even spanning to the entire volumes. Luke chapter 24 and Acts chapter 1 examined a main primary chiasm that joined or connected both volumes as a single book.

In addition to this chiasmus structure, Luke and Acts, throughout both works, contain several main themes and connection features (e.g., Luke 1:1 and Acts 1:1). Several of the features were identified around and within Jesus's three-year travel itinerary from Galilee to Jerusalem.[1] These features were in common with Luke's major themes that centered around the ministry of Christ (Gospel)

---

1. Scholars suggest that Jesus's earthly messianic ministry was approximately three and a half years long. See Köstenberger et al., *Cradle, the Cross, and the Crown*, 142–43.

and the ministry of the apostles (Acts). These were explored as part of Luke's intentional literary structure and design and the Holy Spirit as God's central activity active within the two volumes.

Luke-Acts was written in a narrative sytle (they are quasi-narratives) because the author intended them to be read like a story. They were structured in a way that seemed as if the writer intended to report events to his readers in a chronological sequence of events continuously being unfolded as the story continued to progress. Luke demonstrated this ancient practice of rhetoric throughout Luke-Acts. The narrative design was the author's intention and purpose in his producing a two-volume unified story that abruptly ended shortly after Paul reached Rome. Luke's intentions were proved, that he intended to take Christ and the gospel from Galilee to Rome. He did so by writing one story with vision and purpose, and not two disjointed accounts without having aim or focus.

While moving from a narrative theological approach to a literary approach that dealt specifically with backgrounds, a historical background analysis of the era in which Luke wrote his testimony needed to be examined to reveal the society and culture around Luke that contributed to the writing style in which he wrote Luke-Acts. It was also necessary to explore those external elements within the first-century Roman Empire, as they also contributed to the writing of his two-volume work. The societal and cultural-historical background outside and around the Lukan texts disclosed similar writing trends among his contemporaries.

It also has been shown how modern critics have charged Luke's historicity as inaccurate in recording historical events and that he was not educated. As a result, his writing style, background, and education within his contemporary society were examined. The historical evidence proves that Luke was highly educated and a well-equipped researcher, historian, and theologian. His profession as a medical doctor alone proves he had an advanced education. The historical evidence also proved that the education levels in the first century were also high. Luke, writing in Hellenistic Greek, followed the common writing styles of his era. And not only Luke but also his contemporaries, as the style of the canonical Luke-Acts has similarities to that of Greco-Roman literary writing styles.

The metaphors of a needle, thread, and two garment pieces were used as symbolic expressions in drawing a symbolic picture to explain the chiasm. For example, the Gospel of Luke and the Acts of the Apostles (viz., the two ascension narratives) were seen as individual quilt pieces. The Holy Spirit was seen as the needle, and the thread as the ascension. In this symbolic analogy, Luke, under the Holy Spirit's inspiration, stitched together Luke and Acts with their two ascension narratives. Though the Gospel and Acts both contain an ascension narrative in Luke 24:45–51 and Acts 1:6–11, both are connected by a single chiasm between those two volumes. It was the main/primary chiasm that connects both volumes as part of Luke's literary structure and design.

It also explored how volume 2 (the Acts of the Apostles) is a continuation of the work that Jesus started in Galilee through the Gospel, whereas the *Sitz im Leben* for the end of the Gospel and the beginning of Acts is Jerusalem. It revealed Luke's narrative agenda, where he brought Jesus and his gospel from Galilee to Rome as the sequence of events continued to unfold and progress. Again, this was identified as another intended purpose for Luke, and it was identified as the reason he stopped writing shortly after Paul reached Rome. For Luke, his mission was accomplished. He had successfully taken Jesus and the gospel of Christ from Galilee to Rome, the capital of the then-empire of the pagan world, the seat of Caesar and polytheism.

While so much has been written on Luke and Acts, this book was not an attempt to present an exhaustive study for them. It, however, explained the singleness of the unity of the two volumes. As such, it avoided the use of traditional terms like "the book of Acts." The expression is unique to its current state in the NT canon. No intentions were assumed of any errors or problems with the latter, but the work sought to prove the author's intentions with Luke-Acts based on the way it was received by his original audience. Stated another way, it did not argue for the way Luke-Acts was received and read, but what Luke intended on conjoining them.

CONCLUSION

In any study of these works, their unity goes unnoticed on a fundamental level as an illustrating dictum or truism. Both volumes open with an address to one Theophilus, with the second complementing the first in a sort of jointed literary narrative connection. For any research aimed at suggesting an antithetical approach or view to Luke-Acts, such semantic inscriptions common to ancient writing counter such ventures wherever attempted.

It was proven that Luke and Acts are not rudimental separate and/or independent writings, but writings from the same pen and paper so to speak. Because of the rule for scroll length in ancient (much earlier to the modern era) writing, a continuous work had to be placed on a separate scroll when the current scroll containing the Gospel reached its maximum length. Based on word count, the Gospel of Luke is the longest book in the NT, followed by Matthew, then Acts. Luke-Acts was essentially too long to be placed on the same scroll; hence a second scroll was needed. The NT presents no evidence that there had to be twenty-seven books in its canon. Using a similar example to this point, the TaNaK contains only twenty-four books in comparison to the thirty-nine of the OT.

Again, the axiom "Τὸν μὲν πρῶτον λόγον ἐποιησάμην περὶ πάντων" (Acts 1:1a) calls attention to Luke's former scroll (treatise, account) he wrote concerning all things (that happened among them), and it is a renewed address to his patron, Theophilus. Such dedications belong to the conventions of ancient writing. Even though ancient writing did not follow the rules or protocols associated with modern conventions of writing, such became matters of physical convenience and not evidence of separate origin or publication but an intended signal for marking a continuation of the previous work associated with the current work.[2]

The previous chapter of this book examined how the term "ascension" was used before Jesus's rapture to heaven. Several practical

---

2. The work of Cadbury in *Making of Luke-Acts* was often sourced in this book to annotate such evidence in ancient writing. Works that were addressed to the same patron where people may have not been aware of their source or intention had in such cases denoted that the two volumes were intended to be a single work. The preface at the beginning of both volumes does more to confirm this point rather than to oppose it. See Cadbury, *Making of Luke-Acts*, 8–9.

examples existed in Jewish (the Hebrew Bible or OT) and Greco-Roman thought and literature that prepared people for Jesus's ascension, to make it intelligible, even as Jesus raising Lazarus back to life demonstrated the reality of Christ's resurrection.

In addition to earlier pointing out the importance of chapter 8, "Stitching Luke and Acts Together at the Seams," this book juxtaposed the two ascension narratives discussed throughout Luke 24:45–51 and Acts 1:6–11. While chiasmus exists in the form of several verses, paragraphs, or complete chapters, they encompass the entirety of Luke-Acts. While out of scope, this book used smaller examples of the chiasmus in chapter 8 while demonstrating the ascension narrative as the main primary chiasm for joining together both volumes.

Finally, for all who love and cherish the Lord Jesus Christ and his holy sacred word, it is hoped that each reader will find that this book was intended to teach, inform, enlighten, and contribute to the field of scholarly research and education. Therefore, a thorough examination of the life and works of Saint Luke was desired and achieved. The readers of this book will also be reminded of the depth of Luke's research in the way he produced two amazingly inspired works in the NT, culminating in the reason behind this book project.

Luke, being the only gentile writer in the entire NT, also seeks to encourage humankind and all the rest of those who were not biological descendants of the OT patriarch Jacob. The outcome not only joined gentiles into God's overall plan of salvation history but inserted them as they were direct participants in God's divine work alongside valiant disciples like Peter, John, James, Paul, and others. In the final analysis, Luke has proved himself to be an outstanding researcher, historian, theologian, and disciple of Christ.

Bibliography

Adams, Sean A., ed. *Studies on Baruch: Composition, Literary Relations, and Reception.* Deuterocanonical and Cognate Literature Studies 23. Berlin: de Gruyter, 2016.

Alaharasan, Anthony V. J. *Home of the Assumption: Reconstructing Mary's Life in Ephesus.* Worcester, MA: Ambassador Books, 2006.

Aland, Kurt, and Barbara Aland. *The Text of the New Testament: An Introduction to the Critical Editions and to the Theory and Practice of Modern Textual Criticism.* Translated by Errol Rhodes. Grand Rapids: Eerdmans, 1987.

———. *The Text of the New Testament: An Introduction to the Critical Editions and to the Theory and Practice of Modern Textual Criticism.* 2nd ed. Translated by Errol Rhodes. Grand Rapids: Eerdmans, 1989.

Aland, Kurt, et al., eds. *The Greek New Testament.* 3rd corrected ed. New York: American Bible Society, 1983.

———. *Novum Testamentum Graece.* 27th ed. Stuttgart: Deutsche Bibelgesellschaft, 1979.

Alexander, Loveday. *Acts in Its Ancient Literary Context: A Classicist Looks at the Acts of the Apostles.* London: Bloomsbury, 2007.

———. *The Preface to Luke's Gospel: Literary Convention and Social Context in Luke 1:1–4 and Acts 1:1.* Cambridge: Cambridge University Press, 1993.

Alexander, Phillip S. "A New Translation and Introduction." In *The Old Testament Pseudepigrapha*, edited by James H. Charlesworth, 223–54. Peabody, MA: Hendrickson, 1983.

Andrews, Edward D. *The New Testament Documents.* Cambridge, OH: Christian Publishing House, 2020.

Arndt, William, et al. *A Greek-English Lexicon of the New Testament and Other Early Christian Literature.* Chicago: University of Chicago Press, 2000.

Aune, David E. *The New Testament in Its Literary Environment.* Philadelphia: Westminster John Knox, 1987.

———. "The Text-Tradition of Luke-Acts." *JETS* 7:3 (1964) 69–82.

Balz, Horst Robert, and Gerhard Schneider. *Exegetical Dictionary of the New Testament.* Grand Rapids: Eerdmans, 1990.

Barber, Elizabeth Jane Wayland. *Prehistoric Textiles: The Development of Cloth in the Neolithic and Bronze Ages with Special Reference to the Aegean.* Princeton: Princeton University Press, 1991.

Barclay, William, and F. F. Bruce. *The Making of the Bible.* Nashville: Abingdon, 1961.

Barrett, Matthew M. *God's Word Alone: The Authority of Scripture*. Grand Rapids: Zondervan, 2016.

Barry, John D., et al. *Faithlife Study Bible*. Bellingham, WA: Lexham, 2016.

Barthes, Roland, and Donald G. Marshall. "Textual Analysis of a Tale by Edgar Poe." *Poe Studies* 10:1 (1977) 1–11.

Barton, John. *The Nature of Biblical Criticism*. Louisville: Westminster John Knox, 2007.

Beal, Peter. *A Dictionary of English Manuscript Terminology: 1450 to 2000*. Oxford: Oxford University Press, 2008.

Beale, Gregory K. *Handbook on the New Testament Use of the Old Testament: Exegesis and Interpretation*. Grand Rapids: Baker Academic, 2012.

Beattie, Derek R., and Martin J. McNamara. *The Aramaic Bible: Targums in Their Historical Context*. New York: A&C Black, 1994.

Berg, I. C. "Four Criteria for Identifying the Socially Marginal in the Social Context of Early Christianity Reflected in the New Testament." *Acta Theologica* 40:1 (2020) 6–27.

Bettenson, Henry, and Chris Maunder. *Documents of the Christian Church*. New York: Oxford University Press, 1999.

Biblica. *New Testament: A Presentation of Today's New International Version*. NIV, The Books of the Bible 4. Colorado Springs: Biblica, 2007.

Black, Matthew. *An Aramaic Approach to the Gospels and Acts*. 3rd ed. Eugene, OR: Wipf & Stock, 2020.

Blackaby, Henry. *Experiencing the Word New Testament*. Nashville: Holman, 2008.

Blomberg, Craig L. "The Gospels for Specific Communities and All Christians." In *The Audience of the Gospels: The Origin and Function of the Gospels in Early Christianity*, edited by Edward W. Klink, 111–33. The Library of New Testament Studies. London: T&T Clark, 2010.

———. *A Handbook of New Testament Exegesis*. Grand Rapids: Baker Academic, 2010.

Bock, Darrell L. *A Theology of Luke and Acts: God's Promised Program, Realized for All Nations*. Biblical Theology of the New Testament. Grand Rapids: Zondervan, 2012.

Bonz, Marianne P. *The Past as Legacy: Luke-Acts and Ancient Epic*. Minneapolis: Fortress, 2000.

Borg, Marcus J. *Evolution of the Word: The New Testament in the Order the Books Were Written*. New York: HarperCollins, 2012.

Bousset, Wilhelm. *Kyrios Christos: A History of the Belief in Christ from the Beginnings of Christianity to Irenaeus*. Nashville: Abingdon, 1970.

Bovon, François. *Luke the Theologian: Fifty-Five Years of Research (1950–2005)*. 2nd rev. ed. Waco, TX: Baylor University Press, 2006.

———. "The Reception and Use of the Gospel of Luke in the Second Century." In *Reading Luke: Interpretation, Reflection, Formation*, edited by Craig G. Bartholomew, Joel B. Green, and Anthony C. Thiselton, 379–400. Scripture and Hermeneutics Series 6. Grand Rapids: Zondervan, 2005.

Bowman, Robert M. *Putting Jesus in His Place: The Case for the Deity of Christ*. Grand Rapids: Kregel, 2007.

Brakke, David. *Understanding the New Testament Course Guidebook*. Virginia: The Great Courses, 2019.

Brasfield, Nathan. "Jesus, Ascension of." In *LBD*, edited by John D. Barry et al. Bellingham, WA: Lexham, 2016. Logos software edition.

Bratka, Benjamin D. "Hercules." In *LBD*, edited by John D. Barry et al. Bellingham, WA: Lexham, 2016. Logos software edition.

Breck, John. *The Shape of Biblical Language: Chiasmus in the Scriptures and Beyond.* Crestwood, NY: St. Vladimir's Seminary Press, 1994.

Bromiley, Geoffrey W., ed. *International Standard Bible Encyclopedia: E–J.* Grand Rapids: Eerdmans, 1982.

Brown, Raymond E. *The Birth of the Messiah: A Commentary of the Infancy Narratives in Matthew and Luke.* Garden City, NY: Doubleday, 1977.

Burridge, Richard A. *What Are the Gospels? A Comparison with Greco-Roman Biography.* 25th anniversary ed. Waco, TX: Baylor University Press, 2018.

Buttrick, George Arthur, ed. *The Interpreter's Bible*. Vol. 9: *Acts and Romans*. Nashville: Abingdon, 1954.

Cadbury, Henry J. "Lexical Notes on Luke-Acts: II. Recent Arguments for Medical Language." *JBL* 45:1–2 (1926) 190–209.

———. *The Making of Luke-Acts.* London: Macmillan, 1927.

———. *The Making of Luke-Acts.* 2nd ed. Peabody, MA: Hendrickson, 1999.

Charles, Robert H. *The Assumption of Moses (Translated from the Latin Sixth Century MS).* London: Forgotten Books, 2018.

Charlesworth, James H. *The Old Testament Pseudepigrapha.* Vol. 1: *Apocalyptic Literature and Testaments.* Peabody, MA: Hendrickson, 1983.

Chen, Diane G. *Luke.* A New Covenant Commentary. Eugene, OR: Cascade, 2017.

Clayton, Barbara. *A Penelopean Poetics: Reweaving the Feminine in Homer's Odyssey.* Lanham, MD: Lexington, 2004.

Clouston, Eric. *How Ancient Narratives Persuade: Acts in Its Literary Context.* Lanham, MD: Rowman & Littlefield, 2020.

Comfort, Phillip. *Encountering the Manuscripts: An Introduction to New Testament Paleography and Textual Criticism.* Nashville: B&H, 2005.

Comfort, Philip W., and David P. Barrett. *The Text of the Earliest New Testament Greek Manuscripts.* Vol. 1: *Papyri 1–72.* Grand Rapids: Kregel Academic, 2019.

———. *The Text of the Earliest New Testament Greek Manuscripts.* Vol. 2: *Papyri 75–139 and Uncials.* Grand Rapids: Kregel Academic, 2019.

———. *The Text of the Earliest New Testament Greek Manuscripts: A Corrected, Enlarged Edition of the Complete Text of the Earliest New Testament Manuscripts.* Wheaton: Tyndale, 2001.

Comstock, Gary L. "Two Types of Narrative Theology." *JAAR* 55:4 (1987) 687–717.

Conzelmann, Hans. *The Theology of St. Luke.* Translated by Geoffrey Buswell. Philadelphia: Fortress, 1961.

Copeland, Rita. "Pathos and Pastoralism: Aristotle's Rhetoric in Medieval England." *Speculum* 89:1 (2014) 96–127.

Corbett, Edward P. *Classical Rhetoric for the Modern Student.* 2nd ed. New York: Oxford University Press, 1971.

Cromhout, Markus. Review of *The Social World of the New Testament: Insights and Models*, edited by Jerome H. Neyrey and Eric C. Stewart. *Neotestamentica* 44:1 (2010) 191–96.

Cross, F. L., and E. A. Livingstone. *The Oxford Dictionary of the Christian Church.* New York: Oxford University Press, 1997.

Crowe, Brandon D. *The Hope of Israel: The Resurrection of Christ in the Acts of the Apostles.* Grand Rapids: Baker Academic, 2020.

Crump, David M. *Jesus the Intercessor: Prayer and Christology in Luke-Acts*. Tübingen: Mohr Siebeck, 1992.

Davies, William D., and Dale C. Allison Jr. *A Critical and Exegetical Commentary on the Gospel According to Saint Matthew*. International Critical Commentary 1. London: T&T Clark International, 2004.

De Jonge, Henk Jan. "The Chronology of the Ascension Stories in Luke and Acts." *New Testament Studies* 59:2 (2013) 151–71.

DelHousaye, John. *The Fourfold Gospel: A Formational Commentary on Matthew, Mark, Luke, and John*. Vol. 1: *From the Beginning to the Baptist*. Eugene, OR: Pickwick, 2020.

Demosthenes. *Speeches 60 and 61, Prologues, Letters*. Translated by Ian Worthington. Austin: University of Texas Press, 2006.

Dennert, Brian C. "An Encomium for Jesus: Luke, Rhetoric, and the Story of Jesus." *JETS* 65:1 (2022) 156–57.

Dicken, Frank. *Herod as a Composite Character in Luke-Acts*. Tübingen: Mohr Siebeck, 2014.

———. "Luke." In *LBD*, edited by John D. Barry et al. Bellingham, WA: Lexham, 2016. Logos software edition.

Dio, Cassius. *Roman History*. Translated by Ernest Cary. Vol. 8. London: William Heinemann, 1925.

Diodorus Siculus. *Library of History*. Vol. 4: *Books 9–12.40*. Translated by C. H. Oldfather. LCL 375. Cambridge, MA: Harvard University Press, 1946.

Dodson, Derek S., and Katherine E. Smith. *Exploring Biblical Backgrounds: A Reader in Historical and Literary Contexts*. Waco, TX: Baylor University Press, 2018.

Drazin, Israel. *Maimonides: Reason Above All*. Jerusalem: Gefen, 2009.

Dunn, James D. G. *The Acts of the Apostles*. Grand Rapids: Eerdmans, 1996.

———. *Baptism in the Holy Spirit: A Re-Examination of the New Testament Teaching of the Gift of the Spirit in Relation to Pentecostalism Today*. 2nd ed. London: SCM Press, 1970.

Eadie, John W. *The Conversion of Constantine*. New York: Robert E. Krieger, 1971.

Edwards, James R. "Parallels and Patterns Between Luke and Acts." *Bulletin for Biblical Research* 27:4 (2017) 485–501.

Ellertson, Carol F. "New Testament Manuscripts, Textual Families, and Variants." In *How the New Testament Came to Be: The Thirty-Fifth Annual Sidney B. Sperry Symposium*, edited by Kent P. Jackson and Frank F. Judd Jr., 93–108. Salt Lake City: Deseret, 2006.

Ehninger, Douglas. "On Systems of Rhetoric." In "Selections from Volume 1," special issue. *Philosophy and Rhetoric* 25 (1992) 15–28.

Ehrman, Bart D. *The New Testament: A Historical Introduction to the Early Christian Writings*. 5th ed. New York: Oxford University Press, 2012.

Elgabsi, Natan. "Is There a Problem of Writing in Historiography? Plato and the Pharmakon of the Written Word." *Metodo International Studies in Phenomenology and Philosophy* 7:2 (2019) 225–64.

Enns, Paul. *The Moody Handbook of Theology*. Chicago: Moody Press, 1989.

Education Policy and Data Center. "Literacy and Educational Attainment." 2012. https://www.epdc.org/topic/literacy-and-educational-attainment.html.

Evans, Craig A. *Jesus and His World: The Archaeological Evidence*. Louisville: Westminster John Knox, 2012.

———. *Luke.* Understanding the Bible Commentary Series. Grand Rapids: Baker, 1990.
Fay, Ron C. *Father, Son and Spirit in Romans 8: Paul's Understanding of God with Special Reference to the Roman Recipients.* Deerfield, IL: Trinity Evangelical Divinity School, 2006.
———. "Greco-Roman Concepts of Deity." In *Paul's World*, edited by Stanley E. Porter, 1–31. Leiden: Brill, 2008.
———. "The Narrative Function of the Temple in Luke-Acts." *Trinity Journal* 27:2 (2006) 255–70.
Feinberg, Charles L. *The Minor Prophets.* Chicago: Moody Press, 1990.
Ferguson, Everett. *Backgrounds of Early Christianity.* 3rd ed. Grand Rapids: Eerdmans, 2003.
Ferrero, Mario, and George Tridimas. "Divine Competition in Greco-Roman Polytheism." *Homo Oeconomicus* 35:3 (2018) 143–66.
Fitzmyer, Joseph A. "The Ascension of Christ and Pentecost." *Theological Studies* 45:3 (1984) 409–40.
———. *Luke the Theologian: Aspects of His Teaching.* Mahwah, NJ: Paulist, 1989.
———. *Luke the Theologian: Aspects of His Teaching.* Repr., Eugene, OR: Wipf & Stock, 2004.
———. *The Gospel According to Luke (I–IX).* Anchor Yale Bible Commentaries 28. New Haven, CT: Yale University Press, 1970.
Foakes-Jackson, F. J. *The Beginnings of Christianity.* Part 1: *The Acts of the Apostles, Vol. 1.* Edited by Kirsopp Lake. London: Macmillan, 1920.
———. *The Beginnings of Christianity.* Part 1: *The Acts of the Apostles, Vol. 2.* Edited by Kirsopp Lake. London: Macmillan, 1922.
Forbes, Greg W., and Scott D. Harrower. *Raised from Obscurity: A Narratival and Theological Study of the Characterization of Women in Luke-Acts.* Cambridge, UK: James Clarke & Company, 2016.
Foster, Paul. "Q Source." In *LBD*, edited by John D. Barry et al. Bellingham, WA: Lexham, 2016. Logos software edition.
Frame, John M. "Narrative Theology." The Gospel Coalition, 2020. https://www.thegospelcoalition.org/essay/narrative-theology/.
Freed, Edwin D. *The Stories of Jesus' Birth: A Critical Introduction.* St. Louis: Chalice, 2001.
Fuhr, Alan, and Andreas J. Köstenberger. *Inductive Bible Study: Observation, Interpretation, and Application Through the Lenses of History, Literature, and Theology.* Nashville: B&H, 2016.
Funk, Robert W., Roy W. Hoover, and The Jesus Seminar. *The Five Gospels: The Search for the Authentic Words of Jesus.* San Francisco: HarperOne, 1996.
Gaddis, Michael. *There Is No Crime for Those Who Have Christ: Religious Violence in the Christian Roman Empire.* Berkeley: University of California Press, 2005.
Gallagher, Robert L., and Paul Hertig. *Mission in Acts: Ancient Narratives in Contemporary Context.* New York: Orbis, 2004.
Garbarino, Collin. "Julius Caesar." In *LBD*, edited by John D. Barry et al. Bellingham, WA: Lexham, 2016. Logos software edition.
Garland, David E. *Luke.* Zondervan Exegetical Commentary of the New Testament. Grand Rapids: Zondervan, 2011.

Garrison, Roman. *The Significance of Theophilus as Luke's Reader.* Lewiston, NY: Mellen, 2004.

Gasque, W. Ward. *A History of the Interpretation of the Acts of the Apostles.* Peabody, MA: Hendrickson, 1989.

Gelb, Norman. *Herod the Great: Statesman, Visionary, Tyrant.* Lanham, MD: Rowman & Littlefield, 2013.

Giacobbe, Massimo. *Luke the Chronicler: The Narrative Arc of Samuel-Kings and Chronicles in Luke-Acts.* Biblical Interpretation Series 211. Leiden: Brill, 2023.

Gill, David. "Observations on the Lukan Travel Narrative and Some Related Passages." *Harvard Theological Review* 63:2 (1970) 199–221.

González, Justo L. *Acts: The Gospel of the Spirit.* Maryknoll, NY: Orbis, 2001.

Goodson, Jacob L. *Narrative Theology and the Hermeneutical Virtues: Humility, Patience, Prudence.* Lanham, MD: Lexington, 2015.

Green, Joel B. *The Gospel of Luke.* Grand Rapids: Eerdmans, 1997.

———. "Luke-Acts, or Luke and Acts? A Reaffirmation of Narrative Unity." In *Reading Acts Today: Essays in Honour of Loveday C. A. Alexander*, edited by Steve Walton et al., 110–19. Library of New Testament Studies 427. New York: T&T Clark International, 2011.

———. *Luke as Narrative Theologian: Texts and Topics.* Tübingen: Mohr Siebeck, 2020.

Green, Joel B., and Lee Martin McDonald. *The World of the New Testament: Cultural, Social, and Historical Contexts.* Grand Rapids: Baker Academic, 2013.

Green, Joel B., and Scot McKnight. *Dictionary of Jesus and the Gospels.* Downers Grove, IL: InterVarsity Press, 1992.

Greenlee, Harold J. *Introduction to the New Testament Textual Criticism.* Rev. ed. Grand Rapids: Baker Academic, 1995.

Greever, Joshua M. "The Typological Expectation of Psalm 68 and Its Application in Ephesians 4:8." *Tyndale Bulletin* 71:2 (2020) 253–79.

Grenz, Stanley J., David Guretzki, and Cherith Fee Nordling. *Pocket Dictionary of Theological Terms.* The IVP Pocket Reference Series. Westmont, IL: IVP Academic, 1999.

Grohsebner, Sabrina. "Threads of Life: The Golden Age Midwife Amidst Cloth, Tissue and Antique Deities of Fate." *Avisos de Viena* 1 (2020) 20–28.

Gundry, Robert H. *A Survey of the New Testament.* 4th ed. Grand Rapids: Zondervan, 2003.

Guralnik, David B. *Webster's New World College Dictionary.* 3rd ed. New York: Simon & Schuster, 1986.

Guzik, David. *Luke: Verse by Verse Commentary.* Santa Barbara: Enduring Word Media, 2016.

Hadas, Moses. *Hellenistic Culture, Fusion and Diffusion.* Morning Heights, NY: Columbia University Press, 1959.

Haenchen, Ernst. *A Commentary on the Gospel of John Chapters 1–6.* Philadelphia: Fortress, 1984.

Hall, Stuart G. *Doctrine and Practice in the Early Church.* Grand Rapids: Eerdmans, 1992.

Halley, Henry H. *Halley's Bible Handbook.* 23rd ed. Grand Rapids: Zondervan, 1965.

Hardin, Leslie T., and Derek Brown. "Son of Man." In *LBD*, edited by John D. Barry et al. Bellingham, WA: Lexham, 2016. Logos software edition.

Harris, Ben. "1 Gospel, 4 Acts: Introduction(s) to the Genius of Luke." *Evangelical Quarterly* 89:1 (2018) 3–20.

Harris, W. Hall, III. *The Lexham Greek-English Interlinear New Testament: SBL Edition*. Bellingham, WA: Lexham, 2010.

Hartog, Paul Anthony. "Zeus." In *Eerdmans Dictionary of the Bible*, edited by David Noel Freedman, Allen C. Myers, and Astrid B. Beck, 1419–20. Grand Rapids: Eerdmans, 2000.

Hatina, Thomas R. "Palestine." In *The World of the New Testament: Cultural, Social, and Historical Contexts*, edited by Joel B. Green and Lee Martin McDonald, 560–76. Grand Rapids: Baker Academic, 2013.

Havelock, Eric A. *The Literate Revolution in Greece and Its Cultural Consequences*. Princeton: Princeton University Press, 1982.

Hays, Daniel, and J. Scott Duvall. *The Baker Illustrated Bible Handbook*. Grand Rapids: Baker, 2011.

Hengel, Martin. *Acts and the History of Earliest Christianity*. Eugene, OR: Wipf & Stock, 1979.

Herrick, James A. *The History and Theory of Rhetoric: An Introduction*. Oxfordshire: Taylor & Francis, 2017.

Hill, James H. *The Gospel of the Lord: An Early Version Which Was Circulated by Marcion of Sinope as the Original Gospel*. New York: AMS Press, 1980.

Hobart, William K. *The Medical Language of St. Luke and The Acts of the Apostles*. Dublin: Dublin University Press, 1882.

Holmes, Michael W. *The Greek New Testament: SBL Edition*. Bellingham, WA: Lexham, 2011–13.

Hone, William. *Lost Books of the Bible*. New York: Chartwell, 2016.

Howell, Adam J. Review of *A Biblical Aramaic Reader: With an Outline Grammar*, by Takamitsu Muraoka. *JBTS* 7:1 (2022) 137–39.

Hubbard, Moyer V. *Christianity in the Greco-Roman World: A Narrative Introduction*. Ada, MI: Baker Academic, 2010.

Huffman, Douglas S. "Luke, Gospel of." In *LBD*, edited by John D. Barry et al. Bellingham, WA: Lexham, 2016. Logos software edition.

Hurtado, Larry W. *Destroyer of the gods: Early Christian Distinctiveness in the Roman World*. Waco, TX: Baylor University Press, 2016.

———. *Lord Jesus Christ: Devotion to Jesus in Earliest Christianity*. Grand Rapids: Eerdmans, 2003.

Irenaeus of Lyons. "Against Heresies." In *The Apostolic Fathers with Justin Martyr and Irenaeus*, edited by Alexander Roberts, James Donaldson, and A. Cleveland Coxe, Vol. 1 of *The Ante-Nicene Fathers*. Buffalo, NY: Christian Literature Company, 1885.

James, Montague Rhodes, trans. "Epistle of the Apostles." In *The Apocryphal New Testament*, 485–503. Oxford: Clarendon, 1983.

James, Rob. *The Spiral Gospel: Intratextuality in Luke's Narrative*. Foundations in New Testament Criticism. Cambridge, UK: James Clarke & Co., 2022.

Jamieson, Robert, A. R. Fausset, and David Brown. *Commentary Critical and Explanatory on the Whole Bible*. Vol. 2. Oak Harbor, WA: Logos Research Systems, 1997.

Jerome. "Lives of Illustrious Men." In *Theodoret, Jerome, Gennadius, Rufinus: Historical Writings, Etc.*, edited by Philip Schaff and Henry Wace, translated by Ernest Cushing Richardson. Vol. 3 of *A Select Library of the Nicene and Post-Nicene Fathers of the Christian Church, Second Series*. New York: Christian Literature Company, 1892.

Johnson, Luke Timothy. *The Acts of the Apostles*. Edited by Daniel J. Harrington. Sacra Pagina 5. Collegeville, MN: Liturgical, 2006.

———. *The Gospel of Luke*. Sacra Pagina 3. Collegeville, MN: Liturgical, 1991.

Josephus, Flavius. *The New Complete Works of Josephus: Revised and Expanded Edition*. Translated by William Whiston. Grand Rapids: Kregel, 1999.

———. *Jewish Antiquities*. In *The New Complete Works of Josephus: Revised and Expanded Edition*, translated by William Whiston, 47–644. Grand Rapids: Kregel, 1999.

———. *The Jewish War, or The History of the Destruction of Jerusalem*. In *The New Complete Works of Josephus: Revised and Expanded Edition*, translated by William Whiston, 665–936. Grand Rapids: Kregel, 1999.

Juel, Donald. *Luke-Acts: The Promise of History*. Atlanta: John Knox, 1983.

Julicher, Adolf. *An Introduction to the New Testament*. London: Smith, Elder & Company, 1904.

Kaiser, Walter C., Jr., and Moisés Silva. *Introduction to Biblical Hermeneutics: The Search for Meaning*. Rev. and exp. ed. Grand Rapids: Zondervan, 2007.

Kantor, Mattis. *The Jewish Time Line Encyclopedia*. Updated ed. Oxford: Rowman & Littlefield, 1992.

Keck, Leander E., and J. Louis Martyn. *Studies in Luke-Acts*. Philadelphia: Fortress, 1980.

Keener, Craig S. *Acts: An Exegetical Commentary*. Vol. 1: *Introduction and 1:1—2:47*. Grand Rapids: Baker, 2012.

———. *The IVP Bible Background Commentary: New Testament*. Westmont, IL: InterVarsity Press, 2014.

Kelly, Joseph F. *The Concise Dictionary of Early Christianity*. Collegeville, MN: Liturgical, 1992.

Kiley, Mark C. *Reading Between the Letters of the Gospels*. Eugene, OR: Wipf & Stock, 2024.

Klein, George. *Zechariah: An Exegetical and Theological Exposition of Holy Scripture*. Nashville: B&H, 2008.

Klink, Edward W. *The Audience of the Gospels: The Origin and Function of the Gospels in Early Christianity*. London: T&T Clark, 2010.

Koester, Helmut. *Ancient Christian Gospels: Their History and Development*. Philadelphia: Trinity Press International, 1990.

———. *History and Literature of Early Christianity*. Berlin: de Gruyter, 2000.

Konstam, Angus, and Margaret Keenan. *Rome: A Photographic Journey*. Seattle: Compendium, 2008.

Köstenberger, Andreas J., and Gregory Goswell. *Biblical Theology: A Canonical, Thematic and Ethical Approach*. Wheaton, IL: Crossway, 2023.

Köstenberger, Andreas J., and Richard D. Patterson. *For the Love of God's Word: An Introduction to Biblical Interpretation*. Grand Rapids: Kregel, 2015.

———. *Invitation to Biblical Interpretation: Exploring the Hermeneutical Triad of History, Literature, and Theology*. 2nd ed. Grand Rapids: Kregel, 2021.

Köstenberger, Andreas J., et al. *The Cradle, the Cross, and the Crown: An Introduction to the New Testament*. Nashville: B&H, 2009.

Kremmydas, Christos, and Kathryn Tempest. "Introduction: Exploring Hellenistic Oratory." In *Hellenistic Oratory: Continuity and Change*, edited by Christos Kremmydas and Kathryn Tempest, 1–17. Oxford: Oxford University Press, 2013.

Kummel, Werner Georg. *Introduction to the New Testament*. Rev. ed. Nashville: Abingdon, 1975.

Liddell, Henry George, et al. *A Greek-English Lexicon*. Oxford: Clarendon, 1996.

Lipka, Michael. *Roman Gods: A Conceptual Approach*. Leiden: Brill, 2009.

Litwak, Kenneth D. *Echoes of Scripture in Luke-Acts: Telling the History of God's People Intertextually*. London: A&C Black, 2005.

Livy. *History of Rome*. Vol. 1: *Books 1–2*. Translated by Benjamin O. Foster. LCL 114. Cambridge, MA: Harvard University Press, 1919.

Lorenzen, Thorwald. *Resurrection and Discipleship: Interpretive Models, Biblical Reflections, Theological Consequences*. Eugene, OR: Wipf & Stock, 1995.

Louden, Caleb T. "The Chiastic Arrangement of the Lukan Temptation Narrative." *The Journal of Inductive Biblical Studies* 4:2 (2017) 129–54.

Lyle, Kristopher A., et al. "The Lexham Figurative Language of the New Testament Dataset." In *Lexham Figurative Language of the Bible Glossary*, edited by Joshua R. Westbury et al. Bellingham, WA: Faithlife, 2016. Logos software edition.

MacArthur, John. *The Second Coming: Signs of Christ's Return and the End of the Age*. Wheaton, IL: Crossway, 1999.

MacDermot, H. E. "The Medical Language of St. Luke." *Canadian Medical Association Journal* 40:1 (1939) 80–83.

Maddox, Robert. *The Purpose of Luke-Acts*. Edited by John Riches. Forschungen zur Religion und Literatur des Alten und Neuen Testaments 126. Göttingen: Vandenhoeck & Ruprecht, 1982.

Maier, Paul L. *Eusebius Church History: A New Translation with Commentary*. Grand Rapids: Kregel, 1999.

Marie, Carol. *The Law Fulfilled*. Mustang, OK: Tate, 2009.

Marshall, I. Howard. *Luke: Historian and Theologian*. Cumbria: Paternoster, 1979.

McDonald, Lee Martin. "Anti-Marcionite (Gospel) Prologues." In *AYBD*, edited by David Noel Freedman, 1:262–63. New York: Doubleday, 1992.

McKenzie, Steven L., and John Kaltner. *New Meanings for Ancient Texts: Recent Approaches to Biblical Criticisms and Their Applications*. Louisville: Westminster John Knox, 2013.

Metzger, Bruce M. *The Canon of the New Testament: Its Origin, Development, and Significance*. Oxford: Clarendon, 1987.

———. *The New Testament: Its Background, Growth, and Content*. Nashville: Abingdon, 1965.

———. *A Textual Commentary on the Greek New Testament: A Companion Volume to the United Bible Societies Greek New Testament (Fourth Revision Edition)*. 2nd ed. New York: United Bible Societies, 1994.

———. *A Textual Commentary on the Greek New Testament: A Companion Volume to the United Bible Societies Greek New Testament Third Edition*. London: United Bible Societies, 1971.

Meyer, Anthony R. "Coinage in Biblical Times." In *LBD*, edited by John D. Barry et al. Bellingham, WA: Lexham, 2016. Logos software edition.

Michener, Ronald T. *Postliberal Theology: A Guide for the Perplexed*. New York: Bloomsbury, 2013.

Miller, Jeffrey E. "Theophilus." In *LBD*, edited by John D. Barry et al. Bellingham, WA: Lexham, 2016. Logos software edition.

Moessner, David P. *Jesus and the Heritage of Israel*. Vol. 1: *Luke's Narrative Claim upon Israel's Legacy*. Harrisburg, PA: Trinity Press International, 1999.

Moffitt, David M. *Rethinking the Atonement: New Perspectives on Jesus's Death, Resurrection, and Ascension*. Grand Rapids: Baker, 2022.

Moore, Arthur L. *The Parousia in the New Testament*. Leiden: Brill, 1966.

Morris, Leon. *Luke*. The Tyndale New Testament Commentaries. Downers Grove, IL: IVP Academic, 1988.

Moseley, James Allen. *The Biographies of Jesus' Apostles: Ambassadors in Chains*. Eugene, OR: Resource, 2022.

Moyise, Steve. "Intertextuality and Biblical Studies: A Review." *Verbum et Ecclesia* 23:2 (2002) 418.

———. *Paul and Scripture: Studying the New Testament Use of the Old Testament*. Grand Rapids: Baker Academic, 2010.

Mundhenk, Norm. "Jesus Is Lord: The Tetragrammaton in Bible Translation." *The Bible Translator* 61:2 (2010) 55–63.

Murai, Hajime. "Database System for Archiving the Literary Structure of the Bible." *Journal of the Japanese Association for Digital Humanities* 1.1 (2015) 44–57.

Muraoka, Takamitsu. *A Biblical Aramaic Reader: With an Outline Grammar*. Leuven: Peeters, 2015.

———. "Luke and the Septuagint." *Novum Testamentum* 54:1 (2012) 13–15.

Murray, John. *A Dictionary of Early Christian Biography*. Peabody, MA: Hendrickson, 1999.

Neander, Augustus. *The History of the Christian Religion and Church During the Three First Centuries*. Philadelphia: James M. Campbell & Company, 1843.

Nelson, Peter K. "Theophilus." In *Eerdmans Dictionary of the Bible*, edited by David Noel Freedman, Allen C. Myers, and Astrid B. Beck, 1298. Grand Rapids: Eerdmans, 2000.

Neusner, Jacob, and Bruce D. Chilton. *In Quest of the Historical Pharisees*. Waco, TX: Baylor University Press, 2007.

Newman, Barclay M., and Eugene A. Nida. *A Handbook on the Acts of the Apostles*. UBS Handbook Series. New York: United Bible Societies, 1972.

Neyrey, Jerome H. *An Encomium for Jesus: Luke, Rhetoric, and the Story of Jesus*. Sheffield: Sheffield Phoenix, 2020.

———. *The Passion According to Luke: A Redaction Study of Luke's Soteriology*. Eugene, OR: Wipf & Stock, 2007.

Norris, Steven D. *Unravelling the Family History of Jesus*. Bloomington, IN: WestBow, 2016.

O'Day, Gail R., and David L. Petersen, eds. *Theological Bible Commentary*. Louisville: Westminster John Knox, 2009.

O'Toole, Robert F. *Luke's Presentation of Jesus: A Christology*. Rome: Editrice Pontificio Istituto Bíblico, 2004.

Padilla, Osvaldo. *The Acts of the Apostles: Interpretation, History, and Theology*. Downers Grove, IL: InterVarsity Press, 2016.

Parsons, Mikeal C. *Reading Acts as a Sequel to the Fourfold Gospel*. Waco, TX: Baylor University Press, 2015.

———. "The Text of Acts 1:2 Reconsidered." *Catholic Biblical Quarterly* 50:1 (1988) 58–71.

Parsons, Mikeal C., and Richard I. Pervo. *Rethinking the Unity of Luke and Acts*. Minneapolis: Fortress, 1993.

Parsons, Wilfrid. *A Study of the Vocabulary and Rhetoric of the Letters of Saint Augustine*. The Catholic University of America Patristic Studies 3. Washington, DC: Catholic University of America Press, 1923.

Patzia, Arthur G. *The Making of the New Testament: Origin, Collection, Text and Canon*. Downers Grove, IL: IVP Academic, 1995.

Penner, Ken M. "Philo's Eschatology, Personal and Cosmic." *Journal for the Study of Judaism in the Persian, Hellenistic, and Roman Period* 50:3 (2019) 383–402.

Perdue, Leo G. "Theology, Old Testament." In *LBD*, edited by John D. Barry et al. Bellingham, WA: Lexham, 2016. Logos software edition.

Pervo, Richard I. *Acts: A Commentary*. Hermeneia. Minneapolis: Fortress, 2009.

———. *Profit with Delight: The Literary Genre of the Acts of the Apostles*. Philadelphia: Fortress, 1987.

Peters, John J. *Luke Among the Ancient Historians: Ancient Historiography and the Attempt to Remedy the Inadequate "Many."* Eugene, OR: Pickwick, 2022.

Pettis, Jeffery B. "Ascension." In *Encyclopedia of Psychology and Religion*, edited by David A. Leeming, 71–72. Switzerland: Springer International, 2020.

Pitts, Andrew W. *History, Biography, and the Genre of Luke-Acts: An Exploration of Literary Divergence in Greek Narrative Discourse*. Boston: Brill, 2019.

Pliny the Younger. "The Letters of the Younger Pliny, First Series—Volume 1." Translated by J. B. Firth. In *Epistles*, edited by Heinrich Keil, 1.1.10. New York: Walter Scott, 2020.

Plottel, Jeanine P. *Intertextuality: New Perspectives in Criticism*. New York: New York Literary Forum, 1978.

Plummer, Alfred. *A Critical and Exegetical Commentary on the Gospel According to St. Luke*. International Critical Commentary. London: Bloomsbury T&T Clark, 1989.

Poirier, John. "Some Detracting Considerations for Reader-Response Theory." *Catholic Biblical Quarterly* 62:2 (2000) 250–63.

Porter, Stanley E. *Dictionary of Biblical Criticism and Interpretation*. New York: Routledge, 2007.

———. "The We Passages in the Acts of the Apostles: The Narrator as Narrative Character." *JETS* 52:1 (2009) 162–63.

Porter, Stanley E., and Ron C. Fay. *Luke-Acts in Modern Interpretation: Milestones in New Testament Scholarship*. Grand Rapids: Kregel Academic, 2021.

Porter, Stanley E., and Thomas H. Olbricht. "Rhetoric and the New Testament." In *Essays from the 1992 Heidelberg Conference*, 90–99. London: Bloomsbury, 1993.

Powell, Mark A. *Introducing the New Testament: A Historical, Literary, and Theological Survey*. Grand Rapids: Baker Academic, 2009.

———. *What Are They Saying About Acts?* Mahwah, NJ: Paulist, 1989.

———. *What Is Narrative Criticism?* Minneapolis: Fortress, 1990.

Ramsay, William M. *Luke the Physician and Other Studies in the History of Religion*. Grand Rapids: Baker, 1979.

Resseguie, James L. *Narrative Criticism of the New Testament: An Introduction*. Ada, MI: Baker Academic, 2005.

Reynolds, Benjamin E. *The Son of Man Problem: Critical Readings*. New York: Bloomsbury T&T Clark, 2018.

Richards, E. Randolph. *Paul and First-Century Letter Writing: Secretaries, Composition and Collection*. Downers Grove, IL: IVP Academic, 2004.

———. "Reading, Writing, and Manuscripts." In *The World of the New Testament: Cultural, Social, and Historical Contexts*, edited by Joel B. Green and Lee Martin McDonald, 345–66. Grand Rapids: Baker Academic, 2013.

Rhoads, David, et al. *Mark as Story: An Introduction to the Narrative of a Gospel*. Minneapolis: Fortress, 2012.

Rodgers, Nigel. *Ancient Rome*. England: Southwater Publishing, 2013.

Roisman, Hanna M. *Sophocles' Electra*. Oxford Greek and Latin College Commentaries. Oxford: Oxford University Press, 2020.

Roth, Dieter T. "The Text of Luke and Acts: Witnesses, Features, and the Significance of the Textual Traditions." In *Issues in Luke-Acts: Selected Essays*, edited by Sean A. Adams and Michael Pahl, 51–71. Piscataway, NJ: Gorgias Press, 2012.

Rowe, C. Kavin. "History, Hermeneutics and the Unity of Luke-Acts." *JSNT* 28 (2005) 131–57.

———. "Literary Unity and Reception History: Reading Luke-Acts as Luke and Acts." *JSNT* 29 (2007) 449–57.

Rayan, Samuel. *The Holy Spirit: Heart of the Gospel and Christian Hope*. Maryknoll, NY: Orbis, 1978.

Sailhamer, John H. *Christian Theology*. Grand Rapids: Zondervan, 1998.

———. *Introduction to Old Testament Theology: A Canonical Approach*. New York: HarperCollins, 1999.

———. *The Meaning of the Pentateuch: Revelation, Composition and Interpretation*. Downers Grove, IL: InterVarsity Press, 2009.

———. *The Pentateuch as Narrative: A Biblical-Theological Commentary*. Grand Rapids: Zondervan, 1992.

Sanday, William. *The Gospels in the Second Century: An Examination of the Critical Part of a Work Entitled "Supernatural Religion."* London: Macmillan, 1876.

Sansone, David. *Greek Drama and the Invention of Rhetoric*. Hoboken, NJ: Wiley & Sons, 2012.

Schaff, Philip. *History of the Christian Church*. Vol. 1: *Apostolic Christianity A.D. 1–100*. New York: Charles Scribner's Sons, 1884.

Schmidt, Alvin I. *How Christianity Changed the World*. Grand Rapids: Zondervan, 2004.

Schmitz, Thomas A., and Nicolas Wiater, eds. *The Struggle for Identity: Greeks and Their Past in the First Century BCE*. Stuttgart: Franz Steiner, 2011.

Schnabel, Eckhard J. *Acts*. Zondervan Exegetical Commentary on the New Testament. New York: HarperCollins, 2012.

Schreiner, Thomas R. *Romans*. Baker Evangelical Commentary on the New Testament. Grand Rapids: Baker Academic, 1998.

Schweizer, Eduard. *The Good News According to Luke*. Atlanta: John Knox, 1984.

Shaw, Robert. *Quilts: A Living Tradition*. Fairfield, CT: Hugh Lauter Levin Associates, 1995.

Shin, W. G. "Narrative Development of Israel's Restoration Hope (2): The Exodus 15 Pattern Accomplished by the Davidic Christ." In *The "Exodus" in Jerusalem (Luke 9:31)*, 203–30. Leiden: Brill, 2022.

Sleeman, Matthew. *Geography and the Ascension Narrative in Acts.* Society for New Testament Studies Monograph Series 146. Cambridge, UK: Cambridge University Press, 2009.

Smith, Christopher R. *After Chapters and Verses: Engaging the Bible in the Coming Generations.* Westmont, IL: InterVarsity Press, 2010.

Smith, Daniel Lynwood, and Zachary Lundin Kostopoulos. "Biography, History and the Genre of Luke-Acts." *New Testament Studies* 63:3 (2017) 390–410.

Smith, Robert H. "The Theology of Acts." *Concordia Theological Monthly* 42:54 (1971) 527–28.

Soulen, Richard N., and Kendall R. Soulen. *Handbook of Biblical Criticism.* Cambridge, UK: James Clarke & Company, 1977.

Spencer, Patrick E. "The Unity of Luke-Acts: A Four-Bolted Hermeneutical Hinge." *Currents in Biblical Research* 5:3 (2007) 341–66.

Stadel, Seth. "Gospel Prologues." In *LBD*, edited by John D. Barry et al. Bellingham, WA: Lexham, 2016. Logos software edition.

Staples, Jason A. "Lord, Lord: Jesus as YHWH in Matthew and Luke." *New Testament Studies* 64:1 (2018) 1–19.

Stephens, John, and Robyn McCallum. *Retelling Stories, Framing Culture: Traditional Story and Metanarratives in Children's Literature.* New York: Garland, 1998.

Strauss, Mark L. *Four Portraits, One Jesus: A Survey of Jesus and the Gospels.* Grand Rapids: Zondervan, 2007.

———. *Jesus Behaving Badly: The Puzzling Paradoxes of the Man from Galilee.* Westmont, IL: InterVarsity Press, 2015.

Strong, James. *A Concise Dictionary of the Words in the Greek Testament and the Hebrew Bible.* Bellingham, WA: Logos Bible Software, 2009.

Tacitus, Cornelius. *Annals: Books 13–16.* Translated by John Jackson. LCL 322. Cambridge, MA: Harvard University Press, 1937.

Talbert, Charles H. *Reading Luke: A Literary and Theological Commentary on the Third Gospel.* New York: Crossroad, 1982.

Tannehill, Robert C. *The Narrative Unity of Luke-Acts: A Literary Interpretation.* 2 vols. Philadelphia: Fortress, 1986.

Tilburg, Cornelis V. *Traffic and Congestion in the Roman Empire.* New York: Routledge, 2007.

Thompson, Alan J. *The Acts of the Risen Lord Jesus: Luke's Account of God's Unfolding Plan.* Westmont, IL: InterVarsity Press, 2011.

Thompson, Edward M. *Bible Illustrations.* Oxford: Oxford University Press, 1896.

Thompson, Leonard L. *The Book of Revelation: Apocalypse and Empire.* New York: Oxford University Press, 1997.

Thomson, Ian H. *Chiasmus in the Pauline Letters.* Sheffield: Sheffield Academic, 1995.

Thornburg, Annette. "Narrative's Revelatory Power: Toward an Understanding of Narrative Theology." *Denison Journal of Religion* 5:3 (2005) 2.

Tyson, Joseph B. *The Death of Jesus in Luke-Acts.* Columbia: University of South Carolina, 1986.

Unger, Merrill F. *The New Unger's Bible Dictionary.* Chicago: The Moody Bible Institute of Chicago, 1988.

———. *The New Unger's Bible Handbook.* Chicago: The Moody Bible Institute of Chicago, 2005.

Vermes, Géza. *Jesus the Jew: A Historian's Reading of the Gospels*. Minneapolis: Fortress, 1981.

Vinzent, Markus. *Christ's Resurrection in Early Christianity: And the Making of the New Testament*. London: Taylor & Francis, 2011.

Wace, Henry, and William C. Piercy. *A Dictionary of Early Christian Biography and Literature to the End of the Sixth Century A.D., with an Account of the Principal Sects and Heresies*. Peabody, MA: Hendrickson, 1999.

Walaskay, Paul W. *Acts*. Louisville: Westminster John Knox, 1998.

Wansbrough, Henry. *Jesus and the Oral Gospel Tradition*. New York: T&T Clark International, 2004.

Waterhouse, Steven. *Jesus and History: How We Know His Life and Claims*. Amarillo, TX: Westcliff, 2009.

Welch, John W. *Chiasmus in Antiquity: Structures, Analyses, Exegesis*. Eugene, OR: Wipf & Stock, 2020.

Westcott, Brooke F., and Fenton J. A. Hort. *The New Testament in the Original Greek*. New York: Harper & Brothers, 1882.

Westfall, Cynthia Long. "Roman Religions and the Imperial Cult." In *LBD*, edited by John D. Barry et al. Bellingham, WA: Lexham, 2016. Logos software edition.

Wheeler, James T. *God's Word Unfolded: A Summary of Old and New Testament History, Including the Laws of Moses*. Lancaster, PA: Wentworth, 2019.

White, L. M., et al. "Christianity: Christianity in Asia Minor." In *AYBD*, edited by David Noel Freedman, 1:927–79. New York: Doubleday, 1992.

Widengren, Geo. *Tradition and Literature in Early Judaism and the Early Church*. Leiden: Brill, 1963.

Wilder, Amos. "Variant Traditions of the Resurrection in Acts." *JBL* 62:4 (1943) 307–18.

Witherington, Ben, III. *The Acts of the Apostles: A Socio-Rhetorical Commentary*. Grand Rapids: Eerdmans, 1998.

———. "Education in the Greco-Roman World." In *The World of the New Testament: Cultural, Social, and Historical Contexts*, edited by Joel B. Green and Lee Martin McDonald, 188–94. Grand Rapids: Baker Academic, 2013.

Womble, T. Scott. *Bringing the Depths into Focus: Engaging Difficulties in Biblical Interpretation*. Eugene, OR: Wipf & Stock, 2021.

Woolsey, Theodore D. *The End of Luke's Gospel and the Beginning of the Acts: Two Studies*. London: Forgotten Books, 2018.

Wright, N. T. *Surprised by Hope: Rethinking Heaven, the Resurrection, and the Mission of the Church*. New York: HarperOne, 2008.

Wright, N. T., and Michael F. Bird. *The New Testament in Its World: An Introduction to the History, Literature, and Theology of the First Christians*. Grand Rapids: Zondervan Academic, 2019.

Young, T. Cuyler, Jr. "Persecution of the Early Church." In *AYBD*, edited by David Noel Freedman et al., 5:231–36. New York: Doubleday, 1992.

Zeichmann, Christopher B. "Roman Empire." In *LBD*, edited by John D. Barry et al. Bellingham, WA: Lexham, 2016. Logos software edition.

Zwiep, Arie W. *The Ascension of the Messiah in Lukan Christology*. Leiden: Brill, 1997.

Index

Aaron, 180
Abraham, 71, 101, 137, 171, 174, 187, 284
accuracy, xvii, 20–21, 62–64, 80, 95, 132, 243
accurate, xvii, 10, 20–22, 27, 30, 61, 63–64, 78–79, 94, 128, 151, 206
accurately, 6, 65, 97, 136, 143, 258
accusations, 80, 156
Achaia, 87–88, 155, 160, 185
acta, 86, 304
Adam, xvi, xx, 2, 35, 49–50, 60, 72, 101–2, 105, 138, 171–72, 174, 215–16, 234, 279, 303, 309, 314
Admetus, 210
Adonai, 111
Adriatic, 185
advent, 108, 208, 258, 265, 272
Aeneid, 65
aesthetic, 239, 247, 263
aesthetically, 262
afterlife, 209
agnostic, 19
agony, 163, 197
Agrippa, 127, 131, 183, 194
Alcestis, 210
Alexandria, 105, 137
Alexandrian, 47, 67, 146–47, 150–52
Alexandrinus, 143, 147, 151
allegory, 98
alliteration, 158
alma, 111–13
almah, 112

Almighty, 179, 214
amanuenses, 133
amanuensis, 32, 137
amateur, 60–61, 136, 162
Amphipolis, 185
Ananias, 54, 166, 168
ancestors, 240
ancestry, 174
anciens, 82
ancient, 1, 12–13, 17, 19, 33–34, 37, 41, 49–50, 64–65, 67, 72, 78–80, 82–83, 85–86, 90, 94, 98–99, 108, 115, 118, 120, 125–26, 129–30, 132–34, 136–39, 141, 153, 157, 159, 162–63, 169, 172, 190, 211–13, 225, 229–30, 232–38, 258, 260, 270, 277–80, 296, 299, 301, 303–5, 307, 310–11, 313–14
Andrew, 20–21, 56, 92, 132–35, 137–38, 141, 145, 149–50, 159, 303, 313
angel, 53, 111, 131, 154, 163, 197, 221, 288
angelic, 251, 256, 285, 291, 293
angels, 103, 119, 213, 217, 255–56, 258, 282–85, 288
annals, 64, 155, 315
anointed, 49, 53, 108
anointing, 256
anointings, 108
anonymous, xvii, 8, 19, 22, 46, 63, 130, 144, 148, 160, 203, 297–98
anonymously, xvii, 144, 149

INDEX

Antioch, 30, 46, 84–85, 105, 127, 159–60, 168, 175, 185
Antiochene, 85, 159
Antipas, 80, 187, 194
antiquities, 216, 310
antiquity, 20, 41, 61, 132–33, 191, 200, 229, 250–51, 278–79, 316
antithetical, 5, 229, 293, 301
antitypes, 170
Antonius, 200
aorist, 119
Apion, 77, 79, 280
apocalyptic, 35, 294, 305
apocryphal, 89, 114, 130, 152, 218, 279, 309
Apollo, 212
Apollonia, 185
Apollonius, 237
Apollos, 92, 213
apologetic, 29, 93
apologetically, 20
apologist, 21
apostatize, 156
apostle, xvi, xviii, 3, 12, 36–37, 44–45, 49, 73, 77, 81, 89, 103–4, 131, 141, 155, 164, 193, 217, 263, 294, 297
apostles, xvi, xix, 2–4, 8, 11–12, 15, 22, 24, 26–27, 30, 34, 38, 40–42, 44–46, 51–54, 58, 61–62, 64–65, 68, 71, 73, 77, 81, 84, 86, 88, 91–93, 95, 105, 110, 115–16, 124, 128, 130–31, 138–40, 144, 157, 160, 164, 166, 170–72, 183–84, 187–90, 192–94, 196, 198–99, 201–2, 204–5, 207, 210, 216–21, 223–25, 228, 235, 238, 241–44, 246, 249–51, 254, 258, 260–61, 265–66, 269–71, 277–78, 281, 284–86, 288, 290–91, 297, 299–300, 303, 305–310, 312–13, 316
apostolic, xvii, 5, 14, 39, 46, 75, 131, 138, 164, 225, 261, 265, 271–72, 274, 280–81, 286, 288, 290, 292, 295–96, 309, 314
apotheosis, 6, 37, 118, 211–12, 214, 217, 294, 296

appearance, 4, 8, 19, 56, 59–60, 74–75, 96, 103, 163, 197, 215, 255, 298
appearances, 60, 87, 206, 239
apprentice, 133
Aquila, 92
Aramaic, 113–15, 134–35, 137, 145, 159, 165, 175, 304, 309, 312
Aramaisms, 159
archangel, 215
Archelaus, 194
archeological, 21
archeologists, 22
archetypal, 137
architectural, 175
Areopagus, 295
Aretaeus, 163
Arimathea, 198
Aristarchus, 161
Aristotle, 5, 33, 79, 158, 295, 305
Armageddon, 246
armies, 214
armor, 68
army, 212, 215
arrangement, 3, 12, 15, 78–79, 229, 240–41, 250–51, 282, 284, 291, 295, 311
arrival, 35, 38, 74, 84–85, 94, 129, 183, 186, 200, 208, 228, 268, 270
Artemis, 112
artisan, 214
artistic, 262
ascension, vii, xii, xvii–xviii, 1–7, 14–15, 19, 24, 28, 31, 36–43, 45, 48, 50–51, 56, 59, 84, 92, 130, 160, 168, 171, 199–231, 235–39, 241–48, 252–77, 279–98, 300–302, 304, 306–7, 312–13, 315–16
ascensions, 1, 211, 219
ascent, 227, 265, 268, 291
Asia, 31, 45, 86, 250, 316
Asos, 185
atheistic, 19
atheists, 24, 106
Athena, 112
Athenian, 79
Athens, 105, 112, 158, 183, 185
atone, 2, 256
Attalia, 185

attic, 34, 146
audibly, 129
audience, 3, 7, 13, 16–18, 28–29, 34–35, 41, 45–46, 49, 55, 63, 71, 79, 86, 94, 118, 129, 157, 167–68, 205, 263, 294–95, 300, 304, 310
audiences, xv, 5, 7, 114–15, 118, 237, 264
Augustine, 295, 313
Augustus, 145, 153–54, 312
authentic, 101, 109, 307
authenticity, xvii, 63, 102, 111, 128, 144, 166
authoritative, xvii, 7, 10, 41, 44–45, 77, 111, 115, 131, 144, 168, 171, 186, 201
authoritatively, 111
authority, xvi–xvii, 6–7, 10, 41, 43–45, 48, 63, 182, 192, 215, 256–57, 265, 277, 281, 285–86, 289–91, 294, 296, 298, 304
authorship, xvi–xvii, 8, 16, 23–25, 44, 62, 77, 81, 83, 90, 100, 128–29, 138, 144, 153, 160, 162–64, 166
autograph, 20, 29, 32–33, 46–47, 137–39, 144
autographs, 18, 20, 29, 46, 78, 81, 83, 137–39, 142, 145–46, 151, 298
axiom, 301
axis, xviii, 266
Azotus, 184

Babel, 192
Babylon, 72, 130, 178
Babylonian, 114–15
baptism, 11–12, 31, 53–54, 195, 243–45, 256, 268, 288, 306
baptismal, 11–12
Baptist, 13, 50, 74–75, 93, 102–4, 116, 118–19, 145, 173–74, 187, 190, 194–95, 245, 251, 260, 297, 306
baptize, 54
baptized, 11, 13, 53, 187, 244, 268
baptizing, 11, 13, 151
barbarians, 130
Barnabas, 30, 46, 84, 92–93, 106, 153, 161, 168, 175, 181, 198
Baruch, 279–80, 303
beatitudes, 240

begotten, 105
believers, xv, 1, 28–30, 44–45, 51–52, 67–68, 73, 84, 86, 95, 106, 115–17, 127–131, 142, 144, 147, 193, 196, 221, 242, 256, 269, 288, 290
Bénédictine, 82
benefactor, 144
Berea, 185
Bethabara, 204–5
Bethany, 184, 204–5, 257, 282–84
Bethlehem, 95, 103, 119, 188
Bethphage, 184
Bethsaida, 56
bethulah, 112
Bezae, 84, 144, 147, 152, 164, 222–23
Bible, iv–v, xii, xvi–xvii, xxii–xxiii, 1, 9–10, 18–20, 24–25, 29, 33–34, 44, 47, 50, 53–54, 62, 72–73, 78, 83, 88, 92, 97–99, 102, 104, 109, 113–14, 121, 129, 134–135, 146, 149, 153, 155, 162–63, 170, 174, 186–88, 195, 197, 208, 212–14, 218, 223–27, 230, 233, 245–47, 257–59, 276, 280, 292, 302–5, 307–312, 315
Bibles, iv, xvi, 153, 219
biblical, xi, xv–xvii, xxii, 1, 5, 12, 16–20, 22, 25, 29, 33–34, 46–47, 49–53, 60, 75, 90, 97–100, 107, 109, 114, 121, 123, 136–38, 145, 149, 158, 161, 165, 172–73, 180, 186, 190, 211–12, 216, 224, 228–30, 232–33, 238–39, 241, 250, 271, 277, 279, 286, 293, 296, 304–6, 308–316
biographer, 72
biographic, 57, 125
biographical, 34, 41, 59–60, 125, 136, 298
biography, 10, 41, 57, 60, 62–63, 77, 83–84, 125, 131, 191, 277–78, 305, 312–13, 315–16
biological, 102, 105, 302
birth, xii, xvi, 13, 29, 31, 50, 53–55, 59, 81, 101–8, 110–12, 115, 118–19, 128–31, 151, 153–54, 159, 171, 173, 188, 202, 210, 246, 251, 262, 296, 305, 307
birthed, 101, 143

INDEX

birthplace, 292
births, 104, 173, 251–52
bishop, 105, 139
blasphemy, 111
blessed, 37, 178, 240, 253, 257, 267, 284
blesses, 257, 282–83
blessing, xx, 205, 256–57, 284–85, 287, 289
blood, 50, 152, 163, 180, 197, 224, 255–56
bodiless, 214
bodily, 53, 95
Bodmer, 67, 147, 150–51, 164, 220–21, 223
body, 51, 73, 117, 210, 212, 216, 234
Boeotia, 86
booths, 116
bright, 74, 216
brilliance, 110, 264
brilliantly, 29
broad, 120, 144
broader, 6–7, 29, 40, 52, 86, 98, 101, 233, 238, 262–63, 275, 280, 282, 285–86, 294, 296
brother, xx, 27, 92, 94, 117, 131, 197, 212, 316
burial, 14, 36, 233
Byzantine, ix, 67, 130, 143, 146, 149, 152, 221

Caesar, 7, 24, 37, 94, 154–55, 166, 175, 178–80, 197, 211, 242, 300, 307
Caesarea, 88, 105, 155, 184–85, 195, 219
Caesarean, 146
Caiaphas, 194
Caligula, 94, 211
calligraphy, 150
calvary, 206
Canaan, 224
canon, xvi–xvii, 4, 8, 21–22, 25, 40, 44, 56, 63, 73–74, 76–78, 84, 89–90, 120, 125, 137, 160, 203, 236–37, 273, 277, 298, 300–301, 311, 313
canonical, vii, xvii, 25, 28, 41–42, 45, 52, 58, 63, 73, 76–77, 87, 89, 110, 123, 125, 138, 144, 149, 176, 193, 227, 237, 252, 254, 277, 300, 310, 314

canonically, 122
canonicity, 149
canonization, 25, 142, 203
canonized, 4, 77, 142, 242, 277
Capernaum, 56, 180, 195
Capra, 212
Carmel, 213
carpenter, 133
cataclysmic, 246
Cauda, 185
CEB, iv census, 80
central, xviii, 1, 5–6, 39–40, 46, 51–52, 65, 102, 122, 170, 175, 189, 229–30, 236, 241, 250, 252, 260–61, 263, 272, 275, 283, 285, 289, 291, 293–94, 299
centuries, 16, 21, 23, 28, 67, 74, 77, 105, 109, 114, 130, 138, 143, 148, 150, 155–156, 167, 186, 199, 208, 312
centurion, 198
century, xvi, 5–8, 13, 16–17, 22, 25, 29–32, 34, 40–41, 44–47, 50, 57, 59–61, 63, 72, 75–78, 82–84, 89, 93–95, 103, 108–9, 113, 115, 121, 123–25, 127–28, 130–135, 137, 140–48, 150–52, 155–58, 165–67, 169, 175–76, 186, 194, 210–11, 214, 237, 293–95, 298–99, 304–5, 314, 316
CEV, iv, xxii, 68, 263
characters, 27, 97, 100, 196, 232, 243, 261, 263, 275
chariots, 216
cheaper, 141
Cheltenham, 78
cherubim, 215
chiasm, 3, 5, 14–15, 36, 38, 40, 168, 228–31, 239, 241, 250–52, 254, 260–62, 281, 298, 300, 302
chiasmatically, 262
chiasmic, 228
chiasms, 12, 14, 28, 38, 230–31, 251–52, 272, 281, 298
chiasmus, vii, 5–6, 19, 36, 201, 229–30, 239–41, 248, 250–51, 266, 292, 294, 298, 302, 305, 315–16

INDEX

chiastic, i, iii–iv, xvii–xviii, 2–6, 8, 10, 12, 14–16, 18, 20, 22, 24, 26, 28, 30, 32, 34, 36, 38, 40, 44, 46, 48, 50, 52, 54, 56, 58, 60, 62, 64, 66, 68, 70, 72, 74, 76, 78, 80, 82, 84, 86, 88, 90, 92, 94, 96, 98, 100, 102, 104, 106, 108, 110, 112, 114, 116, 118, 120, 122, 124, 126, 128, 130, 132, 134, 136, 138, 140, 142, 144, 146, 148, 150, 152, 154, 156, 158, 160, 162, 164, 166, 168, 170, 172, 174, 176, 178, 180, 182, 184, 186, 188, 190, 192, 194, 196, 198, 200, 202, 204, 206, 208, 210, 212, 214, 216, 218, 220, 222, 224, 226, 228–30, 234, 236, 238, 240–42, 244, 246, 248–52, 254, 256, 258, 260–64, 266, 268, 270–72, 274–76, 278–82, 284–86, 288, 290–94, 296–98, 300, 302, 311

Chios, 185

Christ, v, vii, xv–xix, 1–2, 4–13, 15, 22, 24, 29–31, 35–42, 45, 47–48, 50–52, 54–61, 64, 67, 69–70, 72–73, 75–77, 84, 88–89, 91, 94–96, 99, 101–3, 105–6, 108, 110–12, 114–19, 125, 127–28, 130–31, 133–34, 138, 141, 144, 152–57, 159–60, 163, 165–66, 168, 170–72, 174–81, 187–88, 191, 193, 197–98, 200–202, 204–5, 208–213, 215, 217–19, 221–25, 227–30, 235–36, 238, 240–46, 254–59, 261–62, 264–68, 270–75, 277, 279, 281, 283–87, 289–93, 295–300, 302, 304–5, 307, 309, 311, 314, 316

Christian, iv–v, xv, xvii–xviii, xxii, 6, 19, 22, 24, 28–30, 32, 35, 39, 44, 46, 51–52, 54–55, 60–61, 63–64, 72–73, 75, 77, 82–86, 92, 94–95, 105, 111, 117–18, 127, 130–31, 138–39, 141, 144–45, 148, 150, 153, 159, 170–71, 191, 238, 241, 247, 261–62, 264–66, 268–69, 280, 287, 291, 294, 303–7, 309–310, 312, 314, 316

Christianity, xviii, 11, 23–24, 27, 29, 32, 45, 52, 61, 64, 73, 91–92, 95, 129–30, 133–36, 138, 143, 148, 156, 159–60, 162, 167, 171, 175, 179, 199, 202, 208–210, 217, 236, 274, 288, 290, 304, 307, 309–310, 314, 316

Christians, 8, 23–25, 32, 44, 47–50, 53–54, 58–59, 68, 73, 80, 84, 92, 106, 127, 130, 135, 140, 143, 145, 148, 154–57, 160, 170–71, 178–79, 197, 199–200, 208–209, 256, 266, 281, 290, 304, 316

Christological, 103, 109, 264, 270

Christology, 6, 53, 266, 294, 306, 312, 316

Christos, 110–11, 304, 310

chronicle, 72, 85, 93, 239, 254

chronicled, 74–75

chronicler, 64, 92–93, 286, 308

chronicles, 72–73, 93, 164, 272, 308

chronicling, 277

chronological, xvii, 17, 41, 53, 153, 299

chronology, 203, 306

Chrysostom, 203

Church, xii, xv–xxi, 3–6, 8, 10–11, 13–16, 23, 29, 31–32, 35–36, 39, 42, 45, 47, 50, 52–56, 58, 60–61, 68, 71, 73–76, 82–87, 90–94, 100–101, 104–6, 115–16, 118, 120, 129–31, 137, 145, 155, 159–64, 166, 170–75, 177, 179, 181, 187–88, 190, 193, 195–97, 202, 213, 215, 225, 235–38, 241–48, 260, 262, 264–65, 267–73, 275–79, 281–94, 296, 304–5, 308–9, 311–12, 314, 316

Churches, v, 29, 45, 148

Cilicia, 30

circuit, 4, 12, 28, 30, 35, 85, 169, 181, 184

circulated, 25, 47, 83, 144, 147, 309

circulation, 57, 83

circumcision, 131, 157

Claromontanus, 78, 147, 152, 164

classical, xxii, 5, 34, 79, 93, 132, 136, 159, 228, 233, 293–95, 305
climactic, vii, 39, 271, 274, 283, 286, 288
climate, 258
climax, xii, 7, 245, 274, 276
cloak, 256
cloth, 270, 303, 308
Codex, 78, 82, 84, 109, 140–41, 144, 147, 164, 219
codices, 109
coherence, 6, 240, 260–61, 263, 294
coherent, i, iii–iv, vii, 2–6, 8, 10, 12, 14, 16, 18, 20, 22, 24, 26, 28, 30, 32, 34, 36, 38–40, 44, 46, 48, 50, 52, 54, 56, 58, 60, 62, 64, 66, 68, 70, 72, 74, 76, 78–80, 82, 84, 86, 88, 90, 92, 94, 96, 98, 100, 102, 104, 106, 108, 110, 112, 114, 116, 118, 120, 122, 124, 126, 128, 130, 132, 134, 136, 138, 140, 142, 144, 146, 148, 150, 152, 154, 156, 158, 160, 162, 164, 166, 168–70, 172, 174, 176, 178, 180, 182, 184, 186, 188, 190, 192, 194, 196, 198, 200, 202, 204, 206, 208, 210, 212, 214, 216, 218, 220, 222, 224, 226, 228, 230, 232–36, 238, 240, 242, 244–48, 250, 252, 254, 256, 258, 260–64, 266, 268, 270–72, 274–98, 300, 302
coherently, 272
cohesion, 5, 232, 241, 251, 271, 273, 276, 283, 292, 295
cohesive, xvii, 43, 233–34, 239, 245, 264, 274–77, 280, 282–83, 292
cohesiveness, 43, 232, 241, 262, 278
coinage, 180, 311
collection, 23, 25, 45, 58, 62, 64, 99, 140, 164, 169, 183, 191, 313–14
Colossians, 163
commentaries, 26, 307, 312, 314
commentary, 10, 12, 23–27, 47, 50, 53–54, 65, 82, 85–86, 89, 113–14, 136, 147, 152, 168, 170, 174, 186–87, 195, 201, 213–14, 223, 225, 237, 245–47, 257, 305–316
comparative, 84

comparison, 1, 11, 31, 44, 59, 73, 147, 150, 211, 301, 305
compassion, 248
composition, 12, 22, 144, 214, 229, 233, 251, 260, 269, 272, 275, 279–80, 303, 314
compositional, 38
compositions, 15, 59, 277–78, 280, 292
comprehensible, 113
comprehension, 43, 263
comprehensive, 3, 53, 94, 201, 241, 247, 252, 267, 274
condemned, 48, 69, 156, 180, 209, 229
condemns, 121
congregation, 61, 144
congregations, 29, 45, 142, 146, 149, 280
conjoin, 231
conjoined, iii–iv, 3, 7, 40, 166, 297
conjoining, 237–38, 300
conjoins, 228, 281
connectedness, 262
connection, xii, xvi–xvii, 3–4, 8, 12, 19, 28, 38, 40, 103, 124, 170, 197, 228, 241, 244, 262, 286, 298, 301
connections, xiii, xvi, 28, 32, 186, 189, 192, 210, 232, 238–39, 245, 251, 276, 296
connector, 270
Constantias, 86
Constantine, 130, 148, 156, 306
Constantinople, 86
context, vii, 3, 5–9, 13, 16–17, 20, 32–34, 37, 43, 52–53, 64, 66, 99–100, 109–112, 115, 121, 126–29, 131–33, 135–37, 139, 141, 143, 145, 147, 149, 151, 153, 155, 157, 159, 161, 163, 165, 167, 170, 172–73, 213, 220, 226–27, 230, 234–35, 238, 245, 254, 259, 272, 294–95, 303–5, 307
contexts, 57, 152–53, 275, 294, 306, 308–9, 314, 316
contextual, 8, 153, 189–90, 192, 226, 238
contextualizing, 233, 238
contextually, 18, 98, 110
continua (scriptio), 139
continuous, xvii–xviii, 5–8, 36, 45, 76, 78, 86, 97–98, 122–24, 149,

161, 168, 184, 246–47, 269, 271, 275–77, 279, 281–82, 290, 293, 297–98, 301
copulation, 105, 112
copyist, 20, 150
Corinth, 185
Corinthians, 69, 204, 209
Cornelius, 30–31, 183, 315
corporeality, 65
corpus, 235, 264, 273
correlated, 110, 192, 235
correlation, 78
correlations, 232
corruption, 47, 83, 259
costly, 138–39
coterie, 117
council, v, 30, 131, 161, 200, 249
counterarguments, 294
covenant, 72, 74, 187, 208, 224, 244, 255, 258, 284, 305
coworker, 138
coworkers, 161
creator, 81
Crete, 185
crime, 32, 148, 155, 307
crimes, 32, 156, 209
crucified, 39, 101, 134, 171, 177, 206, 229, 246, 252
crucifixion, 1–2, 15, 31, 35–36, 42, 50–51, 54, 56, 59, 129, 169, 176–77, 183, 205–6, 209–210, 215, 217–19, 224, 238, 244–46, 252, 255, 263, 284, 287
CSB, iv, xxii, 69, 138
culminated, 35
culminates, 35, 291
culminating, xviii, 40, 42, 187, 269, 288, 302
culmination, 3, 14, 39, 55, 265, 287
cult, 104, 154, 175, 179, 184, 211, 316
cultic, 209
cults, 177
cultural, vii, 5, 7, 13, 16, 18, 28, 32–34, 48, 66, 100, 103, 109, 121, 126–29, 131–33, 135, 137, 139, 141, 143, 145, 147, 149, 151–53, 155, 157, 159, 161, 163, 165,
167, 179, 208, 217, 227, 234–35, 294–95, 299, 308–9, 314, 316
culture, xviii, 18, 37, 64–65, 69, 104, 106–7, 132, 134–35, 143, 145–46, 157–158, 175, 179, 200, 209, 217, 227, 259, 263, 299, 308, 315
cultures, 132, 135, 139, 217
currency, 142
Cyprian, 152, 203
Cyprus, 30, 185
Cyrus, 72

dais, 226
Damascus, 54, 168, 184
damnation, 107
Dan, 7, 49, 108, 114, 296
Daniel, xx, 49, 108, 258, 309–310, 315
David, 3, 9, 14, 23–24, 49, 55–56, 70, 88, 96, 105, 119, 124, 158, 175–76, 219, 257–58, 303–9, 311–14, 316
Davidic, 16, 72, 314
days, 2, 14, 32, 49–51, 53–54, 108, 116, 130, 134, 137, 169, 195, 203, 205–6, 208, 222–24, 238, 246, 248, 257
deacon, 30
deacons, 54, 71, 166, 171, 189
deadly, 155
death, 2, 14, 36–37, 48, 59, 69, 88, 124, 131, 154–55, 158, 163, 178, 180, 183, 194, 199, 206, 209–212, 214–15, 218, 223–24, 244, 266, 268, 270, 277, 287, 312, 315
decade, 65
decades, 72, 74, 150
Decapolis, 71, 153, 182
deception, 216, 234
dedication, xx, 29, 86, 93, 138–39, 142, 161, 177, 191
dedications, 159, 201, 278–79, 301
Deianira, 213
deified, 154, 296
deities, 104, 178, 180, 208, 210, 308
deity, 104, 154, 178, 180, 208–9, 211, 304, 307
demiurge, 81
demonic, 179
demons, 182

Demosthenes, 79, 306
denouement, vii, 39, 247, 274
Deorum, 177
departure, 36, 106, 116, 216, 264, 269, 274, 281, 283, 285–88, 290–91
dependence, 145, 287
dependent, 91, 146, 149, 202, 289
Derbe, 185
descendancy, 105
descendant, 49
descendants, 70, 102, 105, 172, 302
descension, 243–44
descent, 37, 49, 51, 54, 241, 246, 265, 293
desecration, 180
desideratum, 268
Desiderius, 143
destined, 84, 131, 178, 266
destiny, 176–77, 233, 252
destroyer, 23, 32, 155–57, 208, 224, 309
deus, 154
devil, 216
devils, 195
dialect, 114, 188
dialogue, 6, 94, 224, 294
dialogues, 98
diaspora, 136, 175
diatribe, 5–6, 293–94
dictionary, xxii, 17–18, 37, 50–51, 62–63, 80–81, 83–84, 86, 88–89, 116, 122, 131, 140, 159, 163, 170, 179, 188, 190, 258, 271, 303–5, 308–310, 312–13, 315–16
dictum, 301
Didache, 160
dimension, 289, 291
dimensions, xviii, 141, 295
Diocletian, 148
Diodorus, 60, 212–13, 306
Dionysius, 60
Dioscorides, 163
discernment, 260
disciple, 86, 181, 209, 302
disciples, 5–6, 9, 11, 14, 36, 38, 45, 51, 54, 56, 71, 81, 86, 104, 106, 115–16, 118, 132, 169, 177–78, 181–82, 193, 195–98, 201, 204–6, 217, 222–24, 240–41, 243–45, 253, 256–58, 265–68, 270, 274, 281–90, 292–93, 302
discipleship, 11, 225, 238, 243, 252, 256, 270, 311
disclosed, 40, 101, 122, 161, 236, 299
discloses, 3, 28, 52, 127
disease, 180
disjointed, 172, 247, 271, 299
dissected, 90
distinct, xvi, 7, 10, 21, 79, 171, 187, 209, 220, 236, 252, 272–73, 275–78
divine, xviii, 6–7, 9, 12, 24, 27–28, 37, 48–50, 52–53, 55, 59, 62, 101, 103–4, 106–7, 109–110, 132, 154–55, 159, 168–69, 175–76, 178–79, 200, 208–215, 217, 224, 234–35, 243, 248, 262, 266, 268–70, 272–73, 275, 281, 284–94, 296, 298, 302, 307
divinely, xv, 4, 31–32, 35, 109, 173, 271, 285
divinity, 9, 37, 265–66, 268, 270, 296, 307
divinized, 217
Divus, 154
doctrinal, 1
doctrine, xvii, 9–10, 13, 64, 84, 131, 138, 266, 308
doctrines, 1, 131
documentation, 76, 86
dollars, 142
dominion, 258, 290
Domitian, 141, 179, 211
dossier, 161, 166, 223
dozens, 83
drachma, 180
drachmas, 180
durable, 73, 141
dynasty, 194

earthly, xvi, 5–6, 10, 35, 39, 43–44, 59, 116, 145, 169–70, 181, 188, 199, 224–225, 235, 238, 243, 245–47, 260, 265, 268–69, 272, 274, 276, 278, 283, 285–86, 288–89, 291–93, 298
Easter, 208, 223

eastern, 156, 211
Ebionite, 45
Ebionites, 131
ecclesia, 53, 71, 82, 91, 101, 115, 172, 297, 312
ecclesiastical, 51, 195
ecclesiological, 271
Eclogues, 65
economic, 32, 133
economy, 129
edict, 156
edification, 266
edition, iv, xxii, 82, 143, 149, 222, 304–311, 313, 315–16
editions, 143, 223, 303
editor, 203, 236
education, v, 22, 132–36, 139, 158, 299, 302, 306, 316
educational, 132, 134, 306
Egypt, 5, 180, 211
Egyptian, 80
elders, 50, 216
Eleazar, 216
elementary, 132–33, 158
Elijah, 6–7, 74–75, 102, 211–16, 219–21, 224, 256, 259, 291
elimination, 161
Elisabeth, 102, 104, 173
Elisha, 256, 291
elite, 114, 133
Elizabeth, 103, 303
Elkanah, 173
Elkosh, 188
embodied, 179, 291
embodiment, 117, 263
Emmaus, 86, 184, 206–7
Empedocles, 158
emperor, 49, 154, 156–57, 178–79, 211
emperors, 94, 104, 154, 179, 211
Empire, 13–14, 22, 24, 27–28, 30, 32, 48, 51, 60, 80, 88, 91, 94, 106, 127–30, 132–35, 137, 142–43, 145–46, 148–49, 153–55, 157, 165–66, 170, 177–80, 208, 211, 242, 272, 299–300, 307, 315–16
empire, 13–14, 22, 24, 27–28, 30, 32, 48, 51, 60, 80, 88, 91, 94, 106, 127–30, 132–35, 137, 142–43, 145–46, 148–49, 153–55, 157, 165–66, 170, 177–80, 208, 211, 242, 272, 299–300, 307, 315–16
empirical, 107
empowered, 54, 56, 172, 201, 243, 256, 260, 269, 272, 274, 276, 281–85, 289, 294
empowering, 52, 55, 243, 277
empowerment, 54, 265, 284, 286, 288, 292
empowers, 42, 236, 291
emptied, 9
emptying, 9–10
enabler, 48, 52
encapsulate, 241
encapsulated, 3
encapsulates, 252, 260, 270, 289, 291
encomium, 158, 306, 312
encyclopedia, 96, 114, 305, 310, 313
endpoint, 268
enemies, 37, 127, 179, 218, 221
enemy, 204
Enoch, 6–7, 211–12, 214, 216, 221
enthroned, 49, 221
enthronement, 6, 285–86, 294
entrusted, 266, 268, 284, 286
environment, xix, 16, 32, 46, 121, 129, 143, 145, 153, 157, 303
environmental, 7, 12, 16–18, 32, 128–29, 133, 152–53
Epaphroditus, 80
Ephesians, 219, 308
Ephesus, 45, 50, 104, 148, 185, 208, 303
Ephraemi, 147, 151
epic, 64–65, 93, 304
epicenter, 14–15, 35–36, 38–39, 95, 116, 129, 169–70, 175, 228
epics, 65
epiphany, 154
epistle, 6, 73, 131, 216–17, 309
epistles, 11, 27, 50, 52, 69, 78, 82, 84, 144–45, 152, 156–57, 164, 174, 277, 313
epistolary, 52
era, 27, 48, 59, 104, 108, 110, 115, 127, 132, 134–35, 146–48, 153, 162, 166, 173–74, 187–88, 218, 229, 245, 270, 285, 288, 296, 299, 301

eras, 187, 232
Erasmus, 143
eschatological, 103, 108, 215, 246, 263, 265, 268–69, 271, 288, 290–91, 295
eschatology, 6, 115, 217, 294, 313
ESV, iv, xxii, 93, 105, 169, 218, 239, 248, 288
eternal, 2–3, 16, 70, 84, 107, 121, 198, 209, 214, 287
eternity, 209
Ethiopian, 54–55
ethnic, 129, 157, 291
ethnicity, 191
ethos, 5, 294–95
eunuch, 54–55
Euphrates, 91
Eusebius, 85, 89, 311
evangelical, xxii, 121, 307–8, 314
evangelicals, 121
evangelism, 157, 265, 268, 272, 282, 293
evangelist, 39, 171
Evangiles, 82
Eve, 105, 215, 234
evil, 69, 179, 218
evolution, 153–54, 280, 304
exaltation, 6, 56, 202, 285, 287, 290, 292, 294
exalted, 50, 110, 197, 209, 268, 274, 292
examination, xvii, 12–13, 17–19, 31, 33, 40, 84, 99, 127–28, 183, 235, 238, 264, 302, 306, 314
excommunicated, 82, 199
excommunicators, 45
executed, 232
execution, 156
exegesis, 16, 24–25, 36, 172, 190, 216, 290, 294, 304, 316
exegetical, 12, 19, 23–24, 26, 85–86, 89, 112–14, 116, 179, 303, 306–7, 310, 313–14
exhaustive, 24, 94, 163, 180, 300
exile, 97
exilic, 98
existence, 9–10, 23–24, 37, 50, 58, 88, 91, 114, 141, 150, 208, 211–12, 215, 225, 236, 243, 258, 281, 290

existent, 49
exodos, 290
Exodum, 217
eyewitness, 19, 57, 59, 61, 64, 89–90, 117, 159, 164, 183, 190, 204, 207, 215, 256, 296
eyewitnesses, 7, 58–59, 183, 204, 253, 256, 266, 283
Ezekiel, 37, 224
Ezra, 72, 114, 130

fables, 295
fabric, 42, 232–36, 238, 242, 245, 247, 262, 270–71, 275
fabricated, 61
fact, 14, 68, 85, 96, 106, 132, 161, 163, 257, 259, 278
facts, 20, 98, 207–8, 298
factuality, 1
faith, xix, 1, 10, 19–20, 34–35, 48, 52–55, 64, 68, 70, 72, 93–95, 105, 119, 126, 133, 153, 156–57, 165, 181–82, 189, 197, 199, 205, 215, 224, 240–41, 262, 285, 287
faithful, 9, 48, 147, 151, 172, 289
faithfulness, 243, 289
faithless, 70
fate, 233, 308
fearful, 156
feast, 2, 116, 176–77, 206
Felix, 200
festival, 208
festivals, 116, 209
Festus, 200, 219
fictional, 93
fictitious, 64
financial, 142, 162
financially, 56
firmament, 217
first-century, xvi, 5–7, 13, 16–17, 22, 32, 34, 40–41, 45–46, 57, 61, 63, 72, 75, 77, 93–95, 113, 121, 125, 127, 132, 137, 142–43, 146, 157, 166–67, 293–94, 299, 314
firstfruits, 116, 206
flint, 169, 229
forerunner, 181

INDEX 327

forever, 238, 252, 269
forged, 155
forging, 179
forgiveness, 96, 244, 284
formation, xvi, 4, 21, 57, 283, 304
formative, 265
former, xvi, 42, 72, 86–87, 140–41, 154, 171, 183, 202, 219, 223, 237, 242, 251, 254, 257, 279, 301
formulation, 186
fourfold, 45, 125, 140, 164, 242, 292, 306, 312
framework, xvii–xviii, 7, 27–28, 72, 97–98, 101, 107, 145, 260, 262–63, 271, 275, 283–85, 289, 293
fulfill, 10, 64, 215, 224, 289
fulfilled, 6, 45, 70, 87–88, 96, 101–3, 183, 187–88, 191, 206, 224, 257–58, 290, 311
fulfiller, 192
fulfilling, 110, 116, 169, 191, 286
fulfillment, xviii, 2, 5, 42, 49, 51, 55, 93, 102–3, 108, 116, 118, 168, 170, 173, 192, 195, 206, 224, 228, 245, 264, 268, 272, 275, 282–83, 286–90, 293, 296
fulfillments, 45, 257
full, 9, 19, 54, 59, 86, 91, 93, 100, 145, 162, 170, 172, 242, 245, 258
fullness, 69
fully, 6–7, 35, 53, 110, 167, 200, 248, 275
functional, 135, 245, 247
future, 2, 7, 9, 39, 55, 64, 71–72, 94, 144, 170, 187, 215, 255, 257–58, 261, 290

Gabriel, 53, 111, 154–55
Gadara, 182, 195
Gaius, 161
Galatia, 30–31, 131, 185
Galatians, 73, 131
Galilean, 80, 114, 181
Galileans, 188, 255
Galilee, vii, xviii, 4–5, 8–9, 12–13, 15, 35–36, 38–40, 56, 71, 75, 95, 116, 129, 153, 166–67, 169–71, 173, 175, 177, 179, 181–85, 187–89, 191–95, 197, 199–200, 229, 242, 250, 252, 260, 298–300, 315
Gamaliel, 199
gap, 4, 16, 122, 245, 285
gaps, 232
garment, 14, 38, 41, 228, 234, 236, 242, 245, 248, 260, 270–71, 300
garments, 14, 38, 228, 256
Gath, 188
genealogy, xvi, 35, 101, 104, 171, 187
generation, 53, 75, 89, 122, 157
generations, xv, 47, 144, 170, 266, 315
Genesis, 42, 97, 102, 112, 246, 270–71, 273
genre, xi, 10, 16, 22–23, 26, 32, 40–41, 44–45, 56–57, 59–62, 65, 87, 97, 99–100, 120, 125, 149, 153, 158, 164, 167, 191, 276–78, 280, 298, 313, 315
genres, 4, 10, 25, 35, 40–41, 56–57, 98, 107, 121, 277, 298
gentile, xv, 28, 35, 52, 55, 72, 84–86, 105–6, 110, 138, 154, 157, 170–71, 173–175, 177–78, 210–11, 217, 258, 284, 302
gentiles, xv, 3, 9, 23–24, 35–36, 45, 49, 56, 67, 69–72, 84, 86, 104, 106–7, 113, 116, 118, 129, 154–55, 161, 168, 170–71, 173–74, 178–80, 186, 188, 191–92, 194, 198–200, 209–210, 213, 217, 243–46, 249, 258, 262, 279, 284, 291, 293, 297, 302
geographical, 100, 153, 171, 204, 246, 250, 277, 284, 291
geography, 18, 205, 247–48, 315
Gerasenes, 182
German, 58, 222
Gethsemane, 36, 39, 163, 197, 204
global, 266, 268–69, 272, 277, 290, 292
glorification, 245, 287, 295
glorified, 202
glorious, 214–15
glory, 14, 16, 168, 211, 214
Gnosticism, 45
GNT, iv, xxii, 57, 112, 188, 190, 206, 216

INDEX

God, xv–xvi, xx, 1–3, 9–10, 15–16,
   20, 23–25, 32, 34–35, 37, 44,
   48–56, 59–60, 62, 64, 66–71,
   74, 81, 84, 92–94, 98, 101–110,
   115–119, 122, 125, 130, 133, 138,
   143–144, 149, 154–57, 168–80,
   182–83, 186–89, 191–92,
   194–98, 202, 206, 208–214,
   216–17, 219–21, 224–26, 234,
   238, 240–47, 252, 255, 257–59,
   261–65, 267–68, 270–73, 281,
   284–93, 296–99, 302, 304, 307,
   309–311, 315–16
god, xv–xvi, xx, 1–3, 9–10, 15–16, 20,
   24–25, 34–35, 37, 44, 48–56,
   59–60, 62, 64, 66–71, 74, 81, 84,
   92–94, 98, 101–110, 115–19,
   122, 125, 130, 133, 138, 143–44,
   149, 154–56, 168–80, 182–83,
   186–89, 191–92, 194–98, 202,
   206, 208–9, 211–212, 214,
   216–17, 219–21, 224–26, 234,
   238, 240–47, 252, 255, 257–59,
   261–65, 267–68, 270–73, 281,
   284–93, 296–99, 302, 304, 307,
   310–11, 315–16
goddess, 112
goddesses, 178
gods, 23–24, 32, 81, 104, 106, 154–57,
   177–79, 208–213, 309, 311
Goliath, 224
gospel, xii, xv–xix, 2–5, 8–15, 19, 21,
   23, 26–32, 35–36, 38–46, 48–61,
   63, 65–67, 69–74, 76–84, 86–91,
   93, 95, 98, 100–103, 105–6,
   108–111, 114, 116–20, 122–25,
   128–31, 134, 137–40, 142,
   144–45, 148–53, 155, 159–64,
   166, 168–84, 186–87, 189–90,
   192–207, 210, 217–19, 221–25,
   228–29, 235–39, 242–48, 250–
   52, 254–258, 260, 262–66, 270–
   72, 274–79, 281–92, 296–301,
   303–4, 306–316
gospels, xi, 8, 11–12, 21, 25, 44–46,
   56–59, 73, 76–78, 82–84, 87, 89,
   93, 97–98, 103–4, 106, 108, 114,
   125, 144–45, 147, 149, 151–53,
   159, 164, 183, 188–89, 191,
   198–99, 202, 206, 212, 219, 242,
   244, 252, 277–78, 280, 304–5,
   307–8, 310, 314–16
government, 105, 211
governor, 194
grafted, 70–71, 186
grain, xi, 206
grammar, 20, 145, 188, 230, 309, 312
grammatical, 36, 150, 152, 239
grandson, 199
grave, 2, 100, 215, 218, 266
graven, 180
Grecian, 79
Greco, vii, xi, xv, 5–7, 12–13, 28–29,
   32–33, 36–37, 57, 60, 65–66,
   77, 125, 128, 133–34, 137–39,
   141, 143, 151, 154, 191, 200,
   208–211, 214, 217, 219, 228,
   277–278, 280, 293–94, 296, 300,
   305, 307, 309, 316
Greece, 88, 105, 132, 134, 160, 185, 209,
   309
Greek, xxii–xxiii, 13, 22, 24, 26, 29,
   33–34, 47, 54, 58, 62–63, 67,
   78–79, 82–83, 85, 93, 104, 106–
   7, 109–114, 124, 130, 134–37,
   139, 142–50, 157–59, 161–62,
   165, 173–75, 200, 210, 212–14,
   219–22, 228, 259, 290, 299, 303,
   305, 309, 311, 313–16
Greeks, 17, 134, 145, 158, 211, 314
groupings, 119, 146

half, 27, 34, 91, 97, 99, 104, 161, 180,
   194, 298
halves, 142
handbook, 9–10, 18–19, 33, 72, 88, 103,
   109, 129, 146, 155, 162, 197,
   218–21, 304, 306, 308–9, 312,
   315
handbooks, 158
Hannah, 173
harmonious, xviii, 261, 291, 293
harmoniously, 276
harmonization, 152, 266
harmonized, 37, 63, 272
harmonizes, 16

harmonizing, 203, 207
harmony, 108, 151
hatred, 234
HCSB, 138
hearers, 118
heart, 9, 32, 51, 104, 114, 155, 199, 286, 314
hearts, 54, 74
heaven, 1–2, 36–37, 39, 45, 48–49, 53, 59, 68, 108, 120, 171, 202, 204–7, 210, 212–23, 226–28, 238, 240, 253–55, 257, 259, 267–68, 274, 283, 287–88, 290, 296, 301, 316
heavenly, 6, 130, 220, 255, 269, 285–86
heavens, 37, 53, 211, 216–17, 288, 296
Hebraisms, 113, 159
Hebrew, 6, 50, 54, 78, 96, 108, 111–14, 135, 137, 159, 178, 211, 213–14, 216, 229, 302, 315
Hebrews, 219
Hebron, 176
hell, 218
Hellenism, 17, 134–35, 145, 175
Hellenistic, 12–13, 31, 33–34, 49, 59, 61, 85, 104, 111, 113, 124, 128, 134, 143, 157–59, 162, 167, 195, 224–25, 230, 263, 278, 296–97, 299, 308, 310, 313
Hellenization, 134
helmet, 68
helper, 48, 244
hemorrhage, 162
Hepher, 188
Heracles, 211–13
Hercules, 104, 210–11, 305
heresies, 160, 309, 316
heresy, 131
heretic, 81–82
heretics, 199
hermeneutic, 100
hermeneutical, xi, 7, 16–17, 26, 112, 120, 149, 167, 217, 236–38, 308, 310, 315
hermeneutically, 25, 167
hermeneutics, 10, 31, 97–100, 294, 304, 310, 314

Hermes, 93
Herod, 80, 103, 131, 170, 187, 194, 197, 211, 306, 308
Herodian, 184, 194
Hierapolis, 139
highest, 106, 143, 154, 214, 216
Hippocrates, 163
historian, xvi, 7, 13, 20, 32, 63, 65, 72, 84–85, 98, 113, 136, 162, 212, 263–64, 299, 302, 311, 316
historians, 20, 60, 65, 72, 94, 130, 162, 225, 296, 313
historic, 20, 165
historical, xii, xv–xviii, 5, 7, 10, 16, 18–24, 26–27, 32–33, 35–36, 40, 52–53, 60–64, 72, 74–75, 84, 86–87, 90–91, 93–94, 98–100, 103–4, 109, 115, 121, 124, 127–130, 133, 136, 152–53, 159, 162–64, 166–67, 175–76, 186, 191, 201, 207–8, 214, 218, 227, 234, 237, 245, 247, 268–69, 274, 276–78, 280, 283, 294–96, 299, 304, 306, 308–9, 312–14, 316
historical-critical, 36, 62–63, 90, 109
historical-theological, 86
historically, xvii, 6, 61, 92, 237, 294
historicity, 20–21, 24, 64, 207, 299
histories, 72, 280
historiographic, 295–96
historiographical, xviii, 277, 296
historiography, xv, 75, 93, 162, 167, 278, 306, 313
history, xvi, xviii, 3, 5, 9–10, 18–20, 23, 25–27, 31, 33, 41, 45, 51–55, 60–65, 72–73, 75, 77, 80, 84, 88–89, 91–94, 99, 101, 103, 109, 114, 116–17, 120, 122, 124–25, 127–29, 131, 135–36, 141–42, 145, 149, 158, 160–62, 164, 167, 169–70, 172, 175, 178, 180, 186–89, 191, 195, 207, 211–13, 217, 227, 233, 236–37, 242, 244–47, 252, 256, 258–59, 261, 263, 272, 280, 286–87, 289–93, 296–98, 302, 304, 306–316
holiness, 179

holy, iv–v, xvi–xviii, 2–3, 5, 8–12, 14–15,
    20, 36, 38–43, 50–56, 64, 70, 72,
    78, 85–87, 89, 95, 102, 105, 109,
    113, 116, 118, 138, 163, 165,
    171–73, 175, 192–93, 196–97,
    201–2, 204–6, 208, 216–17,
    223–25, 228, 236, 238, 241–47,
    253, 256–258, 260–61, 263,
    265–70, 272, 274–75, 278–79,
    282–93, 296, 298–300, 302, 306,
    310, 314
Homer, 13, 34, 65, 93, 104, 233, 305
Homeric, 12
hostile, xviii, 30, 32, 48, 52, 61, 153, 155
hour, xix, 198
household, 30, 133
huge, 137
human, 1, 9–10, 24, 35, 37, 48–49, 51,
    53, 55, 62, 64, 74, 102, 104–7,
    109–110, 132, 138, 159, 165,
    197, 209, 212, 214, 218, 223–24,
    234, 243, 285, 298
humanity, xvi, 9, 35, 55–56, 62, 68, 81,
    101–2, 107, 116, 159, 171–72,
    178, 206, 213, 244, 252, 267,
    285, 287, 292, 298, 312
humankind, 3, 9, 271, 273, 302
humanness, 62, 109–110, 165
humans, 60, 62, 102, 104, 106, 212–13
humiliation, 10
hundreds, 22, 150
hymns, 156
hyperbole, 294
hyphen, 21, 26, 167
hypothesis, 4, 58, 76, 85, 104, 123, 159,
    205
hypothesize, 58
hypothetical, 46, 88

Iconium, 185
idiomatic, 158
idioms, 78
idiosyncratic, 222, 226, 258
idolatry, 9, 157, 177, 179, 181, 197
ignorance, 188
ignorant, 44, 79
Iliad, 34
illegal, 51

illiteracy, 132, 188
illiterate, 19, 22, 132–34, 136
immanence, 36
immanent, 9
Immanuel, 111–12
immersed, 134, 145
imminence, 202
imminent, 71, 73, 130, 268
immortal, 210
immovable, 69, 214
imparted, 241
impending, 42, 131, 181, 215, 266, 283,
    289
imperator, 154
imperial, 104, 114, 129, 153–54, 175,
    179, 184, 211, 316
impossible, 90, 127, 161
inaccuracies, 63–64, 205
inaccuracy, 63, 225, 255
inaccurate, 19–20, 61, 95, 186, 299
inaugural, 195, 271
inaugurate, 246
inauguration, 245, 272, 282, 284–85,
    288
incarnate, 159
incarnation, 9, 37, 55, 243
incense, 113, 157, 198
inclusio, 5, 168, 293
incomprehensible, 202
inconceivable, 214
inconclusive, 158
incorrect, 119, 255
incorrectly, 111
independent, xvi–xvii, 4, 8, 10, 12, 16,
    40, 44, 97, 104, 110, 162, 167,
    242, 277–278, 292, 297, 301
independently, 3, 138, 149, 168, 186,
    201, 235
indescribable, 214
indoctrinated, 24
indwell, 192, 286
indwelling, 8, 257–58, 292
inerrant, 74
inexpressible, 220
infancy, 104, 118–19, 194, 305
infant, 103, 155
infants, 103
inferences, 168

infilled, 246
infilling, 116
ingathering, 177
ingenious, 128, 247
ingeniously, 14, 145
ingrained, 135, 209
inhabitants, 108
inherent, 43
inherited, 6, 102, 258, 291
inheritors, 71
initiation, 54–55
initiative, 285
inmost, 234
innocent, 194
inscriptions, 22, 301
inspiration, xvi–xvii, xix, 20, 44, 62–64, 74–75, 109, 138, 165, 205, 298, 300
institution, 52, 278
institutions, 22, 135, 179
instructions, 51, 71, 115, 122, 172, 207, 213, 245, 254, 265
instructor, 255
intellectual, xx, 18
intelligence, 135
intelligibility, 135
intelligible, 302
intercalating, 62
intercede, 290
intercession, 269, 287
intercessor, 269, 306
intercessory, 238
interchangeably, 28, 80, 120
interconnected, xviii, 118, 233, 235–36, 242, 247, 260–62, 270
interconnectedness, 28, 42, 234, 241, 245, 262, 272
interconnection, 233
interconnections, 240
intercourse, 112
interdependence, 241
internal, 20, 22, 30, 46, 129, 161, 164, 237
international, v, xxiii, 114, 135, 304–6, 308, 310, 312–13, 316
interpolation, 202–3, 205
interpolations, 19, 203, 297–98

interpretation, 5, 20, 26, 64, 88, 90–92, 98–100, 103, 108, 112, 124, 145, 186, 190, 218, 230, 233, 248, 250–51, 260, 282, 286, 293–94, 304, 307–8, 310, 312–316
interpretations, 121
interpretative, 16, 294
interpreter, 92, 190, 305
interpretive, 6, 251, 294, 311
interrelates, 6
intertextual, 102, 296
intertextuality, 103, 107–8, 233, 312–13
intertextually, 108, 111, 311
intertwining, 43
intervention, 53, 293
interweaves, 261
interwoven, 271, 277
intimate, 234, 271
introduction, vii, 1, 3, 5, 7, 9, 11, 13, 15, 17, 19, 21–23, 25, 27–29, 31, 33–39, 41, 80–81, 88, 97–100, 104, 110, 141, 162, 201, 203, 205, 216, 303, 305–311, 313–314, 316
invaluable, xix–xx, 20, 59
investigation, 19, 22
investigative, 7, 63
inwardly, 15
Irenaeus, 82, 84, 152, 160, 304, 309
irony, 24
irrational, 1
Isaac, 173
Isaiah, 37, 53, 102, 108, 111, 133, 173, 191–92, 195, 269
isolation, 126, 260
isolationism, 186
Israel, xv, xviii, 3, 5–6, 14, 48, 55–56, 65, 67, 69–72, 74, 93, 108, 110, 115–16, 121, 130, 168, 170, 174, 178, 180, 187, 190, 193, 209, 211, 216, 245, 247, 253, 257–58, 267, 284, 305–6, 312, 314
Israelites, 70, 177, 190
Italy, 87, 185
itinerary, 28, 116, 161, 182, 192, 298

Jacob, 120, 302, 308, 312

INDEX

James, v, xx, xxii–xxiii, 27, 30, 44, 58–59, 65–66, 88, 92, 94, 115, 123, 131, 138, 149, 157–58, 194, 204, 216–17, 302–3, 305–7, 309, 312–13, 315–16
Jebus, 96
Jebusites, 96, 176
Jeremiah, 279
Jericho, 184
Jerome, 85, 105, 158, 161, 305, 309, 312
Jerusalem, xviii, 2, 4–5, 9, 14–15, 30, 35–36, 38–40, 45, 52, 85, 92, 95–96, 116, 124, 128–31, 136, 161, 169–72, 174–77, 179–85, 192–93, 197, 204–5, 207, 211, 215, 218–19, 223, 228–30, 241–42, 246, 248–50, 252–53, 256–57, 260, 265–68, 275, 277, 282–85, 287–89, 291–93, 296, 298, 300, 306, 310, 314
Jesus, xii, xvi–xix, xxi, 1–16, 22, 24–25, 27–28, 30–31, 34–40, 42–45, 47–51, 53–60, 64, 67–71, 73–77, 81, 84, 86, 88–92, 94–96, 100–112, 114–20, 124–25, 128–36, 139, 141, 145, 151, 153, 155, 158, 160–61, 163, 166, 168–84, 187–202, 204–219, 221–29, 235–36, 238, 240–63, 265–72, 274, 276–98, 300–302, 304, 306–9, 312, 315–16
Jew, 28, 93, 105, 112, 161, 174, 198, 316
Jewish, xv, xviii, xxii, 5–6, 45, 52, 61, 65, 69–70, 72, 75, 96, 101, 103, 106, 130, 135–37, 143, 146, 157, 170–71, 174–75, 177, 180, 184, 187, 192, 194, 198, 200, 208, 210–11, 214, 216, 278, 280, 289, 291, 293–94, 296, 302, 310
Jewishness, 209
Jewry, 291
Jews, xv, 9, 23–24, 27, 30, 35–36, 39, 45, 49–50, 54, 56, 67, 69–72, 80, 86, 92, 105, 107, 110–11, 113–14, 119, 129, 131, 133, 135, 137, 145, 151, 153–55, 157, 161, 170–71, 174–77, 179–80, 186, 188, 194, 198–200, 208–211, 213, 217, 244–46, 249, 262, 268, 297
Joanna, 56
Job, 136
Joel, 6, 23, 31, 48, 51, 99, 133, 175, 192, 196, 304, 308–9, 314, 316
John, iii–iv, xi–xii, xv–xvi, 9–10, 13, 27, 29–30, 36–38, 44–46, 48–51, 55–56, 63–64, 69–70, 74–77, 80, 82–83, 86–88, 92–93, 96, 102–6, 108, 111, 116–20, 122–23, 131, 135, 138, 141–42, 145, 150–51, 155–56, 158, 160–61, 164–65, 169, 172–74, 176–77, 179, 181–82, 184, 187–90, 194–96, 198, 201–2, 204, 206–7, 210, 212, 214, 219, 221, 228–29, 236, 238–39, 243–46, 251–52, 254–58, 260, 263, 277, 297, 302–316
Jonah, 188, 224
Joppa, 30, 185
Jordan, xx, 13, 151, 184, 187, 195
Joseph, 9, 29, 80, 104–5, 111, 124, 133, 176, 198, 224, 307, 310, 315
Josephus, 72, 75, 77, 79–80, 91, 180, 216, 279–80, 310
Joshua, 216, 308, 311
JPS, xxii, 112
jubilee, 107–8
Judah, 70, 97, 130, 258
Judaicus, 180
Judaism, 24, 27, 81, 95, 131, 153, 157, 170, 174–77, 184, 313, 316
Judaistic, 143, 157
Judaizers, 131
Judaizing, 24, 45, 110–11
Judas, 80, 236
Jude, 131, 138, 215–16
Judea, 14, 39, 45–46, 71, 87, 92, 95, 116, 128, 131, 153, 166, 171, 182–85, 199, 250, 260, 268
Judean, 114
judgment, 48, 258
judgments, 168, 176
Julius, 154, 211, 307
Jupiter, 93, 180
justice, 122
Justifiable, 164, 203

Justin, 60, 309
juxtapose, 31, 128, 200
juxtaposition, vii, 36, 78, 191, 201, 203, 205, 207, 209, 211, 213, 215, 217, 219, 221, 223, 225, 227, 229, 231, 262, 264
Juxtapositional, 202

kenosis, 9, 133
kerygmatic, 264
king, v, xxii–xxiii, 2, 37, 135, 149, 176, 178, 238, 252, 258, 268–69, 290
kingdom, 14, 50, 56, 72, 84, 174, 179, 182–83, 186, 191, 196, 202, 214, 218, 225, 240, 242–43, 247, 253, 258, 267, 281, 286, 289–90
kingdoms, 164
Kings, 37, 97, 164, 178, 216, 238, 258, 308
kings, 37, 97, 164, 178, 216, 238, 258, 308
Kippur, 256
KJV, v, xxii, 74, 93, 108, 116, 138, 143, 168, 204, 215, 221, 238
knowledge, xiii, xx, 1, 22, 75, 84, 102, 105, 121, 132, 158, 163
koine, 134–35, 145–46, 149, 158
Kurios, 48–49, 101, 108–110
kurios, 48–49, 101, 108–110

Lactantius, 203
lamb, 106, 116, 206, 224, 257
language, xvii, 7, 17–18, 22, 33, 46–47, 49, 51, 78–79, 107, 111–12, 114, 122, 128, 134–35, 137, 141–42, 145–46, 149, 162–63, 165, 173, 175, 179, 188, 193, 208, 229–30, 305, 309, 311
languages, 18, 22, 47, 54, 79, 114, 129, 134–35, 137, 142, 165, 193, 221, 259
large, 24, 29, 113, 126, 140, 150–51, 233, 280
largely, 52, 153, 175
larger, 99, 101, 110, 115, 124, 126, 146–47, 159, 169, 210, 233, 261–62
largest, 73
lastly, 294

Latin, 82–83, 93, 104, 134–35, 137, 140, 142–43, 145, 147, 165, 305, 314
Latins, 82
Law, 49, 81, 96, 103, 108, 135, 157, 176, 187–88, 206, 208, 255, 289, 311, 316
law, 49, 96, 103, 108, 135, 157, 176, 187–88, 206, 208, 255, 289, 311
laws, 81, 157, 316
Lazarus, 210, 302
Leben, 46, 103, 182, 300
lectio, 223
legalized, 156
legends, 86
length, ix, 7, 76–77, 139–42, 144, 186, 239, 301
lengthier, 80
lengths, 76, 141, 158
lengthy, 105, 141–42
letter, 34, 59, 139, 143, 146–47, 158, 163, 259, 314
letters, 22, 25, 44, 47, 52, 75, 82, 91, 134, 137, 139, 141, 143, 146, 239–41, 280, 284, 287, 294, 306, 310, 313, 315
Levite, 249
Levites, 74
Levitical, 170, 255
Leviticus, 108, 206
Lexical, xi, 163, 305
liberalism, 99, 120–21
liberalist, 99
libraries, 22, 134
library, xxii, 137, 212–13, 304, 306, 308–9
life, xv–xvii, xix–xxi, 2, 15–16, 30, 45, 47, 51–55, 57, 59–60, 64–65, 69–70, 74, 76–77, 80, 84, 88, 91, 93–94, 99, 103–5, 107, 117–18, 125, 138, 143, 145, 156, 161, 165, 171–72, 178, 181, 183, 189, 191, 196, 198, 202, 209–210, 214, 216, 218, 233–35, 238, 241–42, 244–48, 252, 269–70, 274, 277–78, 287, 298, 302–3, 308–309, 316
linear, 261
linen, 255

linguistic, 84, 143, 146
literacy, 22, 131–35, 158, 306
literal, 9, 61, 98, 114, 159, 166, 207, 220–21, 234, 270
literalism, 190
literally, 100, 130, 213, 220, 223, 227
literarily, 263
literary, vii, xi–xiii, xv–xviii, 4–7, 12–19, 25–28, 31–34, 36, 38–43, 56–57, 61–62, 65–66, 82, 86–87, 89, 98–100, 107, 115, 122–29, 131–33, 135, 137, 139–41, 143, 145, 147, 149, 151–53, 155, 157, 159, 161–63, 165–67, 170, 183, 189–91, 208, 210, 227, 230, 232–34, 236–39, 241, 245–48, 250–51, 254, 260, 262, 264, 269, 271–72, 274–83, 291–93, 296, 298–301, 303, 305–6, 312–15
literate, 134–35, 137, 309
literature, xxii, 1, 13, 18–19, 33–34, 36, 72, 84, 93, 97–98, 110, 117, 123, 128, 134–36, 143, 175, 186, 191, 195, 210, 212–14, 217, 219, 228–29, 232, 239, 271, 278, 302–3, 305, 307, 309–310, 315–16
litmus, 156
liturgically, 290
Livius, 212
Livy, 212, 311
logia, 51, 138
logos, 5, 108, 294–95, 304–9, 311, 313, 315–16
longer, 45, 47, 55, 76, 80, 82, 140, 147, 152, 203, 222–23, 225, 286
longest, 92, 102, 139, 144–45, 162, 186, 301
lords, 37, 178, 238, 258
lovers, 219
Lucifer, 37
lucre, 199
Lukan, vii, 8, 16, 20, 24–25, 31, 35–36, 61, 75, 79, 82–83, 90, 111, 128, 157, 167, 169, 171, 173, 175, 177, 179, 181, 183, 185, 187, 189, 191, 193, 195, 197, 199, 210, 235, 264, 267, 269, 271, 273, 299, 308, 311, 316

Luke, i, iii–iv, vii, ix, xi–xiii, xv–xix, 2–210, 212–316
Luke-Acts, i, iii–iv, vii, xi–xiii, xviii, 2–10, 12–14, 16–34, 36, 38–168, 170, 172, 174, 176, 178, 180–82, 184, 186, 188–92, 194–96, 198, 200, 202, 204, 206, 208, 210, 212, 214, 216, 218–26, 228, 230–31, 233–34, 236–42, 244–48, 250, 252, 254, 256, 258, 260–64, 266–72, 274–308, 310–11, 313–15
LXX, xi, xxii, 36, 49–50, 55, 110–13, 136–37, 145, 159, 173, 200, 220, 226, 259
Lycaonia, 185
Lydia, 31
Lystra, 30, 185

Maccabees, 104
Macedonia, 31, 88, 185
Magdalene, 56
main, xi, 14, 27, 36, 38, 104, 119, 168, 172, 178, 183, 225, 228, 230, 250, 280, 298, 300, 302
majesty, 217
Majority, 21, 40, 59, 149, 165, 175, 221
majority, 21, 40, 59, 149, 165, 175, 221
majuscule, 147
Malachi, 35, 74–75, 102, 110, 145, 166, 229
malady, 213
Malta, 185
mammon, 199
manifest, 9, 37
manifestation, 35, 43, 85, 216, 281, 291
manifested, 9, 32, 37, 51, 69, 110, 154, 243
manifesting, 68, 108
mankind, 102, 116, 172, 178, 215
mantle, 238, 291
manuscript, xxii, 21, 29, 32, 46–47, 67, 83, 109, 128, 137, 140, 142–43, 145–46, 149, 151, 219, 236, 259, 278–80, 304
manuscripts, 20–21, 29, 41, 67, 82–83, 109–110, 114, 139, 141–52, 219, 222, 275, 305–6, 314

Marcion, 81–84, 152, 309
Marcionism, 84
Marcionite, 82–83, 160, 311
Maritima, 184–85
Markan, 46
marriage, 133, 178
Martius, 212
martyrdom, 30, 60, 86, 155
martyrdoms, 94
martyred, 32, 86–87, 178
martyrs, 73
Mary, 53, 56, 88, 102–4, 111–12, 173, 176, 193, 197, 303
masculine, 109
Matthean, 11
Matthew, xv, 9, 11–13, 16, 30, 44–46, 48–49, 58, 63–64, 71, 73, 76–77, 80, 86–88, 101, 103–4, 106, 111–12, 114, 116, 123, 137–38, 153, 160, 162–64, 171, 174, 176, 184, 187, 202, 218, 252, 301, 304–6, 315
Matthias, 236
maximum, 141, 301
measurement, 134
mediator, 287
medical, 7, 33, 128, 136, 162–63, 299, 305, 309, 311
medicine, 163
medicines, 85
meditating, 170
Mediterranean, 109, 133–34, 158, 177
mélet, 180
membrorum, 252
memorabilia, 77
merciful, 9
Mercury, 93
mercy, 55
messenger, 74, 102
messengers, 182
Messiah, xii, 16, 24, 42, 49, 55, 70, 81, 96, 104, 108, 111, 119, 125, 168, 170, 182, 189, 192–93, 195, 197–98, 202, 220, 224, 248, 252, 255–56, 259, 272, 305, 316
messiahship, 256
messianic, 5, 28, 35, 39, 42, 50, 56, 72, 103, 153, 170, 181, 187, 191–93, 195, 241, 243, 245, 247, 252, 254, 265, 298
Metalepsis, 295
metalepsis, 295
metaphor, 98, 214, 232–36, 238–39, 241, 244–45, 247–48, 275
metaphoric, 38, 41, 59, 228, 235
metaphorical, 234, 241, 275
metaphors, 70, 233, 275, 300
method, 8, 17–18, 62, 100, 109, 128
Michael, 148, 215–16, 307, 309, 311, 314, 316
middle, 14–15, 19, 38, 92, 98, 148, 151, 158, 228, 230, 251–52
Midrashic, 5, 293–94
Miletus, 185
milieu, 52
military, 22, 129, 213
millennia, 153
millennial, 176
millennium, 246, 258
ministry, iv, xvi, xviii, 2, 4–6, 10–11, 13, 15, 28, 30, 35, 39–40, 42, 44, 46–47, 51–53, 55–56, 59, 69, 74, 76, 85, 95, 103–4, 106, 111, 113, 116–19, 129–30, 145, 153, 160, 166, 169–70, 172–73, 176, 181, 183, 187–93, 195–97, 200–202, 210, 217, 223–25, 235–36, 238, 241, 243, 245–47, 252, 254–55, 260–62, 267–70, 272, 274, 276–80, 282–86, 288, 290–93, 298–99
miracle, 34, 103, 112, 138, 189, 192, 266
miracles, 69, 99, 106, 196, 210, 256, 274
miraculous, 39, 103, 154, 171, 210, 293
misapplied, 16
misguided, 121
misinterpretation, 100, 153
mispronunciation, 188
missiological, 115, 268, 271
mission, xv, xvii–xviii, 5–6, 14–15, 35–36, 39–40, 49–50, 52–55, 71, 84, 92–93, 101, 115–16, 118, 130, 168–69, 174, 177, 181, 189, 192, 196–98, 215, 229, 236, 238, 243–49, 252, 260–62, 265–74, 276–77, 279, 281–93, 295–96, 300, 307, 316

missional, 14, 269, 289
missionaries, 72
missionary, 30, 42, 74, 116, 161, 192, 269–70
missions, 92, 271
mister, 48, 109
Mitylene, 185
modern, xvi, 1, 4, 11, 16, 19–20, 22, 29–30, 32, 41, 43–44, 46–47, 52, 61–63, 65, 75, 82, 90, 99, 107, 120–21, 131–36, 141, 143–47, 149, 153, 158, 168–69, 185–186, 210, 219, 222–23, 225, 227, 229–30, 232, 259, 276, 278, 280, 293–95, 299, 301, 303, 305, 313
monarch, 226, 258
monarchs, 178
monarchy, 258
monastery, 222
monetary, 180
money, 180, 197
monks, 130, 222
monograph, xviii, 61, 186, 278, 315
monographs, 136
monotheism, 154, 209, 213
monotheistic, 24, 65, 106, 208
months, 134
monumental, 130
monumented, 86
Mosaic, 108, 157, 255
Moses, 45, 96, 103, 155, 157, 170, 173–74, 176, 180, 187, 190, 208, 211–12, 214–216, 221, 224, 305, 308, 316
motif, 122, 233, 296
motifs, 17, 28, 41–42, 107, 169, 201, 284, 293
movement, xviii, 61, 73, 121, 127, 135, 148, 153, 155, 176–78, 181, 195, 197, 200, 261, 268, 282, 284, 291–92
movements, 213
MS, xxii, 82, 280, 305
MSS, 21, 203, 222, 258–59, 280
mulcted, 180
multicultural, 157
multilingual, 78
multitude, 214

multitudes, 196
multivolume, 280
Muratorian, 63, 84, 160
mutilated, 81
myriad, 233
mystery, 3, 69, 174
myth, 105–7, 210
mythological, 104
mythology, 104, 106, 211
myths, 1, 37, 50, 104, 106–7, 110, 210

Nahum, 188
narrate, 91, 93–94, 210
narrated, 53, 61–62, 64, 94, 123, 217
narrates, 174, 190, 219, 244
narrating, 107
narration, 12, 79, 89, 247, 286
narrative, vii, xii–xiii, xv–xviii, 5–9, 12–18, 23, 25–29, 31–32, 34, 36, 38–43, 52–53, 55–56, 59–62, 76–78, 86, 90–92, 95–105, 107–111, 113, 115–27, 149, 152, 158–59, 166–69, 171, 173–75, 177, 181, 183, 186–89, 191–92, 200–201, 203–4, 206, 208, 210, 213, 223, 225, 228, 232–39, 241–42, 245–48, 250–52, 254, 257, 260–64, 268–69, 271–72, 274–85, 287–302, 305, 307–9, 311–15
narratives, vii, 1–2, 4–5, 7, 12, 15, 19, 28, 31, 34–38, 40–41, 43, 55–56, 58, 62, 73, 81, 92, 95, 97–98, 101, 103, 105, 107, 111, 115, 117–20, 122, 124, 126, 151, 159–60, 162, 166–71, 173–75, 177, 179, 181–83, 185, 187, 189, 191, 193, 195, 197, 199–205, 207, 209–211, 213, 215, 217, 219, 221, 223–25, 227–29, 231–35, 237–38, 241–42, 245–47, 251–52, 254, 258, 261–74, 280–81, 283, 286, 293–94, 297–98, 300, 302, 305, 307
NASB, v, xxiii, 9, 108, 111, 113, 138, 182, 190, 204, 206, 214, 268
nascent, 42, 52–53, 71, 235, 247, 270,

INDEX

Nathan, 55, 304
Nathaniel, 92
nation, 70, 161, 170, 174, 180, 198
national, v, 64, 291
nations, xviii, 11, 35, 39, 71, 96, 116, 154, 176, 198, 218, 253, 256, 258, 260, 266–67, 284, 288, 304
native, 129
natural, xvii, 1, 43, 90, 102, 141, 172, 209, 257
naturally, 1, 9, 70, 254
nature, xv, 10, 18, 42, 89, 102, 105, 110, 156, 159, 179, 261, 264, 304
natures, 110
Nazarenes, 199
Nazareth, 39–40, 53, 56, 95, 107, 181, 188, 195, 200
Nazarite, 173
Nehemiah, 130
Nepos, 41
Nero, 85, 94, 155, 186, 211
Neronic, 148, 155
Nestorianism, 159
news, iv, xxii, 53, 56, 73, 95, 125, 151, 154, 166, 199, 270, 314
newspapers, 22
Nicodemus, 188, 198, 218
Nineveh, 224
NIV, v, xxiii, 37, 45, 58, 71, 74, 87, 89, 96, 103, 105–6, 117, 140, 151, 163, 182, 193, 204, 214–15, 219–20, 234, 252, 304
NKJV, v, xxiii, 11, 37, 106, 138, 204, 220, 254
NLT, v, xxiii, 93–94
Noah, 208, 214, 224
nominative, 192
non-interconnected, 247
normative, 9
norms, 7, 121, 145, 208, 295
nostalgic, 213
novel, 24, 64
novels, 65
NRSV, v, xxiii, 53, 112
NT, xxiii, 2–4, 9, 12, 16, 20–22, 24–25, 29, 31–34, 36–37, 40–41, 44–45, 47–48, 50, 52, 54, 58, 67, 73–78, 82, 84–85, 89–90, 93, 95, 98, 101–3, 105–110, 113–14, 116, 127–28, 130–32, 135–39, 141, 143–54, 157–59, 162–63, 166–67, 175, 180, 198–200, 206, 210, 213–15, 217, 219–20, 222, 224, 226, 236, 244–45, 247, 257–259, 264, 266–68, 277, 297, 300–302
numerology, 224

oaths, 156
obedience, 243, 289
objections, 39, 276–78, 294
objective, 5, 31, 36–37, 99, 121, 157, 264
objectively, 121, 196
obligation, 113, 285
obliterate, 165
obscure, 147
obscurity, 20, 307
observable, 255, 259
observance, 176
observation, 125, 165, 307
observations, 181, 308
observers, 189, 266
Octavian, 154
Odyssey, 34, 233, 305
Oeta, 213
Oeuvre, i, iii–iv, 2–4, 6, 8, 10, 12, 14, 16, 18, 20, 22, 24, 26, 28, 30, 32, 34, 36, 38, 40, 44, 46, 48, 50, 52, 54, 56, 58, 60, 62, 64, 66, 68, 70, 72, 74, 76, 78, 80, 82, 84, 86, 88, 90, 92, 94, 96, 98, 100, 102, 104, 106, 108, 110, 112, 114, 116, 118, 120, 122, 124, 126, 128, 130, 132, 134, 136, 138, 140, 142, 144, 146, 148, 150, 152, 154, 156, 158, 160, 162, 164, 166, 168, 170, 172, 174, 176, 178, 180, 182, 184, 186, 188, 190, 192, 194, 196, 198, 200, 202, 204, 206, 208, 210, 212, 214, 216, 218, 220, 222, 224, 226, 228, 230, 234, 236, 238, 240, 242, 244, 246, 248, 250, 252, 254, 256, 258, 260, 262, 264, 266, 268, 270–72, 276, 278, 280, 282, 284, 286, 288, 290, 292, 294, 296–98, 300, 302

offerings, 209
old, xv, xviii, xxiii, 5, 7, 19, 33, 38, 45, 49–50, 84, 106, 108, 112, 114, 122, 137, 153, 174–75, 186, 214–15, 234, 244, 259, 284, 287, 303–5, 312–14, 316
older, 107, 143, 145
oldest, 67, 147
Olives, 38, 204–5, 245–46, 257, 282–83
omission, 222–23, 295
omissions, 165, 222
omit, 59, 84, 152, 182
omnipotence, 10, 243
omnipresence, 9–10, 243
omnipresent, 9
omniscience, 10, 243
Onkelos, 114–15
onlookers, 189, 268
ontological, 202
ontologically, 209
Opistrograph, 141
opus, 41, 43, 275
oral, 5, 57–58, 73–74, 78–79, 88–89, 95, 104, 113, 117, 128, 132, 139, 143, 145, 171, 213, 236, 263–64, 293–94, 316
orally, 128, 139, 263
orator, 158
oratorical, 34
oratory, 34, 79, 128, 157, 310
ordo, 12
origin, 3, 25, 61, 64, 88, 116, 144, 158, 171, 198, 223, 268, 280, 301, 304, 310–311, 313
original, xvi, 7, 16–21, 46–47, 71, 73, 76, 78, 81, 83, 88, 95, 99, 103, 107–9, 129, 137, 139, 142–45, 147–49, 151–52, 154, 159, 167–68, 186, 190, 203, 205, 219, 222, 258–59, 263, 266, 281, 295, 300, 309, 316
originality, 219
originally, xvii, 3, 73, 78, 82, 113, 124, 200, 208, 222, 236, 280
originals, 150
originate, 100
originated, 32, 109, 116, 138, 143, 158, 229

originating, 101
originator, 171, 200
origins, xviii, 72, 83, 162, 288, 291, 293, 295
outlawed, 32
outlier, 280
outpouring, 2, 14–15, 42, 51, 116, 171, 206, 224, 236, 266, 289
outwardly, xviii, 14–15, 39, 166, 171, 229
oversight, 223, 225
overt, 13
overturned, 180
Oxyrhynchus, 151

pagan, 93, 165, 208–9, 300
paganism, 175
pagans, 155
Palestine, 175, 211, 309
Palestinian, 91, 114, 258
Pamphylia, 185
Paphos, 185
Papias, 12, 139
papyri, 135, 147, 150–51, 305
papyrus, 25, 67, 76, 109, 125, 140–42, 150–51, 258–59
parable, 98, 248
parables, 183, 234
Paraclete, 51
paradise, 218, 220
parallelism, 5, 13, 190, 229, 251, 263, 275, 282–83, 292–93, 295
parallelismus, 252
parallelomania, 65
paraphrase, 225
paraphrases, 152
paraphrasing, 294
paraphrastic, 295
parchment, 140–41
parchments, 141
parousia, 51, 68, 312
parse, 56
parsed, 119
parsing, 43
partakers, 70, 174
parthenos, 112
passion, xviii, 35, 129, 183, 271, 312

INDEX

Passover, 2, 116, 176, 206, 208, 223–24, 257
pastoralism, 33, 305
Patara, 185
Pathos, 5, 33, 294–95, 305
Patmos, 141
patriarch, 302
patriarchs, 55, 70, 81
patrimony, 157
patron, 29–30, 162, 301
patronage, 29, 138
patrons, 80
Paul, xvi, 3, 6, 9, 13–14, 25–27, 30–31, 36–37, 39–40, 42, 44–47, 50, 52, 54, 59–60, 63, 68–70, 73–75, 77, 81–82, 84–86, 88–89, 91–95, 100, 103, 106, 116, 124, 127, 131, 133, 135, 137–38, 140, 143, 149, 155, 160–61, 163–64, 166, 168, 170–71, 174–76, 178, 180–81, 186, 192–94, 196–200, 204, 208–210, 213, 215, 217–21, 242–243, 290, 293–97, 299–300, 302, 306–7, 309, 311–12, 314, 316
Pauline, 11, 78, 82, 152, 164, 239–41, 315
Pax (Romana, Deorum), 153, 177
pedagogical, 262
pedagogically, 263
Peloponnesian, 280
Penelope, 233
Pentateuch, 14, 38, 115–16, 137, 172, 314
Pentecost, 2, 6, 30–31, 39, 42, 51, 53–55, 61, 93, 104, 116, 118, 171, 175, 192, 195, 197, 202, 206, 208, 219, 223–24, 236, 243, 246, 257, 265, 289–91, 293, 295, 307
Peraea, 182
percent, 22, 132–33, 137, 150, 152, 199–200
percentage, 151
Perea, 71, 153
Perga, 185
Pergamon, 136

period, xvii, 24, 51, 75, 93, 104, 107, 127–28, 130, 132, 135–36, 164, 174, 207–208, 211, 280, 288, 313
periods, 187, 208, 245
perish, 68, 199
perished, 142, 258
permanent, 73, 131, 175, 192, 288
permanently, 2
perpetrators, 155
perplexed, 156, 311
persecuted, 32, 85, 192, 240
persecutes, 48
persecution, 23, 42, 47–48, 71, 92, 106, 148, 155, 170, 172, 194, 221, 241, 316
persecutions, 36, 155
persecutor, 39, 171
persecutors, 197
personified, 104, 178, 214
persons, 22, 159, 212
perverse, 156, 208
Peter, 6, 11–12, 27, 30, 42, 44–45, 51, 56, 68, 92, 94, 110, 116, 127, 131, 133, 137–38, 178, 180, 183, 188–90, 192, 194–97, 199, 244, 249, 295–96, 302, 304, 312–13
Pharaohs, 211
Pharisee, 183
Pharisees, 69, 176, 188, 214, 312
phenomenal, 86
phenomenon, 132
Philadelphus, 137
Philip, 39, 45, 54, 60, 92, 166, 171, 305, 309, 314
Philippi, 85, 185, 195
Philippian, 9
Phillip, 30, 56, 92, 199, 303, 305
Philo, 135, 217, 313
Philoctetes, 213
philosophy, 34, 121, 135, 306
Phoenicia, 71, 153, 182, 185
phraseology, 49, 63
Phrygia, 30–31, 185
physical, 7, 21, 36–37, 51, 85, 101–2, 117, 128, 134, 163, 189, 202, 209, 211–214, 220–21, 225, 234, 246, 269, 277, 280–81, 285, 291, 301

physically, xvi, 4, 9, 30, 59, 85, 110, 176, 182, 193, 210, 212, 286–87
physician, xvi, 7, 20, 33, 63, 77, 85, 105, 127, 136, 138, 149, 158, 160–64, 166–167, 297, 313
picturesque, 147
Pilate, 80, 134, 165, 171, 200, 218
pilgrimage, 116
pilgrimages, 177
pinnacle, 179, 245
Pisidia, 185
plagiarism, 146
plagues, 180
platform, 37, 91, 226
Plato, 79, 98, 306
plethora, 135
Pliny, 32, 72, 91, 141, 156–57, 208, 313
plurality, 178, 208
Plutarch, 41
Pneumatological, 51, 268, 270
poet, 13, 138, 158
poetic, 59, 229
poetry, 22, 34, 98, 229
political, 18, 33, 80, 108, 129, 154, 294
politics, 153–54
polymorphous, 89
polytheism, 9, 175, 177, 209, 300, 307
polytheistic, 24, 106
Pontius, 80, 134, 165, 171, 200
Pontus, 81
poor, 20, 53, 100, 199, 240
populace, 179
population, 132–33, 135
populations, 135
Porcius, 200
possession, 108
possessions, 199
possessive, 161, 238
postal, 134
posthaste, 71
postliberal, 120, 311
postmortem, 212
pouch, 140
poverty, 31
powerful, xv, 34, 191, 235, 247
practical, 2, 15, 20, 38, 73, 122, 135, 171, 197, 225, 228, 238, 275, 280, 301

prayer, 42, 55, 152, 156, 193, 197–98, 282–83, 289, 306
prayers, 197, 209, 221, 226
preached, 15, 96, 160, 179, 209, 256, 258, 260, 284
preaching, 42, 84, 95, 106, 178, 196, 242, 266, 288, 290
predate, 151
predated, 99
predestined, 69
prediction, 110, 249
predictions, 249, 270
predisposed, 154
preface, vii, xv–xviii, 29, 80–81, 86–87, 159, 191, 237, 301, 303
prefaces, 87
prefix, 80
prefixed, 83
pregnant, 68, 112
prehistoric, 232, 234–35, 303
preindustrial, 132
prejudices, 165
prelude, 287
presence, xix, 36, 43, 50, 160, 212–14, 243, 246, 269, 272, 278, 280–81, 284–87, 291–92, 296
preserved, 21, 60, 67, 83, 128, 140, 258, 277
presumptuously, 210
prevailed, 24, 143
priest, 72, 186, 216–17, 224, 249, 255, 269, 287
priestly, 114, 170, 255–56, 287
priests, 69, 74, 113, 130
primitive, 109
principal, 204, 316
principalities, 218
Priscilla, 92
prison, 88, 187, 194
privy, 90, 107, 120
proclamation, 64, 111, 195, 246–47, 262, 291
procurators, 200
profession, 33, 85–86, 137, 163, 299
professional, 16, 29, 32, 128, 133, 150, 163
professionals, 137
prognostication, 183, 255

INDEX

progression, xvii–xviii, 43, 169, 176–77, 180, 197, 200, 225, 270, 283, 291–93
progymnasmata, 158
prolepsis, 295
proliferation, 272
prologue, 29, 79–83, 87, 160, 183, 187, 239, 254, 264, 279, 296
prologues, xvii, 10, 13, 28–31, 42, 65, 78–83, 90, 191, 278–79, 306, 311, 315
prominent, 56, 60, 92, 146, 157
prominently, 248
proof, 8, 13, 16, 79, 84, 87, 186, 203
proof-texting, 8, 186
propagate, 266
propagated, 138
propagation, 2
property, 108
prophecies, 6, 49, 55, 81, 252, 265
prophecy, xviii, 59, 74, 102, 111, 119, 168, 173, 191–92, 229, 233, 246, 258, 286, 296
prophet, 35, 42, 45, 74–75, 102, 111, 133, 138, 145, 166, 173, 175–76, 179–80, 188–89, 191, 195–96, 208, 229
prophetic, 103, 119, 173, 190, 215, 252, 256, 258, 275, 284, 288, 291, 293
prophets, xxi, 3, 45, 48–49, 55, 74, 81, 93, 96, 102–3, 111, 119, 137, 173, 187–188, 190, 195, 240, 245, 284, 307
propinquity, 87
proportion, 24, 135, 165
proposition, 83, 236
prose, 62, 158, 229
proto, 151
protocols, 145–46, 301
prototypes, 189
prototypical, 159, 179
Proverbs, 234
providential, 174, 247
province, 88, 144
provinces, 88
Psalm, 218, 308
psalmist, 234
Psalms, 49, 96, 103

pseudepigrapha, 214–15, 303, 305
pseudepigraphic, xvii, 22, 63, 89, 114, 130, 214–15
Ptolemais, 185
Ptolemy, 137
punishable, 32, 155
punishment, 179, 209

Quaestiones, 217
quality, 98, 143, 234, 263
quasi-narratives, 56, 97
quelle, 58, 88, 104
questionable, 61, 74, 84
quilt, 14, 38, 55, 228, 233–35, 238, 241, 300
quilting, 239
quilts, 38, 228, 234, 314
quintessential, 271
Quirinius, 80
Qumran, 114–15
quotidian, 137

Rabbi, 115, 199
rabbinic, 176, 216
rabbis, 115
racial, 191
radical, xiii, 260
rapture, 215, 252, 259, 301
raptured, 220
ratification, 156
ratified, 111
readable, 137
readers, xviii, 1, 4, 9, 14, 16, 18, 20, 23, 25, 30, 34–35, 38–39, 41, 44, 46, 52, 61, 63–65, 67, 74, 76, 80, 86–87, 90, 93–94, 97–100, 103, 107, 110, 121, 128, 149, 161, 167, 169–70, 187, 192, 209–210, 225, 230, 235, 239, 242, 247–48, 260, 271–272, 276, 281, 285, 298–99, 302
realm, 1, 196, 211, 215
realms, 214, 269
rebellion, 37, 101
rebuking, 198, 298
recant, 156
recanted, 157
recapitulated, 224

recapitulation, 294
recapitulatory, 237–38
recast, 196
Receptus, 21, 143, 149
recipients, 18, 33, 110, 129, 283, 307
redaction, 3, 123, 312
redactions, 81, 83
redactor, 219, 225
redemption, 71, 108, 119, 121, 155, 170, 187, 266, 271, 289
redemptive, xv–xvi, 51, 103, 155, 215, 218, 264, 271–72, 284–85, 287–92, 296
region, 56, 91, 134, 145, 182–84, 188, 198, 205, 217
regional, ix, 184–85
regions, 31, 71, 109, 131, 153, 177, 182
relatable, 1
relation, 27, 123, 202, 229, 306
relations, 237, 303
relationship, 40, 56, 87, 99, 107, 244, 270
relationships, 18, 33, 70, 129
relative, 10
religion, xxii, 32, 106, 131, 153–54, 175–76, 199, 208–9, 213, 311–15
religions, 104, 178, 210, 316
religious, 18, 33, 111, 122, 129–30, 169, 176, 184, 188, 194, 208, 210, 217, 235, 307
relocated, 56, 104, 195
Remus, 212
repent, 11, 68
repentance, 96, 197, 253, 256, 260, 266, 284, 288
repetition, 5, 43, 74, 229, 239, 247, 263, 274, 281–82, 293–94
repetitions, 17
researcher, 299, 302
resseguie, 123, 313
restoration, 234, 244–45, 249, 258, 314
resurrected, 39, 101, 221, 246
resurrection, xviii, 1–2, 14–15, 31, 36, 38, 42, 48, 50–51, 54, 56, 59, 71, 77, 116, 172, 183–84, 199, 203–8, 210, 212–13, 217–19, 223, 238, 243–46, 253–55, 258, 260–61, 263, 266, 270, 277, 287, 290, 302, 305, 311–12, 316

Revelation, 36, 49, 103, 109, 141, 153, 169, 179, 181, 215, 221, 256, 258, 277, 287, 298, 314–15
revelation, 36, 49, 103, 109, 141, 153, 169, 179, 181, 215, 221, 256, 258, 277, 287, 298, 314–15
revelatory, 121–22, 315
revenues, 156
revue, 82
rewriting, 47
rhetoric, 5, 33–34, 79, 97, 115, 128, 157–58, 162, 166, 233, 260, 293–95, 299, 305–6, 309, 312–14
rhetorical, xvii–xviii, 5–7, 12, 16–17, 27, 33–34, 38–40, 60, 79, 87, 126, 128, 136, 157–58, 162, 169, 171, 190, 229–30, 239, 241, 248, 263, 293–95, 316
rhetorically, 264
rhetoricians, 17
Rhodes, 185, 303, 309
rhythm, 158, 271
rhythmic, 223
rich, xvi, xx, 53, 81, 183, 234, 240, 245, 271, 275, 311
righteous, 199
righteousness, 241, 244, 256
rightly, 47, 124, 128, 165, 224
rigorous, 271
river, 13, 151
road, 54, 184
roads, 134
Roma, 154
Roman, vii, xi, xv, xviii, 5–7, 12–13, 22, 24, 27–29, 32–33, 36–37, 48, 51, 57, 60, 65–66, 75, 77, 80, 88, 91, 94, 104–6, 125, 127–30, 132–35, 137–39, 141–43, 145–46, 148–49, 151, 153–56, 165–66, 177–80, 184, 191, 200, 208–212, 214, 217, 219, 228, 272, 277–78, 280, 293–94, 296, 299–300, 305–9, 311, 313, 315–16
Romana, 153, 177
Romanization, 134
Romans, 6, 17, 39, 69–70, 89, 104, 106, 130, 133, 145, 154, 176–77, 180, 211, 219, 305, 307, 314

Rome, vii, xviii, 4–5, 9, 12–15, 35–36,
    38–40, 42, 45, 52, 75, 81–82,
    84–86, 88, 91–92, 94–95, 104,
    124, 129–30, 132, 134, 153–55,
    160, 166–67, 169–71, 173–75,
    177–81, 183–87, 189, 191–95,
    197, 199–200, 211–12, 229, 242,
    249–50, 291–93, 296, 299–300,
    310–12, 314
Romulus, 212, 296
rounded, 146–47
royal, 212
rudimental, 301
ruler, 104, 183, 211
rulers, 154, 194

sacred, 65, 72, 138, 144, 149, 234, 292, 302
sacrificial, 244
Sadducees, 176, 210, 214
safeguards, 139
saint, xv, 302, 306, 313
saints, 127, 174, 218, 221
Salamis, 185
salient, 151, 169, 222
salutis, 12, 56
salvation, xv, xviii, 3, 9, 15, 31, 35, 45,
    48, 52, 55–56, 62, 70, 100, 108,
    110, 119, 122, 125, 131, 153,
    155, 168–70, 172, 174, 178, 186–
    89, 191, 198, 205, 215, 244–47,
    252, 256, 261–64, 266, 272, 275,
    281, 285, 287–93, 296–97, 302
salvific, 8, 119, 170, 242, 244, 247, 261, 272, 284, 286
Samaria, 14, 30, 39, 45–46, 71, 92, 128,
    131, 153, 166, 171, 182, 184,
    199, 250, 268
Samaritan, 184, 248–49
Samaritans, 71, 182, 210
Samos, 185
Samothrace, 185
Samson, 173
Samuel, 164, 173, 187, 308, 314
sanctioned, 178
sanctuary, 180
Sanctus Scriptura, 63, 76, 149
Sanhedrin, 30, 69, 135, 198

sarcastically, 188
Satan, 108, 195, 197, 215–16, 218
Saul, 39, 54–55, 153, 170–71
Savior, 9, 16, 56, 70, 101–2, 110, 119,
    153–54, 172, 178
savior, 9, 16, 56, 70, 101–2, 110, 119,
    153–54, 172, 178
sayings, 58, 89, 114, 117, 138
scarce, 263
scattered, 65, 75, 95, 142, 146, 148–49,
    177, 193, 206, 236
schema, 264
schematic, 95, 272
school, 22, 116, 307
schools, 158
scientific, 16–18, 33, 46, 128–29, 152
scribal, 152, 223
scribe, 137–38, 150, 222
scribes, 20, 29, 133, 151, 188, 222
script, 139
scriptio (continua), 139
scriptorium, 144
scriptural, 7, 160, 293–94
Scripture, xvii, 10, 20, 42, 44–45, 49, 54,
    62, 64, 74, 89–90, 95, 99, 103,
    107, 116, 120–21, 131, 133, 138,
    154, 157, 161, 178, 180, 191,
    226–27, 230, 255, 283, 290, 304,
    310–12
Scriptures, iv–v, 8, 13, 16, 44–46, 50,
    64, 89, 96, 98, 109, 111, 114,
    137–38, 148, 188, 230, 253, 266,
    277, 282–83, 305
scroll, 7, 18, 53, 76–77, 100, 132–33,
    140–42, 171–72, 191, 202–3,
    254, 266, 301
scrolls, 6–7, 29, 76, 114–15, 140–42,
    162, 186, 261, 268
Sea, 6, 114–15, 184–85, 195
seam, 14, 40, 228, 235–36, 269–70, 275,
    277, 292
seams, vii, xii, 14, 38, 228, 232–33, 235,
    237, 239, 241–43, 245, 247, 249,
    251, 253, 255, 257, 259, 261,
    263, 265, 267, 269, 271, 273, 302
seamstress, 234–35
sects, 131, 316
Secundus, 161

Seleucia, 185
semantic, 107, 301
semantics, 259
Semites, 229
Semitic, 114, 159
separation, xvii, 8, 41, 75–76, 90, 124–25, 139, 186, 276–77, 288, 292, 298
Sepphoris, 195
Septuagint, xxii, 50, 55, 65, 78, 111–12, 137, 159, 312
Septuagintal, 118
sequel, 26, 42, 149, 279, 312
sermon, 30, 42, 59, 158, 195, 199, 240, 295
sermonic, 35
sermons, 195
serpent, 215
servant, 16, 141, 269
servants, 58, 194, 214
severe, 148
severed, 77, 124–25, 140
Shakespeare, 234
Shavuot, 116, 118
sheaf, 206
sheep, 69, 71
sheets, 141
shekel, 179–80
shepherds, 103
shin, 274, 276, 278–80, 282, 314
shorten, 150
shorter, 139, 147, 151
shroud, 233
Sicilian, 158
Sicily, 158
sick, 195–96
Sidon, 185
siege, 130
siglum, 150
Silas, 30–31, 85, 161
silence, 76
Silvanus, 137–38
Simeon, 168, 173
simile, 98
Simon, 92, 308
Sinai, 208, 222
Sinaiticus, 143, 147–48, 151, 219, 222–23

sinful, 102, 105
sinless, 102, 106
sinners, 179, 218
Sinope, 81, 309
sir, 48, 109
Sirach, 214
Sitz, 46, 103, 182, 300
skeptical, 22
skeptics, 47
skilled, 160, 248
sky, 37, 213, 220–21, 287
slavery, 178
smooth, 251, 262, 267
socio, 12, 16–18, 27, 32–34, 103, 128–29, 152–53, 235, 316
sociolinguistics, 32
sociological, 7, 121
Socrates, 133
soldiers, 130, 212
Solomon, 14, 55, 95, 170, 257
son, 5, 11–12, 35, 37, 48–49, 53, 55–56, 81, 104–6, 108, 111–12, 116, 154–55, 171, 192, 211, 221, 252, 296, 307–8, 313–14
Sopater, 161
soteriological, 244, 270–71
soteriology, 244, 312
soul, 163, 217
sovereign, 286, 293
sovereignty, 215, 272
spacetime, 98
spanned, 17, 153, 157, 187
spans, 97, 129, 186, 252
speaker, 17, 79, 93, 157, 183, 254–55
speakers, 92, 178, 255
spectacle, 197, 266
spectators, 216, 255–56
speech, 17, 30, 38, 51, 59, 79, 89, 117, 126, 162, 165, 183, 190, 195, 204, 233, 239, 256
speeches, 34, 79, 98, 118–19, 124, 126, 157, 173, 183, 224, 254, 264, 295, 306
spirit-empowered, 272, 276, 282–84, 294
spiritual, 6, 108, 117, 202, 220, 224, 235, 281
spiritually, 285, 289

INDEX 345

stater, 180
static, 52
stationary, 95
Stephen, 27, 30, 49, 60, 69, 92, 166, 183, 196, 233–34, 238, 315
Stichoi, 142
stichometry, 78
stigma, 188
stitchwork, 234
stories, xii, 25, 31, 50, 61, 65, 93, 98–99, 101, 107, 119, 122, 173, 190, 205, 210–14, 224, 232–34, 238, 247, 271, 306–7, 315
story, xii, xvii, 3, 5, 9, 13, 15, 17–18, 27, 31, 34, 36, 40–43, 45, 48, 57, 59–61, 64, 73–74, 76–77, 90–93, 97–99, 101–2, 107–8, 115, 120–25, 139, 149, 153, 161–162, 164–65, 167–69, 174, 176, 184, 186–87, 190–91, 200–201, 204, 210, 212, 233–35, 237–38, 242, 244, 246–47, 261–63, 276–78, 281, 283, 295, 297–99, 306, 312, 314–15
storyteller, 122
storytelling, 233, 248
Strabo, 60
strophes, 230
structural, xi–xii, xvi, xviii, 7, 39–40, 43, 262, 272, 275–76, 279–80, 282–85, 291–93, 296
structurally, 6, 281, 283, 294
stylistic, 89, 150, 152, 239, 263, 279–80
stylometry, 46
subjective, 134
substance, 199
substructural, 27
subversive, 176–77, 197
subversively, 7
Suetonius, 72, 91, 155
suicide, 178, 213
Sukkot, 116
superhuman, 138
supernatural, 1, 34, 74, 102, 104, 106, 163, 210, 214, 314
superpowers, 210
superstition, 155–56, 208
superstitious, 155

supremacy, 211
Susanna, 56
suttee, 213
syllogism, 15
symmetrical, xviii, 251, 257
symmetry, 6, 194, 261–62, 274, 282–83, 292
symphonic, 271
synagogue, 53, 56, 191, 195
synagogues, 136, 199
synoptic, 63, 73, 108, 277
synoptics, 58, 73, 123
synthesis, 16
synthetic, 5, 293
Syracuse, 158
Syria, 30, 85, 175, 184–85, 199
Syriac, 114, 135
Syrian, 85
systematic, 99, 121, 271, 290

tabernacle, 173, 296
tabernacles, 95, 116, 176–77
tablet, 141
tablets, 140
Tabor, 215
Tacitus, 72, 75, 91, 148, 155, 208, 315
Takamitsu, 114, 309, 312
tale, 93, 210, 304
tales, 64, 93, 210
Talmud, 115
Tanak, 50, 55, 65, 78, 137, 301
Tanakh, 112
tapestry, xii, 53, 232, 234–35, 239, 242, 245–46, 271–72, 275
Targum, 114–15
Targums, 114, 304
Tarsus, 39, 55, 84, 153, 170–71
Tatian, 152
teacher, 255
teachings, 25, 57–59, 73, 95, 114, 131, 134, 144, 234, 238, 241–42, 252, 264–66, 269–70, 274, 277–78, 281, 283, 285, 290
tedious, 137
temple, xii, 35, 38, 55, 70, 72, 95, 100, 103, 110, 113, 128–30, 164, 166, 169–170, 173, 175–76, 180, 197–98, 205, 211, 228–29, 252, 257, 285, 287, 291–92, 307

temples, 156, 178, 209
temptation, 108, 197, 311
terminus, 148
terrestrial, 265, 270, 272
tertiary, 158
Tertius, 137–38
Tertullian, 152, 203
Testament, xv–xvi, xviii, xxii–xxiii, 2, 5–7, 19–20, 22–23, 25–26, 38, 44, 49–50, 56, 58, 63, 67–68, 73, 79–80, 85, 103, 110, 112, 114, 116, 122–25, 132–35, 137–153, 158, 162, 164, 173, 177, 179, 183, 186, 189–94, 196–201, 203, 205, 209–210, 214–15, 217, 220–21, 237, 265, 268–69, 277, 284, 287, 303–316
Testaments, 19, 97–98, 102, 108, 305, 311
testimony, 57, 64, 75, 88, 92, 104, 139, 164, 183, 207, 233, 256, 285, 296, 299
tête têtes, 90, 161
Tetragrammaton, 49, 109, 312
tetragrammaton, 49, 109, 312
Tetrevangelium, 44, 46–47, 125
textiles, 232, 234–35, 303
textual, 16–17, 47, 77, 107–9, 146–48, 151–52, 161, 203, 222–23, 233, 269, 272, 303–6, 308, 311, 314
texture, 233
textured, 238
Textus, 21, 143, 149
Thebes, 86
thematic, xii, xvi–xvii, 5, 42–43, 174, 186, 189, 191, 245, 269–70, 272, 276, 278–279, 282, 292–93, 310
thematically, 278
theme, 172, 188–89, 225, 229–30, 245, 250, 252, 284, 289, 291
themes, vii, xii, xvii–xviii, 3–6, 12–13, 17, 23, 27–28, 35–36, 38, 40, 42, 52, 115, 149, 166–69, 186, 188–89, 191–92, 195, 198, 200–201, 225, 228, 232–33, 235, 238–39, 241, 248, 250–51, 260–61, 263–64, 268, 270, 272, 275, 279, 283, 293, 295–96, 298
theocracy, 106
theological, xi–xii, xv, xviii–xix, xxii, 5–7, 9–10, 15, 23–25, 27, 29, 31, 34–35, 39–41, 43, 50, 52–55, 59, 62, 64, 73, 83, 86, 93, 99, 103, 108, 111, 115, 118, 121–122, 127, 138, 149, 163, 170–71, 174, 183, 186–90, 195, 205, 207–8, 214–15, 223, 227, 234, 236–38, 241, 243, 245–48, 257, 262, 264–65, 268–69, 271–72, 274–84, 286, 289, 291–96, 299, 307–8, 310–15
theological-historical, 247
theology, 3, 9–10, 16, 20, 25–26, 31, 38, 41–42, 49–51, 55–56, 99, 107, 110, 116, 118–22, 124, 126, 140, 149, 153, 155, 159, 167, 175, 182, 186, 203, 208, 210, 233, 267, 269, 286, 304–8, 310–16
Theophilum, 4, 164
Theophilus, 28–30, 47–49, 63, 65–66, 80, 86, 93–94, 97, 105–7, 117, 119–20, 139–140, 142, 144, 161–62, 164, 191, 201–2, 205, 210, 219, 242, 251, 255, 278–79, 301, 308, 311–12
thesis, 3, 5, 39–40, 60, 124, 167, 231
Thessalonians, 197
Thessalonica, 68, 185
Theudas, 80
Thomas, v, 70, 92, 309, 313–14
thousands, 22
thread, 38, 40–41, 204, 228, 234–36, 238, 241–42, 246–47, 260–61, 269–71, 275, 300
three-year, 10, 28, 35, 298
throne, 37, 175, 214, 220, 226, 258
Thucydides, 280, 296
thunderstorm, 212
Tiberias, 195
Tiberius, 184
Tigris, 91
timeline, 206–7
timetable, 203

Timothy, 30–31, 85, 89, 140, 161, 310
Tischendorf, 222
Titus, 56, 199, 212
Toletanus, 82
tome, 83, 270
Torah, 45, 115
tradition, 4, 12, 21, 47, 58, 61, 69, 73–74, 81, 104–5, 114, 117, 128, 139, 143, 145–47, 157, 160, 174, 195, 215, 235–36, 278–80, 284, 293, 303, 314, 316
traditional, 24, 40, 61, 77, 86, 152, 156, 221, 300, 315
traditionally, 4, 30, 51, 81, 128, 236, 297
traditions, 5–6, 58, 65, 69, 88, 100, 109, 117, 170, 203, 209, 213, 219, 222, 236, 293–94, 314, 316
tragedies, 234
tragedy, 107
Trajan, 32, 156
trajectories, 271
trajectory, xi, 275, 292
transcend, 157, 275
transcendent, 122, 291
transcends, 272
transfiguration, 215
translation, iv–v, xxii–xxiii, 21, 47, 78, 93, 112, 115, 137, 140, 159, 190, 211–212, 215–16, 303, 311–12
translations, xvi, 9, 47, 82, 112, 135, 138, 140, 147, 149, 171, 214–15, 219, 223, 227–28, 259
translators, 114, 148
transmission, 21, 74–75, 89, 139, 141, 259, 264
travelers, 177, 193
travel-route, 4
treatise, xviii, 87, 171, 238, 242, 251, 255, 279, 301
treatises, 108, 278
tribe, 70, 137
tribes, 70, 176
tripartite, 14
triumphal, 176
triumphant, 107, 177
Troas, 31, 74, 85, 140, 185

Trophimus, 161
truism, 301
trustworthiness, 4, 21, 62–63, 205
trustworthy, 21, 61, 64, 74, 81, 96
truth, 22, 47, 56, 64, 75, 94, 99–100, 105–6, 121, 207, 210, 242, 244, 252, 263, 298
Turabian, 146
Turkey, 185
twenty-five, 74, 106, 142
two-volume, xviii, 3, 16, 23–24, 26, 32, 47, 66–68, 74, 86–87, 124, 128, 142, 144, 153, 166, 168, 186, 190, 225, 242, 260, 262, 276, 279, 296, 299
Tychicus, 161
typological, 6, 218, 308
Tyre, 185
Tyrian, 179

ubiquitous, 128
unadulterated, 83
unbelief, 72, 198
unbelievers, 172, 192
unbelieving, 71, 155, 171
unbroken, 8–9, 31, 36, 40, 43, 149, 168, 242, 286
uncial, 146–47
uncial-majuscule, 147
Uncials, ix, 147, 150, 305
uncials, ix, 147, 150, 305
uneducated, 19
unfamiliar, 1
unfastening, 167
unfolding, xv, xvii–xviii, 32, 166, 234, 242, 262, 286–87, 289, 291, 315
unfulfilled, 263
ungodly, 48
uninspired, 64
unique, xv, 4, 28, 40, 46, 48, 50, 52, 56, 73, 102, 104, 125, 162, 183–84, 187, 213, 217, 233, 235, 245–46, 268, 279, 298, 300
uniquely, 50, 102, 189, 221, 235
uniqueness, 102, 242

INDEX

unity, i, iii–iv, vii, xi–xii, xvii–xviii, 2–6, 8–10, 12, 14, 16, 18, 20–28, 30–32, 34, 36, 38, 40, 42–44, 46, 48, 50, 52, 54, 56, 58, 60–62, 64, 66–68, 70, 72, 74, 76–78, 80, 82, 84, 86, 88, 90–92, 94, 96, 98–100, 102, 104, 106, 108, 110, 112, 114, 116, 118, 120, 122–24, 126, 128, 130, 132, 134, 136, 138, 140, 142, 144, 146, 148–50, 152, 154, 156, 158, 160, 162, 164, 166–68, 170, 172, 174, 176, 178, 180, 182, 184, 186, 188–90, 192, 194, 196, 198, 200, 202, 204, 206, 208, 210, 212, 214, 216, 218, 220, 222, 224, 226, 228, 230, 232, 234–48, 250–52, 254, 256, 258, 260–262, 264, 266, 268–70, 272, 274–76, 278–80, 282, 284, 286, 288, 290–94, 296–298, 300–302, 308, 313–15
universal, xv–xvi, 49, 134–35, 165, 218, 265, 270, 291, 293
universality, xviii, 52
universally, 134, 156
universe, 81, 133
university, xx, 82, 303–315
unjust, 79
unrepentant, 68
unrighteous, 199
unrighteousness, 241, 246
unrolled, 16, 140
unsettled, 107
unsound, 132
unstable, 44
unstitch, 233
unsubstantiated, 65
unwarranted, 76
unwavering, xix–xx, 287
unweaving, 233
upright, 69, 84
uprightly, 156
upwardly, 37
ushered, 202, 286
usurped, 37
utilitarian, 235
utilitarians, 135
uttermost, 285

validate, 144
validated, 265
validation, 245
vanishes, 8
vast, 13, 175
vastly, 23
vastness, 180
Vaticanus, 143, 147–48, 151, 219, 222
vehicle, 162
vellum, 258
vengeance, 191
verbally, 179
version, iv–v, xxii–xxiii, 11, 16, 46, 55, 57, 80–81, 93–94, 111–13, 137, 143, 149, 176, 192, 197, 208, 220, 223, 254–55, 259, 304, 309
versions, 169, 237, 276, 280
vicinity, 204–5, 257
vindicate, 213
vindicated, 2, 268
vindicating, 202
Virgil, 65, 93
virgin, 49, 101–2, 111–13, 131
virgins, 112
virtue, 80, 128, 216
virtues, 120, 308
visible, 50, 207, 218, 236
vision, xviii, 6, 49, 53, 215, 236, 244, 258, 271–72, 276, 291, 299
visions, 108
visitation, 35
vocabulary, 140, 159, 295, 313
vocative, 29
void, 10, 171
Volume, iii–iv, ix, xvi–xviii, 2–8, 10, 12–16, 19, 23–26, 28, 31–32, 35–36, 38–43, 47, 58, 62–64, 66–68, 73–74, 76–78, 80, 86–87, 90–91, 94, 99, 101, 108, 116–17, 119, 122–26, 128, 139–42, 144, 149–50, 153, 155, 160–64, 166–71, 173–75, 182–186, 188–91, 199–200, 203–7, 223, 225, 228, 231, 233, 235–38, 241–43, 245–48, 251–52, 254, 257, 260–62, 264, 266, 273–83, 285, 287, 291–93, 295–302, 306, 311, 313

INDEX 349

volume, ix, xvii–xviii, 3, 10, 12, 16, 23–24, 26, 32, 40, 42, 47, 66–68, 73–74, 76–77, 86–87, 91, 94, 116–17, 119, 124, 126, 128, 139–40, 142, 144, 150, 153, 161–162, 166, 168, 171, 173–75, 182–86, 190, 200, 203, 205–7, 225, 237, 242, 251, 254, 257, 260, 262, 276, 279, 287, 293, 296–97, 299–300, 306, 311, 313
volumen, 140
volumes, iii–iv, xvi–xviii, 2–8, 10, 12–16, 19, 25–26, 28, 31–32, 35–36, 38–43, 58, 62–64, 76–78, 80, 86, 90–91, 94, 99, 101, 108, 122–26, 140–42, 149, 155, 160, 163–64, 166–71, 182–83, 186, 188–89, 191, 199–200, 204, 223, 225, 228, 231, 233, 235–38, 241–43, 245–48, 251–52, 261–62, 264, 266, 273–78, 280–83, 285, 291–93, 295, 297–302
voluntarily, 10
voyage, 194
vulgate, 83, 143

Washingtonianus, 152
wealth, 31, 42, 199, 240
wealthy, 29, 139, 162
weaver, 234
week, 2, 35, 116, 129, 134, 206
Weeks, 2, 116, 134, 206
Weltanschauung, 217
Western, 47, 67, 130, 146–48, 152, 164, 203, 222
widespread, 132, 134–35
wilderness, 6, 53, 108, 195, 208
wisdom, xix, 16, 54, 98, 103, 213–14, 288
womb, 111, 234
word, xix, 9, 20, 33–34, 48, 51–52, 55, 58, 62, 85, 88, 102, 109, 111–13, 139, 143, 146, 152–54, 176, 190, 198, 208, 215, 226–27, 232, 243, 258–59, 270, 284, 301–2, 304, 306, 308, 310, 316
wording, 114, 148, 203, 207, 225, 228, 258–59, 295

words, xii, 2, 11–12, 16, 18, 27, 44–46, 57–59, 69, 71, 77, 86, 91, 95, 98–99, 106–107, 109, 112–13, 116, 125, 130, 132, 135, 137–39, 142, 144–46, 149, 151–52, 159, 163, 178–79, 181, 187–88, 190, 199, 204–5, 207, 216, 225, 227–29, 238–239, 249, 259, 263, 268, 288, 294, 307, 315
world, xx, 3, 9, 13, 16–17, 24, 29, 33, 35, 48–50, 52, 57, 66, 68–69, 74, 78–80, 84–85, 93, 95, 101–2, 110, 115–16, 118–19, 121, 123–24, 129–30, 132–34, 136, 138–39, 143, 151, 153–55, 157–60, 163, 169–71, 174–77, 179–81, 186–87, 193, 196, 202, 208–210, 217, 247, 252, 254, 256, 258, 262, 278, 280, 282, 285, 287–88, 290, 293, 300, 305–9, 314, 316
worldview, 117, 208
worldwide, v, 61, 175
worship, 72, 95–96, 154–55, 157, 176, 197, 282, 287–88
worshiped, 106, 154–55, 178, 205, 211
worshiping, 179, 285
worthy, 155, 212, 235
writer, xv, 17, 33–34, 47–48, 64, 80, 85, 87, 90, 97–99, 101–3, 106, 122, 138, 141, 145, 155–58, 160, 162, 165, 169, 172, 176, 196, 207, 216, 219, 234, 242, 254, 299, 302
writers, xv–xvi, 1, 5–6, 22, 29–33, 37, 44–45, 69, 75, 78–80, 88–90, 102–3, 106–108, 110–14, 125–26, 128, 130–31, 133, 137–38, 141–43, 145–46, 154, 157–58, 161, 163, 165, 169, 176, 184, 186, 203, 206, 208, 210, 213–14, 217, 219, 225, 293–296
writings, xi–xii, xv, xvii, 6, 13, 19, 22–23, 25, 32, 35, 44–46, 49–50, 57, 60, 62, 64–65, 72, 75–78, 83, 85–89, 97, 108, 110, 114, 133, 136–40, 148, 163, 165, 187, 219, 228–29, 237, 280, 294, 301, 306, 309

year, 10, 28, 35, 84, 87–88, 107–8, 148, 177, 298
years, 20, 35, 84, 95, 98, 129, 151, 177, 186, 208, 265, 298, 304
YHWH, 35, 48–49, 70, 95, 109–111, 166, 180, 187, 218, 258, 315
yhwh, 35, 48–49, 70, 95, 109–111, 166, 180, 187, 218, 258, 315
YLT, 112
yom, 255
young, 106, 111–13, 133, 178, 316
Younger, 156, 313
youths, 133

Zacchaeus, 183
Zebedee, 92, 131
Zechariah, 9, 102, 113, 119, 124, 173, 186, 198, 246, 310
Zeus, 93, 104, 211, 213, 309
Zion, 96, 246

ἁγίου, 11
ἀκριβῶς, 113
ἁμαρτιῶν, 11
ἀναβαίν, 226
ἀναβαίνω, 14, 37, 200, 238
ἀνάβαση, 227
ἀναλαμβάνομαι, 220, 259
ἀναλημφθ, 227
ἀναλημφθεὶς, 220, 228, 238, 259
ἀνάληψη, 227
ἀνατάξασθαι, 89
ἀνελήμφθη, 220, 227, 238, 259
ἀνεφέρ, 227
ανεφερετο, 220–21, 228, 238, 259
ἀνεφέρετο, 220–21, 228, 238, 259
ἀνθρώπου, 49, 106, 110
ἄνωθεν, 113
απ, 58, 108, 220
ἀποθέωσις, 210
ἁρπαγησόμεθα, 215
ἀρχῇ, 102
ἀρχῆς, 58, 108
αὐξάνειν, 187
αὐτὸν, 220, 257
αὐτόπται, 58, 183
αὐτούς, 11, 220, 257
αὐτῶν, 220

ἄφεσιν, 11
αφήγημα, 100

βαθμ, 226
βαθμός, 226
βαπτίζοντες, 11
βαπτισθήτω, 11
βῆμα, 226
βιβλίον, 141
βίβλος, 141
βίοι, 57, 77, 125, 278

γαστρὶ, 111
γενόμενοι, 58
γράψαι, 63

δὲ, 11, 187
δεῖ, 187
διδάσκειν, 254
διέστη, 220
διεστη, 220
διήγησιν, 89
διήγησις, 79, 100
δύναμιν, 257
δωρεὰν, 11

ἑαυτὸν, 9
εγενετο, 220
ἐγένετο, 220
ἐγὼ, 192
ἔδοξε, 113
ἔθνη, 11
ἔθνος, 243, 260
εἰκών, 180
εις, 11, 220–21, 226–27, 259
ἕκαστος, 11
ἐκεῖνον, 187
ἐκένωσεν, 9
ἐκκλησία, 117
ἐλαττοῦσθαι, 187
ἐλεημο, 226
ἐλεημοσύν, 226
ἐλεημοσύνη, 226
ἐμέ, 187, 195
ἐν, 102, 111, 187, 220
ἕξει, 111
ἔξοδος, 290
ἐπ', 195

ἐπήρθ, 227
ἐπήρθη, 228, 238, 259
ἐπὶ, 11
ἐπίλογος, 79
ἐποιησάμην, 63, 301
εται, 227
ετο, 227
εὐαγγέλιο, 143, 150
εὐαγγέλιον, 76–77, 87, 125, 140, 161, 170
ευλογειν, 220, 257
εψαγγελιον, 12

ἡμέραν, 116
ἡμέρας, 220
ἡμῖν, 58, 108, 187
ἦν, 102
ἧς, 220

θάνατος, 210
θεόπνευστος, 138
θεόφιλε, 29, 63

ἰατρός, 85
ἰδοὺ, 111
ἰησοῦ, 11, 143
ἰησοῦς, 110, 254

καθὼς, 58, 108
και, 11, 58, 111, 220–21, 254
κἀμοὶ, 113
κατά, 12, 150, 161
κενός, 9
κοινά, 117
κράτιστε, 29, 63
κράτιστος, 144
κυριος, 48–49, 109–111
κυρίου, 195

λαμβάν, 227
λαμβάνεται, 227
λαμβάνω, 227
λήμψεσθε, 11
λόγοι, 264
λόγον, 63, 301
λόγος, 102
λόγου, 58
λουκάν, 73, 76, 140, 150, 161

μαθητεύσατε, 11
μαθθαιον, 12
μὲν, 301
μεταθέσεως, 214

οἱ, 58, 108
ομένου, 227
ὄνομα, 11–12
ὀνόματι, 11
ὅς, 226
οὖν, 11
οὐρανόν, 220–21, 226–28, 259
οὐρανός, 221
οὐρανούς, 226

πάντα, 11
πάντων, 63, 301
παράκλητος, 290
παρέδοσαν, 58, 108, 111
παρηκολουθηκότι, 113
παρθένος, 111–12
παρθένου, 112
παρουσία, 130
πᾶσιν, 113
πατρὸς, 11
πεντηκοστή, 116
πεντηκοστῆς, 116
πεπληροφορημένων, 187
περὶ, 63, 301
πέτρος, 11
πίστις, 79
πνεῦμα, 195
πνεύματος, 11
ποιεῖν, 254
πολλοί, 88–89
πορευ, 227
πορευθέντες, 11
πορευομένου, 228, 238, 259
πραγμάτων, 187
πράξεις, 73, 76–77, 140, 161
προοίμϊον, 79
πρὸς, 11
πρόσωπον, 169
πρῶτον, 63, 301

σοι, 63
σώσει, 180

τὰ, 11
τάξις, 79
τε, 254
τέξεται, 111
τὴν, 11, 116
τῆς, 112, 116
τό, 11–12, 125, 161
τὸν, 220–21, 259, 301
τοῦ, 11, 49, 58, 106, 110, 143
τοὺς, 226
τῷ, 11, 220
τῶν, 11, 187

υἱόν, 111
υἱὸς, 49, 106, 110
υἱοῦ, 11
ὑμῶν, 11
ὑπηρέται, 58

φησίν, 11
Χχριστοῦ, 11, 143

יסובי, 96

עצבמ, 96

www.ingramcontent.com/pod-product-compliance
Lightning Source LLC
Chambersburg PA
CBHW071147300426
44113CB00009B/1112